THE GRAND BAZAAR ▲ 193 | SÜLEYMANIYE CAMI'I ▲ 214 | NORTHERN WALLS ▲ 229

BEŞIKTAŞ

KURTULUŞ

KSIZ

KASIMPAŞA

DOLMABAHÇE

DOLMABAHÇE
SARAYI

GALATASARAY

DOLMABAHÇE
CAMI'I

GALATASARAY
LİSESİ

BEYOĞLU

ORNI)

GALATA TOWER

GALATA

BOSPHORUS

KIZ KULESİ

SÜLEYMANIYE
CAMI'I

EMİNÖNÜ

SİRKECİ
GARI

ÜSKÜDAR

YAZIT

TOPKAPI

GRAND BAZAAR

HAGIA SOPHIA

BLUE MOSQUE

MKAPI

SULTANAHMET

PRINCES' ISLANDS ▲ 271 | BOSPHORUS ▲ 274 | DOLMABAHÇE ▲ 276

charming, popular neighborhoods.
EYÜP
The mosque is one of the most venerated in Turkey. Its cemetery, a sea of green, is a model of romanticism.

GALATA TOWER
Pinnacle of the Genoese fortifications, it has an unrivaled 360° view.
PRINCES' ISLANDS
The sea, the *yalı*, the pine forest and even the bicycles all contribute to make a

perfect weekend getaway in a busy, fashionable seaside resort.
BOSPHORUS
Mythical link between Europe and Asia, between the Slavic and Mediterranean worlds, it bustles with

the hypnotic to-ing and fro-ing of boats.
DOLMABAHÇE
Last home of the sultans. Its façade, a blend of oriental and rococo styles, is reflected in the waters of the Bosphorus.

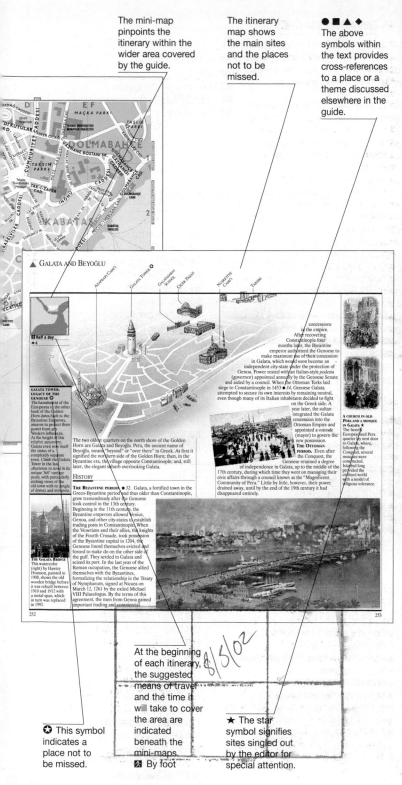

The mini-map pinpoints the itinerary within the wider area covered by the guide.

The itinerary map shows the main sites and the places not to be missed.

● ■ ▲ ◆
The above symbols within the text provides cross-references to a place or a theme discussed elsewhere in the guide.

▲ GALATA AND BEYOĞLU

AZAPKAPI CAMİİ ✪   GALATA TOWER ✪   GALATASARAY SCHOOL   ÇIÇEK PASAJI   NUSRETİYE CAMİİ ✪   TAKSİM

⏱ Half a day
● C

GALATA TOWER, LEGACY OF THE GENOESE ✪
The banishment of the Europeans to the other bank of the Golden Horn dates back to the Byzantine Emperors, anxious to protect their power from any Western influences. At the height of this relative autonomy, Galata even won itself the status of a completely separate town. Climb the Galata Tower in the late afternoon to revel in its unique 360° vantage point, with particularly striking views of the old town with its tangle of domes and minarets.

THE GALATA BRIDGE
This watercolor (right) by Hawiry Hvanson, painted in 1908, shows the old wooden bridge before it was rebuilt between 1910 and 1912 with a metal span, which in turn was replaced in 1992.

The two oldest quarters on the north shore of the Golden Horn are Galata and Beyoğlu. Pera, the ancient name of Beyoğlu, means "beyond" or "over there" in Greek. At first it signified the northern side of the Golden Horn; then, in the Byzantine era, the village opposite Constantinople; and, still later, the elegant suburb overlooking Galata.

HISTORY

THE BYZANTINE PERIOD ● *32*. Galata, a fortified town in the Greco-Byzantine period and thus older than Constantinople, grew tremendously after the Genoese took control in the 13th century. Beginning in the 11th century, the Byzantine emperors allowed Venice, Genoa, and other city-states to establish trading posts in Constantinople. When the Venetians and their allies, the knights of the Fourth Crusade, took possession of the Byzantine capital in 1204, the Genoese found themselves evicted and forced to make do on the other side of the gulf. They settled in Galata and seized its port. In the last year of the Roman occupation, the Genoese allied themselves with the Byzantines, formalizing the relationship in the Treaty of Nymphaeum, signed at Nicaea on March 12, 1261 by the exiled Michael VIII Palaeologus. By the terms of this agreement, the men from Genoa gained important trading and commercial concessions in the empire. After recovering Constantinople four months later, the Byzantine emperor authorized the Genoese to make maximum use of their concession in Galata, which would soon become an independent city-state under the protection of Genoa. Power rested with an Italian-style *podesta* (governor) appointed annually by the Genoese Senate and aided by a council. When the Ottoman Turks laid siege to Constantinople in 1453 ● *34*, Genoese Galata attempted to secure its own interests by remaining neutral, even though many of its Italian inhabitants decided to fight on the Greek side. A year later, the sultan integrated the Galata concession into the Ottoman Empire and appointed a *voivode* (mayor) to govern the new possession.

THE OTTOMAN PERIOD. Even after the Conquest, the Genoese retained a degree of independence in Galata, up to the middle of the 17th century, during which time they went on managing their civic affairs through a council known as the "Magnificent Community of Pera." Little by little, however, their power drained away, until by the end of the 19th century it had disappeared entirely.

A CHURCH IN OLD PERA AND A MOSQUE IN GALATA ★
The heavily Europeanized Pera quarter lay next door to Galata, where, following the Conquest, several mosques were constructed. Istanbul long provided the civilized world with a model of religious tolerance.

252
253

✪ This symbol indicates a place not to be missed.

At the beginning of each itinerary, the suggested means of travel and the time it will take to cover the area are indicated beneath the mini-maps.
🚶 By foot

★ The star symbol signifies sites singled out by the editor for special attention.

03

● Encyclopedia section

▲ Itineraries

◆ Practical information

FROM SARAY BURNU TO THE FIRST HILL
▲ 128
The landing piers and the lively Spice Market.

HAGHIA SOPHIA
▲ 138
Stroll in the Tribunes, between the soaring columns and Byzantine mosaics, under the vault adorned with angels.

TOPKAPI SARAYI
▲ 150
Once called the "summary of the universe", its alcoves evoke pomp and intrigue.

BLUE MOSQUE ▲ 174
Masterpiece of Ottoman religious art, built on the remains of old Byzantine palaces.

THE GRAND BAZAAR, THE BEYAZIDIYE AND THE SÜLEYMANIYE
▲ 186
A huge area where commerce rubs shoulders with religion and philosophy.

FETHIYE CAMI'I ▲ 220
The religious center of old Istanbul, dotted with former Byzantyne churches now converted into mosques

THE BYZANTINE LAND WALLS ▲ 224
Currently being restored, more than three miles of walls bear witness to the city's history.

THE GOLDEN HORN AND EYÜP ▲ 238
The Golden Pavilions have given way to other treasures; alleyways teeming with life, delightful churches and mosques.

GALATA AND BEYOĞLU ▲ 252
A modern neighborhood that has always been particularly open to Western influences.

ÜSKÜDAR AND THE PRINCES' ISLANDS
▲ 264
This rich Anatolian suburb boasts superb monuments, while the islands reveal natural treasures.

THE BOSPHORUS
▲ 274
Utilized for both transport and leisure, it is lined with palaces, fortresses and sleepy villages.

IZNIK ▲ 292
The site of ancient of Nicaea, it has retained the old grid systems of the streets and is world-famous for its faiences

BURSA ▲ 298
The cradle of modern Turkish civilzation, it was the first capital of the Ottoman empire.

EDIRNE ▲ 308
Once popular with the empire's sultans and viziers, who endowed it with sumptuous buildings such as the famous Selimiye Cami'i.

THE DARDANELLES
▲ 322
A major strategic asset since the Byzantine era, the strait is bordered by citadels and military cemeteries.

→ **NUMEROUS SPECIALISTS AND ISTANBUL ENTHUSIASTS
HAVE CONTRIBUTED TO THIS GUIDE.**

● **Encyclopedia section**

■ NATURE
Marc-Henri Lebrun, W. D. Nesteroff
■ HISTORY
John Freely, Stéphane Yérasimos,
Michel Gilquin
■ LANGUAGE
Altan Gokalp
■ ARTS, CRAFTS AND TRADITIONS
Gérard Georges Lemaire
(palaces and gardens, hammams,
costumes, cafés)
Ersu Pekin (music)
Mme Onger (shadow theater, food)
Henri Daumas (carpets and kilims)
Altan Gokalp (religion, Byzantium)
Arthur Thévenart (fountains)
■ ARCHITECTURE
Augusto Romano Burelli, Ugur Tanyelli,
Stéphane Yérasimos
■ ISTANBUL AS SEEN BY PAINTERS
Abidine Dino
■ ISTANBUL AS SEEN BY WRITERS
Lucinda Gane

▲ **Itineraries**

Zeynep Avçi, Murat Belge, John Freely,
Michel Gilquin

◆ **Practical information**

Christophe Bardèche,
Catherine Laussucq, Nathalie Phan,
Meltem Savçi, Mehmet Ipekel,
Fadime Deli

EVERYMAN GUIDES
Published by Everyman Publishers Plc

© 2001 Everyman Publishing Plc

Originally published in France by
Nouveaux-Loisirs, a subsidiary of
Editions Gallimard, Paris, 1992
© 1992 Editions Nouveaux-Loisirs.

First published 1993
Further editions, revised and updated:
September 1995, July 1997,
September 2001

Istanbul – ISBN 1-84159-015-0

ISTANBUL
■ EDITOR
Anne Nesteroff *assisted by* Catherine Bray,
Sybille d'Orion, Gwenhaelle Le Roy,
Samuel Péron, Solène Bouton (updates)
■ GRAPHICS
Elisabeth Cohan
■ PICTURE RESEARCH
Anne Nesteroff
■ LAYOUT
Philippe Marchand
■ CORRECTIONS
Lorène Bücher
■ MAPS
Pierre-Xavier Grézaud, Jean-François Binet,
Philippe Pradel, Samuel Tranlé
■ CARTOGRAPHY
Edigraphie
■ ILLUSTRATIONS
NATURE: Sophie Lavaux,
Jean-François Péneau, Philippe Pradel
ARCHITECTURE: Françoise Brosse
ITINERARIES: Norbert Soussot
■ PHOTOGRAPHY
Ara Güler (Istanbul), Guido Rossi,
Gérard Degorges, Arthur Thévenart,
Éduoard de Pazzis, Hâluk Özözlü

WE WOULD LIKE TO THANK
Pierre de Gigord, Godfrey Goodwin
and Vahit Canbas

EDITED AND TYPESET BY
Book Creation Services Ltd, London

Printed in Italy by Editoriale Lloyd

EVERYMAN GUIDES
Gloucester Mansions, 140a Shaftesbury Avenue,
London WC2H 8HD
guides@everyman.uk.com

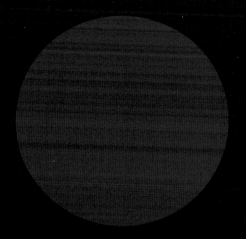

Encyclopedia section

"No woman of any rank whatsoever is permitted to go in the street without two muslims, one that covers her face all but her eyes and another that hides the whole dress of her head and hangs half way down her back: and their shapes are wholly conceal'd by a thing they call a *Feridge*, which no woman of any sort appears without."
Lady Mary Wortley-Montagu

The thermal baths of Eski Kaplıca in Bursa, at the base of the hill of Çerkige, are the oldest baths ever built by the Ottomans in their first capital: "copied from the Thermæ of Diocletian in Rome, although very much smaller" (Penzer, 1540).

The Orthodox Church opened special schools and seminaries for Bulgarian children in Adrianople (Edirne).

The rococo palace of Küçüksu on the shores of the Bosphorus was built in 1856–7 by the architect Nikoğos Balyan for the sultan Abdül Mecit I.

Nature

■ THE GEOLOGY OF TURKEY

Mining Research
and Exploitation
Institute of Turkey.

Anatolia, or Asian Turkey, is composed of a central plateau with an average height of 2,900 ft, bordered by the Pontides and Taurus mountain ranges which reach an altitude of 10,000 ft. This plateau slopes gently from the eastern mountain ranges to the Aegean Sea in the west. Three hundred million years ago the area that is present-day Turkey was part of the supercontinent of Gondwana, which was bordered to the north by the paleo-Tethysian sea, which separated it from the Eurasian continent. Throughout the following ages this area experienced a series of tectonic upheavals, causing the Tethys sea to split and fill with sediments. When it closed up it was squeezed between the two continental blocks, which forced all of its rock formations (sediments, oceanic crust, ophiolites) to the surface. In the early Miocene period (23 million years), Anatolia was a compact continental block situated between the Black Sea and the eastern Mediterranean, and subjected to pressure from the surrounding plates.

Quaternary	Paleogezoic	Triassic	Paleozoic
Neogene	Mesozoic	Mesozoic-Paleozoic	

Anatolia and the Aegean Sea are caught in a vice between the African-Arabian plate, which is moving north, and the Eurasian fixed plate. To the west the collision is absorbed by the plunging of the northern border of the African plate beneath an Aegean Crete-Cyprus arc. This subduction transformed the Aegean Sea into a zone of expansion.

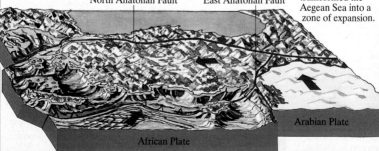

North Anatolian Fault   East Anatolian Fault

Arabian Plate

African Plate

SHALE AND LIMESTONE ROCKS

The shores of the Bosphorus are lined predominantly with shale and limestone, as well as platy limestone (**6**) (**7**) from the Devonian era (410 to 360 million years). Granitic batholiths reach the surface in massifs like the Ulu Dağ near Bursa. Fractures in the granite (**9**) sometimes reveal dendrites (**10**). More recent rocks like clay, marl, sandstone, sand, and volcanic tuffs now fill the ancient sedimentary basins.

PETROGRAPHY

A wide variety of petrographic rocks exist. The ophiolithic series are made up of fragments of ancient oceanic crusts (ophioliths), raised during the paleo-Tethys and neo-Tethys eras. These rocks form the mountains bordering the Anatolian plateau: the Taurus mountains to the south and the Pontides to the north. In cross-section, it is also possible to observe the oceanic crust from the base towards the surface: peridotites (**5**), gabbros (**3**) basalts (**4**), pillow lavas (**8**) and finally cherts (**1**) and bauxites (**2**).

Meanwhile, to the east, the Arabian plate continued its climb, colliding with Anatolia. Caught in a pincer-like movement, the Anatolian block moved (over 11 million years) towards the west and the Aegean Sea, alongside the old sutures of the East and North Anatolian faults. This movement continues, and it is along the North Anatolian fault that the most significant quakes are registered today.

MARBLES, PLAQUES AND PILASTERS

Marble revetments, most of them from the quarries of Anatolia, cover the walls of the basilica of Haghia Sophia. The architects of the Hellenistic period used marble for the supporting elements of the ornamentation. In the mosques there were delicately carved sculptures on the small marble columns and on the pillars that framed doors and windows.

17

■ THE BOSPHORUS AND MIGRATORY BIRDS

Twice a year millions of migratory birds fly over the Straits of the Bosphorus, which is situated beween their nesting sites in Europe and western Asia and their East African winter homes. For most of the birds, this involves a journey of thousands of miles. Birds of prey and other gliders (cranes and storks, for example) are reluctant to fly over the open seas, so instead they cross by the isthmuses and straits. They use thermals over the land to gain altitude, which enables them to then glide over long distances, saving valuable energy.

GREY CRANE
Crane flocks migrate primarily in the month of October.

BLACK KITE
These are often seen along the Golden Horn scavenging for dead fish.

WHITE STORK
Approximately 315,000 fly over the Bosphorus each year.

OLIVACEOUS WARBLER
Large numbers of these warblers nest in the hills of Çamlka.

RED-BACKED SHRIKE
On their journey to East Africa these birds pause in the bushes in the hills around Istanbul.

Swallows

Black kites

Honey buzzards

Storks

Lesser spotted eagles

Sparrowhawks

EGYPTIAN VULTURE
Only 300 to 500 of these birds fly over the Bosphorus each year, primarily during August and September.

LESSER SPOTTED EAGLE
Nearly 18,000 of these birds migrate across the Bosphorus in the fall.

HONEY BUZZARD
25,000 cross in the fall on their way from central and western Europe.

THE BOSPHORUS
The strait is like a river with its abrupt curves, flowing between fairly steep-sided banks, with cultivated and forested hills on either side. The speed of its current varies depending upon the season. The fall migration is more spectacular than that of the spring because it also includes the young birds, which were hatched only a few months earlier.

■ LAKE MANYAS

CHLIDONIAS HYBRIDA

WHISKERED TERN

Lake Manyas – also called Kuş Gölü, "bird lake" – is situated between Bursa and Çanakkale, 50 feet below the level of the Sea of Marmara. It covers an area of approximately 65 square miles, next to the small Kuş Cenneti national park. Its waters are home to a multitude of amphibians (especially frogs) and twenty types of fish. Fishing is an important part of the area's economic life. Large reed beds line the banks, and a little willow forest near the mouth of the Sigirci river is a perfect habitat for herons, pelicans, and cormorants, which return to nest there every year. However, this exceptional bird life is under threat from excessive draining, poaching, and industrial pollution, which has already resulted in Lake Iznik, once home to numerous species, being abandoned by most birds.

IBIS FALCON
With its curved beak, it resembles a curlew.

DALMATIAN PELICANS
Lake Manyas is one of the few places in Turkey where this endangered species nests.

EGRET
In the springtime its neck and wings are decorated with long white feathers.

GREAT CORMORANT
600 pairs of this fish-eating bird nest around the lake. In the spring the birds display themselves in the willows where they nest.

MARSH HARRIER
They nest in the reed-beds.

GREY HERON
This is the most common heron. It fishes in the lake's shallow water. Grey heron numbers range from 300 to 600 pairs.

THE GREY HERON'S HEAD
The bird holds itself still, its neck stiff, or folded up.

CRYING EAGLE
A few birds manage to stay during the fall.

NIGHT HERON
In the spring, the head of this little heron, which feeds at night, is decorated with a long white crest.

GREAT CRESTED GREBE
This fish-eating bird can be seen along the lake, primarily in the winter.

The limestone cliffs of the Black Sea are not sheer. There are vertical fractures within them that cause rock falls, which then accumulate as embankments with steep-sided faces. These formations provide that crucial initial foothold for scrub vegetation to establish itself. At water level a deep cleft carved into the limestone rock face can be seen, distinguished by its dark, gray-black color. This cleft is not due to erosion by the waves, but is in fact caused by blue-green algae, which grows on and into the rock, perforating it. This algae thrives in the perpetually humid environment, and destroys the limestone little by little.

SEASIDE VEGETATION

The vegetation on top of the cliffs is mostly low scrub, including rock-roses and laburnum which begin to flower in the early spring and sometimes continue until the fall(1). The sea grasses are singed by seaspray which drenches them in salt. In the spring miniscule romulea flower on the rocks, and wonderfully scented narcissi grow in the crevices. Mesembryanthemums cover large stretches of the coast, along the beaches and on the rocks (3).The plants and animals that live on the rocky coasts between the spring and neap tides are divided among a number of zones. The supralittoral level is the zone where such creatures as acorn shells and limpets are found, as it is rarely under water (4). The laminaria grow in the area where the tides turn, as well as in the infralittoral zone (5). Living in the sand are many species of crustaceans, anemones, and worms.

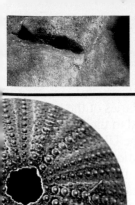

THE SEA BED

The rocky bottom of the Black Sea makes it easy to explore when diving. There is a wide variety of habitats in the first 30 feet beneath the surface while on the bottom, among the algae, it is possible to find numerous shellfish and invertebrates, and in the sand and silt there are many flatfish.

1

2

3

4

5

1. SEA URCHIN
Its shell is green and it clings on to rocks, stones, and algae from the edge of the cliff down to a depth of 100 feet.

2. PEARLY NUCULE
This bivalve lives in the sand at depths of up to 500 feet.

3. ABALONE
The abalone lives among the rocks. The inside of its shell has an opalescent sheen.

4. DRILLER
This mollusk lives on silty and sandy beds.

5. ACORN SHELL
The carapace of this rock-clinging crustacean is made up of six smooth plates.

MENDOLE
Also known as the cackarel, it lives in coastal waters and estuaries.

COMMON MACKEREL
The common mackerel travels in shoals that stay near the coast.

SPANISH MACKEREL

SPRAT This fish lives near the coast and in briny waters.

CHINCHARD Rarely found, this fish lives in the open sea.

THE ULU DAĞ NATIONAL PARK

The creation of a large skiing area poses a threat to the park's natural beauty and the whole environment.

The road within the park crosses a scrub of lavender and juniper, then runs on through the various types of woodland, past rivers and torrents.

Syrian woodpeckers, warblers, and birds of prey nest in the pine trees.

The boundaries of the national park extend to the southern slopes of the Ulu Dağ massif. The vegetation is divided into four zones, from 1,600 to 8,000 feet in altitude. The first zone is the Mediterranean level, from sea-level to 2,000 feet, where lavender, arbutus, and green oak flourish (1). The second or upper Mediterranean level, from 2,000 to 4,000 feet, is characterized by Byzantine hazel trees, lindens, eastern beech trees, and oaks (2). The mountain level, from 3,000 to 5,900 feet, has firs and pines (3). Above 5,900 feet, in the meadows of the subalpine level, lies the area designated for skiing.

In the scrubland little orchids and sweetly scented hyacinths bloom in springtime.

This thick forest of conifers and deciduous trees harbors a great variety of wildlife. *Cervidae* – red (4) and fallow deer (5) – are found there as well as boar and sometimes bears and wolves.
The Ulu Dağ national park was created to protect this natural site, and to safeguard the animal population, which includes many endangered species.

MOUFFLON
A type of wild mountain sheep, the moufflon is found on the highest summits of the Ulu Dağ.

THE VEGETATION is made up of rockroses, arborescent briar bushes, mastic trees, pistachio trees, and honeysuckle.

GRASSHOPPERS AND BEES
The national park is home to numerous insects. Many of the species are found only in this part of Turkey and are completely unknown in Europe. The best time to see them is during the summer months.

CREEPING CYCLAMEN
These cyclamen mix with violets and ranunculae in shrubs growing at the highest altitudes in the forest.

APOLLO
This remarkable butterfly is indigenous to the mountain regions and rarely descends below 2,000 feet.

25

In the 18th and 19th centuries landscape gardeners were charged with creating parks for the sultans' palaces, embassies and yalı by the Bosphorus. For these gardens, they selected a mixture of forest, fruit, and ornamental trees and created arbors from a variety of plants and flowers, which were either transplanted or grown from cuttings. They had to fight against the established tradition of more modest gardens but they won, and the resulting parks and town squares are beautiful creations of great artistry.

JUDAS TREE

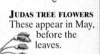

JUDAS TREE WITH PODS

JUDAS TREE FLOWERS
These appear in May, before the leaves.

ROSE BUSH FLOWER
Rose bushes with large flowers are used as ornamental shrubs. They are remarkable for their size and for the scent of their flowers.

HOLM-OAK (ILEX)
This oak has long-lasting leaves, and is planted in parks.

EUCALYPTUS
An imported tree, which tends to sterilize the soil.

OLIVE TREE
This tree has silvery leaves and heavily scented flowers.

BALKAN PINE (OR BOSNIAN PINE) This type of pine is cultivated in the gardens of the Bosphorus.

History and language

ORIGINS. Turkey, a cradle of civilizations and a crossroads of history, is the meeting place of East and West. The first human settlements date back to 10,000 BC and archeological excavations have shown that, from around this time, communities had been established at Çatalhüyük and possibly other unexcavated sites in Central Anatolia. Millennia later, the Neolithic site at Hacilar is much less sophisticated. In the early 3rd millennium BC, peoples crossed the straits and settled along the Aegean and on the site of Troy. In the 2nd millennium BC, the Hittites moved into Asia Minor. There were further numerous migrations from the end of the 2nd millennium.

THE NEOLITHIC PERIOD

8000–1200 BC
Anatolia is settled.

THE FIRST CITIES. The oldest known city, Çatalhüyük, perished in about 5500 BC. Simple agriculture, metallurgy and weaving began in Anatolia before their later development in Europe.

THE BRONZE AGE

4000 BC
Influx of Neolithic people.

3600 BC
Troy I is founded.

2600 BC
Anatolian migrations to Crete.

2100 BC
Troy II is invaded and destroyed.

2000 BC
The Ionians invade Greece.

1400–1200 BC
The Dorians invade Greece.

THE SITE OF TROY. Archeological excavations in Anatolia began in 1870, with Schliemann's work at the site of Troy on the Asian side of the straits, which were known to the Greeks as the Hellespont. The fortified city was founded layer by layer between 3600 and 2500 BC, that is, between the end of the Chalcolithic period and the beginning of the Bronze Age. Throughout the Bronze Age, the city was continuously inhabited and was in contact with the Aegean and Cycladic peoples. Around 2100–2000 BC, Troy was destroyed by people who left no trace of their culture behind. A new civilization appeared around 1800 BC.

THE HATTIANS. Writing was introduced to Anatolia in the Middle Bronze Age (2000–1500 BC) by Assyrian merchants from Hattian cities. The Hattians were a people indigenous to Asia Minor whose civilization produced some very beautiful works of art – such as a golden ewer found at Alaca Hüyük. They dominated the area for over 500 years and, at the beginning of the 2nd millennium BC, were supplanted by the Hittites, a warrior people who seem to have come from

southern Russia. The Hittites (2000–1800 BC) conquered Anatolia and founded their capital at Hattuşaş, now known as Boğazköy. They were the first great fortress builders: the city of Hattuşaş was surrounded by curtain walls set with towers, and five great temples and a complex with shops have been uncovered.

THE HITTITE KINGDOM. Hattuşaş was the capital of the Hittite Kingdom (1700–1450 BC) and of the Hittite Empire (1450–1200 BC). During the Late Bronze Age the Hittite rulers rivalled the Egyptians in their power, and in 1286 BC when Ramses II was pharaoh, these great empires fought one another at the famous battle of Kades in Syria. This conflict was settled by the earliest-known peace treaty, signed in 1269 by Hattousil and Ramses II. The clay tablet on which it is recorded is preserved at the Museum of the Ancient Orient in Istanbul.

THE SEA PEOPLE. Around 1200 BC all the great cities of the Late Bronze Age – most notably Troy, Mycenae and Hattuşaş – were destroyed, perhaps by the warrior race that the Egyptians knew as the Sea People. This was followed by an obscure period in Anatolian history, which lasted several centuries (1180–750 BC) and during which there is little or no evidence of civilization.

THE NEO-HITTITE STATES. Something of the Hittite culture survived in southeastern Anatolia and in Syria in the period c. 1000–700 BC. But in western and central Anatolia the Phrygians dominated the Hittites between 900 and 650 BC. Their kings were named Midas or Gordius and they were conquered by the rich Lydians who ruled until they, in turn, were defeated by the Persians under Cyrus. During the same period, the Urartians took control of the eastern part of the subcontinent.

GRECO-ANATOLIAN CIVILIZATION. From the 14th century BC, the Greeks settled along the Anatolian coast and established important Greek cities like Miletus and Ephesus which in the 7th century BC colonized the Bosphorus and the Black Sea.

ANATOLIA UNDER THE PERSIANS. The former Lydian empire was to remain under Persian rule from 546 to 334 BC, when Alexander the Great crossed the Dardanelles.

1230–25 BC
Fall of Troy and destruction of Mycenae and Hattusa.

753 BC
Foundation of Rome.

600 BC
Foundation of Marseilles.

490 BC
Battle of Marathon.

448–30 BC
Pericles reaches the height of his power at Athens.

FOUNDATION OF BYZANTIUM

According to tradition, Byzantium was founded by the hero Byzas the Megarian, who led an expedition of colonists from Megara and Athens to establish a new city on the Bosphorus. Byzas chose a site on a steep, sharp-topped hill, opposite the Golden Horn and the Bosphorus. At this confluence, the Megarian leader built an acropolis, surrounded with ramparts. This hill town, with its port in a sheltered cove below, was the embryo of a city that would endure until the early 4th century AD.

HISTORY

FROM ALEXANDER THE GREAT TO THE ROMAN EMPIRE

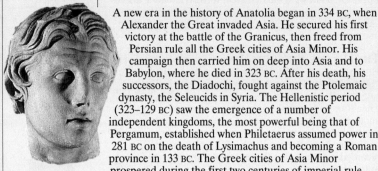

A new era in the history of Anatolia began in 334 BC, when Alexander the Great invaded Asia. He secured his first victory at the battle of the Granicus, then freed from Persian rule all the Greek cities of Asia Minor. His campaign then carried him on deep into Asia and to Babylon, where he died in 323 BC. After his death, his successors, the Diadochi, fought against the Ptolemaic dynasty, the Seleucids in Syria. The Hellenistic period (323–129 BC) saw the emergence of a number of independent kingdoms, the most powerful being that of Pergamum, established when Philetaerus assumed power in 281 BC on the death of Lysimachus and becoming a Roman province in 133 BC. The Greek cities of Asia Minor prospered during the first two centuries of imperial rule, this prosperity reaching its peak with the Emperor Hadrian (117–138), under whose rule temples, theaters and monuments were built.

88–63 BC
The Romans re-conquer Asia Minor.

27 BC
Octavian is crowned Emperor.

THE GREAT INVASIONS. From 263 BC, the Goths started to invade western Asia Minor. Descending in successive waves they brought death and destruction and paved the way for other invaders who eventually destroyed all the Greek cities of Asia Minor.

CONSTANTINOPLE, THE SECOND ROME

70 AD
The Romans sack Jerusalem.

CONSTANTINE THE GREAT. While the great cities of the Greco-Roman world were suffering destruction, a new empire was taking shape in Constantinople. In 330 Constantine the Great proclaimed the city capital of the Byzantine Empire, and the entire history of this empire was to revolve around Constantinople, the Byzantium of the Greeks.

253–60
The Franks and Alamans invade Gaul.

BYZANTIUM AND RIVAL POWERS. During the six centuries of its existence, Byzantium often fell under the control of more powerful states: first Persia, then Athens and Sparta during the Peloponnesian War, later Alexander and his successors, and then Rome. Byzantium was destroyed and rebuilt several times in the course of its history, notably in 196, when it fell to the Roman emperor Septimius Severus after a two-year siege. The city was then enlarged and the walls around the acropolis were strengthened and extended to embrace an area between the Golden Horn and the Sea of Marmara. In 324, Constantine the Great took Byzantium after his victory over Licinius, which made him the sole ruler of the Roman Empire.

260
The Persian Sassanids in Central Anatolia.

324–37
Reign of Constantine the Great.

325
Council of Nicaea and the establishment of the Christian Creed.

340–63
The Persians and Romans fight over northern Mesopotamia.

> «THE PROSPECT OF BEAUTY, OF SAFETY, AND OF WEALTH, UNITED IN A SINGLE SPOT, WAS SUFFICIENT TO JUSTIFY THE CHOICE OF CONSTANTINE.»
>
> EDWARD GIBBON

THE CITY OF CONSTANTINE.

Constantine decided to move the capital of the Roman Empire from Rome to Byzantium, and rebuild the old Greek city on a much larger and grander scale in keeping with its new imperial status. The  new capital was dedicated on May 11, 330 as Nova Roma, but popularly it came to be known as Constantinople, the City of Constantine. The new capital, covering an area five times larger than that of the old city of Byzantium, now had ramparts running more than two miles from the Golden Horn to the Sea of Marmara. In the first hundred years of its history, the capital grew rapidly and soon spread beyond the limits defined by its founder. In the 5th century Theodosius replaced Constantine's walls with a new and stronger line of defence walls topped by ninety-six towers. These walls have defined the limits of the old city from that time on, although subsequent expansion took place on the other side of the Golden Horn and along the shores of the Sea of Marmara and the Bosphorus. The area thus enclosed included seven hills, the same as in old Rome, with the acropolis of ancient Byzantium on the First Hill.

FROM THE ROMAN TO THE BYZANTINE EMPIRE.

Great changes in the Roman Empire took place during the two centuries following the reign of Constantine the Great (324–337). After the death of Theodosius I in 395, the Empire was divided between his two sons, Arcadius and Honorius. Arcadius took command of the empire from Constantinople eastwards and Honorius governed from Rome westwards. In the following century, the western part of the Empire was invaded by barbarians and in 476 its last Emperor of the West was deposed, leaving the Emperor of the East in Constantinople sole ruler of what was left of the Roman Empire. Classical Greco-Roman traditions were gradually obliterated as the Empire's Christian and Greek culture took hold. This brought about a profound change in the character of the Empire, which from now on was centered around lands populated largely by Greek-speaking Christians, even though Latin remained the official language of the court until the 6th century. By choosing Byzantium, Constantinople's original name, as the generic name of the Empire, the Emperor declared his intention to break the ties of the Greek Christian state with the old imperial, pagan Rome. Thenceforth the influence that Christianity had on Byzantium was not only religious but also political and economic.

361
Reign of Julian the Apostate and reinstitution of paganism.

379
Theodosius I becomes Emperor at age 16.

391
Christianity becomes the state religion.

395
Death of Theodosius I. Final division of the Western and Eastern Empires.

410
Alaric plunders Rome.

429
The Vandals invade Africa.

431
The Council of Ephesus

441–51
Attila and the Huns overrun the Western Empire.

622
Mahomet flees to Medina (the hegira).

913–59
Reign of Constantine VII Porphyrogenitus,

THE REIGN OF THE EMPEROR JUSTINIAN. The Byzantine Empire reached the pinnacle of its greatness during the reign of Justinian (527–565), who recaptured many of the lost dominions of the Roman Empire. By the end of Justinian's reign, the Empire embraced a large part of the Mediterranean world, reaching as far west as Spain, eastward into Persia, northward as far as the Danube and south into Egypt, an area only slightly less than that of the Roman Empire under Augustus. Capitalizing on the opulence that his vast empire could provide, Justinian built magnificent churches, palaces and public buildings with such zeal that no other city in the world could rival the splendor of Constantinople. It was he who built the Basilica of Haghia Sophia, completed in 537 and dedicated to the Holy Wisdom, a symbol of the universal radiance of the Byzantine Empire.

THE DECLINE OF THE EMPIRE. The Byzantine Empire endured for nearly a thousand years after Justinian, even though on his death decline had already begun. During the Middle Ages, its dominions were reduced to Asia Minor and the southern Balkans, including what is now Greece. The Selçuk Turks inflicted a cruel blow when they routed the Byzantine army at the battle of Mantzikert in 1071. In the same year the Normans took Bari, the last Byzantine possession in Italy.

THE LATIN KINGDOM

1067
The Selçuk Turks occupy Caesarea.

1204–61
The Greek Empire of Nicaea.

1209–12
The Venetians conquer Crete.

1256–1335
Mongol Dynasty in Persia.

THE FOURTH CRUSADE. In 1204 the Byzantine Empire was almost destroyed again when the Venetians joined forces with the knights of the Fourth Crusade, organized by Pope Innocent III to 'come to the aid of' the Holy Land. The French crusaders, under the command of Count Thibaud de Champagne, and the Doge of Venice undertook to join and finance the Crusade; the Venetians suggested that the Crusaders take Constantinople. Having reached the city, even though Pope Innocent III had been banned and excommunicated, the Crusaders placed Alexius IV Angelus on the throne. He was unable to produce the money that the Crusaders demanded and in March 1204 they decided to do away with him and establish a Latin kingdom. By April 13, the Crusaders had torched and taken control of every quarter of

the city. Constantinople was sacked, thousands of Greeks massacred, churches pillaged and relics stolen and sent back to the West. On May 9, 1204, after the spoils had been divided, Baldwin of Flanders was crowned Emperor and Tomaso Morosini patriarch. The victors divided up the land between them and, as Baldwin of Flanders put it, laid their hands on riches both physical and spiritual. This kingdom lasted for more than half a century. However, certain provinces of the empire kept their independence during this period, notably Nicaea in northwestern Asia Minor, the capital of an empire ably ruled by the Lascarid dynasty which began

the rebirth of Byzantine power. Finally, under Michael IX Paleologus the Greeks captured the city in 1261. Over two centuries before it finally fell, the Byzantine Empire was gradually disintegrating, suffering repeated attacks from the Osmanlı Turks, known in the West as the Ottomans.

1261
Foundation of the Palaeologus dynasty.

1331
Nicaea taken by the Turks.

THE OSMANLI TURKS

THE FIRST OTTOMAN CONQUESTS. In 1326, the Osmanlı captured Prusa (Bursa), which Sultan Orhan Gazi established as the capital of the burgeoning empire. From then on, they were unstoppable. In the mid-14th century they crossed the Dardanelles and took Adrianople (Edirne), where in 1371 Sultan Murat I founded the new capital of the Ottoman Empire. In 1422, Murat II invaded Greece and the Peloponnese, conquering Thessalonika in March 1430. In 1438 the *devşirme* was instituted. This was a system for recruiting young Christian slaves given by their families in payment of tribute due to the sultan. Educated in the palace barracks, they formed the backbone of the powerful Turkish army and were later to make up the famous élite corps known as Janissaries. In 1440, Belgrade, a powerful and well defended city, managed to fend off a six-month siege but Ottoman expansion was only briefly thwarted and Venice intervened.

1328
Victory of Orhan Gazi over Andronicus III Palaeologus.

1369–1403.
Mongolian incursions in Asia Minor.

1402
Beyazıt I vanquished by Tamerlane.

1422
First Ottoman siege of Constantinople.

THE BYZANTINE EMPIRE IS REDUCED TO CONSTANTINOPLE. By the mid-15th century, the Ottomans had conquered most of Asia Minor and reached southern Europe, even though the popes had the Christian princes to raise armies to halt their progress. The Byzantine Empire was reduced to little more than the town of Constantinople and its immediate environs. Pope Nicholas V would only give his support on condition that the Greeks joined the Catholic Church. Emperor John III was forced to accept these terms and on December 12, 1452, Cardinal Isidore, the Pope's envoy, celebrated Roman Catholic mass at Haghia Sophia. However, help from the Christian powers of Europe was not to materialize.

1423
Venice promises to defend Thessalonika, until it falls in 1430.

1453
End of the Hundred Years War.

1456
Ottomans take Athens.

● THE FALL OF CONSTANTINOPLE

February 3, 1451: Mehmet II, born March 30, 1432, succeeded his father to the Ottoman throne.

February 14, 1452: The Venetian senate informed the Byzantine ambassador of unprecedented preparations by the Turks for the siege of Constantinople.

March 26: Mehmet II reached the Bosphorus and started building a fortress, the Rumeli Hisarı, on the western bank to control seaborne traffic. It faced the fortress of Anadolu Hisarı, built by his grandfather Beyazıt I in 1396.

September 3: The construction of the fortress was completed. After inspecting his 50,000 troops, as well as Constantinople's

defenses, the Sultan returned to Edirne, the new capital of the Empire, where he set up his winter quarters and carefully planned the siege.

September 10: Mehmet agreed another peace treaty with Venice.

October 26: Cardinal Isidore of Kiev, sent by the Pope, arrived in Constantinople to seal the union between the Orthodox and Catholic churches. He was accompanied by a troop of 200 men. The city was thus divided into two camps: those who were for and those against the union.

December 12: The union of the churches was solemnly proclaimed in Haghia Sophia by the Emperor Constantine XI and Cardinal Isidore.

January 26, 1453: Seven hundred Genoese mercenaries arrived in Constantinople, led by Giovanni Giustiniani. He was put in charge of defending the walls. These were the only Western reinforcements.

February 26: Seven Venetian ships with 700 men aboard secretly sailed out of Constantinople despite a promise given to the emperor that no one would flee the city.

March 1 to 15: The Turkish forces gathered in front of the city.

April 2: Preceded by cannons and siege engines, Mehmet arrived at the city walls.

April 4: The start of the siege. About 17,000 men defended the ramparts. The Turkish

army was estimated to be 250,000 men, and had the most powerful artillery ever amassed.

April 18: The first attack was repulsed.

April 20: Three Genoese merchant ships and a Byzantine ship brought reinforcements to break the blockade of the Ottoman flotilla, prying open the enormous chain that closed the entrance to the Golden Horn and joining the besieged citizens.

April 22: Aiming to enter the harbor and command the Golden Horn, Mehmet had some 50 ships transported overland on wooden rollers from the Bosphorus. His navy thus avoided the Genoese city of Galata and reached the Golden Horn, where it reinforced the troops already attacking Constantinople. He built a bridge.

May 7: The second assault began at four in the morning. The 30,000 attackers were repulsed, with heavy losses.

> "And the greatest of all this, that you will capture a city whose renown has gone to all parts of the world."
>
> Mehmet II

May 11: Constant bombardments seriously damaged the walls of Constantinople.

May 12: A third assault of 50,000 men was launched at midnight. Serious losses on both sides.

May 16: Galleries dug by Serbian miners

for the Sultan were parried by a system of counter-galleries designed by a German engineer who was working for the Byzantines.

May 19: Mehmet II had a bridge built on the Golden Horn to allow him to attack the sea walls.

May 22: Two other Turkish galleries were

put out of action. A partial eclipse of the moon terrified those under siege.

May 23: A brigatine sent to meet the

Venetian navy returned to report that no reinforcements were in sight.

May 26: Before the city was taken, Mehmet II ordered three days of solemn fast and prayer.

May 28: The final assault was announced for the following day.

May 29: Three hours before daybreak, Mehmet II gave orders for the final assault to begin. At dawn, Saint-Roman Gate (known as Top Kapi today) was destroyed and taken by the infantry which poured into the city. The Western defenders fled back to

their ships. Emperor Constantine died in the battle and, even though the citizens,

exhausted after seven weeks of siege, put up a fight, the Turks poured into the city. The fall of Constantinople, on May 29, 1453, marked the end of the Byzantine Empire.

35

FROM THE EMIRATE TO THE OTTOMAN EMPIRE

A.GRECIAN

Through his physical appearance and his majestic bearing Süleyman projected an image worthy of such a powerful monarch.

The Anatolian Selçuk kingdom, created after the Turkish conquest two centuries earlier, collapsed at the end of the 13th century under Mongolian pressure. Of the 15-odd tribal principalities set up opposite Byzantium, it was in fact the smallest, founded by Osman, an obscure tribal chief, that was constantly waging war on its neighbors. In 1326 his son, Orhan, consolidated Osman's conquests by taking Bursa. He transferred the Selçuk capital there and, in the following years, took possession of Nicaea (Iznik) and Gallipoli (Gelibolu). Not content with taking over the other principalities, the Ottomans were to establish the last great near-eastern empire, worthy successors to the Romans, the Byzantines and the Arabs. No longer hemmed in by rival powers, the Ottoman emirate contemplated a Byzantine world in crisis and, beyond, the Balkans.

A.EGIPTIA

OTTOMAN SULTANS
Osman I (1280–1324)
Orhan Gazi (1326–1359)
Murat I (1360–1389)
Beyazıt I (1389–1413)
Mehmet I (1413–1421)
Murat II (1421–1451)
Mehmet II (1451–1481)
Beyazıt II (1481–1512)
Selim I (1512–1520)
Süleyman I (1520–1566)
Selim II (1566–1574)
Murat III (1574–1595)
Mehmet III (1595–1603)
Ahmet I (1603–1617)
Mustafa I (1617–1618)

A.ASSYRIAN

A.ARABIAN

A.PERSIAN

> "The sultan of sultans of the east and the west, he who lavishes crowns upon monarchs throughout the land, the shadow of God on Earth..."

OTTOMAN SULTANS
Osman II (1618–1622)
Mustafa I (1622–1623)
Murat IV (1623–1640)
Ibrahim (1640–1648)
Mehmet IV (1648–1687)
Süleyman II (1687–1691)
Ahmet II (1691–1695)
Mustafa II (1695–1703)
Ahmet III (1703–1730)
Mahmut I (1730–1754)
Osman III (1754–1757)
Mustafa III (1757–1774)
Abdül Hamit I (1774–1789)
Selim III (1789–1807)
Mustafa IV (1807–1808)
Mahmut II (1808–1839)
Abdül Mecit I (1839–1861)
Abdül Aziz (1861–1876)
Murat V (1876, deposed)
Abdül Hamit II (1876–1909)
Mehmet V (1908–1918)
Mehmet VI (1918–1922)
Abdül Mecit II (1922, caliph, abdicated in 1924)

HIS WIFE

HIS WIFE

HIS WIFE

HIS WIFE

HIS WIFE

The age-old rivalry between the Turks and Venice caused seven wars, totalling 71 years of conflict over two and a half centuries – wars that exhausted both states. At the same time the abandonment of the traditional Mediterranean trade routes and the discovery of the new worlds resulted in the rise of the Atlantic powers.

The emirate, founded in 1299, took root 50 years later in the Balkans, and with the fall of Constantinople in 1453, reached from the Adriatic to the Danube. The conquest of the Byzantine capital conferred imperial stature, and its position inevitably led to direct confrontation with the other great powers of the time.

● THE BATTLE OF LEPANTO

Under the reign of Sultan Selim II, son of Süleyman, the empire suffered a number of set-backs, but, between the victory of Preveza (1538) and the defeat at Lepanto (1571), the Ottomans ruled the sea. Their naval supremacy in the Mediterranean put the Christians on the defensive. Pope Pius V called for a Holy War and took the lead of the Holy League (Philip II's Spain, Naples, Genoa, and Venice). The Christian fleet gathered in Messina under the command of Don Juan of Austria. The Ottoman armada, strengthened by a privateer fleet from Algeria and Tripoli, was made up of galleys crewed by Greek sailors under the command of Ali Paşa. After this naval defeat, the Grand Vizier Sokollu set to rebuilding his fleet which would take Tunis in 1574.

THE ROLE OF THE INFANTRY
The fleet blocked the Gulf of Corinth near the city of Lepanto. Just before the engagement began the four Venetian galleys opened fire with their formidable artillery causing considerable losses among the Turkish ranks. Boarding maneuvers and hand-to-hand combat followed. Throughout the afternoon the Italian and Spanish troops fought the Janissaries along the length of both fleets. The Turkish Grand Admiral Müezzinzade Ali Paşa was killed.

THE BATTLE
At dawn on October 7, 1571, the two fleets found themselves face to face. The Christian fleet consisted of 208 galleys; the Ottoman fleet of 260 galleys. In the center, the two flagship galleys; the galley of Ali Paşa and that of Don Juan faced off. In three hours the fleet was destroyed and only 30 ships managed to return to their home port.

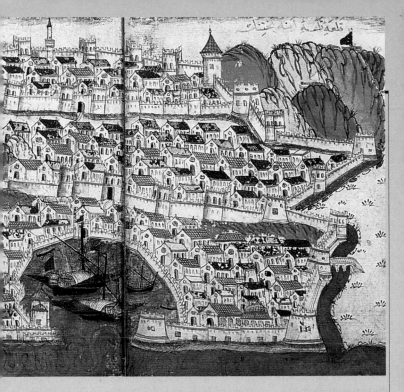

عقلة قتله ابن ختان

MINIATURE OF THE CITY OF LEPANTO

This detailed map of Lepanto was made around 1540. The city and its port were conquered by Sultan Beyazıt II in 1499. Kasim Bey, Süleyman's vizier, then governor of the Moors, built fortifications. The citadel was surrounded by moats and protected by Janissaries. Because of its location, Lepanto controlled the entrance to the Gulf of Corinth.

THE ATLAS OF ALI MACAR RE'IS

The Ottoman seafarers possessed precise maps such as this one of the western Mediterranean made in 1567. It consists of nine maps drawn on parchment. The coastline is marked in blue and islands and important cities are highlighted in green. The names of the ports are written in Turkish.

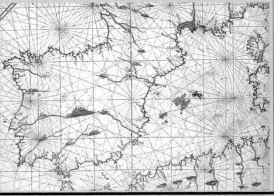

39

● THE RISE AND FALL OF THE OTTOMAN EMPIRE

In the 16th century the Ottomans negotiated the first "capitulations" between Süleyman and François I, then with the English (1580) and the Dutch (1612). At its height the empire included Mesopotamia, Syria, most of the coast of the Arab peninsula, Egypt, and the coast of North Africa. It engaged in a merciless fight against the Hapsburgs, who controlled not only the German empire, but also that of Spain and soon Portugal (1580–1640). The struggle took place on two fronts: Central Europe, with the conquest of Hungary (1526) and the siege of Vienna, and the Mediterranean, where the Ottomans maintained their supremacy from the victory of Preveza (1538) through to their defeat at Lepanto (1571).

At the end of the 16th century the Ottomans had an inadequate army and were at a disadvantage when engaging the Hapsburg army, which used numerous technical innovations paid for by the gold from the recently discovered Americas.

The European Wars of Religion, especially the Thirty Years War (1618–1648), interrupted this struggle. When it began again in the second half of the 17th century the Ottoman Empire had a fragile economy, and was in a weak position.

> "The over joyous souls in these countries are
> like children treated to halva."
>
> Süleyman the Magnificent

After the defeat of the Turks outside Vienna (1683) the Hapsburgs began to take back Central Europe. At the same time the Russian Empire showed signs of expanding, which was to lead to a long conflict: there would be nine Russo-Turkish wars between 1683 and 1918. In 1699, the Ottomans signed the Treaty of Karlowitz (the first to be unfavorable to them) and lost important territory. In the 19th century the treaty of San Stefano (1878) pushed Turkey out of Europe. Serbia, Romania, and Bulgaria were given independence, Bosnia and Herzegovina were occupied by the Austrians, and western Anatolia by the Russians.

In 1891 Russia obtained free passage for its commercial ships through the straits.

MAP OF THE OTTOMAN EMPIRE
Turkey and other countries under Ottoman sovereignty in 1626: in Europe, Greece, Albania, Bulgaria, Bosnia, Hungary, Romania, Serbia and Bessarabia; in Asia and Africa, Algeria, Tunisia, Libya, and Egypt. At this time the empire had several setbacks at the hands of the Iranians in Georgia and in Azerbaijan.

At the turn of the century national movements led to the subdivision of the empire. In addition to the Balkan revolutions there was the National Arab Movement which, along with World War I, brought about the end of the empire. New states were founded upon its remains. The treaty of Lausanne, signed on July 24, 1923, recognized that Turkey's permanent borders included Thrace and the territories under dispute: Smyrna, Cilicia and the Eastern provinces.

TURKEY AND THE TANZIMAT (1839–1878)
This great modernizing movement was pushed forward by the ministers and the sultans. The reforms affected the administration and the state machinery, such as the army, the law, and education. Influenced in its innovations by the great powers (Britain, Germany, and France), Turkey created the first Ottoman Constitution in 1876. The Westernization of the society can be seen in the arts as well: literature, painting, and theater were all inspired by Western models. Newspapers also played an important role. But the 19th-century sultans remained caliphs and took part in traditional ceremonies just as their predecessors did.

THE END OF THE EMPIRE

THE YOUNG TURKS. A revolution led by officers in 1908 restored the constitution and introduced an elected parliament. Power now lay in the hands of the Young Turks and the Union and Progress Committee, which was led by the generals Cemal and Enver Paşa and the future Minister of the Interior Talat Paşa. This triumvirate persuaded the Sultan to fight on the German side in the First World War.

August 2, 1914
Secret pact with Germany.

THE DARDANELLES. It was this alliance that led to the Allies' expedition to the Dardanelles in 1915, to force a passage through the straits then blocked by German ships. The resistance put up by the Turkish army under the command of Mustafa Kemal, Enver Paşa and the German General Liman von Sanders, together with strategic errors on the part of the Allies, resulted in failure. This was to be the first and last resounding success that the Turkish troops would have during the war, as they were all but wiped out in the bloody campaigns fought on the Russian front and in Palestine. The defeat of Germany and other Axis powers in November 1918 led to the collapse of the Ottoman Empire. The Ottomans lost their territories in the Arab Near East and all their European territories except the western part of Istanbul.

ENVER PAŞA

THE OCCUPATION OF ISTANBUL. Early in 1919 the British and French occupied Istanbul and took control of the Straits and other strategic coastal areas in Turkey, while the Greeks landed in Smyrna (Izmir) and soon afterwards advanced into western Asia Minor. On August 10, 1919, the completely powerless Mehmet VI was forced to sign the Treaty of Sèvres, by which the Ottoman Empire lost almost all

November 13, 1918
The allied fleet occupies Istanbul.

June 28, 1919
Treaty of Versailles.

August 10, 1919
Treaty of Sèvres.

of its territory in Europe and in Asia retained only those parts of Anatolia that were not claimed by the Greeks, Italians and the French.

1920
The first Great National Assembly at Ankara. The war of independence begins.

TURKISH NATIONALISM AND MUSTAFA KEMAL.
The great majority of Turks refused to bow to the diktat of the western powers. Nationalist fervor began in Anatolia. Mustafa Kemal, an officer who had distinguished himself in the Dardanelles, mobilized the Anatolian population, which consisted largely of peasants, and embarked on a war of national

1922
Smyrna is recaptured.

Moustafa Kiemal Pacha

liberation. On April 23, 1920, Mustafa Kemal, later acclaimed as Atatürk, Father of the Turks, presided over the new National Assembly at Ankara, which formed a government in opposition to the Sultan's postwar puppet regime in Istanbul.

1922–1924
Short reign of the last Ottoman calif, Abdul Mecit.
1922–1923
Exchange of Greek and Turkish nationals.

THE TURKISH REPUBLIC

The Turkish Nationalists then defeated the Greek army in several engagements in Anatolia, forcing them to flee to Greece in September 1922. During the following year more than a million Greeks were forced to leave Asia Minor and resettle in Greece, while about half a million Turks left Crete and Greece. This population exchange was one of the consequences of the Treaty of Versailles, signed in July 1923, which established the boundaries of Turkey essentially as they are today.

July 24, 1923
Treaty of Lausanne.

October 19, 1923
Ankara becomes the capital of Turkey.

MUSTAFA KEMAL ATATÜRK, FIRST PRESIDENT OF THE TURKISH REPUBLIC. The Turkish National Assembly abolished the sultanate on November 1, 1922, and Mehmet II fled Istanbul aboard a warship. His younger brother Abdül Mecit II succeeded him as Caliph. On March 3, 1924, the National Assembly abolished the caliphate, and the Caliph, accompanied by his whole family, was driven to the frontier. On October 29, 1923, the National Assembly created the Republic of Turkey, with Mustafa Kemal as its first president and Ankara as the new capital.

1928
The Latin alphabet is adopted.

TURKEY BETWEEN THE WARS. Kemal Atatürk's political agenda caused far-reaching change in the politics of Turkey as a whole. The new republic was modeled on the Constitution of April 30, 1924. Atatürk pursued a policy of secularization; judicial law replaced the Koran and religious education was banned in schools.

October 1939
Aid pact signed with France and Great Britain.

One of the most dramatic changes was the banning of the Arabic alphabet, which has few vowels, in favor of the Latin alphabet. European dress became popular and Mustafa Kemal favored helmets and hats over the fez that was worn by Ottoman officials. Industrialization became a priority for the republican Turkey of the 1930's, and a Turkish bourgeoisie slowly took the place of the great Greek and Armenian families. At the same time, the population of Istanbul changed: Armenians, Greeks and Serbs were replaced by Muslim Turks abandoning rural Anatolia. In 1938, on the death of Mustafa Kemal, Ismet Inönü became President of the Republic. Turkey remained neutral during World War II.

TURKEY TODAY

1938–50
Presidency of Ismet Inönü.

1950–60
Government of Menderes.

1960
General Gürsel's military coup

1961–5
Inönü's coalition government.

1965–71
Demirel's coalition governement.

1974
Turkish troops invade Cyprus.

1974 and 1977–9
Ecevit's coalition governments.

During the Cold War, Turkey became more closely allied to the West: it received Marshall Plan aid from 1947 and joined NATO in 1952. In the 1950's Menderes' government gave agriculture a boost by introducing mechanization.

INDUSTRIALIZATION. Based on five-year plans, industrial policy until the end of the 1970's was geared to financing food imports. Later, after the liberalization that took place in the 1980's, it was oriented towards exports. Thus, having initially built steelworks and refineries and geared itself to heavy industry, Turkey subsequently turned to producing consumer durables.

AGRICULTURE. Turkey is one of the few countries with a rapidly expanding population which is still able to feed itself. Agricultural mechanization introduced in the 1950's was followed by major irrigation and sanitation projects. One of these is GAP, the ambitious project in southeastern Anatolia to increase the region's agricultural and energy-producing potential by building dams on the Euphrates and opening irrigation channels. Agriculture is moving away from tobacco and dried fruits and towards industrial crops such as cotton and oil-producing plants and greenhouse fruit and vegetables grown for export.

> "There is no land or city that is like
> No place to live that can compare with it."
>
> Nâbî (1642–1712)

ISTANBUL'S DEMOGRAPHIC EXPLOSION. Today Turkey has 52 million inhabitants, five times more than in 1920. The increase has been considerable in Istanbul. In 1920 there were about 500,000 living in Istanbul, half of whom were not Turks. In 1990, a census counted over 7,500,000, of whom only 20,000 to 30,000 were from ethnic minorities (Greek, Armenian or Jewish). Istanbul's demographic explosion has been caused by the continuous influx of people from country areas who have given up agriculture in the hope of improving their quality of life. They settle in hurriedly built areas of Istanbul, and often live in makeshift buildings known as *gecekondu*.

FATIH MEHMET BRIDGE

OPENING UP TOWARD EUROPE

The state of the Turkish economy is dependent on a number of factors, both internal (government instability) and regional (conflicts in the Caucasus, the Balkans, Cyprus and the Near East). The budget deficit and especially inflation (90% in 1997) are sapping Turkey's sustained growth (7.4% in 1996). Trade with Europe, its main commercial partner, continues to grow and it is exporting more and more manufactured goods. France has been the leading foreign investor in Turkey since 1994. But membership of the European Union, first discussed in 1987, has been delayed, despite pressure from Ankara. Faced with these difficulties, Turkey has begun new economic relationships: significant Turkish investments, notably in public works, are underway in central Asia, the Arab countries and Russia, while projects for pipelines transporting petrol from the Caspian Sea via Anatolia are the subject of fierce negotiations. These economic breakthroughs remain modest, however, and money sent back by Turks living in western Europe and in the Arab countries continues to help the balance of payments, as it has for the last thirty years.

THE BREAK-UP OF THE SOVIET UNION. The dramatic upheaval that the Balkans and especially the Caucasus have experienced in recent years, together with the troubles in northern Iraq, are a source of concern to Turkey but also underline its indisputable role as a powerful influence in the region: Turkish is spoken in Azerbaijan, Uzbekhistan, Turkmenistan, and Kirgiztan, as well as by small groups in Bulgaria, Greece, Moldavia, Iran, Afghanistan, Russia, and China.

September 12, 1980
Military coup. General Evren becomes head of state.

June 14, 1993
Mrs Tansu Ciller, President of the DYP party, is elected prime minister.

March 6, 1995
Signing of customs agreement with Europe.

1996–7
For the first time in the history of republican Turkey, a Muslim, Necmettin Erbakan, becomes prime minister. Tension with the secular forces of the army.

1997
Mesut Yilmaz becomes prime minister.

45

A little

ORIGINS

The so-called Turkish languages of the Ural-Altaic family (Turkic and Mongolic) make up a huge linguistic group of some 180 million speakers (in Siberia, Central Asia, Altai, etc.), a third of whom live in Turkey. The fact that this young republic was associated with the residual Ottoman Empire gave Turkey's Turkish prestige and a status as the standard

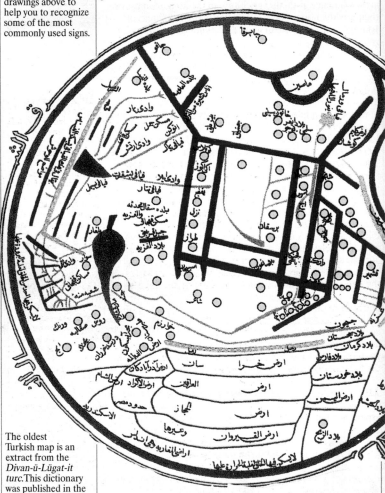

The oldest Turkish map is an extract from the *Divan-ü-Lügat-it turc.* This dictionary was published in the 11th century by Kâşgartlı Mahmut, and is a summary of all of the languages and customs of the Turkish tribes. It was written to be presented to their new allies, the caliphs of Baghdad. This map shows the Caspian Sea to the right.

of reference for other Turkish-speaking communities. A distinction is generally made between contemporary Turkish and historic "Ottoman Turkish", which is hardly spoken at all now.

LINGUISTIC REFORM

Today the Turkish spoken in Turkey is standardized – the product of significant linguistic alterations and planning undertaken during the Atatürk reforms from 1928 onwards.

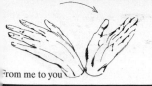
From me to you

Come towards me   Go away

The reforms took into consideration the recommendations of various contemporary linguists and philologists who worked together to define the *yeni türkçe* (new Turkish), or *öz türkçe* (purified Turkish). The policy of reform adopted by Atatürk had two aims: to break completely with the Ottoman system, notably by abandoning the Arabic alphabet and replacing it with the Latin equivalent, and to give a noble written form to the popular Turkish dialect which was the living heritage of the ancient Central-Asian pre-Islamic Turkish languages.

RETURN TO OTTOMAN ORIGINS. The results of the linguistic reform are impressive: in July 1932, 35 percent of the Turkish vocabulary was of Turkish origin; by 1946 it was 46 percent, and today it has reached 80 percent. The one thousand Turkish words most used today were "born" following the 1932 reform.

THE STRUCTURE OF THE LANGUAGE

Turkish is an agglutinative language. Its basic structure is made up of verbal or nominative roots of two or three syllables. To these are attached some 200 suffixes, with various grammatical functions, ranging from declension suffixes, to those for plurals, conjugations, adverbs, etc. All suffixes are added according to a rule of concatenation which is structured according to vocal harmony.
Vowels are divided into two groups: those pronounced at the back of the mouth (e, i, ö, ü), and those pronounced at the front (a, ı, o, u). Other criteria also come into play, such as open/closed and high/low. This phonology also governs consonants.

CONSEQUENCES OF THE REFORM

The abrupt linguistic break, along with the banning of the Arab alphabet, had disastrous consequences. The teaching of the Ottoman language and literature in the Arabic alphabet could have formed the basis of learning about a great culture, just as does Latin or Ancient Greek. Though steeped in an architectural and historic environment rich in inscriptions – there are more than 55 million in the Ottoman archives – the children of the Republic cannot even decipher the inscription on their grandfathers' tombstones.

CONTEMPORARY TURKISH LITTERATURE
The new Turkish literature, recognized both nationally and internationally and including for example the poems of Nazım Hikmet and novels of Yaşar Kemal, has given modern Turkey its literary prestige.

THE RUNES OF THE FUNERARY STELAE
The funerary stelae of Central Asia were carved in the 6th century. They relate the heroic deeds of the Turkish chiefs of the region – such as government and political councils – and were commissioned by the deceased during their lifetime. These funerary stelae constitute a written history of a nation of nomadic pastoralists. The vocabulary and syntax of this language is very close to that of Anatolian Turkish: drawing on archaic scources *öz türkçe* was inspired by the language of these runic inscriptions.

● THE TURKISH LANGUAGE

PHONETICS

Turkish has few sounds that are difficult for an English-speaker. It is usually pronounced as it is written. There are 29 letters in the Turkish alphabet. Below are listed only those letters that are additional to or are pronounced differently from English. The letters Q, W, and X do not exist: their equivalents are K, V and KS.

CONSONANTS	PRONOUNCIATION	VOWELS	PRONOUNCIATION
c	'j'	e	'e' as in bed
ç	'ch' as in chair	ı	'i' in flirt
g	'g' as in gift	ö	'u' as in furniture
ğ	silent	u	'u' as in you
s	'z'	ü	the French 'u'
ş	'sh' or 's' in sugar		

Head tilted back: no

Movement of the head up and down: yes

Movement of the head from left to right: expresses doubt

Hand over the heart: thank you

To ward off bad luck you pinch the lobe of your right ear with your right hand, and whistle, then knock wood three times.

Arts, crafts and traditions

A SUMMER-HOUSE BY THE BOSPHORUS
The strait is the site of many yalı and summer houses. In the 19th century several new palaces were built there for the sultans.

The Dolmabahçe Sarayı was built for Sultan Abdül Mecit between 1842 and 1856. It was designed by the Armenian architect Balyan, and is surrounded by a large tree-filled park, interspersed with beds of scented flowers and shrubs which are reflected in a pond with a fountain. Abdül Aziz succeeded his brother and had Balyan construct a palace for him at Beylerbeyi, on the opposite side of the river. The park is planted with rare trees arranged in terraces on the hillside. His successor, Abdül Hamit II, established himself in the Yıldız palace where he built many summer-houses in landscaped grounds among tree-lined rivers and lakes.

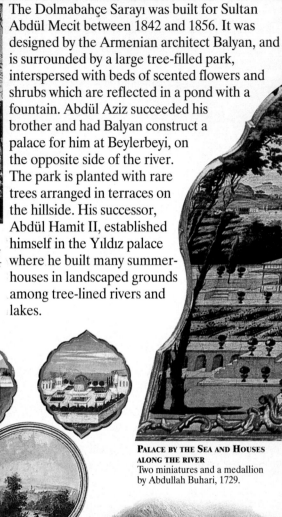

PALACE BY THE SEA AND HOUSES ALONG THE RIVER
Two miniatures and a medallion by Abdullah Buhari, 1729.

THE PRINCES' ISLANDS
An engraving by Thomas Allom. These mountainous islands remained relatively isolated until the arrival of the first steamships at the end of the 19th century. From then on people from Istanbul began building yalı among the pine forests and on the coasts.

SUMMER-HOUSE WITH FAIENCE FAÇADE Painting by Gedikpaşalı, 1889.

YILDIZ PALACE AND GARDEN Painting by Şevki, 1891.

KAĞITHANE MOSQUE Painting by Mustafa, 19th century.

SUMMER-HOUSES AND GARDENS Mural painting, 1789–1807.

The style of mural painting inaugurated in the Topkapı Sarayı at the end of the 18th century was imitated in numerous yalı and *konak*: whether the paintings represent houses surrounded by gardens or open countryside, water is always part of the picture.

The yellow salon in the ceremonial wing of the Yıldız palace is famous for the landscapes painted on the ceiling.

The Turkish concept of the ideal house has hardly changed since Mehmet II's palace and gardens were constructed on a promontory overlooking the Golden Horn on one side and the Sea of Marmara on the other. The summer-houses within the parks and the yalı on the shoreline are constructed following the same basic principles: they are built in wood and can be thrown wide open to the outdoors, where the water and greenery create a fresh and beautiful backdrop.

51

The most splendid Ottoman costumes were made of precious fabrics such as brocades, silk velvets, and marbled organdy. The Bursa workshops span raw silk which was imported from Iran, doubled, milled, and dipped in baths of vegetable dye before being woven or used for embroidery. The printed or embroidered patterns and weaves were especially intricate on womens' costumes. They tended to be very detailed, showing primarily flowers (such as eglantine, hyacinths, carnations, roses, tulips, and cherry or pomegranate tree blossoms) which were either lifelike or stylized in arabesques, palmettes, or foliage. Collections of Istanbul's most beautiful costumes are shown at the Topkapı and Sadberk Hanem museums.

FUNCTIONARIES AND JANISSARIES
Their leader wore a "bonnet of crimson velvet, in the shape of a brimless cap, lined with cotton, and around which they wrap a turban. The turban is made up of a fabric or silk scarf which is several yards long, and as wide as the fabric bolt: they wrap it around a number of times [...]; there are several ways to wrap it. You can identify the condition and quality of a man by the way he wears his turban."

J. Thévenot, *Voyage au Levant*

KIZLAR AĞASI
The chief eunuch and leading dignitary of the seraglio, painted by J.B. Van Mour (1671–1737), is dressed in a *ferace* of green and white silk, and a red silk robe clasped with a decorated buckle. On his head is a red muslin turban.

In the 17th century the Turks wore a sort of fabric dolman, made of taffeta, satin, or cotton, beneath their shirts. This dolman was knotted at the waist by a wide fabric or leather belt with a gold or silver buckle. One or two daggers were tucked into the belt, along with handkerchiefs and a tobacco pouch. They then donned a *ferace*, a large floor-length coat with very long sleeves. In the 19th century, with the arrival of the Reform era, the Turks adopted a Western-style costume characterized by a long redingote in a dark color called stambouline. The turban was eventually abandoned in favor of the fez, a stiff red cap. In the 20th century, with the end of the Ottoman Empire, the wearing of the fez was abolished by Atatürk.

WOMEN'S COSTUMES IN THE 18TH CENTURY

They wore a long coat which was usually green, and an ankle-length *ferace* made out of satin or tafetta with such long sleeves that their fingers could not be seen. The embroidered brocade dress was open and covered wide pants, known as shalvar, which were knotted at the ankles. The long-sleeved silk smocks, (*bürümcek*) were embroidered with skill. A wide embroidered velvet, satin, leather, or cashmere belt was worn around the waist. In the winter the *ferace* was lined with fur. The hem of the fabric was sewn onto yellow or red leather slippers (*mest*) over which they pulled babouches.

WOMEN'S COSTUME IN THE 19TH CENTURY

These women adopted the Western style, but their head was covered with a veil, a *mahrem*, which consisted of two pieces of muslin: the first covered the face up to the nose, the second was wrapped around the head and neck and knotted.

ISTANBUL MERCHANT AND HIS WIFE

He wore the traditional costume, while his wife was dressed in an *entari*, a long jacket with a train and wide pants.

YOUNG GROOM, COUNTRY PEASANT

The groom was clothed in a *yelek*, a jacket made of a rich fabric with blue and black stripes, embroidered in wool and silk.

MUSLIM WOMAN

The woman's dress was held together by a silver belt decorated with gold and silver buckels.

53

Classical Turkish music draws its inspiration from various Islamic cultures, and was further enriched during the Ottoman era by influences from conquered lands. In the 8th century traditional songs and poetry recitals were accompanied by instruments such as the *def* (drum), the *tanbûr* (lute), and the *ney* (flute). The repertoire, as well as the variety of instruments, increased during the 13th century, a period in which some very important music was written, during which the great poet Mevlâna composed a number of works. The apogee of Ottoman music coincided with the brilliant reign of Süleyman the Magnificent (1520–66). Along with vocal music (*fasil*), instrumental music was also developed, notably that played by the Janissaries (*mehter*).

PERCUSSION INSTRUMENTS IN A JANISSARY REGIMENTAL BAND The *kös*, large copper kettledrums, are predominant in the *mehter*, with their sound resembling thunder. The *davul* is the most common drum: players wear it hung from their necks, and beat it with a drumstick.

TANBUR lute.

ÇANK harp.

KEMENÇE A long-necked lute and bow.

THE SANTUR
Of Persian origin, this 72-chord zither is played with drumsticks and is very popular in Turkey.

THE SAZ
There is evidence that this instrument has been in use since the 12th century, and it is still played in some traditional Turkish music. This type of lute can be easily recognized by its long neck which is bent backwards, and by its pear-shaped drum.

In the 18th century, Gluck integrated Turkish kettledrums into his *Iphigénie en Tauride* and Mozart was inspired by the music of the Janissaries in his opera *Escape From the Seraglio*.

Today little is known for certain about the origins of shadow theater. It is thought to have been imported from Java by the Arabs, and was then developed in Egypt where Selim I encountered it when he conquered that country in 1517.

Early in the 16th century, a typically Turkish form of the imported shadow theater developed. It was named after its principle character, Karagöz, literally "black eyes". For three centuries these comic plays were the only arena for political and social criticism.

There are a number of female characters in the Karagöz theater but usually they play only minor roles as wives, young marriageable girls, servants, old women, dancers or witches.

The puppeteer moves the figures about in front of a fabric screen which is strongly lit from behind. The jointed marionettes are made of camel skin and painted with bright colors, and they are moved around by means of a stick attached to them.

Some of the plots are taken from ancient myths or traditional folk tales. They can involve fantastical characters, demons from the underworld or mythical animals.

Karagöz and his accomplice Hacıvat are at the center of all the plots and intrigues. The comic element is reinforced by figures called Taklits who are caricatures of merchants, the middle classes, country-dwellers, and foreigners.

57

The Ottoman conquerers retained much more of Byzantium's heritage than one might imagine, including the institution of public baths. The baths both surprised and impressed most of the Western travelers who discovered them. In the 18th century, Jean Thévenot described them minutely in his *Voyage au Levant*: "I will describe the one at Tophana, next to a superb mosque, since it is one of the most beautiful that I have seen. You enter by a large square room, about 20 feet long, with a very high ceiling. This room is lined with stone benches built against the surrounding wall. They are as wide as the wall, and half as high, and all are covered with matting." The Turkish hammams retain the structure of Roman baths, with the tepidarium, the frigidarium and the caldarium; where there were thermal springs, the baths are called kaplicas.

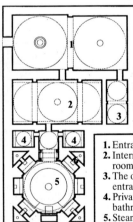

THE STEAM ROOM OF YENI KAPLICA
This gives access to the private bathrooms which were originally reserved for dignitaries.

1. Entrance hall.
2. Intermediate room.
3. The old private entrance.
4. Private bathrooms.
5. Steam room.
6. Alcoves.

PLAN OF THE YENI KAPLICA, IN BURSA
These public baths were founded in 1550 by the Grand Vizier Rüstem Paşa. They include an entrance hall, often with a decorative fountain, and a cloakroom; an intermediate room to allow you to get used to the heat; and an octagonal steam room with a great circular pool in the middle and baths in alcoves round the sides. The wash-basins provided hot and cold water.

Some kaplicas had a pool in the center of the steam room where the clientèle could bathe after being washed.

TURKISH BATHS

Western imagination has transformed the hammam and the harem into erotic fantasies which are reinforced by the works of the French and Italian painters who visited Istanbul. Lady Mary Wortley-Montagu's visits to the Turkish baths in Edirne and later in Istanbul, and her admiration for the beauty of Turkish women's bodies, provided the inspiration for a painting by Ingres (shown left): *The Turkish Bath* (1862). Lady Mary noted that the hammam was for women what the café was for men – a chance to socialize.

"Turkish women, following an ancient Asian and Greek custom, go to the baths in all weathers, less for their health than to beautify themselves. The other, and main, reason is because it gives them an excuse to get out of their houses."

Nicholas de Nicolay

There were separate hammams for men and women except in small towns, where they bathed at different times. Until the turn of the 20th century, young boys bathed with the women until puberty.

59

CARPETS AND KILIMS

The origins of kilim decorations go back to prehistoric times, with motifs symbolizing goddesses.

The importance of carpets in Turkish life is a result of the lifestyles of the Turkish people. Carpets or kilims were essential for providing shade from the sun and lining the insides of tents, thus giving protection from the rigors of the climate. When the nomadic tribes of Anatolia converted to Islam, carpets acquired a new function as prayer mats. The different types range from knotted carpets woven of wool or silk to tapestry weave kilims. *Cicims* were embroidered kilims.

ÇUVAL
Carpet bag from Malatya.

KILIMS
In nomadic tribes and in villages, kilims were kept for domestic use. The techniques and motifs of each tribe and region were passed on from one generation of women to the next. Therefore the styles were not altered by commercial pressures until this century.

THE STITCHING OF KILIMS
The diversity of styles results from the different techniques developed from one tribe to the next.

CARPET WORKSHOPS
The carpets which decorated the palaces of sultans and dignitaries came from great workshops which, from the 16th century, exported examples to Europe. The workshops of Uşak, Kumkapı and Hereke were among the better known.

Elibelinde   Burdock   Rose

UŞAK CARPET (16TH CENTURY)
The geometric Turkish patterns are influenced by the Persian safavid style.

A COURT CARPET OF HEREKE STYLE (LATE 16TH CENTURY). In the symbolic mihrab niche is a tree of life – here an almond tree with birds perching on it – surrounded by a floral border.

PRAYER RUG FROM ERZURUM
The central image is an alcove in a mosque pointing in the direction of Mecca, which is known in Turkish as *Mirhab*.

CARPET WEAVING
The women knot the weft to two strands of warp to evolve a traditional pattern.

The method of knotting differs from place to place. The double or Ghiordes knot, also used in Europe, made the carpets strong. The Persian, Sehna knot resulted in more intricate patterns and gave a beautiful finish.

RELIGION IN TURKEY

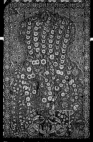

Panels of tiles in a mosque.

In the middle of the 11th century the khans of the Oğuz Turks of central Asia adopted Islam in order to control the silk route, in alliance with their former enemies the Arabs. It was an entirely political conversion, and was only a matter of convenience. Until the mid 16th century the epics of the time celebrate the ancient divinities of the Turkish religion, while affirming the strength of their Muslim faith in opposition to the Christians. The Ottoman version of Turkish Islam is primarily political: the sultan is the swordsman of Islam and Allah's shadow on earth. With the coming of the Republic in 1923, Mustafa Kemal Atatürk pursued a policy of secularization, because religion had become synonymous with attachment to the past.

Some of the finest examples of Ottoman art are found in the decoration of the mosques and the ornamentation of religious objects, such as sumptuously illuminated copies of the Koran, with leather covers embossed with gold, silver, or sometimes precious stones, or Koran stands made of ebony inlaid with mother-of-pearl and bone. The religious manuscript shown here, and its rich tabernacle, are remarkable for the fineness of the calligraphic writing as well as for their pastel-toned floral decoration.

With the revival of the Islamic religion over the past few years, Koranic schools and places of worship are proliferating. Here a *softa* or older student is reading the Koran in the Bursa Ulu Cami.

WOMEN AND ISLAM
The Turkish state, deeply secularized since the Kemalist reforms of forced secularization, have multiplied measures in favor of the equality of the sexes. The 1926 civil code defines the rights of women in marriage, divorce, inheritance, and education. The right to vote was granted in 1935, well before many European countries.

THE NAME OF ALLAH
The name of Allah is
painted on the walls of
mosques in majestic Arabic
calligraphy.

**SCENE FROM A
WEDDING AT EYÜP**
The assistance of an
imam is still often
required for the blessing
of civil marriages. Some
families continue to
practice the henna ritual
of dyeing the bride's
palms and the soles of
her feet. Few brides
wear the old-style
embroidered red robe;
most prefer a Western-
style white dress.

**19TH-CENTURY
STREET SCENES**
The picture below
shows elders
reading the
Koran outside a
mosque.

A characteristic style emerged at the beginning of the 6th century: a fusion of classical realism with the symbolic figurativeness of Roman art. The majority of known works date from after the iconoclastic period (726–843). The fresco technique was developed sometime in the 10th century, but it was not considered to be a serious alternative to the more expensive mosaics. The latter are the true masterpieces of Byzantine art and are the product of sophisticated techniques. The modeling of the faces is accomplished with graded colors of stone, and their luminous appearance is achieved by varying the position of the tiles, so the light is caught at different angles.

CHRIST IN MAJESTY, A 9TH- TO EARLY 10TH-CENTURY MOSAIC
This mosaic (right) decorates the tympanum of the Imperial Gate and the entrance to the nave of Haghia Sophia basilica.

A 14TH-CENTURY FRESCO
One of the angels surrounding the Virgin and Child in the funerary chapel in the old Saint-Savior-in-Chora church (Kariye Cami'i).

From the 9th century onwards the positioning of the tableaux and the hierarchy of the characters represented in Byzantine churches were obliged to follow an official schema, probably decreed by Michael III. Christ Pantocrator, or Master of the Universe, always had to be placed in the center of the main cupola.

BYZANTINE IVORIES
In the center of this fine example of a Byzantine ivory (left), which dates from the 6th century (527–65), is the emperor Justinian (527–65), along with the symbolic figures of Victory and Earth. In the bottom section it portrays the conquered people of India, who are presenting offerings, including an elephant tusk, to the emperor.

ICON OF SAINT EUDOXIA
This 11th-century icon represents the Empress Eudoxia, wife of Theodosius II (408–450). Her dress and her crown are incrusted with precious stones. Imperial dignity was considered to be synonymous with divine selection, and Byzantine monarchs and their spouses were frequently portrayed wearing halos.

A 14TH-CENTURY FRESCO OF THE ANASTASIS OR HARROWING OF HELL.
This fresco dominates the Pareclesion of the Church of Saint Savior-in-Chora. Christ rescues Adam and Eve from their tombs.
The locks of the gates of Hell surround Satan bound at his feet.Other figures are St John the Baptist, David, Solomon and Abel.

A 14TH-CENTURY MOSAIC OF THE GENEALOGY OF CHRIST
Christ, in the center, is surrounded by his ancestors, from Adam to Ersom Japhet and the eleven sons of Jacob. This mosaic (left) decorates the southern dome of the inner narthex of Saint Savior-in-Chora.

Istanbul has many fountains. Their sites were chosen according to the needs of the city's residents and travelers, as well as for aesthetic reasons. There were two types of public fountain: the *çeşme* or public fawcet for filling jugs and the *sebil* where drinking water was given to passers-by from behind a grille.

The grandest fountains combined most functions. The *şardıvan*, or ablution fountain had an almost sacred status; at the Eyüp mosque the faithful would leave the fountain fawcets open so that the water – the symbol of their destiny – could flow freely. Behind high walls were the ornamental fountains of private mansions and the *yalıs* of the Bosphorus.

HOLY FOUNTAINS
Building a fountain was a good deed, a philanthropic act according to the teachings of Islam. Accordingly the sultans, princes, ladies of the seraglio, and dignitaries vied with each other to endow them.

THE FOUNTAIN OF SULTAN AHMET III

This Baroque-style fountain, built in 1728, is the most famous of all. A basin flanked with niches in the shape of a mihrab occupies the center of each of its four faces. The *sebil* of the angles are closed by bronze gates.

PRECIOUS MARBLE

The Baroque style was used to great effect on many of the pediments and façades of fountains. These often have fanciful complicated forms, such as delicate drapery and marble carved to represent flowing water.

ENGRAVED PEDIMENTS

Fountains are often engraved with calligraphy. The most common inscription of all is a verse from the Koran: "By water all things have life."

ÇEŞME, STREET FOUNTAINS

The citizens of Istanbul carried water in earthenware jugs. Watersellers carried it in porous skins which kept the water at a refreshingly cool temperature.

MONUMENTAL FOUNTAINS

Antoine-Ignace Melling (1763–1831) painted *Procession in Honour of a Turkish Wedding* (below). It shows the traditional order of the people who took part in the procession, as well as the bride's chariot, in great detail. The crowd of characters gathered around the fountain is carefully portrayed, all of them dressed in costumes and turbans in a myriad of colors.

One visit to the Grand Bazaar is enough to convince you of the diversity and richness of the Turkish craft industry. First, of course, are the rugs (*halı*) and kilims, but you might also be tempted by the leather and suede goods. Equally famous is the golden jewelry decorated with precious stones, as well as the traditionally shaped pieces in silver. There are also copper objects and onyx trinkets, as well as pottery and ceramics from Iznik and Izmir. Smokers will appreciate the meerschaum pipes and the hookahs, while gourmets will prefer the canned stuffed vegetables or the spices and dried fruits that can be bought in bulk at the Egyptian or Spice Bazaar.

The pistachios that are served as snacks all day long are also a common ingredient in Turkish cuisine, as are dried apricots and raisins from Smyrna (Izmir).

PASTIRMA. Spiced meat dried with fenugreek.

SOME SPICES. Pul biber, a flaked pepper (1), aniseed (2), fenugreek (3) and sumak (4). An aromatic infusion prepared from mint and lemon (5) is a drink to aid digestion.

1

2

3

ZEYTINYAĞLI DOLMALAR
These are vegetables stuffed with onions, rice, and olive oil: stuffed peppers (Biber Dolması), stuffed vine leaves (Yaprak Dolması) and stuffed eggplant (Patlıcan Dolması).

BAKLAVA
Puff pastry layered with walnuts or pistachios.

TURKISH PASTRIES
Often very sugary and rich in butter. They combine almonds, hazelnuts, sesame seeds, and, as here, pistachios.

These squares of pistachio-flavoured almond paste are found in Bebek.

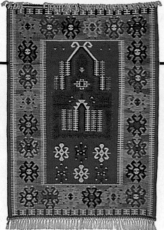

TURKISH JEWELRY

The jewelers draw their inspiration from many sources: traditional motifs, reinterpretation of Ottoman and Byzantine designs (see the earring, right), and variations on the romantic style, as with this hair ornament in silver filigree (below).

KELIM. This kilim in shades of blue, red and unbleached wool, is an example of those currently made in Uşak.

SMOKING ACCESSORIES
A pipe with a meerschaum bowl carved in the shape of a head is a typical product made by Turkish craftworkers.

THE TURKISH DAILY PRESS
The large-circulation daily papers are *Cumhuriyet* (*The Republican*), *Milliyet* (*The Nation*), *Sabah* (*The Morning*), *Hürriyet* (*The Independence*), *Türkiye* (*Turkey*), and *Yeniyüzyil* (*The New Century*).

4

5

SWEETS
Rose jelly (*Gül Reçeli*), fig jam (*Incir Reçeli*) and dried rose petals are used to flavor tea, desserts and nargile, or hookah, water.

ALCOHOLIC BEVERAGES
Those include Buzbağ, a Turkish red wine produced in the Elaziğ vineyards, and Rakı, an aperitif made from grapes and aniseed.

69

CHICKEN WITH APRICOTS AND ALMONDS

In the 16th century the Ottoman Empire dominated the Mediterranean, uniting diverse lands and cultures. The influence of Turkish cuisine spread to Greece, North Africa, and the Middle East. A refined court cuisine, partly inherited from the Byzantine imperial court, was developed in Istanbul, in the sumptuous palaces of the sultans and in the *konaks.*

INGREDIENTS FOR 4 TO 6 PERSONS
1 free-range chicken (3 lb), 1 large onion, 1 tablespoon honey, 1 cup dried apricots, ½ cup almonds, 3 tablespoons Izmir raisins, 5 tablespoons of butter, 2 cups of rice, salt and pepper.

1. Cut the chicken into 8 parts and finely chop the onion.

2. In a thick-bottomed skillet melt 3 tablespoons of butter, then brown the chicken pieces all over.

3. Add the chopped onion and allow to brown for several minutes.

> "... Dinner came in, which was served one dish at a time...
> Their sauces are very rich, all the roasting very well done.
> They use a great deal of spice."
>
> Lady Mary Wortley-Montagu

4. While the onions brown, mix the apricots, raisins, honey, salt and pepper.

5. Add this mixture to the skillet and moisten with ½ cup of water.

6. Cover and simmer over a low heat for 30 minutes.

7. Soak the rice in warm, salted water.

8. After 30 minutes rinse and drain the rice. Pour the rice over the chicken and add 2 cups of water.

9. Cover and simmer for a further 10 to 15 minutes, over a low heat.

10. While the chicken cooks melt the remaining butter in a skillet and brown the almonds in it.

11. Arrange the chicken in a serving dish and sprinkle with the almonds. Serve hot.

● THE CAFÉS

Coffee was first drunk in the 9th century and was for a long time very rare and expensive, available only to the powerful of Arabia. At the beginning of the 16th century it was still served with great pomp in the court of

Süleyman. It became more popular and widely available in 1555 when two Syrian traders, Hakim and Shams, opened the first coffee shop in Istanbul. It was an enormous success and they soon opened many more establishments. Coffee was nicknamed "milk of chess players and thinkers" and became the favorite drink of intellectuals. The coffee shops were places for discussion and relaxation where one came to smoke a chibouk or a hookah. Soon they would offer their clientèle a range of entertainments: musicians and dancers would perform, and crowds would gather to hear the storyteller or *meddah*, or to watch the shadow theater, the Karagöz.

Pierre Loti particularly loved to go to a small Eyüp café that looks over the Golden Horn. Today the café is named after him and this has helped to keep it in business.

During the 19th century, some cafés became specialized. The *kıraathâne* were reading rooms that provided newspapers, magazines, and sometimes the latest literary creations. The *algılı kahveleri*, or "instrumental cafés", were reserved for music. In the *aşık kahveleri*, "cafés of love", poetry readings were held, sometimes accompanied by a soloist or small group of musicians.

TURKISH CAFÉ IN THE 18TH CENTURY
Engraving by A. I. Melling.

Architecture

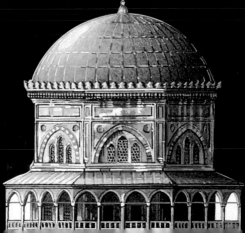

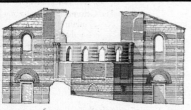

REAR FAÇADE OF THE CHURCH OF ST JOHN OF STUDIUS. A classic example of a basilica erected around 450 but now in ruins.

Although Istanbul contains some magnificent examples of Byzantine architecture, very little from that period remains, scarcely enough to provide even a representative selection of an architecture that spread across three continents and eleven centuries. Apart from Haghia Sophia and a few land walls, there is almost no civil architecture, and barely thirty churches are still in existence today.

HAGHIA SOPHIA
Built in five years (532-537), from foundations to completion, Haghia Sophia is a unique structure in both conception and size, without precedent and unrivaled until the building of the Ottoman mosques. The dome, with a diameter of more than 100 feet and a height of more than 180 feet, borders on the miraculous, given the technology that was available. Subsequent generations actually believed Haghia Sophia to be the product of supernatural intervention.

THE CHURCH OF STS SERGIUS AND BACCHUS
Erected by Justinian between 527 and 536 to an octagonal plan inscribed within a circle. A foretaste of Haghia Sophia – hence its present Turkish name, Küçük Ayasofya ("Small Haghia Sophia") – the church was converted into a mosque at the end of the 15th century. Its elegance makes Sts Sergius and Bacchus one of the best examples of Byzantine architecture from this period.

BYZANTINE CAPITALS
Three examples, from the Theotokos Pammakaristos (Fethiye Cami'i) (**1**), Haghia Sophia (**2**), and Saint Eirene (**3**).

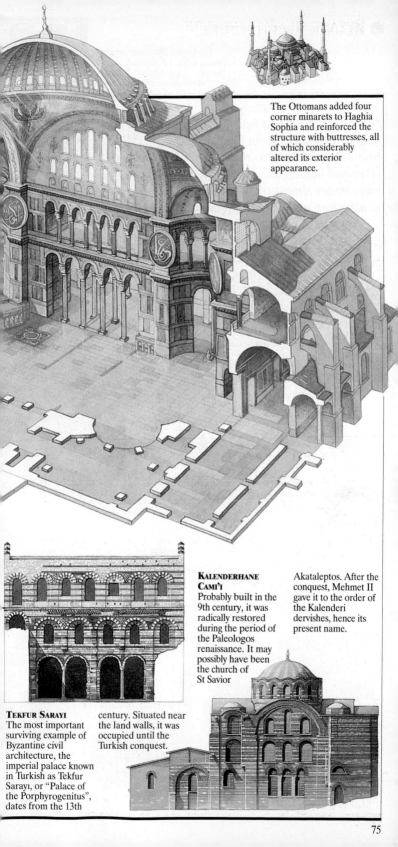

The Ottomans added four corner minarets to Haghia Sophia and reinforced the structure with buttresses, all of which considerably altered its exterior appearance.

KALENDERHANE CAMI'I
Probably built in the 9th century, it was radically restored during the period of the Paleologos renaissance. It may possibly have been the church of St Savior Akataleptos. After the conquest, Mehmet II gave it to the order of the Kalenderi dervishes, hence its present name.

TEKFUR SARAYI
The most important surviving example of Byzantine civil architecture, the imperial palace known in Turkish as Tekfur Sarayı, or "Palace of the Porphyrogenitus", dates from the 13th century. Situated near the land walls, it was occupied until the Turkish conquest.

● AQUATIC ARCHITECTURE

The largest Byzantine covered cistern is the *Yerebatan Sarayı* or *Sarnıcı* ("Underground Palace"). It measures 360 by 230 feet.

Istanbul needed a steady, reliable source of fresh water for it was built on an arid peninsula and at several points in its history the population reached as many as several hundred thousand inhabitants. So the Byzantines, who were under almost constant threat of siege, constructed a system of aqueducts together with a vast array of cisterns, the latter both covered and also open to the sky. The interlinked dams and aqueducts culminated in a network of fountains which were spread throughout greater Istanbul.

CORINTHIAN CAPITAL
One of the 5th-century capitals which crown the majority of the 336 columns in the Justinian cistern of Yerebatan Sarayı. They were of many designs and clearly job lots because not intended to be seen.

TURKISH BATHS
A standard feature of the Ottoman city, the public baths could be quite magnificent buildings, particularly if founded by a member of the imperial family or the high administration.

The chambers are surmounted by cupolas which are pierced with bell-shaped glass lights.

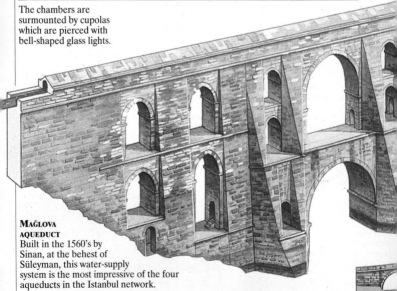

MAĞLOVA AQUEDUCT
Built in the 1560's by Sinan, at the behest of Süleyman, this water-supply system is the most impressive of the four aqueducts in the Istanbul network.

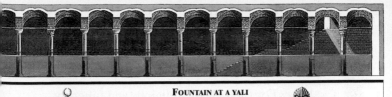

FOUNTAIN AT A YALI
In the 18th century, ahead of the city's expansion, a system of aqueducts was created for the quarter situated on the Asian bank opposite the Golden Horn. The new water supply would primarily serve the houses of the wealthy.

AHMET III FOUNTAIN
The public fountain was the charitable gesture par excellence for the rich or powerful Ottoman eager to perpetuate his good name by means of a dedicatory inscription. The imperial fountains are very grand, like this one erected in front of Topkapı Palace.

FOUNTAIN IN THE LIBRARY OF AHMET III (1719)
The fountain seen here was built in 1578 by the architect Sinan in front of the library in the third court of Topkapı Palace. It is decorated with Iznik faience in floral motifs.

BÜYÜK ÇEKMEÇE
This 28-arch bridge, constructed by Sinan in 1565-67, spans Lake Büyük Çekmeçe, at the point where it flows into the sea, on the Edirne road some 25 miles from Istanbul.

● OTTOMAN ARCHITECTURE

For their classic religious and funerary architecture, the Ottomans adopted forms already established in Arabia and Persia and brought to Anatolia by the Seljuk Turks. From the end of the 13th century, the architectural structures became more elaborate and in this area, the Ottoman builders benefitted from Byzantine expertise. Many religious works were built: mosques, *medreses* (colleges), and *türbes* (mausoleums). In the 14th century Ottoman architects began to use local techniques and materials.

THE GREEN MOSQUE
Built in 1378 in Iznik, this is a classic example of a square-plan mosque with a single dome.

PORTICO OF THE MOSQUE OF BEYAZIT I
This is one of the earliest of the porticos that would become so characteristic of the imperial mosques; it was built in Bursa, 1379–1402.

THE GREEN MOSQUE
Built by Mehmet I (1413–21) it is, by virtue of its size and the beauty of its decor, one of the most important works in Bursa. Here, two cupolas succeed one another within a rectangular plan, the first crowned by a 19th-century lantern.

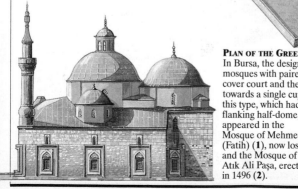

PLAN OF THE GREEN MOSQUE
In Bursa, the designs for the first mosques with paired successive domes, to cover court and then prayer halls, evolved towards a single cupola. The earliest of this type, which had a flanking half-dome, appeared in the Mosque of Mehmet II (Fatih) (**1**), now lost, and the Mosque of Atık Ali Paşa, erected in 1496 (**2**).

Ottoman "stalactite" capitals, with wood used for those of the first period based directly on Seljuk models (**1**), and stone for those in the 15th-century Green Mosque in Iznik (**2**) and the 16th-century Süleymaniye in Istanbul (**3**).

TÜRBE. The architecture of these Ottoman mausoleums is derived from that of tombs in Iran and Central Asia, as well

as Armenian and Georgian architecture.

Originally intended to house the tombs of the reigning family, *türbe* became more widespread in the 15th century when high state officials began to build them. Illustrated on the left is the octagonal Seljuk mausoleum of Princess Hüdavend Hatun at

Niğde, central Anatolia. The center image represents the Green Mausoleum of Mehmet I at Bursa, decorated with turquoise ceramics. On the right is the Mausoleum of

Süleyman in Istanbul, one of the most elaborate structures of its kind; an octagonal building encircled by a gallery and capped by a double cupola, its interior is ornamented with ceramic panels.

THE COMPLEX (KÜLLIYE) OF BEYAZIT II AT EDIRNE. Constructed in 1484–88, this is one of the supreme works of Ottoman architecture. The complex comprises a mosque in the center, a public soup kitchen (*imaret*) on the left, a medical college on the extreme right, and a hospital for the mentally ill with a magnificent octagonal hall.

THE BEYAZIT II MOSQUE IN ISTANBUL
Shown here in cross-section with its grand forecourt, this mosque dates from 1500–5. It is a typical mosque with its design of a single dome on two half-domes modeled on the Haghia Sophia.

PLAN OF THE ATIK ALI PAŞA MOSQUE BUILT IN 1496

THE SELIMIYE OF EDIRNE, IMPERIAL MOSQUE

The mosque at Edirne, built by Sinan between 1569 and 1575 for Sultan Selim II, was considered by the architect himself, by contemporaries, and also by posterity, as his masterpiece and as the finest example of Ottoman architecture ever built. The building is admired for its originality and renowned for a dome with a diameter of 90 feet and a height of 160 feet, identical to that of Haghia Sophia.

STRUCTURE
The huge cupola, set on eight piers surmounted by eight segments of a circle, appears almost to float on air. Meanwhile, the absence of bearing walls made it possible to pierce windows at every level, thereby flooding the mosque with natural light.

GENERAL PLAN
While reducing the need for external buttressing, numerous side aisles and galleries also create isolated or private spaces, reserved for prayer or the recitation of the Koran, as well as for the superb imperial loggia decorated with the most beautiful Ottoman tiles. The great variety of the spaces within is reflected on the exterior, with its wonderful mix of façades. The four minarets mark the cardinal points.

The ablutions fountain at the center of the large courtyard.

MINARET
Shown in section, this is one of the minarets on the forecourt side, with its triple-spiral stairway providing a separate access to each of the balconies. This astonishing feature is unique in Ottoman architecture, but unfortunately it is not open to the public.

MIHRAB
A prayer niche (above) oriented towards Mecca.

MIMBAR
The pulpit in the Selimiye is made entirely out of marble and is crowned with a ceramic cone surmounted by a gilded copper crescent.

81

● TOPKAPI PALACE

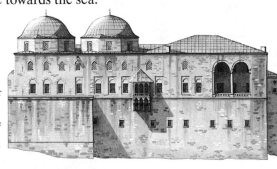

In 1463, Mehmet II walled in an area of the city stretching between Haghia Sophia and a point facing the Bosphorus. He outlined the ground plan of a palace which would have offices distributed throughout a number of wings situated in interior courtyards and throughout the gardens. The four courtyards lead progressively from the public to the private. The private apartments in the garden areas are connected to the state offices that face towards the sea.

THE HOUSE OF FATIH
In the palace's third courtyard, Mehmet II built a pavilion of freestone on massive foundations. It includes a small belvedere in the center and, on the Sea of Marmara side, a loggia. The vaults have housed the imperial treasure since the 16th century.

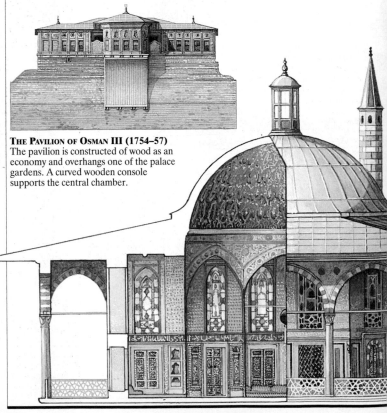

THE PAVILION OF OSMAN III (1754–57)
The pavilion is constructed of wood as an economy and overhangs one of the palace gardens. A curved wooden console supports the central chamber.

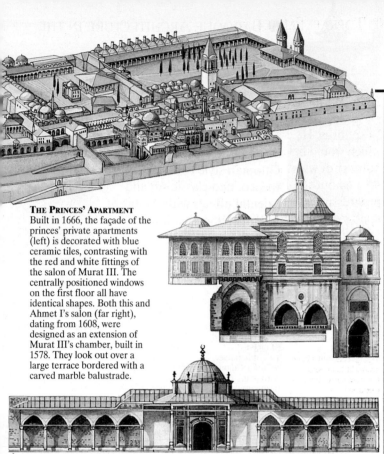

THE PRINCES' APARTMENT
Built in 1666, the façade of the princes' private apartments (left) is decorated with blue ceramic tiles, contrasting with the red and white fittings of the salon of Murat III. The centrally positioned windows on the first floor all have identical shapes. Both this and Ahmet I's salon (far right), dating from 1608, were designed as an extension of Murat III's chamber, built in 1578. They look out over a large terrace bordered with a carved marble balustrade.

THE GATE OF FELICITY OR OF THE WHITE EUNUCHS
This passage, between the second and third courtyards, leads to the Throne Room.

The arcaded entranceway is surmounted by cupolas, and was used only by dignitaries and ambassadors.

BAGHDAD PAVILION
Murat IV constructed this house in 1635, over-looking the Golden Horn to mark the taking of Baghdad. Its cross-shaped layout is inscribed in an octagon and covered with a cupola.

The walls are covered with blue ceramic from Iznik, and the interior decoration of the cupola is painted. The house is illuminated by the light that comes through the stained-glass windows, and is encircled by an exterior gallery.

CHAMBER OF MURAT III
This was the state room of the sultan. Symmetrical cabinets and alcoves with low sofas and a fireplace mark the center. The walls are decorated with ceramic panels. A splendid wall with a superb central *çeşme* is an outstanding feature.

● BAROQUE ARCHITECTURE IN THE 19TH CENTURY

At the end of the 18th century, the influence of western architecture was overturning the rules of Ottoman civil and religious architecture. Thus was born the Baroque Ottoman style which mixed rococo, neo-classicism and oriental effects with Arabic or Indian elements reimported from the west. The development was due to Ahmet III in the early 18th century.

BAS-RELIEFS FROM THE KÜÇÜKSU HOUSE
Sculpture decorated windows, doors, palace façades and public fountains with rococo motifs.

HOUSE IN ARNAVUTKÖY
The eclectic Ottoman style can be seen in the façades of this wooden house.

KÜÇÜKSU
This little palace, built in 1870 on the Asian bank of the Bosphorus, reflects the influence of the École des Beaux-Arts at this period. Two bowed balconies on consoles add to the elaboration of the façade.

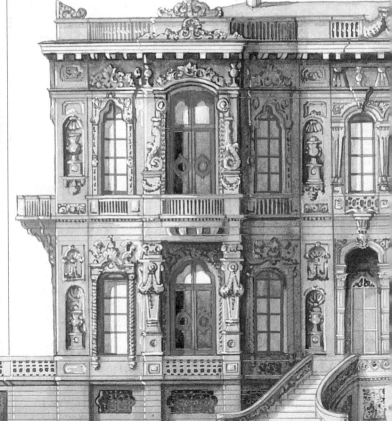

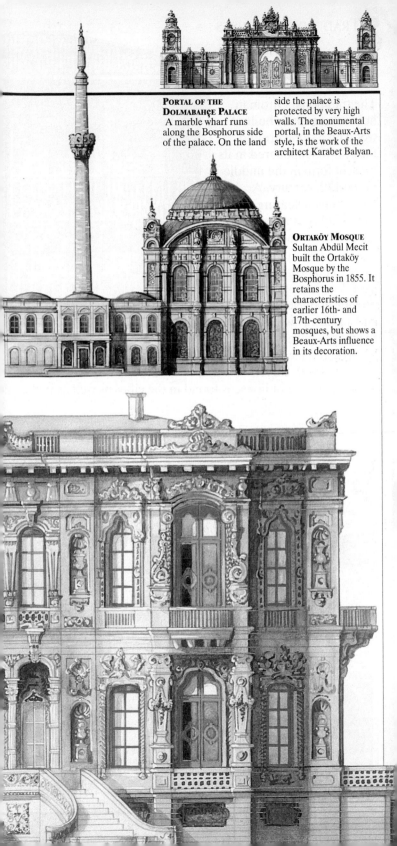

PORTAL OF THE DOLMABAHÇE PALACE
A marble wharf runs along the Bosphorus side of the palace. On the land side the palace is protected by very high walls. The monumental portal, in the Beaux-Arts style, is the work of the architect Karabet Balyan.

ORTAKÖY MOSQUE
Sultan Abdül Mecit built the Ortaköy Mosque by the Bosphorus in 1855. It retains the characteristics of earlier 16th- and 17th-century mosques, but shows a Beaux-Arts influence in its decoration.

● TRADITIONAL HOUSES

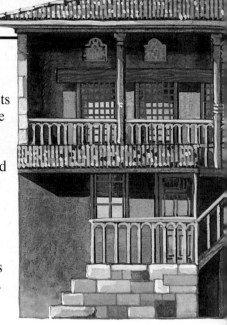

The traditional Ottoman house was usually built of wood on a stone ground floor. It first appeared in its present form in the middle of the 17th century. A characteristic feature of such a house is its corbeled construction: each floor is supported by a corbeled wooden platform. It has many windows which provide good ventilation, and a stairway which leads to an open gallery (*hayat*). The painted façades are decorated with carved wood. This type of house is found in the cities as well as in the country.

CORBELED CONSTRUCTION
The wooden floor of an Ottoman house is built on a stone or adobe wall, and overhangs the front of the house.

Plan illustrating the evolution of the *hayat* into a *sofa*.

A TRADITIONAL HOUSE IN BURSA
The floor plan of an Ottoman house often has to allow for an irregularly shaped plot and twisting roads, and through the use of complicated corbeling on the upper floors ensure that the rooms on the upper floors are rectangular.

HAYAT

The oldest example of an Ottoman house has a first-floor gallery, called a *hayat*. It is reached by exterior stairs from the courtyard, which all the rooms open onto. These rooms were originally entirely lit from the courtyard side, while the street side of the house was filled in. The raised parts of the *hayat* are used as the main living space in summer. This form did not necessarily originate in the country, but it has survived for a long time in rural areas.

MAIN ROOM with cabinets and alcoves.

HOUSE FLOOR PLAN
The central space (*sofa*) is surrounded by four corner bedrooms (*oda*).

HALF-TIMBERED OTTOMAN HOUSE

This house is built around a wooden framework which is then filled in with rubble or scrap material, and covered with an ochre-, brick-, or indigo-colored roughcast. In Istanbul, from the mid-19th century, horizontal wooden slats were added.

SOFA HOUSE

During the 19th century, and especially in the cities, it became increasingly inconvenient to use the *hayat*. These open galleries were enclosed by glass or by rooms added on piecemeal. On the courtyard side the room would become an interior antechamber, or *sofa*. Houses with a *sofa* were composed of a central space and four corner rooms often projecting on corbels.

THE "YALI"

The yalı are summer residences built of wood and situated along the banks of the Bosphorus (the word *yalı* also means shore). Their symmetrical design was influenced by being on the seafront, and includes two entrances – one facing the sea, the other the land. The main rooms jut out from the front of the house and have wide bay windows which open onto the sea.

INTERIOR OF A YALI
This view shows the low *sedir* (divan) which runs along the painted wood partitions.

CLASSIC YALI WITH INTERIOR "SOFA"
The *sofa*, or central room, is framed by four corner rooms (*oda*) built out from the façade.There was also a family or harem wing.

THE AMCAZADE HÜSEYIN PAŞA YALISI
The yalı of the celebrated Köprülü family, shown below, dates from the end of the 17th century. It is the oldest example of an Ottoman house in existence. The row of openings protected by horizontally opening shutters was a typical feature of the yalı by the sea.

Yalı are luxurious houses which belonged to the great dignitaries of the Empire. Along the Bosphorus more modest wooden houses can also be found, for example at Arnavutköy and Yeniköy on the European side.

The ground floor of the yalı sometimes includes a shelter for caiques or skiffs.

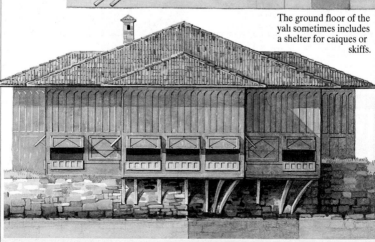

Istanbul
as seen by painters

> "The most majestic, most varied, most magnificent, and most untamed site that a painter could hope to find."
>
> Lamartine

In the 18th century in an attempt to save the empire from its successive defeats, the Ottoman élite adopted the most efficient Western military and civil systems. Thanks to this opening up towards Europe, a number of orientalist painters moved to Istanbul. When their paintings were displayed in the Seraglio they were admired, and little by little they began to change the perceptions about art of those who saw them. J.-E. Liotard, known as the "Turkish painter" (1702–89), is the creator of the *Portrait of Richard Pococke* (1), an archeologist and English traveler. The background of the portrait shows a view over Seraglio Point and the Bosphorus, the blues of which are in harmony with those of the sky and the turquoise of the oriental costume. Jean-Baptiste Hilair's blue-toned *The Point of the Seraglio as seen from Galata* (2) is seen from the eye-level of the people in the foreground. To the left, the Sepetçiler Köşkü, to the right Haghia Sophia, Haghia Irene, and the smokestacks of the Topkapı Sarayı. In the background is a ship with its sails unfurled. Fabius Brest, who painted the *View of the Bosphorus* (3), lived in Istanbul during the 19th century.

	2
1	
	3

Devrim Erbil,
General View of Istanbul,
1986.

Cihat Burak (1915–94) was born in Istanbul. As both an architect and a gifted, original writer, his taste for realism did not preclude either the strange or the humorous. His *Interior View of the Süleymaniye* (1), painted in 1975, gives an idea of the splendid displays during the investiture ceremonies of the Ottoman sultans. Fikret Muallâ (1904–69), who was born in Turkey but

died in France, has admirers in both countries. The portrait of his friend Avni Arbas (4) was painted in 1948. Despite a life full of misery and drama, his work is pure exaltation, full of the charm and color of everyday city life, as in his *Countryside* (3) painted in 1945. Istanbul and Paris were his two great passions. Namik Ismail (1890–1935) excelled in a number of genres, especially that of female portraiture. In 1925 he painted the lyrical work, *Full Moon over Istanbul* (5).

2		
1	3	4
	5	

In his early works
Bedri Rahmi
(1913–75) was greatly
influenced by Turkish
popular art. He
created his own lively
and colorful language
in order to celebrate
his Anatolian home,
although he did not
neglect the charm
and colors of
Istanbul, as in the
façade of his *Kariye
cami'i* (1). Hüseyin
Avni Lifij
(1889–1927) was a

student of the great
painter Osman
Hamdi. Avni did his
studies at the Paris
École des Beaux-
Arts. His canvases are
imbued with a
nostalgic fervor, and
celebrate the light of
Istanbul like no other
painter before him.
His landscapes are
interspersed with an
intense interior life.
He touches upon
allegorical themes
that appeal to
Ottoman taste, as in
this Zeyrek
landscape, *Zeyrekten
Görünü* (2). The
watercolors of
Mustafa Pilevneli, a
contemporary of Lifij,
are inspired by the
Ottoman miniaturists
of the 18th century.
Pilevneli's favorite
subject was the
depiction of scenes
from the daily life of
the city.

3

2

1

A bidine Dino (1913–93) adopted the city of Istanbul as his subject, finding in it both reality and mystery. He was the founder of the first Turkish avant-garde group, the D group (1933) as well as the "Port" group (1939). Abstraction, figurative work, sculpture, writing, and film-making all influenced him at different periods in his quest for uncompromising plastic purity. Shown here are *Seraglio Point* (1), *I dreamt of Istanbul* (2), and *Portrait of Nazim Hikmet* (3). Abidine

has exhibited regularly in Paris and other European capitals as well as in his own country.

1

2

3

Istanbul
as seen by
writers

Ralph Waldo Emerson's statement, "A city lives by remembering", has a great deal of truth in it. Today's Istanbul has a memory that spans twenty-seven centuries. The city reverberates with the whispers of history and the murmurs of human drama. It is full of songs of joy, elegies and paeans from all of its centuries. Authors from many cultures listen to Istanbul and give new echoes to it. The city lives by remembering and listening.

IMPERIAL CONSTANTINOPLE

VIEW FROM THE SERAGLIO

Pierre Gilles (Petrus Gyllius, 1490–1555) spent several years in the Ottoman capital between 1544 and 1550. His extensive work on the history and topography of the city was published posthumously: "Three Books on the Thracian Bosphorus" and "Four Books on the Topography of Constantinople and on its Antiquities".

❝ Though all the hills of Constantinople afford a very pleasing prospect, there is none that entertains you with such peculiar delight as the first hill, where the Sultan lives in a licentious and luxurious manner. He has before him, whether he is walking in his gardens or in his chambers of the Seraglio, a full view of the Bosphorus and both its shores, which are green and flourishing with woods belonging to the neighboring farms. On the right hand he beholds a spacious field of Chalcedon covered with his own gardens; he sees the Propontis, islands without number, and the woody mountains of Asia. If he looks an immense distance behind him he beholds Mount Olympus always clothed in snow. If he takes a shorter prospect he views before him the wonders of his own city, the Church of Saint-Sophia and the Hippodrome. If he casts his eyes to the left, he beholds the seven hills on which the city is seated, and more remotely he looks around the immeasurable, spacious fields of Thrace. If he extends his prospect over the seas, he views a moving scene of ships passing and repassing before him; some sailing from the Hellespont or the Black Sea, others again coming into his port from all the coasts of the Propontis; while at the same time other vessels are sailing up and down the Bay of Ceras, where there is also an abundance of ferries and small boats always rowing from side to side. And if he looks below him, he has the agreeable pleasure of beholding the three sides of the first hill, dressed with trees, flowers, and plants of all kinds. He not only has a fine prospect from the palace but is entertained with several delightful vistas from the top of the gardens rising on the hills. If he has an inclination to take a view of his Seraglio from the point of land that projects so far into the sea and that, as I observed, divided the Bosphorus, here he beholds it in all its glory, strengthened with large pillars of marble and fanned with gentle, refreshing breezes. Here he often sits with small osier lattices before him, so that, like another Gyges, he discerns all that sail near him, though he himself is visible to none. And if at any time he is weary of the company of his domestics, he can divert himself with the ridiculous drollery of the watermen fixing their oars and boat-poles to the shore as they tug against the violent stream of the Bosphorus, which is much more rapid than the Rhone. **❞**

PIERRE GILLES, *FOUR BOOKS ON THE TOPOGRAPHY OF CONSTANTINOPLE AND ON ITS ANTIQUITIES*, LONDON 1729, TRANSLATED BY JOHN BALL

HUNDREDS OF PALACES

Lady Mary Wortley-Montagu (1689–1762) was in the Ottoman imperial capital in 1718 as the period later named "The Tulip Age" was about to start. She was the wife of the British consul. Her letters describing life in the city and its environs are remarkable for their observations, style, and understanding of Ottoman culture.

❝To Lady Bristol – Pera of Constantinople, 10 April 1718

The pleasure of going in a barge to Chelsea is not comparable to that of rowing upon the canal of the sea here, where for twenty miles together down the Bosphorus the most beautiful variety of prospects present themselves. The Asian side is covered with fruit trees, villages and the most delightful landscapes in nature. On the European side stands Constantinople, situated on seven hills. The unequal heights make it seem as large again as it is (though one of the largest cities in the world), showing an agreeable mixture of gardens, pine and cypress trees, palaces, mosques and public buildings, raised one above another with as much beauty and appearance of symmetry as your ladyship ever saw in a cabinet adorned by the most skilful hands, jars showing themselves above jars, mixed with canisters, babies and candlesticks. This is a very odd comparison, but it gives me an exact image of the thing. ... I have taken care to see as much of the Seraglio as is to be seen. It is on a point of land running into the sea: a palace of prodigious extent, but very irregular; the gardens a large compass of ground full of high cypress trees, which is all I know of them; the buildings all of white stone, leaded on top, with guilded turrets and spires, which look very magnificent, and indeed I believe there is no Christian king's palace half so large. There are six large courts in it all built round and set with trees, having galleries of stone: one of these for the guard, another for the stables, the fifth for the divan, the sixth for the apartment destined for audiences. On the ladies' side there is at least as many more, with distinct courts belonging to their eunuchs and attendants, their kitchens, etc.[...]Nothing can be pleasanter than the Canal, and the Turks are so well acquainted with its beauties, all their pleasure-seats are built on its banks, where they have at the same time the most beautiful prospects in Europe and Asia. There are near one another some hundreds of magnificent palaces ... I was yesterday to see that of the late Grand Vizier ... The extent of it is prodigious; the guardian assured me there is eight hundred rooms in it ... The garden is suitable to the house, where arbors, fountains, and walks are thrown together in an agreeable confusion.**❞**

LETTERS OF THE RIGHT HONOURABLE
LADY MARY WORTLEY-MONTAGU,
LONDON, 1763

About the Bosphorus

Lord Byron (1788–1824), traveled extensively in the western parts of the Ottoman Empire and visited Istanbul. He was active in support of the Greek independence movement against the Turks and lost his life during that struggle. He wrote both acerbic and admiring verses about Ottoman Turkey.

III

The European with the Asian shore
Sprinkled with palaces; the ocean stream
Here and there studded with a seventy-four;
Sophia's cupola with golden gleam;
The cypress groves; Olympus high and hoar:
The twelve isles, and the more than I could dream,
Far less describe, present the very view
Which charm'd the charming Mary Montagu.

V

The wind swept down the Euxine, and the wave
Broke foaming o'er the blue Symplegades;
'Tis a grand sight from off "the Giant's Grave"
To watch the progress of those rolling seas
Between the Bosphorus, as they lash and lave
European and Asia, you being quite at ease:
There's not a sea the passenger e'er pukes in,
Turns up more dangerous breakers than the Euxine.

Lord Byron, *Don Juan*, Canto V, 1819–24

The fall of Byzantium

Joseph von Hammer-Purgstall (1774–1856) served as an Austrian diplomat in Constantinople. He was renowned for his academic studies of oriental languages, and for his magnum opus, "The History of the Ottoman Empire".

❝No miracle was to save the Empire. The gates were hacked down by axes; the Turks flooded the streets; looting started, a looting which nothing was to stop, neither weeping women and girls, nor cries of the children nor the oaths of the wounded. No restraint could curb soldiers intoxicated with victory. The only criteria that affected the fate of the trembling creatures were those of youth, beauty and fortune. Without any distinction of rank or sex, prisoners were tied two by two with their belts or veils. Next it was the turn of the churches: pictures of saints were torn from their walls and cut up; sacred vessels were destroyed; vestments were turned into coverings; the crucifix, capped by a Janissary's bonnet, was carried around the streets; altars were profaned and used as dining-tables, or as beds to violate girls and boys, or as stalls for horses. 'Aya Sophia,' says Phranzes, 'God's sanctuary, the throne of His glory, the marvel of the earth, was transformed into a place of horrors and abominations.' Thus antique Byzantium fell, 1125 years after having been built by Constantine. The siege, which had lasted fifty-three days, ended on 29 May 1453; it was the 29th it had undergone since its foundation.❞

Ritter J. von Hammer-Purgstall,
The History of the Ottoman Empire, Paris, 1835,
translated by Marie Noële Kelly and Lawrence Kelly

SULTAN MURAD III

Evliya Çelebi (1611–1682) was the premier travel writer of the Ottoman Empire. In 1630 he had a dream which urged him to travel: first he toured all over Istanbul, then the far-flung territories of the empire.

❝ Murad III never himself took the field, but the conquests of the empire were multiplied every year by his generals. He was buried beneath a separate cupola with his children, in the harem (court-yard) of Aya Soifiyah. He was the first Ottoman sovereign who lived and died at Constantinople without having once left it. Being much given to women and pleasure he had an immense number of male and female children, altogether three hundred and twenty-six. It is stated that in one single night fifty five of his women were lying in. At his death nineteen princes were killed according to the bloody code of the Ottoman empire. One of them, a very young boy, was eating chestnuts at the moment the executioner came in, to whom he said, 'Let me eat my chesnuts, and strangle me afterwards.' A request with which the executioner did not comply. Another was torn from his mother's breast and put to death, emitting at the same time his mother's milk by the nose, and his soul by his mouth. Twenty six daughters, some of them married to vezírs, survived their father. They all now lie buried in his sepulchre. God's mercy upon them! ❞

EVLIYA ÇELEBI EFENDI, *NARRATIVE OF TRAVELS IN EUROPE, ASIA, AND AFRICA IN THE SEVENTEENTH CENTURY*, LONDON 1834, TRANSLATED BY RITTER J. VON HAMMER-PURGSTALL

THE SULEYMANIYE

❝ Then he heard his Royal Chief Architect's impatient voice cry out from the top of the scaffolding surrounding one of the gigantic granite monoliths, to say something like this: 'No! No! That's not the way to cut stalactites. Here, give me that mallet and chisel. I'll show you how to carve the capital.

Then, standing at the base of the pillar, the Sultan had to put up his hand to shield his eyes as the chips flew and the marble dust rained down. He may then have smiled. I doubt that he interrupted Sinan as he cut the geometrical crystalline stalactites in the round to come out right.

Sinan finished the Süleymaniye in 1557. It is an enormous space, full of light by day, once lit by twenty-two thousand flames by night. In the seventeenth century, when the mosque was not a century old, Evliya Çelebi saw ten 'Frankish infidels skillful in geometry and architecture' take off their shoes and put on slippers to enter the southwestern portal. He followed them to watch the great spaces of the Süleymaniye take their effect. Heads back, the ten men shuffled along in their

baboushes; they walked on thick carpets woven to Sinan's patterns at Ushak instead of on the rush matting and scatter rugs of today. ... Each of the ten Frankish infidels

raised his right hand and laid his forefinger across his open mouth. 'They tossed up their hats and cried out ... "Mother of God!" ' ...

(Sinan) was a robust man of sixty-eight when he climbed up onto the dome to put the burnished finial in place. According to legend, when he got down again, he said to the Sultan, 'I have built thee, O Padishah, a mosque which will remain on the face of the earth till the day of judgement, and when Hallaj Mansur comes and rends Mount Demavend from its foundations, he will play tennis with it and the dome of this mosque!' **99**

ARTHUR STRATTON, *SINAN*, LONDON, 1972

THE HAREM
Ottaviano Bon (1551–1622) was a diplomat at the Sublime Porte, the court of the Ottoman sultans, between 1604 and 1607.

66 If he should require one of them for his pleasure or to watch them at play or hear their music, he makes known his desire to the Head Kadin, who immediately sends for the girls who seem to her to be the most beautiful in every respect and arranges them in a line from one end of the room to the other. She then brings in the King, who passes before them once or twice, and according to his pleasure fixes his eyes on the one who attracts him most, and as he leaves

throws one of his handkerchiefs into her hand, expressing the desire to sleep the night with her. She, having this good fortune, makes up as well as she can and, coached and perfumed by the Kadin, sleeps the night with the King in the Royal chamber in the women's apartments, which is always kept ready for such an event. And while they are sleeping the night the Kadin arranges for some old Moorish women ... to stay in the room ... There are always two torches burning there, one at the door of the room, where one of the old women is, and the other at the foot of the bed ... On rising in the morning the King changes all his clothes, leaving the girl those he was wearing with all the money that was in the purses: then, going to his other rooms, he sends her a present of clothes, jewels, and money in accordance with the satisfaction and pleasure recieved. The same procedure holds good for all the others who take his fancy, lasting longer with one than with another according to the pleasure and affection he feels for her. And she who becomes pregnant is at once called Cassachi Sultan – that is to say, Queen Sultana – and if she bears a son its arrival is heralded with the greatest festivities. 99

OTTAVIANO BON, *PURCHAS HIS PILGRIMS*, LONDON 1625

EUNUCHS

Thomas Dallam (fl. 1599–1615) was an English organ-maker who traveled to Constantinople in 1599 to take a gift of an organ to Sultan Mehmed III from Queen Elizabeth I. While there, he looked into the Harem at Topkapi through a wall grating, one of the few people ever to do so and live to tell the tale.

66 When he (a black eunuch) had showed me many other thinges which I wondered at, than crossinge throughe a litle squar courte paved with marble, he poynted me to goo to a graite in a wale, but made me a sine that he myghte not goo thether him selfe. When I came to the grait the wale was verrie thicke, and graited on bothe the sides with iron verrie strongly; but through that graite I did se thirtie of the Grand Sinyor's Concubines that weare playinge with a bale in another courte. At the firste sighte of them I thoughte they had bene yonge men, but when I saw the hare of theiir heades hange doone on their backes, platted together with a tasle of smale pearle hanginge in the lower end of it, and by other plaine tokens, I did know them to be women, and verrie prettie onew in deede.

Theie wore upon theire heades nothinge but a little capp of clothe of goulde, which did but cover the crowne of her heade; no bandes a boute their neckes, nor anythinge but faire cheans of pearle and a juell hanginge on their breste, and juels in their ears; their coats weare like a souldier's mandilyon (cloak), some of reed sattan and som of blew, and som of other collors, and grded like a lace of contraire collor; they wore britchis of scamatie, a fine clothe made of coton woll, as whyte as snow and as fine as lane (muslin); for I could desarne the skin of their thies throughe it. These britchis cam doone to their mydlege; som of them did weare fine cordevan buskins, and som had their leges naked, with a goulde ringe on the smale of her legg; on her foute a velvett panttoble (high shoe) 4 or 5 inches hie. I stood so longe loukinge upon them that he which had showed me all this kindnes began to be verrie angrie with me. He made a wrye mouthe, and stamped with his foute to make me give over looking; the which I was verrie lothe to dow, for that sighte did please me wondrous well. 99

THOMAS DALLAM, *DIARY, 1599–1600*, IN *EARLY VOYAGES AND TRAVELS IN THE LEVANT*; ED. J.T. BENT, HAKLUYT SOCIETY 1ST SERIES, VOL. 87, 1893

A CITY OF THE SENSES

A DIFFERENT ISTANBUL

Sait Faik (Abasıyanık, 1906-1954), one of Turkey's best-loved short story writers, used the vivid scenes and colorful characters of Istanbul in most of his fiction. His selected stories are available in translation in books published in France, Spain and the United States.

❝ I have realized that the Istanbul of our dreams is more beautiful than the real city. Or is it, really? Are we happier beside a mean Galata Bridge, an ugly Beyazıt Tower, a mighty dome of the Mosque of Süleyman, or St Sophia the amiable giant?… Could it be that the Istanbul we miss, even when we are just an hour's distance away from it, is the Istanbul of our visions, dreams and memories?

I feel joyous when I create an Istanbul lovelier than Istanbul on three feet of snow… Actually, I used to get sad thinking that I could not create Istanbul within Istanbul. There is an Istanbul more beautiful than Istanbul. You ought to know that. This Istanbul is a different one that we construct, through our imagination, at all sorts of places — the plain through which a train hurtles at a hundred kilometres per hour, the sea through which a ship goes swishing, or a mountain covered with knee-deep snow. ❞

SAIT FAIK, *ESSAY*, 1930,
TRANSLATED BY TALAT SAIT HALMAN

SAILING TO BYZANTIUM

William Butler Yeats (1865–1939), Irish poet and dramatist, won the Nobel Prize for Literature in 1923. "Sailing to Byzantium" is considered one of the masterpieces of the English language.

That is no country for old men. The young
In one another's arms, birds in the trees
— Those dying generations — at their song,
The salmon-falls, the mackerel-crowded seas,
Fish, flesh, or fowl, commend all summer long
Whatever is begotten, born, and dies.
Caught in that sensual music all neglect
Monuments of unageing intellect.

An aged man is but a paltry thing,
A tattered coat upon a stick, unless
Soul clap its hands and sing, and louder sing
For every tatter in its mortal dress,
Nor is there singing school but studying

Monuments of its own magnificence;
And therefore I have sailed the seas and come
To the holy city of Byzantium.

O sages standing in God's holy fire
As in the gold mosaic of a wall,
Come from the holy fire, perne in a gyre,
And be the singing-masters of my soul.
Consume my heart away; sick with desire
And fastened to a dying animal
It knows not what it is; and gather me
Into the artifice of eternity.

Once out of nature I shall never take
My bodily form from any natural thing,
But such a form as Grecian goldsmiths make
Of hammered gold and gold enamelling
To keep a drowsy Emperor awake;
Or set upon a golden bough to sing
To lords and ladies of Byzantium
Of what is past, or passing, or to come.

WILLIAM BUTLER YEATS, *SAILING TO BYZANTIUM,* 1926

DELIGHT IN SEEING

Abidine Dino (1913–93)was born in Istanbul. Painter and writer, journalist, cineast and sculptor, he is a founder of the Avant-Garde Turkish group D of painters (1933). In the following excerpt, he writes of his feelings about his country.

66 Whenever I am asked about my country, Turkey, I am always haunted by a feeling that no one has ever really seen it, neither I nor anyone else. Its essence always seems to escape me. A land and a people steeped in tragedy, coulours turning in a flash from drabness to moving intensity, frenzied agitation beneath outward calm, the wild anger of nature and of men that suddenly fades away, the antagonism of man and of dispro-portionate space, doldrums and seismic shocks, silences so thick one can touch them, but occasionally torn by the endless screeching of an ox cart or a son howled as wildly as if the singer were on the rack. But there is gentleness, too. The eyes of women, the hair of camels, the fields of narcissus, and spreading tectonic movement – as the geographers say. Zones of weakness, broken topography, slumped ridges...Then the lakes, salty and turquoise, the phenomenal waterfalls of Pamukkale "Cotton Fortress" and their terraced basins so dazzlingly white that Marx Ernst might have signed them. No, I could never finish this list of "delights to be seen." Every summer the Turks placidly watch foreign migrations flowing into their country, those same Turks who had at one time practised, and admittedly more belligerent form of migration. But the old motive is still there: a delight in seeing the world. Today the verb "see" is gaining

ground: one learns to see, one is able to see, one occasionally loses all hope of seeing. We try to see with paintings, photography, films and television, with the eyes of others and with our own. Nothing is ever totally satisfying. I still remember one morning in 1953 at Vallauris, where Picasso said, with a note of sadness: "A man sees only once or twice in a lifetime." It is true, but also shattering. How does one approach this Turkey? Should you forget about seeing and instead, taste grilled swordfish or Bosphorus strawberries?Or the contraband alcohol known as bogma "stangler" or lamb grilled over vine shoots?To glimpse Turkey would it be better to prance dead drunk to the beat of an enormous drum on the roofs of a village in round dances of another era? Or is the answer to sit at the bow of a Bosphorus boat under the finger of light piercing a snow storm at night?Perhaps one could guide a plough behind a bony ox or suffocate from dust on a road while jeeps race by.Or would it be better to go to Bergama, ancient Pergamum, with its temple to Aesculapius the healer and spend a night there to cure an imaginary ailment? But what can one do to see this Turkey since crayons and brushes have been of no help to me? Turkish miniaturists were not able to grasp much of it either, even though the Matrakis and the Levnis and others are magnificent. Perhaps only Siyah Kalem saw things clearly. Then there is the music of Dede Effendi but it represents only Istanbul. Are the songs of Anatolia enough in themselves? As a last resort, if one is in Uskudar, one can still visit a friend who is an expert in preparing colours for illuminated manuscripts.One can also draw spirals with a quill facing Leander's tower, unless one races to the other end of the country to sketch the day labourers at Adana bridge. One can sail for Trebizond, wander in Kayseri, try to board Noah's Ark if it is ever found on Mount Ararat, drop in at Raman to watch the oil wells, come back to Istanbul to look at the city from the top of the Hilton or, even better, take the measure of Galata Tower from a rowboat. **"**

ABIDINE DINO, *UNPUBLISHED EXCERPT*, 1993

THREE CIVILIZATIONS

A LAND AND WATER CITY

Lord Kinross (1905–1976) traveled extensively in Turkey and wrote several memorable books about its history and cultural landscapes. His biography of Atatürk is regarded as perhaps the best in any language and his one-volume "The Ottoman Centuries: The Rise and Fall of the Turkish Empire" is one of the most readable accounts of Ottoman history.

" The land-and-water city which I now explored was a world in itself, on three neighbouring seas: the deep Bosphorus linking the Black Sea, with its dark Russian storms, to the Sea of Marmara, as pellucid and calm as an enclosed Mediterranean. It was a world of two seasons. When the wind blew from the South, we could stay in the cool of the Bosphorus, braced by its sparkling waters. When it blew from the North, we would seek relaxation and shelter on the beaches and in the shallows of the pine-clad islands of the Marmara.

The city itself, looking out to these seas over the remains of its medieval walls, is a world of three civilisations — the Byzantine, the Ottoman, the Western European. In essence the skyline is still Byzantine, the flat, sixth-century dome of St Sophia matched a thousand years later — the art of building on such a scale having lapsed meanwhile — by the more rounded domes of the great mosques of the incomparable Ottoman architect, Sinan. But now, giving to the city of the Greeks an oriental character, there were minarets, tall and slender as pencils, to punctuate the array of domes, much as in a landscape cypresses punctuate the dome-shaped trees beneath them. Minarets, domes of all sizes whether of mosques or tombs or baths, courtyards colonnaded, cooled by fountains, flanked by the libraries and schoolsand hospitals and workhouses of the medieval Welfare State — such, architecturally, is Istanbul.

But there is some of it still, besides St Sophia, that is wholly Byzantine. There are the Kahriye and the Fethiye Mosques (St Saviour in Chora and St Mary Pammakaristos), still yielding to the restorer lost masterpieces of fresco and mosaic. There are some two dozen other churches, one, St Sergius and St Bacchus, a miniature replica of St Sophia, by the sea, others hidden away amid the slums, the Phanar and in the outskirts of the city. There are the Byzantine "Golden Gate", through the city walls, and just within them the ruins of the monastery of St. John the Baptist, which grew from a Greek basilica.

Thus does Christian Constantinople dovetail into Muslim Stamboul. Opposite, the modern quarter of Péra, now Beyoğlu, climbs vertiginously upwards beyond the Golden Horn, while the ornate nineteenth-century palaces of the Sultans decorate, like triumphs of confectionery, the shores of the Bosphorus beyond.

If, in their architecture, the Turks learnt from the Greeks in the West, in their decorative arts they learnt from the Persians in the East. For a century before venturing, in 1453, to besiege Byzantium and thus assume control of the remainder of its Empire, the Ottoman Sultans reigned in Brussa, a city burgeoning amid gardens on the lower and more fertile slopes of the snow-capped Mount Olympus. Here they absorbed, by observing the Greeks, the art of good administration, meanwhile enriching their city with the arts of decoration which they had absorbed on their progress through Persia. Persians were employed to build their mosques and to embellish them with a wealth of tile work and copper work, of carpets and textiles, of wood-carving and stone-carving. The geometric motifs of their earlier Seljuk forbears, austere as some fugue by Bach, had sprouted, as the centuries went on, into tendrils and leaves and flowers as naturalistic as those of the Persian garden. Whith these, after the conquest, they adorned the mosques and the palaces of Istanbul, reaching an apotheosis of elegance in the Grand Seraglio, its palatial precincts disposed around gardens on a point commanding the Bosphorus, the Marmara and the Golden Horn. Here in Istanbul, between East and West, is the flavour of Ottoman Turkey. **"**

LORD KINROSS, INTRODUCTION TO
TURKEY,
ED. BY ROBERT MANTRAN, 1959

THE SPIRIT OF THREE CITIES

Michel Butor, born in 1926, is a leading proponent of the nouveau roman, and he also enjoys fame as a poet, critic, and travel writer. He taught at Manchester, Geneva, and Thessalonika in the 1950s. This passage is from a chapter entitled "Istanbul" in his "Le Génie du lieu".

❝ It was lucky for me there was rain and fog the first time I crossed the floating bridge of Galata, which breathes gently under your feet every time a tugboat goes by. The bridge is in fact both a bridge and a railway station with two levels, with many iron stairways, flanked by loading quays with landing steps, for the Bosphorus, the Princes' Islands or Eyüp; with ticket windows, waiting rooms, shops and cafés, congested with a crowd of fishermen dropping their lines, leaning on the railings or crouching on the edges, and with travellers carrying their baskets, or people walking by, dressed in European style...

The coast of Asia was barely visible... large caiques with sails, long strings of black barges, to the left the big ships that ran to Smyrna and Alexandria, to the right the cranes, the smoke from the trains, the trees of Gulhane Park, and, above the roofs of the Seraglio with its odd bell tower like a French church, the cupola of Saint Irené, then the Sophia looking as though it were floating, as though it were being borne away in a very slow, imperturbable flight by its four enormous buttresses.

It may be that I never again felt so profoundly the effect of this immense and solemn spectacle, this animated maritime crossroads, this unfolding ceremony... as I watched it I was delighted by the pearl and amber light that was so wonderfully diffused, reflected, set in motion by the shimmer of the omnipresent water, I was delighted by all the minarets on the hills like the tent poles of some sumptuous camp, or like reeds in an angel's pool; then, in the evening, everything becoming transfigured in the contagion of the sky's dripping gold, flashing back from that immense luminous horn that plunges into the interior of Europe, dyeing the domes and the depots, dyeing the eyes of men, entering their blood, entering my blood, entering my hands...The Spirit of Three cities are superimposed on one another, and as one wanders one unravels them, three cities born of profoundly different structure, three cities born of three invasions. ❞

MICHEL BUTOR,
THE SPIRIT OF MEDITERRANEAN PLACES, 1986,
TRANSLATED BY LYDIA DAVIS

NATURAL BEAUTY

MISTRESS OF THE WORLD

Augier Ghislain de Busbecq (1522–1592) was born in Flanders. He served as the Habsburg Ambassador at the Court of Süleyman the Magnificent in the mid-1550s. He stayed for seven years in Constantinople. His letters, written in Latin, contain great insights into the Ottoman life of the time, government, and culture.

❝ As for the situation of the City itself, it seemed to me, to be naturally placed as fit to the Mistress of the World; it stands in Europe, and hath Asia in view, and on its right, hath Egypt and Africa, which though Countries not adjacent to it, yet by reason of frequent intercourse and naval commerce, they seem as it were, contiguous: on its left hand is the Euxin Sea, and the Palus Maeotis, whose banks are inhabited round about by many Nations, and so many navigable Rivers have influx into them, that there is no thing that grows in any of the Countries there about, fit for man's use, but there is a great conveniency of transporting it by sea to Constantinople. ❞

AUGIER GHISLAIN DE BUSBECQ,
TRAVELS INTO TURKEY, 1744

THE BOSPHORUS

Julia Pardoe (1806–1862), a British poet, went to Istanbul with her father in 1835 and, in the following year, published her enchanting book entitled "The City of the Sultan and the Domestic Manner of the Turks". Later she wrote "The Romance of the Harem" and "The Thousand and One Days".

❝To be seen in all its beauty, the Bosphorus should be looked upon by moonlight. Then it is that the occupants of the spacious mansions which are mirrored in its waters, enjoy to the fullest perfection the magnificence of the scene around them. The glare of noonday reveals too broadly the features of the locality; while the deep, blue, star-studded sky, the pure moonlight, and the holy quiet of evening, lend to it, on the contrary, a mysterious indistinctness which doubles its attraction. The inhabitants of the capital are conscious of this fact; and during the summer months, when they occupy their marine mansions, one of their greatest recreations is to seat themselves upon the seaward terraces, to watch the sparkling of the ripple, and to listen to the evening hymn of the seamen on board the Greek and Italian vessels; amused at intervals by a huge shoal of porpoises rolling past, gambolling in the moonlight, and plunging amid the waves with a sound like thunder: while afar off are the dark mountains of Asia casting their long dusky shadows far across the water, and the quivering summits of the tall trees on the edge of the channel sparkling like silver, and lending the last touch of loveliness to a landscape perhaps unparalleled in the world.

Shakespeare must have had a vision of the Bosphorus, when he wrote the garden scene in Romeo and Juliet!

All the Orientals idolize flowers. Every good house upon the border of the channel has a parterre, terraced off from the sea, of which you obtain glimpses through the latticed windows; and where the rose trees are trained into a thousand shapes of beauty sometimes a line of arches risen all bloom and freshness above a favourite walk – sometimes the plants are stretched round vases of red clay of the most classical formation, of which they preserve the shape – ranges of carnations, clumps of acacias, and bosquets of seringa, are common; and the effect of these fair flowers, half shielded from observation, and overhung with forest trees, which are in profusion in every garden, is extremely agreeable.❞

JULIA PARDOE, *THE CITY OF THE SULTAN*,
LONDON, 1837

A CITY UNDER SNOW

❝I shall never forget my first impression of Constantinople. It has been my good fortune since then, to see it again and again, at every time of year, and under every possible aspect, but no subsequent picture has had either the vividness or the beauty of the first. I remember that it was in February and we steamed up the Sea of Marmora to the entrance of the Bosphorus in a heavy snow-storm. The flakes fell so thick and fast that scarcely a single building was distinctly visible. Then, suddenly, just when we were opposite St. Sophia, the snow ceased to fall, the clouds parted in a bright blue rent, and the clear morning sun, rising behind us, shone full upon Stamboul. It was a marvellous sight. Every dome and minaret and tower was

frosted with thick silver. It was as though the whole beautiful city were moulded in precious metal finely chiselled and richly chased. The slender minarets shot up like rays of light, the dark cypresses were changed to silver plumes, even the Seven Towers, far on the western wall, were as white as Parian marble. Only the sea had colour. A moment earlier it had been grey and dull as weather-beaten lead, but under the touch of the Eastern sun it flashed all at once to a deep opaque blue, more like lapis lazuli than sapphire.

The glory of the scene was beyond description, and, in its way, surpasses anything I have witnessed in any part of the world. A few minutes later it was gone, the wintry clouds rolled together, the light went out, snow fell again, then rain, and then more snow, and my second impression was of dismal, slushy, filthy streets, dripping eaves, marrow-biting air, and an intense longing for a comfortable room and a good fire. Perhaps the contrast has served in memory's gallery to throw the first picture into unreasonable prominence, but

remembrance may have exaggerations which one does not regret. **99**

F. MARION CRAWFORD,
CONSTANTINOPLE, 1895

BUILDINGS OF THE CITY

THE FAIREST SHOW

Edward Lithgoz, the intrepid British traveler, visited Constantinople in the early years of the 17th century and wrote extensively about the city and the life of its inhabitants, in his "Rare Adventures and Painefull Peregrinations".

66 I beheld (...) the Prospect of that little World, the great City of Constantinople; which indeed yeeldeth such an outward splendor to the amazed beholder, of goodly Churches, stately Towers, gallant Steeples, and other such things, whereof now the World make so great accompt, that the whole earth cannot equal it.

For indeed outwardly it hath the fairest show, and inwardly in the streets being narrow, and most part covered, the filthiest & deformed buildings in the world; the reason of its beauty, is, because being situate on moderate prospective heights, the universal textures, a farre off, yeeld a delectable show, the covertures being erected like the backe of a Coach after the Italian fashion with gutterd tyle. But being entred within, there is nothing but a striking deformity, and a loathsome contrived place; without either internal domesticke furniture, or externall decorements of fabricks palatiatly extended. Notwithstanding that for its situation, the delicious wines, & fruits, the temperate climat, the fertile circumjacent fields, and for the Sea Hellespont, and pleasant Asia on the other side: it may truely be called the Paradise of the earth. **99**

EDWARD LITHGOZ, *RARE ADVENTURES AND PAINEFULL PEREGRINATIONS*, LONDON, 1640

THE GREAT WALLS OF STAMBOUL

Pierre Loti, born Louis Marie Julien Viaud (1850–1923), achieved wide-spread popularity with his novels and travel writing about exotic places. His name became virtually synonymous with "Ottoman romance". His "Les Désenchantées" and "Aziyadé", set in Istanbul, are touching romantic novels.

❝ It was a bright winter afternoon and we were out wandering together, she and I, rejoicing like a couple of children to be out in the sun for once, and roaming the countryside. But we had chosen a cheerless region for our walk. We were strolling along by the great wall of Stamboul, the most solitary spot in the world, where nothing seems to have stirred, since the days of the last Byzantine Emperors. ... The ancient ramparts are steeped in a silence, such as broods over the approach to a necropolis. Here and there a gate has been built in the thickness of these walls, but to no purpose, for never a soul goes in or out. These queer, little, low doors have an air of mystery, and above the lintels are gilded inscriptions and curious decorations. Between the inhabited quarters of the town and the fortifications, lie great tracts of waste land, dotted with suspicious-looking hovels, and with crumbling ruins, dating from every epoch of history. There is nothing from without to break the eternal monotony of these walls, save here and there the white shaft of a minaret, rising in the distance. Always the same battlements, the same turrets, the same dark hues, laid on by the hand of time, the same regular lines, running straight and dreary, till they are lost on the far horizon. **❞**

PIERRE LOTI, *CONSTANTINOPLE* (*AZIYADÉ*),
TRANSLATED BY MARJORIE LAWRIE, 1927

ARRIVING BY SEA

Rose Macaulay (1881-1958), the prolific British novelist and essayist, is perhaps best known for her novel entitled "The Towers of Trebizond", which contains vivid scenes from various parts of Turkey and long descriptions of Istanbul and its streets, shops and cafés.

❝ ... Before dark Istanbul could be seen ahead, and it is true that it must look more splendid than any other city one comes to by sea. Even Father Chantry-Pigg, who did not think that Constantine's city and the Byzantine capital ought to have had all those mosque-domes and minarets built on to its old Byzantine shape, of which he had engravings in a book, even he thought the famous outline climbing above the Bosphorus and the Sea of Marmara, with all its domes and minarets poised against the evening sky, was very stupendous. ... I saw Istanbul, the mosques and palaces and the Seraglio and the cisterns and the Turkish cemetery and the walls and the Bazaar, and the excavations going on in Justinian's palace... and one day I went up the Bosphorus and saw the castles and palaces and mosques and old wooden houses and villages on the shores. But in the evenings I wandered about old Stamboul, down by the quays and among the narrow streets and cafés and old shops, and watched the ships in the harbour and the people. **❞**

ROSE MACAULAY, *THE TOWERS OF TREBIZOND*, 1956

THE GARBAGE HILLS

Latife Tekin was born in 1957 in Karacafenk, in the Turkish province of Kayseri. Her first book "Dear Cheeky Death", ("Sevgili Arsız Ölün"), was published in 1983. John Berger wrote that "In Berji Kristin, a shanty-town community becomes the center of the world, holding the stage and addressing the sky."

111

66 One winter night, on a hill where the huge refuse bins came daily and dumped the city's waste, eight shelters were set up by lantern-light near the garbage heaps. In the morning the first snow of the year fell, and the earliest scavengers saw these eight huts pieced together from materials bought on credit – sheets of pitchpaper, wood from building sites, and breezeblocks brought from the brickyards by horse and cart. Not even stopping to drop the sacks and baskets from their backs, they all ran to the huts nd began a lively exchange with the squatters who were keeping watch.A harsh and powerful wind kept cutting short their words and at one point almost swept the huts away.The scavengers pointed out that the ramshackle walls and makeshift roofs would never stand up to the wind, so the squatters decided to rope down the roofs and nail supports to the walls.

When the garbage trucks had come and gone, the simit-sellers on the way to the garbage heard that eight huts had been built on the slopes and spread the news throught the neighbouring warehouses, workshops and coffee houses. By noon people had begun to descend on the hillside like snow. Janitors, pedlars and simit-sellers all arrived with pickaxes, closely followed by people who had left their villages to move in with their families in the city, and by others roaming the hills behind the city in the hope of building a hut. Men and women, young and old, spread in all directions. Kneeling and rising they measured with feet and outstretched arms.Then with their spades they scratched crooked plans in the earth. By evening Rubbish Road had become a road of bricks and blocks and pitchpaper. That night in snowfall and lantern-light a hundred more huts were erected in the snow.

Next morning, by the garbage heaps – downhill from the factories which manufactured lightbulbs and chemicals, and facing the china factory – a complete neighbourhood was fathered by mud and chemical waste, with roofs of plastic basins, doors from old rugs, oilcloth windows and walls of wet breezeblocks.

Throughout the day bits and pieces arrived to furnish the houses, and remaining women and children, with sacks on their backs and babies in arms, entered their homes. Mattresses were unrolled and kilim-rugs spread on the earthen floors. The damp walls were hung with faded pictures and brushes with their blue bead good-luck charms and cradles were slung from the roofs and a chimmey pipe was knocked through the side wall of every hut. 99

LATIFE TEKIN, *BERJI KRISTIN, TALES FROM THE GARBAGE HILLS*, 1993

KAGITHANE

Evliya Çelebi Efendi, the Ottoman travel writer, collected his vivid impressions of his journeys in his ten-volume "Seyahatname" ("Book of Travels"). His monumental work is a treasure-house of geographic data, anthropological knowledge, oral history and personal observation.

❝ While my humble self was lodging with Melek Ahmed Pasha at Topçular (Artillery) Palace, every evening we used to watch thousands of firecrackers reach the sky and hear the report of thousands of guns and rifles. Later, when I enquired of a fellow man-of-pleasure about this feast, he said 'Woe to the hopeless fool who has dissipated his wits, wisdom and yielded to sorrow and despair… Why is it that you are so aggrieved as not to know about Kâgıthane? Ever since this Great Ottoman Empire has existed, never has there been a gayer and more joyful feast than Kâgıthane. Anyone who has not seen this place has seen nothing'.

I then immediately went and got the Pasha's permission to go to Kâgıthane. I spent 40 gold bullions to buy two *kayım*, food and drinks and, together with five or six Agas, pitched our tents in the shadow of the great oak trees along the Kâgıthane river; thus settling, we started our feast of reason and the flow of soul to continue day and night.

During the two months from the beginning of the month of Recep until the holy crescent of Ramazan appears in the sky there has been such amusements and pleasures on these green fields that no words can fully describe. All gentry, noblemen and prodigal sons of the plutocrats of Istanbul adorned the valley with more than three thousand tents. Every night these tents were illuminated with thousands of candles, oil lamps and lanterns. In the evening, the leading groups were entertained by musicians, singers, minstrels and performers like the Ahmed group, Cevahir group, Nazlı group, Garibanu group, Ahide group, Zümrüt group, Postalcı group, Batakoglu group, Hasena group, Samur-ka group, who played many tunes on their 'Ceng-ür Rebab' 'Santur', tambour and 'Ud-u Kanun' until sunrise while a hundred thousand fireworks adorned the sky with lightnings, stars, butterflies, etc., and the entire Kâgıthane was bathed in this radiant splendour. Guns were fired from dawn

to dusk. Besides these tents, scattered along the two banks of the Kâgıthane river, were more than two thousand shops vending not only foods and drinks but also myriad valuables. Every day the clowns, jesters, magicians, weight lifters, ropedancers, acrobats, jugglers, jongleurs, bear, monkey, donkey and dog trainers, puppet shows, bird-men, and swordeaters, about three hundred and sixty entertainers performed and made great profit. Four Janissary platoons were assigned by the palace to maintain order in this area. Most of these Janissaries used to swim in the Kâgıthane river. Never in history there has been such union of gentlemen and scholars. 99

EVLIYA ÇELEBI EFENDI, *SEYAHATNAME (BOOK OF TRAVELS)*
(EXCERPT FROM A SMALL COLLECTION OF PASSAGES PUBLISHED IN THE 1960s BY THE TURKISH MINISTRY OF TOURISM AND INFORMATION)

CAPITAL OF THE WORLD

Gustave Flaubert (1821–80)), the French novelist, is perhaps most famous for "Madame Bovary" (1857). Certain passages were deemed to be offensive to public morals and so Flaubert was tried in the courts but subsequently acquitted. At the age of twenty-nine, he decided to visit Istanbul and the Middle East and compare the reality with the various descriptions he had read in books. He wrote about his impressions to several intimate friends.

66 About Constantinople, where I arrived yesterday morning, I'll tell you nothing today, except to say that I have been struck by Fourier's idea that some time in the future it will be the capital of the world. It is really fantastic as a human anthill. That feeling of being crushed and overwhelmed you had on your first visit to Paris;: here one is penetrated by it, elbowing as one does so many unknown men, from the Persian and the Indian to the American and the Englishman, so many separate individualities which in their frightening total humble one's own. And then, the city is immense. One gets lost in the streets, which seem to have no beginning or end. The cemeteries are forests in the midst of the city. From the top of the tower at Galata, looking out over all the houses and all the mosques (beside and between the Bosphorous and the Golden Horn, both full of ships), the houses too seem like ships – a motionless fleet, with the minarets as masts. (A rather tortuous sentence – skip it.) We walked through (no more that that) the street of the male brothels. I saw bardashes buying sugared almonds, doubtless with bugger-money – the anus thus about to provision the stomach instead of the usual other way round. I heard the sound of a scratchy violin coming from ground-floor rooms: they were dancing a Greek dance. These young boys are usually Greeks. They wear their hair long. 99

GUSTAVE FLAUBERT,
LETTER, 1850

THE GREAT BAZAAR

Edmondo De Amicis (1846–1908), an officer in the Italian army, published "Vita militare" in 1868. He was one of the most perceptive as well as colorful of the 19th-century European observers of Ottoman Istanbul and also an unqualified admirer of the city. The passage below is from his book "Constantinople".

" The Great Bazaar has nothing on the exterior to attract the eye, or give an idea of its contents. It is an immense stone edifice, of Byzantine architecture, and irregular form, surrounded by high grey walls, and surmounted by hundreds of little cupolas, covered with lead, and perforated with holes to give light to the interior. The principal entrance is an arched doorway without architectural character; no noise from without penetrates it; at four paces from the door you can still believe that within those fortress walls there is nothing but silence and solitude. But once inside you stand bewildered. It is not an edifice, but a labyrinth of arcaded streets flanked by sculptured columns and pilasters; a real city, with its mosques, fountains, crossways and squares, dimly lighted like a thick wood into which no ray of sunlight penetrates; and filled by a dense throng of people. Every street is a bazaar, almost all leading out of one main street, with an arched roof of black and white stone, and decored with arabesques like the nave of a mosque. In this dimly lighted thoroughfare, carriages, horsemen, and camels are constantly passing, making a deafening noise. The visitor is apostrophized on all sides with words and signs. The Greek merchants call out in loud voices and use imperious gestures. The Armenian, quite as cunning, but more humble in manner, solicits obsequiously; the Jew whispers his offers in your ear; the silent Turk, seated cross-legged upon his carpet at the entrance of his shop, invites only with his eye, and resigns himself to destiny. Ten voices at once address you; Monsieur! Captain! Caballero! Signore! Eccellenza! Kyrie! My Lord! At every turn, by the side doors, are seen perspectives of arches and pilasters, long corridors, narrow alleys, a long confused perspect of bazaar, and everywhere shops, merchandise piled up or hanging from wall and ceiling, busy merchants, loaded porters, groups of veiled women, coming and going, a perpetual noise of people and things enough to make one dizzy…You may linger a whole day in one bazaar, unconscious of the flight of time; for example, the bazaar of stuffs, and clothing. It is an emporium of beauty and riches enough to ruin your eyes, your brains, and your pocket; and you must be on your guard for a caprice might bring upon you the consequence of sending for help by telegraph. You walk in the midst of towering heaps of brocades from Bagdad, carpets from Caramania, silks from Broussa, linens from Hindustan, muslins from Bengal, shawls from Madras, cachemeres from India and Persia, many tinted tissues from Cairo; cushions arabesqued in gold, silken veils woven with silver stripes, scarfs of gauze in blue and crimson, so light and transparent that they seem like sunset clouds; stuffs of every kind and every design, in which red, blue, green, yellow colors the most rebellious to sympathetic combination, are brought together

115

and interwoven, with a happy audacity and harmony, that makes one stand in open-mouthed wonder; table covers of all sizes, with red or white grounds embroidered all over with arabesques, flowers, verses from the Koran, and imperial ciphers, worthy of being admired for hours, like the walls of the Alhambra. **99**

EDMONDO DE AMICIS, *CONSTANTINOPLE*, 1878

TRANSLATED BY CAROLINE TILTONM

A BARBARIC POPULATION
Virginia Woolf (1882–1941) visited Istanbul on two brief occasions in 1905 and 1910. At one point, she outlined a novel to take place in Galata but did not continue with it. She wrote briefly of her impressions of Istanbul in "Orlando".

66 Orlando's day was passed, it would seem, somewhat in this fashion. About seven, he would rise, wrap himself in a long Turkish cloak, light a cheroot, and lean his elbows on the parapet. Thus he would stand, gazing at the city beneath him, apparently entranced. At this hour the mist would lie so thick that the domes of Santa Sofia and the rest would seem to be afloat; gradually the mist would uncover them; the bubbles would be seen to be firmly fixed; there would be the river; there the Galata Bridge; there the green turbanned pilgrims without eyes or noses, begging alms; there the pariah dogs picking up offal; there the shawled women; there the innumerable donkeys; there men on horses carrying long poles. Soon, the whole town would be astir with the cracking of whips, the beating of gongs, cryings to prayer, lashing of mules, and rattle of brass-bound wheels, while sour odours, made from bread fermenting and incense, and spice, rose even to the heights of Pera itself and seemed the very breath of the strident and multicoloured and barbaric population. **99**

VIRGINIA WOOLF, *ORLANDO*, 1928

LIVING IN ISTANBUL

TURKISH LAW
Lady Mary Wortley-Montagu returned to England in 1718, bringing back several lessons learned in the Turkish capital. One of these was the practice of innoculation against smallpox, an illness by which she had been badly marked herself in 1715. She was also very impressed by Turkish ideas of crime and punishment but fortunately did manage to have them introduced in England.

66 The climate is delightful in the extremest degree. I am now sitting, this present fourth of January, with the windows open, enjoying the warm shine of the sun, while you are freezing over a sad sea-coal fire; and my chamber set out with carnations, roses, and jonquils, fresh from my garden. I am also charmed with many points of the Turkish law, to our shame be it spoken, better designed and better executed than ours; Particularly, the punishment of convicted liars (triumphant criminals in our country, God knows): They are burned in the forehead with a hot iron, being proved the authors of any notorious falsehood. How many white foreheads should we see disfigured, how many gentlemen would be forced to wear their wigs as low as their eyebrows, were this law in practice with us! I should go on to tell you many other parts of justice, but I must send for my midwife. **99**

LADY MARY WORTLEY-MONTAGU, *LETTER*, 1763

The vegetable vendor

❝ But to go back to the vegetable vendor and his bedecked and beflowered animal and bulging baskets. As he ambles slowly through the streets, most of which are paved with cobblestones, the doors of the houses are flung open and the housewife or the cook appears, tray in hand. Even the well-to-do families buy from these ambulant merchants. And what a variety of vegetables they carry in the spring and summer! Purple eggplants, smaller and slimmer than yours, tomatoes, green peppers, green squash and a kind called *asma kabak* which measures several feet in length. The men also sell ochra and artichokes, the hearts of which are as big as saucers but sweet and tender to eat. Other vegetables sold are horse bean (the pods are eaten while tender and the beans inside when big and mealy), several varieties of green beans, shell beans and peas, lettuce and radishes, not to mention those indispensable herbs to a Turkish cook – parsley, dill, fresh mint and scallions.

June is the month of strawberries and they are sold in small round wicker baskets. A sweet and fragrant kind grows on the hills behind the villages along the Bosphorus. No sugar is needed to sweeten them. The berries are picked late in the evening. They are carefully packed in the round baskets, the largest resting on the top. Some twenty baskets are hung on a thick pole which a man then balances over his shoulders. Every evening, while the strawberries are in season, one can see these men, trousers rolled up to their knees, feet and head bare, bringing their heavy loads to the city markets after having walked for miles to get there. As they pass by, the delicious fragrance of fresh strawberries tempts the appetite of all the passers-by.

I should also mention the nut vendors who are seen frequently in the summer. The Turkish people are very fond of fresh walnuts, almonds and hazelnuts and eat a great many of them. The walnut man, his hands black from shelling the nuts, carries his wares in a glass jar filled with water; the almond man, in a flat basket where the nuts rest on fresh leaves or cakes of ice. The outer green shells are carefully removed and the white milky nuts inside, covered with their thin yellow skins, are sold in the streets.

In the fall, the chestnut man and his small brazier appear in the city. He has a special brazier, small, round and with a wide cover in which are many holes. Charcoal is burned in this implement. When the coal turns into red-hot embers and the cover is piping hot, the chestnuts are put on top to roast. Autumn is always connected with the smell of roasting nuts and one can see the merchant and his brazier in almost every street of the city. ❞

SELMA EKREM, *TURKEY OLD AND NEW*, 1967

Smoking Hookahs

Pierre Loti writes here about one of the best-known Turkish pastimes.

❝ As he felt deeply Turkish on this warm, clear evening, when the full moon would soon shine blue on the Sea of Marmara, he returned to Stamboul at nightfall, and climbed up to the heart of the Muslim quarter, to go and sit on the familiar esplanade in front of Sultan-Fatih's mosque. He wanted to dream there, in the pure cool of the evening, and in sweet Oriental peace, smoking hookahs while surrounded by dying splendour, decay, religious silence and prayer.

When he arrived at the square, all the little cafés had lit their modest lamps; lanterns hanging in the trees – old oil lanterns – also cast a discreet light; and everywhere, on benches, on stools, turbanned dreamers smoked, talking little and in low voices, hundreds of hookahs made a curious whispering sound — water bubbling in the flask as the smoker takes a long, deep breath. They brought him one, with small, live embers on leaves of Persian tobacco, and soon like all around him, he felt a gentle semi-intoxication, harmless and thought-inducing. He sat under the trees, where the hanging lanterns cast barely any light, facing the mosque on the far side of the esplanade. The square was empty and full of shadows, with uneven paving stones, dirt and holes; the wall of the mosque filled the entire far side, tall, huge, imposing, severe, like a rampart with only one opening : the thirty-foot-high archway leading to the holy court. **99**

PIERRE LOTI, *LES DÉSENCHANTÉES*,1906, TRANSLATED BY MARINA BERRY

TURKISH BATHS

William Makepeace Thackeray (1811–1863) began his career as a journalist. His first major novel, "Vanity Fair", did not appear until 1847. He died suddenly and this account of his trip "from Cornhill to Grand Cairo" was published posthumously.

66 The spacious hall has a large fountain in the midst, a painted gallery running round it; and many ropes stretched from one gallery to another, ornamented with profuse draperies of towels and blue cloths, for the use of the frequenters of the place. All round the room and the galleries were matted enclosures, fitted with numerous neat beds and cushions for reposing on, where lay a dozen of true believers smoking, or sleeping, or in the happy half-dozing state. I was led up to one of these beds to a rather retired corner, in consideration of my modesty; and to the next bed presently came a dancing dervish, who forthwith began to prepare for the bath.

When the dancing dervish had taken off his yellow sugar-loaf cap, his gown, shawl, etc., he was arrayed in two large blue cloths; a white one being thrown over his shoulders, and another in the shape of a turban plaited neatly round his head; the garments of which he divested himself were folded up in another linen, and neatly put by. I beg leave to state I was treated in precisely the same manner as the dancing dervish.

The reverend gentleman then put on a pair of wooden pattens, which elevated him about six inches from the ground; and walked down the stairs, and paddled across the moist marble floor of the hall, and in at a little door ...But I had none of the professional ability of the dancing dervish; I staggered about very ludicrously upon the high wooden pattens; and should have been down on my nose several times, had not the dragoman and the master of the bath supported me down the stairs and across the hall. ...

The dark room was the tepidarium, a moist oozing arched den, with a light faintly streaming from an orifice in the domed ceiling. Yells of frantic laughter and song came booming and clanging through the echoing arches, the doors clapped to with loud reverberations. ...

When you get into the Sudarium, or hot room, your first sensations only occur about half a minute after entrance, when you feel that you are choking. I found myself in that state, seated on a marble slab; the bath man was gone; he had taken away the cotton turban and shoulder shawl: I saw I was in a narrow room of marble, with a vaulted roof, and a fountain of warm and cold water; the atmosphere was in a steam, the choking sensation went off, and I felt a sort of pleasure presently in a soft boiling simmer, which, no doubt, potatoes feel when they are steaming. You are left in this state for about ten minutes; it is warm certainly, but odd and pleasant, and disposes the mind to reverie.

But let any delicate mind fancy my horror, when, on looking up out of this reverie, I saw a great brown wretch extended before me, only half dressed, standing on pattens, and exaggerated by them and the steam until he looked like an ogre ... This grinning man belabours the patient violently with the horse brush. When he has completed the horse-hair part, and you lie expiring under a squirting fountain of warm water, and fancying all is done, he reappears with a large brass basin containing a quantity of lather, in the midst of which is something like old Miss MacWhirter's flaxen wig that she is so proud of, and that we have all laughed at. Just as you are going to remonstrate, the thing like a wig is dashed into your face and eyes, covered over with soap, and for five minutes you are drowned in lather; you can't see, the suds are frothing over your eyeballs; you can't hear, the soap is whizzing into your ears; you can't gasp for breath ... You little knew what saponacity was till you entered a Turkish bath.

When the whole operation is concluded, you are led – with what heartfelt joy I need not say – softly back to the cooling room, having been robed in shawls and turbans as before. You are laid gently on the reposing bed; somebody brings a narghile, which tastes as tobacco must taste in Mahomet's Paradise; a cool sweet dreamy langour takes possession of the purified frame; and half an hour of such delicious laziness is spent over the pipe as is unknown in Europe, where vulgar prejudice has most shamefully maligned indolence, calls it foul names, such as the father of all evil, and the like; in fact, does not know how to educate idleness as those honest Turks do, and the fruit which, when properly cultivated, it bears. **"**

W.M. THACKERAY, *NOTES OF A JOURNEY FROM CORNHILL TO GRAND CAIRO*, 1865

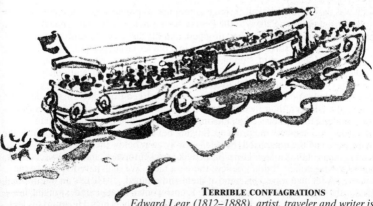

TERRIBLE CONFLAGRATIONS
Edward Lear (1812–1888), artist, traveler and writer is remembered chiefly for his watercolors and for his nonsense verse, including "The Owl and the Pussy-cat". He traveled widely throughout Europe and north Africa and published accounts of many of his trips. The following passage is from a letter to his elder sister, Ann Lear.

❝I must now devote a word to conflagration general & especial. You know that nearly all the houses in Constantinople are of wood – & you may have heard of the frequency of the fires, & their extent, but you will yet be surprised to hear that since I came – (Aug 1st) there have been 8 dreadful burnings – the least of which destroyed 60, & the largest 5,000 houses – & reduced hundreds and thousands to wretchedness. If I had not seen these things, I could not have believed them. ... And now I come to the night of Wed, the 6th – when about 12 everybody was awakened by the waiters (throughout the hotel) with the news that a tremendous fire was raging in Pera, & advancing to the inn. But Misseri said there was no danger - as there was a stone house, & a church (Greek) between him and them, where the flames would stop, & as I guessed from his coolness – he was in the right. However, I packed up, & then joined everybody else on the house top – where wet carpets, & water were all the fashion. A most horrible sight it was. ... The flames were tremendous – & all the city light as day. The houses fell crash, crash, crash, as the fire swept on nearer & nearer – & by 4 o'clock after midnight, it reached within 2 houses of the hotel – but there it stopped ... As it was, only 300 houses were burnt! – no lives lost; they very seldom are – & all the property is carried through the streets by innumerable porters to the cemeteries etc. – & there the poor people live till another wooden suburb arises in less than a year's time. Such is life in Constantinople.!!!**❞**

EDWARD LEAR, *LETTER*, 9 SEPTEMBER 1848

NIGHTLIFE

Graham Greene (1904–92) was a master of many forms of writing from thrillers to travel writing and reportage, and short stories to detective novels and children's books. "Stamboul Train" was his first commercially successful novel.

❝It was easy to talk hard all through dinner and to put his arm round her as they walked from the Pera Palace to the Petits Champs near the British Embassy. The night was warm, for the wind had dropped, and the tables in the garden were crowded. ... On the stage a Frenchwoman in a dinner jacket pranced up and down with a cane under her arm, singing a song about 'Ma Tante', which Spinelli had made popular in Paris more than five years before. The Turkish gentlemen, drinking coffee, laughed and chattered and shook their small dark feathery heads like noisy domestic birds, but their wives, so lately freed from the veil, sat silent and stared at the singer, their faces pasty and expressionless. Myatt and Janet Pardoe walked along the garden's edge, looking for a table, while the Frenchwoman screeched and laughed and pranced, flinging her desperate indecencies towards the inattentive and the unamused. Pera fell steeply away below them, the lights of fishing boats in the Golden Horn flashed like pocket torches, and the waiters went round serving coffee. 'I don't believe there's a table. We shall have to go in to the theatre.' A fat man waved his hand at them and grinned. ... 'There's an empty one.' Under the table their legs touched. The Frenchwoman disappeared, swinging her hips, and a man flung cartwheels on to the stage from the wings. He got to his feet, took off his hat, and said something in Turkish which made everyone laugh. 'What did he say?' 'I couldn't hear,' Myatt said. **❞**

GRAHAM GREENE, *STAMBOUL TRAIN*, 1932

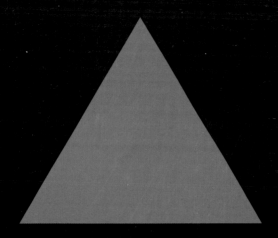

Itineraries

▲ Beyoğlu

Istanbul from Saray Burnu to the Beyazidiye▼

▲ The Süleymaniye Mosque

▲ Topkapı Sarayı   Yedikule ▼

▲ The Blue Mosque and Haghia Sophia   The Grand Bazaar ▼

▲ Fields in Bithynia

▲ Harvesting in Thrace

Shepherds near Bursa▼

Istanbul and the Bosphorus

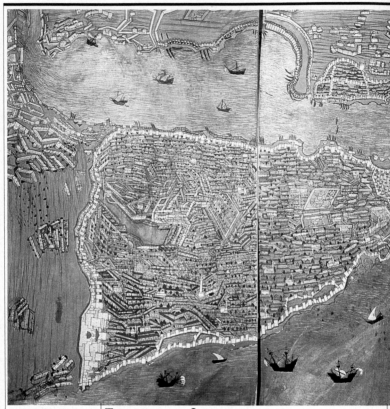

MAP OF THE CITY
A red and silver miniature painted by Seyyid Loqman depicting the districts of Stamboul, Galata, and Pera in 1584, from the *Hunarmana Manuscript* in the Topkapı Museum. The protective shield of walls which completely enclosed the Ottoman capital has been painted in a light, pale color. The green area is the gardens at Topkapı Sarayı.

THE CRADLE OF ISTANBUL

According to legend, it was on the Seraglio Point, called *Saray Burnu* in Turkish, that Byzas the Megarian landed around 660 BC and founded the city of Byzantium ● *29*. The two illustrious capitals that would succeed it, Byzantine Constantinople and Turkish Istanbul, created the heart of the present-day metropolis. Here the waters of the Bosphorus and the Golden Horn meet and then flow on into the Sea of Marmara. Over the centuries this stretch of land and sea has been the site of many epic events, and it is here also that the most spectacular buildings are situated: the Basilica of Haghia Sophia ● *74* ▲ *138*, the temple of the New Rome; and the Topkapı Palace ● *82* ▲ *150*, the center of Ottoman power. The Galata, Üsküdar, and Stamboul quarters sit astride the crossroads between Europe and Asia, facing one another across the water as they have for centuries, and today they remain the heart of the city, whose suburbs stretch along the shores of both strait and sea. At the extreme edge of the promontory, a quiet park has replaced the sultans' gardens, while the great Ottoman palace and its kiosks now open their doors to the public, who come in droves to appreciate the treasures of the imperial past.

128

> "No city has eaten the fruits of the garden of art so richly as the city of Istanbul, birthplace and school of famous men, the nursery of many nations."
>
> Nâbi (1642–1712)

The great basilica of Haghia Sophia is now admired primarily for the beauty of its architecture, after a millennium as the cathedral of Byzantium and a further 500 years as a mosque. In 1923, the basilica became a museum, thanks to Mustafa Kemal Atatürk, the father of modern Turkey ● *42*, whose bronze statue stands on the far edge of the Saray Burnu. Fifty years later, the Boğazıçı Köprüsü bridge over the Bosphorus was inaugurated to commemorate the birth of the New Turkey.

THE SARAY BURNU

GÜLHANE PARK. This park occupies the lower part of the former gardens of Topkapı Sarayı. In the Ottoman period many wooden pavilions were built in the cypress groves, where the court took up residence in summer, but a fire destroyed them in 1863.

THE GOTHS' COLUMN. Tucked away on the park's wooded slopes is one of the oldest monuments in Istanbul, the *Gotlar Sütunu* or Goths' Column, a 50-foot high granite monolith capped by a Corinthian capital. The column takes its name from the Latin inscription on its base: *Fortunae reduci ob devictos Gothos* ("To the prosperity that returned with the defeat of the Goths"). The monument is attributed either to Claudius II the Goth (268–270) or to Constantine the Great (324–337), both of whom had victories over the Goths. According to a Byzantine historian, it was once surmounted by a statue of Byzas the Megarian ● *29*.

THE KIOSK OF THE BASKET-WEAVERS. From Saray Burnu, proceed towards the Galata Bridge, on the near side of which spreads the Eminönü quarter. Along the shore railway tracks run past the docks. En route, you pass the Sepetçiler Köşkü – the Basket-Weavers' kiosk – a seaside pavilion presented in 1643 to Sultan Ibrahim the Mad (1640–48) by the eponymous guild. Today it serves as an International Press Center.

SIRKECI STATION. After the Sepetçiler Köşkü, you come to Sirkeci Istasyon, a station built in 1889 for the first of the great luxury trains: the ORIENT EXPRESS. This celebrated but now slightly less glamorous train makes only occasional trips between Paris and Istanbul today. Further along is the main pier for the ferries calling along the Bosphorus, the Golden Horn, the suburbs of Üsküdar and Kadıköy, and the Princes' Islands ● *271*.

THE GALATA BRIDGE
This 18th-century painting (below left) shows the Third Hill from the Golden Horn with the Mosque of Süleyman the Magnificent in the background. On the right can be seen the wooden bridge that once linked Stamboul to the free quarters of Galata and Pera. Built in 1845, on the orders of Sultan Abdül Mecit, it was replaced at the beginning of the 20th century by an iron bridge. Seriously damaged by a fire in 1992, this structure has now been replaced by a new one, which opened to traffic on June 18, 1992. The present Galata Bridge spans the Golden Horn slightly upstream from the site of the old one.

THE GARDENS OF THE SERAGLIO
The once-private gardens of the sultans, here seen in an engraving by Thomas Allom, are now a public park. It is much favored by the people of Istanbul who, in good weather, come here for family picnics. There is a small café near the Goth's Column. Off-shore, motorized ferries ply waters once sailed by wind-powered caiques.

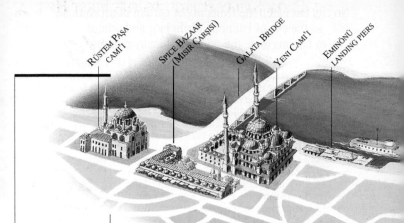

RÜSTEM PAŞA CAMİ'İ   SPICE BAZAAR (MISIR ÇARŞISI)   GALATA BRIDGE   YENİ CAMİ'İ   EMİNÖNÜ LANDING PIERS

⏱ **Four hours**

◆ **E** A1–D3

A JEWISH QUARTER
The area now
occupied by Yeni
Cami'i was for
centuries a Jewish
enclave wedged in
between the Venetian
and Genoese
concessions. The Jews
who first settled there
– all members of the
Karaite sect – arrived
in the 11th century.
They remained until
1660 when they were
expelled to make
room for Yeni Cami'i.
Remnants of the
community survive in
the Hasköy (Royal
Village) quarter a
little further up on
the right bank of the
Golden Horn.

THE EMİNÖNÜ QUARTER

THE GALATA BRIDGE. Spanning the Golden
Horn between Eminönü and Galata, this bridge is the main
artery of Istanbul. Every day vast numbers of people cross it
or pass under its arches in the many ferries that ply the lower
Golden Horn. From the western side it is reached by way of
an enormous square, the EMİNÖNÜ MEYDANI, at the edge of
which looms Yeni Cami'i, the New Mosque.

YENİ CAMİ'İ

Officially known as the Yeni Valide Sultan Cami'i, or the New
Mosque of the Valide Sultan, Yeni Cami'i was commissioned
around 1600 by the Dowager Sultana Safiye, the widow of
Murat III (1574–95) and mother of Mehmet III (1595–1603).
However, the death of Mehmet in 1603 brought construction
to a halt. The half-finished building hovered like a ghost on
the Saray Burnu until 1660, when Turhan Hadice, the mother
of Mehmet IV (1648–87) ordered Mustafa Ağa, the Sultan's
chief architect, to resume work on the abandoned mosque,
which, with its complex, would be completed in 1663 and
dedicated on November 6 of that year.

THE STRUCTURE OF THE MOSQUE. As in all Ottoman
mosques, there is a vast walled-in and porticoed forecourt
in front of Yeni Cami, to the west, called an *avlu*. The
ceremonial entrance is at the western end of the
courtyard, where a broad flight of steps leads to a richly
ornamented gateway. Inside there is a space bordered
all around by a portico of six columns on each side. At
the center stands a pretty octagonal *şadırvan*, an
ablution fountain that, like so many old things today,
serves primarily as decoration, since the faithful now
use the water taps along the south side of the
building. From the corner where the *avlu* and the
mosque join, the slender shafts of two minarets
shoot up, their three *şerefe* (balconies) carried on stalactite

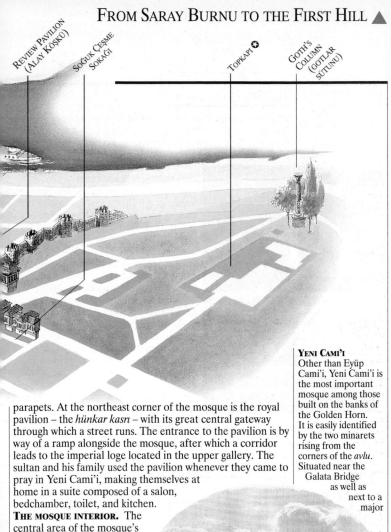

parapets. At the northeast corner of the mosque is the royal pavilion – the *hünkar kasrı* – with its great central gateway through which a street runs. The entrance to the pavilion is by way of a ramp alongside the mosque, after which a corridor leads to the imperial loge located in the upper gallery. The sultan and his family used the pavilion whenever they came to pray in Yeni Cami'i, making themselves at home in a suite composed of a salon, bedchamber, toilet, and kitchen.

THE MOSQUE INTERIOR. The central area of the mosque's interior – measuring 135 feet on each side – is defined by four corner pillars that support the central dome through four great arches, with squinches making the transition from square to circle. At the east end of the nave is the mihrab, the niche that indicates the direction of Mecca, and to its right is the mimbar, or pulpit, from which the imam delivers the sermon at the Friday noon prayer. The royal loge is at the northeast corner of the gallery, screened by a gilded grille.

THE COMPLEX ● 80. Turhan Hadice's *külliye* (complex) originally included a *medrese* (Koranic school), *darü'ş-şifa* (hospital), *mektep* (primary school), *türbe* (mausoleum), and both *çeşme* and *sebil* (fountains), as well as a hammam and a *çarşı* (bazaar). The last two were built to provide income to support the rest. Everything, save the hospital, hammam, and primary school, survive, but only the mosque and bazaar are open to the public.

YENI CAMI'I
Other than Eyüp Cami'i, Yeni Cami'i is the most important mosque among those built on the banks of the Golden Horn. It is easily identified by the two minarets rising from the corners of the *avlu*. Situated near the Galata Bridge as well as next to a major pier, Yeni Cami'i has long been surrounded by the clamor of heavy traffic, with cars, buses, and ferries all intersecting at the very foot of the great basilica.

131

THE EGYPTIAN OR SPICE MARKET

"If you follow the little streets that wind their way from the Yeni Djami leading to the Mosque of Sultan

Bayezid, you will arrive at the Egyptian Bazaar – the Drug Market – an immense hall crossed from end to end by a lane reserved for the movement of both merchandise and consumers. Immediately one is struck – indeed intoxicated – by a penetrating odor composed of scents from all the exotic products. Displayed on every side, in heaps or open sacks, are henna, sandalwood, cinnamon, benzoin, pistachios, ambergris, mastic, ginger, nutmeg, opium, hashish – all watched over by merchants nonchalantly sitting on crossed legs as if they were benumbed from the sheer weight of an atmosphere so steeped in aroma."

Théophile Gautier
Constantinople, 1851

THE SPICE BAZAAR ★

This covered market is the attractive L-shaped building to the southwest of the Yeni Cami. The bazaar is called the *Misir Çarşışı* or Egyptian Market because it once received income from the tax levied on Egypt. Its English name survives from

the time when the market specialized in the sale of spices and herbs, as well as medicinal plants and drugs. The heavy aroma of the Orient that captivated 19th-century travelers has now lost some of its power. Only six shops of the original eighty-eight are still devoted to the traditional products. Inside these the shelves are laden with great, bulging sacks of multicolored spices and jars filled with precious foodstuffs and essential oils. One enters the market through a monumental gatehouse, in the upper story of which there is the restaurant called Pandeli. Two gateways open out at the angle of the bazaar's L shape. The one on the right leads to Hasırcılar Caddesi – the Avenue of the Mat-Makers – which runs parallel with the Golden Horn. Some 200 yards along this avenue on the right is the Rüstem Paşa Cami'i. A vaulted stairway then brings you to the porticoed forecourt of the mosque, built on a terrace overlooking shops and warehouses.

RÜSTEM PAŞA CAMI'I ★

Rüstem Paşa Cami'i is one of the most beautiful of the vizierial mosques built by the great Sinan ▲ *314*, Chief Imperial Architect under Süleyman the Magnificent (1520–66) and his two successors, Selim II (1566–74) and Murat III (1574–95). Sinan built the mosque for Rüstem Paşa, Grand Vizier to Süleyman and the husband of Princess Mihrimah, the Sultan's only daughter. The mosque is entered through a rather curious double porch; the inner porch is composed of a portico with five domed bays, and the outer part has a deep, low-slung penthouse roof supported at its extremity by a colonnade. The plan is an octagon inscribed within a rectangle. At the corners, four half-domes flank the main

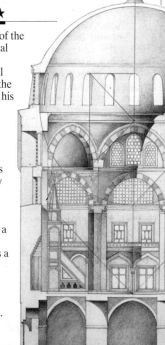

cupola, which rests upon four arches rising from four octagonal columns, two to the north and two to the south, as well as on four pillars projecting from the east and west walls. Alternating pillars of stone and small marble columns support the galleries on the north and south sides.

THE INTERIOR DECORATION. The Rüstem Paşa Cami'i is renowned for the gorgeous tiles that cover most surfaces, not only inside but also on the front of the porch. Possibly even more remarkable is the faience on the gallery level, revealing a different style. As with all great ceramics, those of Rüstem Paşa Cami'i came from Iznik ● 292, ancient Nicea, where the ceramic art attained its apogee in the years 1555–1620 – the golden age of Ottoman architecture. Here the beauty of the floral and geometric motifs spreads radiance over walls, mihrab, mimbar, and even the columns, making a harmonic whole that sets the mosque apart as one of the most spectacular in Istanbul.

THE MAUSOLEUM OF ABDÜL HAMIT

Returning to Yeni Cami'i, walk eastward between the mosque and the Spice Bazaar, then continue along Hamidiye Caddesi. The first turning on the right brings us to the *türbe* of Abdül Hamit (1774–89), which survives from a small *külliye* ● 79 that originally included a *sebil* and a *medrese*. The *medrese* is still there, but the *sebil* has been removed. Buried alongside Abdül Hamit is his son, the mad and murderous Mustafa IV, who was deposed on July 28, 1808 and executed three months later. At the end of Hamidiye Caddesi we turn right on Ankara Caddesi, a busy avenue leading up from the Golden Horn to the ridge between the First and Second Hills. On the left side of the avenue we pass the Vilayet, the headquarters of the governor of the Istanbul province.

THE CAĞALOĞLU HAMMAM

One block beyond the Vilayet turn left, and then proceed for about a hundred yards until, on the left, you see one of the entrances to the magnificent and justly famous Cağaloğlu Baths. Built for Mahmut I they are double baths, one part reserved for men and the other for women. Remarkably,

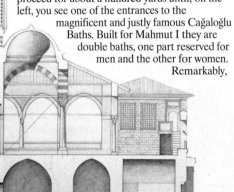

VERTICAL SECTION OF THE CENTRAL AXIS OF THE RÜSTEM PAŞA MOSQUE
The axis cuts through the multicolored mirhab and the monumental entrance way which points towards Mecca.

THE STEAM ROOM OF THE HAMMAM
The ritual of a Turkish bath is an enjoyable way to escape the clamor of the city. It involves a massage before bathing, followed by a relaxing drink of tea. Engraving by Thomas Allom, 1834.

AFFAIR OF THE SOFA
One day in 1677 the Marquis de Nointel entered the Audience Chamber only to discover that his stool was placed not upon the *sofa*, but on the floor below. Furious, the diplomat seized the stool and carried it onto the *sofa* and sat down. And so began the famous "Affair of the Sofa", which was to have diplomatic consequences.

the hammam has remained in operation since it opened in 1741. Mahmut I had the Cağaloğlu built in order to generate income for the library he had established at Haghia Sophia. Istanbul boasts over a hundred Ottoman hammams ● *58*, most of them still frequented by people who do not have baths at home. No Muslim may attend Friday prayers without having first washed from head to toe. In the Cağaloğlu Hammam the most interesting chamber is the *hararet* or steam room, which is cruciform and surmounted by a central dome supported by a circle of columns. The four lateral arms of the chamber are also dome-vaulted. One of the most beautiful public baths, the Cağaloğlu remains almost exactly as it was in Ottoman times.

THE COMPLEX OF BEŞIR AĞA

At the first intersection beyond the hammam turn left onto Alay Köşkü Caddesi, and then take the first turning on the left which places you before a small mosque set upon a platform. The mosque and its *külliye* were built in 1745 on the orders of Beşir Ağa, Chief Black Eunuch in the Topkapı Harem during the reign of Mahmut I. When it was finished the complex also included a *medrese*, a *tekke* (Dervish monastery), and shops installed under the vaults. The monastery was closed in the early days of the Turkish Republic because the dervish orders were disbanded. Both the *tekke* and the *medrese* house a cultural center for the Turks of Western Thrace, now part of Greece.

THE SUBLIME PORTE

At the next intersection Alay Köşkü Caddesi crosses Alemdar Caddesi, running next to the wall of the Topkapı Sarayı and on to the top of the First Hill. On the left is a large gateway decorated in the Turkish rococo style. This is the famous Sublime Porte, or Bab-i-Ali. In the 16th century, the empire of the Osmanlis reached its height. Its capital, which already had almost one million inhabitants by this time, began to worry the Europeans. The Sublime Porte symbolized this power, and was from this point on synonymous with an Ottoman government that was seen as a threat. The present gateway dates from 1843 and leads to the Vilayet, the administrative department of Istanbul.

THE ALAY KÖŞKÜ

Opposite the Sublime Porte, in a corner of the outer defense wall of Topkapı Sarayı, there is a large polygonal gazebo in the Turkish Baroque style. This is the Alay Köşkü, or Review

Pavilion, first built in c. 1565 and then reconstructed in 1819 by Mahmut II (1808–39). From here the Sultan would observe the life of the city, keep an eye on the activities of his Grand Vizier at the Sublime Porte, and attend both civil and military parades. The trade guilds of Istanbul took part in several grand processions in the Ottoman era. The last such event occurred in 1769 during the reign of Mustafa III (1757–74). They were held for various reasons: to mark the circumcision of a young prince; to celebrate a

great victory won by the Ottoman army; or even to take a census. In 1638, for instance, Murat IV (1623–40) used the march-past to determine the health of the capital's trade and commerce on the eve of his campaign in Iraq. A contemporary witness, Evliya Çelebi, describes the procession in his Seyâhat-Nâmé (Chronicle of Travels). It was organized into 57 sections and included 1,001 corporations, though Çelebi describes only 735. Representatives of the guilds filed by in their characteristic garb, pulling floats dedicated to their various trades, while also competing to amuse and amaze the Sultan, who, with his court, looked on from the latticed Alay Köşkü. Sometimes the parade turned into a festival that went on for an entire month. The sheer color and variety of these affairs attracted many painters, as we know from the collection of miniatures in the Topkapı Sarayı Museum. Now restored, the pavilion is used to exhibit the Kenan Özbel collection of Turkish embroideries and carpets. Its suite of rooms can be reached by a ramp from just inside the gate of Gülhane Park, a short distance up Alemdar Caddesi.

PROCESSION OF THE GUILDS

"All these guilds pass in wagons or on foot, with the instruments of their handicraft, and are busy with great noise at their work. The carpenters build wooden houses, the builders raise walls, the woodcutters pass with loads of trees, the sawyers saw them, the masons crunch chalk and whiten their faces. . . . They also build artificial ships, each ship being towed by a thousand men. The sails, masts, prow, and stem of each of the ships are ornamented with fruit kernels. Merchants flock in crowds to enter these fruit-ships to fill their baskets. With the greatest noise and quarreling from these simulated çalebs, they pass the Alay Kiosk. This is a faithful representation of what occurs at the port on the arrival of every fruit-ship. These guilds pass before the Alay Kiosk with a thousand tricks and fits, which it is impossible to describe, and behind them walk their sheikhs."

Evliya Çelebi
Chronicle of Travels
1611–12

SÜLEYMAN THE MAGNIFICENT
Woodcut,
Venice, c. 1550.

Tollbooth on the Galata Bridge at the turn of the 20th century.

THE FISH MARKET
The cuisine of Istanbul is renowned for the variety of the fish it uses – *kefal*, *lüfer* and *barbugna*, for example – all readily available from markets and restaurants. Along the quays of the Golden Horn itinerant vendors offer grilled fish fresh from the sea. The Galatasaray fish market is one of the most famous in Istanbul. It is depicted in the painting on the right by the contemporary Turkish artist Nedim Günsür, a member of the Group of Six who first exhibited their work in 1947.

ZEYNEP SULTAN CAMI'I

Following Alemdar Caddesi to the top of the first hill and then to the right, away from the outer walls of Topkapı, you arrive at a small Baroque mosque, commissioned by Princess Zeynep, daughter of Ahmet III. Its architect, Mehmet Tahir Ağa, completed the mosque and its complex in 1749. The complex included an elementary school, which still exists in the corner of the street just below the mosque, and a small cemetery, where the Princess and members of both her family and her household are buried. At the gate of the graveyard there is a rococo fountain ● 66, also designed by Mehmet Tahir Ağa in 1778 but for the *külliye* of Abdül Hamit, whence it was relocated to the Zeynep Sultan Cami'i in 1950.

SOĞUK ÇEŞME SOKAĞI

A bit further along on the opposite side of Alemdar Caddesi stands the Soğuk Çeşme Sokağı Medrese, a handsome school building erected in the outer precincts of Haghia Sophia soon after the Conquest and recently restored. It is named for the street where the entrance is situated – the Street of the Cold Fountain – which climbs the first hill from Gülhane Park to the defensive walls surrounding Topkapı Sarayı.

OTTOMAN HOUSES. The elegant old Ottoman dwellings that border Soğuk Çeşme Sokağı are the result of a major renovation launched in 1986 by the TTOK (Turkish Touring and Automobile Club). By this time the long-abandoned houses had so deteriorated that their demolition seemed inevitable. It required two years of work to complete the restoration, at which time most of the houses were integrated into a luxury hotel, the AYA SOFYA PANSIYONLARI. With their fronts freshly painted in pastel or bright colors the houses bring great charm to the old cobblestone street as it gently winds its way down towards the sea. The excavations at the lower end of the street uncovered a cistern whose brick vaults rest on six blocks of marble. This remnant of late Roman architecture now houses a deluxe restaurant, the SARNIÇ LOKANTASI, also managed by the TTOK.

THE ISTANBUL LIBRARY. The largest of the old houses on Soğuk Çeşme Sokağı is a wooden *konak* (mansion) built at the beginning of the 19th century. Today it houses a part of the Çelik Gülersoy Foundation, the Istanbul Library and its rich collection of books and prints related to the history of the city.

THE SOĞUK ÇEŞME MEDRESE

Continuing on Soğuk Çeşme Sokağı as far as Caferiye Sokağı, turn right and make your way down the blind alley on the right, where a gateway at the end leads into the Soğuk Çeşme Medrese. This theological school was founded by Cafer Ağa, Chief White Eunuch during the reign of Süleyman the Magnificent. Cafer Ağa died in 1557 while construction was still underway, but Sinan finished it in 1559–60. Owing to the steepness of the land, the architect had first to construct a vaulted substructure under the west end of the complex, along today's Alemdar Caddesi, providing space for four large shops. The domed *dershane*, or lecture hall, occupies the south side of the courtyard, with the student cells (*hücre*) placed around the periphery of the cloister.

BAZAAR OF OTTOMAN ARTS AND CRAFTS ★. Today the *medrese* serves as a bazaar of Ottoman crafts; each specialty – embroidery, bookbinding, paper-marbling – has been given one of the stalls opening onto the court. Two stalls in the right corner have been made into a café, a perfect place to pause after a walk from Saray Burnu, before continuing along Caferiye Sokağı. A left turn at the end leads into Aya Sofya Meydanı, the huge square before Haghia Sophia at the top of the First Hill.

THE SOĞUK ÇEŞME SOKAĞI
Above left is an unrestored house in the midst of a cluster of renovated buildings. The Ayasofya Pansiyonları (above right), on the "Street of the Cold Fountain," is open to visitors interested in knowing more about traditional Ottoman architecture.

THE GOLDEN HORN
A photograph taken in the 1960's of the old tramway crossing the Galata Bridge. Behind the trams looms the massive Yeni Cami.

▲ HAGHIA SOPHIA

🔺 Two hours

◆ E D4

A VIEW OF HAGHIA SOPHIA
In a detail from his panorama of 1557, the Danish painter Melchior Lorichs shows the basilica from the Asian shore.

Haghia Sophia and the old Ottoman houses after the restoration work by the Fossatis in 1852.

THE HISTORY OF THE BASILICA

Haghia Sophia was built at the command of Emperor Justinian in the years 532 to 537. The present basilica is the third church called Haghia Sophia to stand upon this site. The first, known as the Great Church, was finished on February 15, 360, and on that day Emperor Constantius (337–361), Constantine the Great's son and successor, dedicated it to Haghia Sophia, or "Divine Wisdom," an attribute of Christ. This building was destroyed by fire on June 9, 404, during a riot by supporters of John Chrysostomos, the sainted Patriarch of Constantinople who had been deposed by Empress Eudoxia, wife of the Emperor Arcadius (395–408). By 415 a new church had been constructed on the site, and was dedicated on October 10 by Theodosius II (408–450), Constantius' son and successor. Known to archeologists as the Theodosian Church, this building also burned down, during the Nika Revolt of January 15, 532. The insurrection almost cost Justinian his throne, which he retained only through the steadfastness of his Empress, Theodora.

CHRIST BLESSING (BOTTOM RIGHT)
Detail from the mosaic Deisis (Christ flanked by the Virgin and the Baptist). Rather than the stern, judgmental Pantocrator, the iconic face is haloed in other-worldly gold, suggesting kindness and sympathy. Cleared of whitewash in 1932, the mosaic is in the southeast gallery on the right.

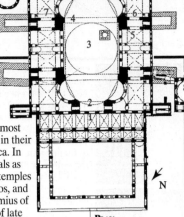

JUSTINIAN'S HAGHIA SOPHIA. Shortly after the revolt was crushed, Justinian set about rebuilding the church on an even grander scale, bringing in workers and artisans from all over the Byzantine Empire. Provincial governors were asked to send the most beautiful parts of ancient monuments found in their regions for incorporation into the new basilica. In this way Justinian gathered the finest materials as well as columns and ornaments from pagan temples as far away as Ephesus, Athens, Delphi, Delos, and even Egypt. The Emperor appointed Anthemius of Tralles, the greatest mathematical physicist of late antiquity, as the principal architect and for an assistant builder he employed Isidorus of Miletus, a renowned geometrician who had been director of the Platonic Academy in Athens. Anthemius died during the first months of the project, whereupon Isidorus took charge, completing the building within five years. The new church was formally opened on December 26, 537, St Stephen's Day, when Justinian and Theodora rededicated it to Haghia Sophia. Two decades later a series of earthquakes severely damaged the basilica, causing the collapse of the eastern part of the great dome along with the arch and half-dome on that side of the building. Because Isidorus of Miletus had died, Justinian entrusted the task of reconstruction to the architect's nephew, Isidorus the Younger, who accomplished it in five years. The building was rededicated on Christmas Eve 563, by an 81-year-old Justinian, less than two years before his death. Haghia Sophia would then serve as the Greek Orthodox cathedral of Constantinople throughout the remainder of Byzantine history, except for the Latin interregnum of 1204 to 1261, when it was a Roman Catholic church administered by the Venetian clergy. After the Ottoman Conquest of Constantinople in 1453, Haghia Sophia was converted into a mosque by Sultan Mehmet II, and it then became known as Aya Sofya Cami'i.

HAGHIA SOPHIA
MUSEUM ★

Haghia Sophia continued to serve as a mosque until 1932, when it was closed and converted into a

PLAN
1. Narthex
2. Imperial door
3. Nave
4. North tympanum
5. Tribunes
6. South gallery
7. North gallery
8. Baptistery

HAGHIA SOPHIA, SUBLIME AND POWERFUL ✪
Legend has it that on the cathedral's opening, Justinian exclaimed: "Solomon, I have beaten you!". A thousand years would pass before the technical feats of Haghia Sophia were surpassed – by Saint Peter's Basilica in Rome. Visit Haghia Sophia early on a sunny morning, to see it in its best light and avoid the crowds. Start with the tribunes, which close early.

▲ HAGHIA SOPHIA

THE LARGEST DOME IN THE ANTIQUE WORLD
The interior surface of the main dome – approximately 100 feet in diameter – is constructed of 40 stone ribs, all decorated with geometric motifs. Around the circumference, a diadem of 40 windows contributes to the sense of this immense cupola floating in airy lightness above the prayer hall below. Gold calligraphy on a black background encircles the emblematic sun at the center.

THE INTERIOR OF THE UPPER GALLERY
The basilica underwent major restoration in the 19th century, between 1847 and 1849. Louis Haghe produced the lithograph (right) from drawings by Gaspare Fossati, one of the architects responsible for the renovation. It gives a clear picture of the way Haghia Sophia looked at that time, far better than any verbal description or photograph from the period.

museum, which opened two years later. The entrance to the museum is in the garden to the west of Haghia Sophia, an area that was once the *avlu*, or outer courtyard, of the church. The west side and rear of the garden are filled with ancient columns and other architectural fragments, all of which were unearthed in various excavations around the city, most of them on the first hill. Approaching the entrance to the museum, it is possible to see the excavated remains of the Theodosian Church, discovered in 1935 by the German archaeologist Alfons Maria Schneider. The remaining fragments of the Theodosian basilica show that this was a building of monumental proportions, comparable in size and grandeur to Justinian's church.

THE STRUCTURE OF THE GREAT CHURCH ● 74.
Before entering the museum, visitors should pause to examine the structure of the building, which the Greeks called *Megale Ekklesia*, the "Great Church." The main ground plan of Haghia Sophia is that of a basilica, which is a rectangle, and measures some 230 by 250 feet. At the center of the east wall there is a projecting apse, semicircular within and three-sided on the exterior, while to the west, in front of the church, is an inner and an outer vestibule, known in Greek as the *narthex* and the *exonarthex*. The central part of the rectangular nave is surmounted by the great dome, one of the great wonders of architecture, as well as by smaller half-domes on the east and west, and by conch vaults over both the semicircular apse at the eastern end and the semicircular exedrae at all four corners. These spherical surfaces cover the central area of the

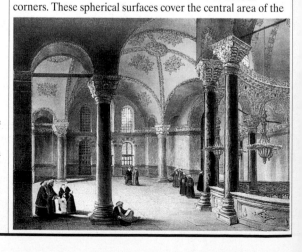

140

nave, which is flanked by side aisles, while upper galleries extend around the sides of the church and also the narthex. This was the basic form of Justinian's church, but engineering problems which developed in the course of construction and damage caused by earthquakes made it necessary to add buttresses all around the building.

Aya Sofya Cami'i

Haghia Sophia gained four corner minarets after the Ottomans converted the church into a mosque. The precincts also acquired a number of structures, some of them introduced by the Byzantines and others by the Ottomans. The additions included the baptistery and the imperial Turkish tombs on the south side. The conversion also involved some minor modifications of the interior, principally the construction of a mihrab and mimbar ● *81*. All of the Ottoman sultans continued to keep Haghia Sophia in good repair, for it would always hold pride of place among the imperial mosques.

THE FOSSATIS' RESTORATION OF HAGHIA SOPHIA. The last and most important restoration in the Ottoman era came at the instigation of Sultan Abdül Mecit (1839–61), who commissioned the Swiss architects Gaspare and Giuseppe Fossati to carry out the work, which was begun in 1847 and completed in 1849. In addition to structural work the Fossatis cleared the figurative mosaics, surviving from Christian times, of the whitewash and plaster that had covered them since the adaptation of the building to Muslim worship. Then, having completed their restoration, the architects re-covered the mosaics for safekeeping. In April 1932, Thomas Whittemore, of the Byzantine Institute of America, began once more to uncover and restore the mosaics, a number of which had disappeared since the Fossatis' time. Whittemore's renovation work continued until 1964, when the galleries of Haghia Sophia were opened to the public for the first time.

The Byzantine Mosaic Décor ● *64*

The present entrance to the church is through the central door of the exonarthex, which is flanked by the two middle buttresses on the west side of the building. You will pass through the exonarthex into the narthex, from which nine large doors open into the nave. Pausing in the narthex, you can see, glittering on the vaults above, some of the original mosaic

THE INSCRIPTION ON THE CENTRAL DOME
The enormous inscription on the intrados of the great dome is by the calligrapher Mustafa Izzet Efendi. Executed between 1847 and 1849 at the time of the Fossati restoration, it preserves the text that had been there before: "Allah is the Light of the heavens and the earth. The similitude of His light is a niche wherein is a lamp. The lamp is in glass. The glass is as it were a shining star."
Koran XXIV:35

THE PAINTED WOODEN PLAQUES
The six enormous *levhas* (inscribed plaques) hanging from the corner pillars at the gallery level were introduced by the Fossatis.

Mustafa Izzet Efendi executed the calligraphy, a golden Arabic script evoking the sacred names of Islam: Allah, the Prophet Muhammad, and the first four Caliphs: Abu Bakir, Umar, Othman, and Ali.

THE EMPEROR ALEXANDER

Alexander came to the throne in May 912, succeeding his elder brother Leo VI. His portrait, the last mosaic uncovered during the restoration work begun in 1932, dates from the brief period of his reign, 912–13. The Emperor is shown full length, clad in the sumptuous ceremonial garb of the Byzantine sovereigns. In his left hand he holds a skull, symbol of the vanity of life on earth.

decoration that survives from Justinian's church. The great dome, the half-domes, the north and south tympana, and the vaults of the narthex, aisles, and gallery – a total of more than four acres – were originally sheathed in gold tesserae. It is clear from the descriptions given by Procopius and other sources that the mosaics in Justinian's church depicted no figurative images, and none would have been permitted during the Iconoclastic period (730–843), when icons were banned throughout the Byzantine Empire. Thus the representational mosaics still extant in Haghia Sophia date from after the end of the Iconoclastic era. Most of the mosaics from Justinian's time survive on the vaults of the narthex and the side aisles, as well as on the thirteen ribs of the original dome. They consist of large fields of gold around architectural forms, articulated by bands of geometric or floral design in various colors. Outline crosses appear again and again on the crowns of the vaults and the soffits of arches, creating a remarkably simple but brilliant décor that must have been quite dazzling.

THE PORTAL OF THE IMPERIAL DOOR. Among the depictive mosaics still in place, one of the most impressive fills the lunette above the huge central door leading from the narthex into the nave, a portal known as the Imperial Door (**2**) and once reserved for the Emperor and his entourage. Here Christ is shown seated upon a jeweled throne, his feet resting upon a stool. He raises his right hand in a gesture of blessing, while in his left hand he holds a book with this inscription in Greek: "Peace be with you, I am the Light of the World." At the left a crowned figure prostrates himself before the throne, his hands upraised in supplication. Above, on either side of the throne, there are two roundels, the one on the left containing a bust of the Blessed Virgin and the other an angel with a staff. The Imperial figure is thought to portray Leo VI, which dates the mosaics to his reign: 886–912.

THE NAVE. You now pass through the Imperial Door into the nave, an immense space shot through with slanting shafts of sunlight falling from the diadem of forty windows at the base of the fabled dome. The central area is defined by four colossal pillars some 100 feet in height. Four great arches rise from these pillars, connected by four corner pendentives to make a continuous base for the circular, slightly elliptical, dome hovering above the square structure below. From this base rises the majestic, fairly shallow dome, with its crown soaring over 180 feet above the floor (about the height of a fifteen-story building). Pairs of subsidiary pillars to the east and west support the main half-domes. These give the nave its great length, about 260 feet, and, from the entrance, allow one to view the whole vast interior as well as the huge cupola – a massive structure that nonetheless creates the uncanny illusion of simply floating overhead. The tympana

**THE MOSAICS OF
THE SOUTH GALLERY**
Two Byzantine
mosaics decorate the
chamber situated at
the far end of the
south gallery. The
first, on the right,
portrays the Blessed
Virgin flanked by the
Emperor John II
Comnenus (1118–43)
and the Empress
Eirene. The second
mosaic, on the left,
shows Christ between
the Empress Zoe and
her third husband,
Constantine IX
(1042–55). The head
of the Emperor was
evidently executed
later than the rest of
the composition. This
effigy had been
preceded, in
succession, by those
of Zoe's first two
husbands, Michael IV
(1034–41) and
Romanus III Argyrus
(1028–34). The
Empress, who died in
1050 at the age of 72,
was deeply mourned
by the great mass of
her people, who
called her "Mama."
In his *Chronigraphica*,
the Court Chamberlain
Michael Psellus
declares himself
profoundly attached
to Zoe. He reports
that, despite her back
stooped with age and
her trembling hands,
she "retained a face
of perfect freshness."

between the central arches on the north and south are pierced
by twelve windows, a row of seven underneath a row of five,
where the three central openings form a kind of arcade.
Between the pillars on the north and south, there are four
huge columns of verd antique which support the upper
galleries, and above these columns are a further six columns
of the same marble supporting the tympanum. At the four
corners of the square nave, semicircular exedrae extend the
space, carried by two massive columns of porphyry below and
six of verd antique above, on which rest smaller half-domes or
conch vaults. The capitals of the columns ● 74 and pillars
are remarkable – among the greatest glories of Haghia
Sophia. Each of them is unique, but all are alike in their
acanthus-leaf and palm-foliage décor, as well as in their
carving, which is so deeply undercut in places that it
creates a snowflake lightness and complexity on a dark
background. Most of the capitals are bowl-shaped,
and those in the nave and gallery arcades boast
abacuses, Ionic volutes, and the imperial
monograms of Justinian and Theodora. Viewed
overall, the central area of the nave, with its
flanking, two-tiered colonnades of columns, becomes
a rhythmic procession which Procopius likened to "a
line of dancers in a chorus." To the east, beyond the
secondary pillars, a semicircular apse with conch
vaulting juts out from the main wall.

Motifs used in
carpets also appear
often in ceramics

**THE MOSAIC ON
THE TYMPANUM OVER
THE NARTHEX DOOR**
Here, the Blessed
Virgin is depicted
enthroned in a
hieratic pose with the
Christ Child on her
lap. She is flanked by
two haloed figures.
On the left, Justinian
– the "illustrious
Emperor," according
to the inscription –
makes a symbolic
offering of Haghia
Sophia, while on the
right, Constantine I –
the "great Emperor
among the saints" –
presents a model of
Constantinople itself.
The mosaic, probably
commissioned by
Emperor Basil II
(976–1024), dates
from around the end
of the 10th century.

ST GREGORY THE MIRACLE-WORKER. Legend has it that St Gregory the Miracle-worker imbued one of the aisle pillars with his healing power. To save the stone it was encased in brass; even so, credulous pilgrims have punctured the metal and worn a hole into the pillar itself, believing the moisture collected in the hollow to be a cure for eye diseases and beneficial for fertility.

THE MARBLE FACING. A great variety of rare and beautiful marbles, from all over Justinian's Empire, were used for the splendid cladding of both pillars and walls. The elaborate, symmetrical pattern of each panel was obtained by sawing thin blocks of marble in two, sometimes in four, and opening them out like a book so that the natural veining of the stone would be duplicated in a mirror image. Among other rare marbles found in the church, the large square of the *opus Alexandrinum* pavement at the southeast end of the nave has always attracted particular attention. It consists mainly of circles of granite, red and green porphyry, and verd antique. According to Antony, Archbishop of Novgorod, who visited the church in 1200, the Emperor's throne stood upon this square, surrounded by a bronze enclosure.

**THE MAUSOLEUM
OF SELIM II**
In the garden around
Haghia Sophia stands
the tomb of Sultan
Selim II (1566–74),
built by the great

THE INTERIOR OF THE MOSQUE. Haghia Sophia, or Aya Sofya, contains a number of structures added after the church was adapted into a mosque, most notably the mihrab and mimbar and the royal loge against the northeast pillar, all of which date from the Fossatis' restorations of 1847 to 1849. Other objects dating from the Ottoman period were given by

Sinan. Completed in
1577, it is one of the
most beautiful
examples of Ottoman
funerary architecture.
Iznik tiles clad the
interior walls and the
façade on either side
of the entrance. Above
the doors calligraphic
inscriptions of
Ottoman verse evoke
the beauties of
Paradise.

various sultans, and some of these gifts are described by Evliya Çelebi, a muezzin in Aya Sofya Cami'i during the reign of Murat IV (1623–40): "Murat III brought from the island of Marmara two princely basins of white marble, each resembling the cupola of a bath. They stand inside the mosque, full of fresh water for all the congregation to perform their ablutions and quench their thirst. The same sultan caused the walls of the mosque to be cleaned and smoothed; he increased the number of lamps and built four raised stone platforms for the readers of the Koran, and a lofty pulpit on slender columns for the muezzins. Sultan Murat IV, the Conqueror of Baghdad, raised upon four marble

columns a marble throne for the preacher. Sultan Murat, who took great delight in this incomparable mosque, erected a wooden enclosure within it near the southern door, and when he went to prayer on Friday he had his attendants hang there cages containing a great number of singing birds, particularly nightingales, so that their sweet notes, mingled with those of the muezzins' voices, filled the mosque with a harmony approaching to that of paradise." Other than the wooden cages for nightingales, all of these objects can still be seen in the nave of Haghia Sophia, along with the gifts of later sultans. The two lustration urns that Evliya mentions stand in the western exedrae. They are late Hellenistic or early Byzantine vases with Turkish lids. An English traveler in the 17th century noted that the vessels were kept full of water "to cool the Mohammedans overheated by their pious gesticulations." The "lofty pulpit" survives in the north arcade. It is made of marble, as are the "raised platforms" for the readers of the Koran, which stand against the four main pillars.

THE OTTOMAN LIBRARY. The finest of the later Ottoman additions is the elegant library that Mahmut I installed beyond the south aisle in 1739. Invested by the Sultan with revenue from the Cağaloğlu Baths, the library consists of several domed rooms enclosed with metal grilles. These rooms, housing some five thousand Ottoman books and manuscripts, are clad in superb Iznik tiles, all found stored in Topkapı Sarayı.

THE NAVE MOSAICS. Little now remains of the mosaics (**3**) that once adorned the nave of Haghia Sophia. The largest and most beautiful of those that survive lines the conch vault over the apse. This mosaic depicts the Mother of God with the Christ Child on her knees, an image unveiled by Patriarch Photius on Easter Sunday 867. At the bottom of the arch framing the apse there is a colossal representation of the Archangel Gabriel. Despite the loss of the upper left side and the tops of his wings, the Archangel makes a fine and striking figure. Opposite him, on the north side of the arch, are only a few surviving fragments of the great wings from a mosaic of the Archangel Michael.

THE MOSAICS ON THE NORTH TYMPANUM WALL. Three other mosaic portraits (**4**) decorate the niches at the base of the north tympanum wall, every one of them visible from the nave. In the first niche on the left appears St Ignatius the

Younger, who served as Patriarch of Constantinople from 847 to 858 and again from 867 to 877. In the central niche is St John Chrysostomos, Patriarch from 398 to 404, and St Ignatius Theophoros of Antioch is portrayed in the fifth niche.

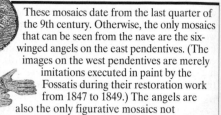

THE MOSAIC ON THE TYMPANUM OF THE IMPERIAL DOOR
This detail, of a Byzantine emperor in supplication before Christ, is thought by most experts to portray Leo VI, which dates the mosaic to the years 886 to 912.

THE IMPERIAL KIOSK
This painting from 1904 by Zeikâi Paşa depicts the Imperial Kiosk of the Haghia Sophia Mosque. The kiosk was an addition conceived by the architect Gaspare Fossati for the Sultan Abdül Mecit I (1839–61). The decorative style blends oriental traditions with the European Baroque, still fashionable in the 19th century. Polygonal in shape, the kiosk is crowned by a dome supported on small columns. The enclosing elements, which shelter the interior from the curious, echo the balustrades of the upper galleries in Haghia Sophia, though in a more elaborate manner.

These mosaics date from the last quarter of the 9th century. Otherwise, the only mosaics that can be seen from the nave are the six-winged angels on the east pendentives. (The images on the west pendentives are merely imitations executed in paint by the Fossatis during their restoration work from 1847 to 1849.) The angels are also the only figurative mosaics not whitewashed by the Ottomans. However, the Fossatis, after restoring the images, covered their faces with gold-starred medallions, which are still in place today. The angel mosaics date from the mid-14th century, when the east pendentives were rebuilt following a partial collapse of the dome in 1346.

THE GYNACAEUM. There are other figurative mosaics in the galleries, which are reached by a corridor leading up from the northern end of the narthex. According to Byzantine sources the galleries were reserved for the *gynacaeum*, or women's quarters, although the two eastern bays of the south gallery seem to have been used by the royal family and, on occasion, by synods of the Greek Orthodox Church. The empress sat upon a throne behind a balustrade at the center of the west gallery, the spot marked by a circle of green Thessalian marble and a pair of double columns of the same material.

THE MOSAICS OF THE SOUTH AISLE. Three of the four surviving mosaics in the galleries are situated at the extreme end of the south aisle. Here the gallery is set apart by a pair of false doors, both richly carved marble screens symbolizing the Gates of Heaven and Hell. The actual doorway lies between them, surmounted by a slab of translucent Phrygian marble. Still higher, a wooden beam, relief-carved with floral designs, forms a cornice stretching across and unifying the entire gateway. Well after Justinian's time, the gateway seems to have been added to close off the end of the gallery for use as a royal enclosure or as a meeting place for church synods.

THE DEISIS ★.
Turning to the right once inside this portal, one sees the most magnificent of all the surviving mosaics in Haghia Sophia, the Deisis (**5**), which is located past the last pillar on the east wall. This is an iconographic type of mosaic, in which Christ appears flanked by the Blessed Virgin and St John the Baptist (who in Greek is known as *Prodromus*, or the Forerunner). Here John stands to the

right and the Virgin to the left, reversing the usual order in Deisis compositions. They lean towards Christ in suppliant attitudes, pleading, so the iconographers tell us, for the salvation of humankind. Christ, holding up his right hand in a gesture of benediction, looks off into space with an expression of sadness, as if his nature were more human than divine – despite the teaching of medieval theology. Although two-thirds of the mosaic has gone, the features of the three figures are miraculously intact, making the Deisis a work of great power and beauty. This mosaic dates from the second half of the 13th century, when Byzantium experienced a renaissance under the Palaeologus dynasty, the last to rule the Empire.

THE MOSAICS OF THE SOUTH GALLERY. The two other mosaics in the south gallery (**6**), both of them Imperial portraits, are on the east wall of the building at the far end of the last bay, flanking a window beside the apse. The mosaic adjacent to the window depicts a royal couple kneeling on either side of Christ enthroned. On the right is the notorious Empress Zoe, one of the few women ever to rule Byzantium in her own right, reigning together with her sister Theodora in 1042. The mosaic to the right of the window shows a royal couple presenting gifts to the Virgin and Christ Child, a composition that continues on the narrow panel of the side wall, where young Prince Alexius has been portrayed together with his parents, John II Comnenus (1118–43) and Empress Eirene, daughter of King Ladislaus of Hungary. The Emperor was known in his time as Kalo Yanis, or John the Good, and Nicetas Choniates wrote of him: "He was the best of all the emperors, from the family of the Comneni, who ever sat upon the Roman throne."

THE MOSAICS OF THE NORTH GALLERY. Another imperial portrait survives in the main bay of the north gallery (**7**), high on

IZNIK TILE PANEL IN THE TOMB OF SELIM II
At the center is an oval medallion on a the shape of a mihrab, a favorite Ottoman motif in carpets as well.

JANISSARIES ACCOMPANYING THE SULTAN TO THE HAGHIA SOPHIA MOSQUE
The scene depicted in this watercolor from the early 17th century often occurred during the period when Haghia Sophia was a mosque. The Sultan never visited the basilica unless accompanied by his Janissaries, an élite corps of the Turkish Army that also served as his personal guard. Here, both dignitaries and soldiers wear ceremonial dress. The captains, or *ağa*, riding between the squadrons, are dressed in velvet and satin, and wear turbans. Next come the officers, identified by their tall plumes and who proceed on foot. Behind Haghia Sophia rise the walls surrounding the Topkapı Palace.

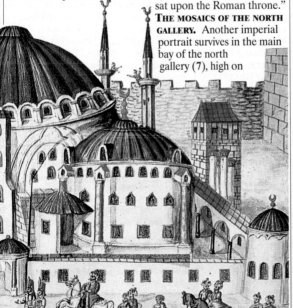

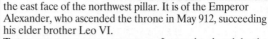

The Fountain of Ahmet III
with Haghia Sophia
in the background.

the east face of the northwest pillar. It is of the Emperor Alexander, who ascended the throne in May 912, succeeding his elder brother Leo VI.

THE VESTIBULE OF THE WARRIORS. Leave the church by the door at the southern end of the narthex. This leads into a hallway known in the Byzantine period as the Vestibule of the Warriors, for it was here that the troops of the imperial guard waited while the emperor attended services in the church.

THE COMPLEX OF HAGHIA SOPHIA

The courtyard of Haghia Sophia harbors a number of minor but fascinating Ottoman structures, all of them part of the *külliye* of Aya Sofya Cami'i. In the center of the courtyard stands the ablution fountain built in the Turkish rococo style for Mahmut I around 1740. The building on the right of the gateway to Ayasofya Meydanı (Square) is the *mektep*, a primary school for the children of the mosque's staff. The little domed structure to the left of the gate is the *muvakithane*, the house and workshop of the mosque astronomer, whose sundial can still be seen on the front of Haghia Sophia near the southwest corner of the building.

THE IMPERIAL OTTOMAN TOMBS. The four domed buildings in the garden just to the south of Haghia Sophia are all imperial Ottoman tombs. The oldest of them is the one on the left as you leave the south end of the narthex. As the form – a domed octagon – would suggest, this was the baptistery of Haghia Sophia. The Ottomans then converted it into a mausoleum for the mad Sultan Mustafa I. A quarter of a century later the Sultan Ibrahim was also interred here, on September 10, 1648, after he had been deposed and executed, on the orders of his own mother.

THREE IMPERIAL TOMBS. These are in the east end of the garden, all of them attractive structures with superb Iznik tile cladding. The oldest tomb is the one in the center. Designed by the great Sinan for Selim II (1566–74), it ranks among the finest Ottoman tombs in the city. The westernmost of the three tombs houses the remains of Murat III (1574–95). This *türbe* was finished in 1599 by Davut Ağa, who succeeded Sinan as Chief of the Imperial Architects. The tomb at the eastern end of the garden is that of Mehmet III (1595–1603), completed in 1603 by Dalgic Ahmet Ağa, Davut Ağa's successor as chief architect.

THE FOUNTAIN OF AHMET III. Walk around the south and east sides of Haghia Sophia to approach the Imperial Gate of Topkapı Sarayı. This brings you, on your right, to the grandest of all Istanbul's Ottoman street fountains. Built in 1728 for Ahmet III (1703–30), the Tulip King, it is a particularly fine example of Turkish rococo architecture. Topped by five small domes and a projecting roof, the fountain is gaily decorated with red and white marble, floral reliefs, elegant columns, and bright calligraphy.

THE TREASURY. Diagonally opposite the Imperial Gate at the upper end of Soğuk Çeşme Sokağı, a large Ottoman gateway, in the rococo style, leads to the northeast corner of Haghia Sophia's precincts. The domed structure inside the

> "The most perfect, the richest, and the most sumptuous of temples, not only in the Orient but also in the world."
>
> Nicolas de Nicolay

THE BYZANTINE CAPITAL

Byzantine architects reinforced the column capital with a crowning impost block or "cushion" formed like a truncated, upside-down pyramid. To overcome the instability of this structure, builders fused the two parts and created the impost-capital, which developed from an undecorated, massive state into the lavishly ornamented "bowls" at Haghia Sophia. Other than the acanthus, decorative themes, such as beasts' heads, were possibly derived from oriental textiles and mosaics, as were many of the techniques. This left the capital deprived of classical plasticity but rich in all-over, filigreed, chiaroscuro pattern, sometimes so delicately as well as intricately carved as to appear chased. However, the relief could also be deep enough to resemble open work. Drawing on the strong, malleable marble from the nearby quarries at Preconnese, the builders and sculptors of Constantinople exported the new impost-capital and consequently spread their influence throughout the Mediterranean world.

gate was part of the church built by Justinian and served as its *skeuphylakion*, or treasury. It housed all of the precious objects used in the liturgies of Haghia Sophia, as well as such sacred relics as the Crown of Thorns from Christ's Passion and fragments of the True Cross, which Constantine's mother, the Empress Helena, had brought back from her pilgrimage to Jerusalem. All of these treasures were looted when the knights of the Fourth Crusade and their Venetian convoy sacked Constantinople in 1204. The Director of the Haghia Sophia Museum now makes his office in the Treasury, which is therefore closed to the public. Here you might pause to look back on Haghia Sophia, for this is one of the best vantage points for viewing the Great Church, before which travelers have stood in awe for more than fourteen centuries. Some thousand years ago an envoy of Prince Vladimir of Kiev reported after his pilgrimage to Haghia Sophia: "We know not whether we were in heaven or on earth. For on earth there is no such splendor or such beauty, and we are at a loss how to describe it. We only know that God dwells there among men, and their service is fairer than the ceremonies of other nations. For we cannot forget that beauty."

TOPKAPI SARAYI

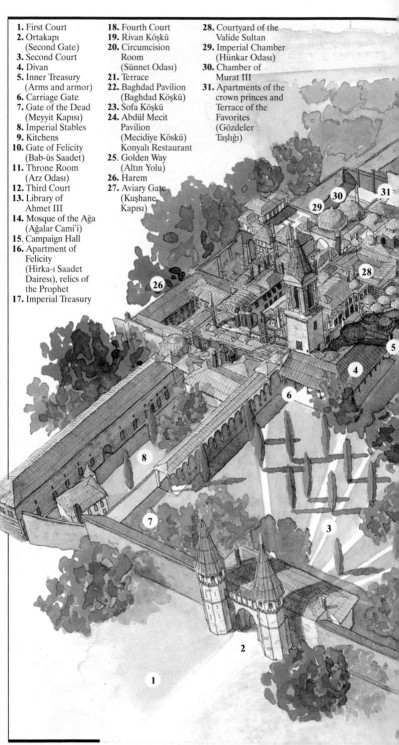

TOPKAPI, PALACE OF THE 1001 NIGHTS ✪

Topkapi Palace is a complex of halls and pavilions built in stages over the centuries. The first four courtyards are given over to the official areas with the private quarters to the rear of the complex. Visit the palace early in the morning; when you arrive go straight to the harem to purchase a ticket there (numbers are limited and you have to make a reservation).

🚶 **Four hours**

◆ **E** D3–E3

151

▲ TOPKAPI SARAYI

THE GREAT PALACE OF THE OTTOMAN SULTANS

In 1461 or 1462, less than ten years after the Conquest ● *34*, Fatih Mehmet ordered the construction of Topkapı Sarayı ● *82*, a palace that would be known as Dar-üs-Saadet, the

THE FIRST COURT OF THE PALACE
Also known as the Courtyard of the Janissaries, the First Court was the mustering place for the Ottoman Army's élite corps while it was on duty at the palace. During the reign of Süleyman the Magnificent there were almost 12,000 Janissaries, and they were described as "the nerve center and the mightiest force in the service of the great Turk". Rank in the corps was identified by the degree of richness and magnificence of the clothing and headgear. There is a collection of Ottoman costumes on display in the Imperial Costume Collection at Topkapı Palace.

HAGHIA EIRENE
This Byzantine church – "Holy Peace" – was once closely linked to Haghia Sophia – "Divine Wisdom." As the administration buildings of Topkapı Palace were built all around the square, the church was eventually isolated within the walled enclosure of the imperial palace grounds.

"House of Felicity." Having found the Great Palace of Byzantium so ruined as to be uninhabitable, Mehmet decided to build a new imperial residence at a different site, on the northern side of the first hill overlooking the Bosphorus where it joins the Golden Horn and the Sea of Marmara. Topkapı Sayarı remained the seat of the Ottoman Sultans until 1853, when Abdül Mecit moved into Dolmabahçe, his new residence on the shores of the Bosphorus ● *85*. More or less abandoned, the old palace would not reopen its doors until 1924, the year that Mustafa Kemal Atatürk inaugurated it as a museum ● *44*.

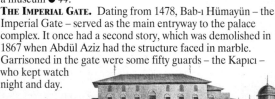

THE IMPERIAL GATE. Dating from 1478, Bab-ı Hümayün – the Imperial Gate – served as the main entryway to the palace complex. It once had a second story, which was demolished in 1867 when Abdül Aziz had the structure faced in marble. Garrisoned in the gate were some fifty guards – the Kapıcı – who kept watch night and day.

Topkapı Sarayı
in 1590

THE FIRST COURT OF THE SARAY

The Imperial Gate opens into the First Court, or the SQUARE
OF CEREMONIES (1), where a number of service buildings
once stood: a bakery, housing for its staff, an infirmary, and a
warehouse for firewood. Here too was the
DARPHANE, the Imperial Mint, which is
still there today, though the structure
dates from a period later than that of
Mehmet II. The vast courtyard was also
used by the Janissaries as a mustering
point, and ceremonies were held there
before the commencement of a military
campaign. The gate next to it leads down
to GÜLHANE PARK and the museums on
the western terrace (details of which will
be given after a tour of the Inner Palace).
In Ottoman times, this gateway was
known as the Kız Bekçiler Kapısı – the
Gate of the Watchman of the Girls – for
the sentries were stationed there to secure
the Harem and prevent intruders from
entering.

GRAND VIZIER

PALACE OFFICIALS

HEAD GARDENERS

HAGHIA EIRENE. While crossing the
courtyard, you should take note of the
Byzantine Church of Haghia Eirene,
dedicated to "Divine Peace," an attribute
of Christ, and one of the most beautiful of surviving
Byzantine churches. Justinian had it built in 537, at the same
time as Haghia Sophia, to replace a church destroyed during
the Nika Revolt of 532. Shortly after the conquest of
Constantinople, the Janissaries took over the building and
made it their arsenal. In 1826, the Sultan Mehmet II decided
to suppress this élite branch of the armed services, whose
power had long been a threat to political stability. The arsenal
was later converted into a military and archeological museum.
Since its restoration in the 1970's the building has been used
as a concert hall during the Istanbul Music Festival, which is
held in the summer.

THE MIDDLE GATE. Continuing along the right, to the bottom
of the First Court,
we arrive at the
Orta Kap (2), or
the Middle Gate,
which is also called
Bab-üs Selam – the
Gate of Salutations.
Dating from the
reign of Süleyman
the Magnificent,

this monumental gateway takes us into the Inner Palace of
Topkapı Sarayı. No one except the sovereign was permitted to
ride a horse past its flanking pair of towers, cone-capped and
linked by an upper walkway concealed behind crenellations.
The suite of rooms to the right of the gate was originally
occupied by the head of the palace guard. The watchmen
under his command lived in rooms on the left, where a small
suite of chambers was also set aside for the chief executioner,
an official who was also employed as principal gardener.

Created in 1850, the
Imperial Costume
Collection began with
an exhibition of 140
figures representing
the former Janissaries.
Théophile Gautier
described it thus:
"Here are assembled,
like specimens of
antedeluvian animals
in the Museum of
Natural History, the
very people suppressed
by Mahmoud's coup
d'état. Here brought
back from the dead is
that fantastic and
fanciful Turkey of the
pastry-mold turbans,
of dolmans trimmed
in cat fur – the Turkey
of comic opera and
fairy tales."

THE COLLECTION OF ARMS AND ARMOR
These treasures are now housed in the Inner Treasury, situated in the Second Court of Topkapı. The display includes many pieces from the 16th century, a golden age in the art of decorating weaponry. The scabbards and

THE SECOND COURT

Once beyond the Middle Gate, we enter a vast court, approximately 430 feet long and 330 feet wide. This is the Second Court, also known as the COURT OF THE DIVAN (3) because up until the 18th century ● 40 the Imperial Council – the Divan – met in the domed chambers in the left corner of the courtyard. Here the Grand Vizier and the chief administrators of the empire met during the first four days of every week to deal with ongoing affairs of state. In the early years after the Conquest, Fatih Mehmet himself presided over all the sessions. Subsequently, he came to prefer following the discussions from an adjacent loge, through a grilled window installed above the Grand Vizier's seat, a practice that his successors would also adopt. On the days the Divan met, the

hafts of even the simplest daggers are carved in ivory and damascened in gold or silver, with the most sumptuous examples inlaid with precious stones. Helmets are engraved and the barrels of cannon chased with calligraphic themes. As for the *rondaches*, or round shields, with their wickerwork surfaces embroidered in silk and silver, dominated by floral motifs, they are just like exquisite miniature tapestries.

courtyard teemed with officials, Janissaries, and other palace guards, making a colorful, noisy crowd of some 5,000 people, and twice that many on special occasions. From the Middle Gate, five paths fan out towards various points in the courtyard. The second path from the left leads to the Divan and its attendant chambers, the whole crowned by the tall, cone-topped towers that make Topkapı Sarayı so easy to distinguish against the swarming panorama of Istanbul when viewed from the Golden Horn. Essentially, the architecture of the complex remains that of Fatih's time, though admittedly there have been many alterations over the centuries.

THE DIVAN ● 83. The Divan (4) is composed of a suite of three dome-vaulted rooms, surrounded by a deep, colonnaded portico with wide, overhanging eves. The first room on the left is the council chamber, around three sides of which there is a low carpet-covered couch, the divan that gave the Council its name. Its lower walls are clad in the finest tiles. The room at the center was the Public Records Office, and that on the right

> "The Palace of Saray Burnu with its Chinese roofs,
> its white crenellated walls, its latticed kiosks, its gardens
> of cypresses, umbrella pines, and sycamores...."

Théophile Gautier

the Office of the Grand Vizier. Today the Public Records Office houses a good part of the Topkapı clock and watch collection. Next to these three rooms is the Treasury or Inner Treasury (**5**), a long hall vaulted with four pairs of domes supported upon three massive pillars. It dates from the end of the 15th century or the beginning of the 16th. In here were deposited the tax receipts and tribute monies collected from all over the Ottoman Empire. This revenue was used to defray the cost of government until quarterly pay days, after which all remaining funds went to the Imperial Treasury in the Third Court. Today, the collection of arms and armor, much of it booty, together with other personal objects once owned by the sultans, is housed where once there was the ring and jingle of money being counted. At the corner of the Divan, south of the tower, is the main door to the Harem, also known as the Carriage Gate (**6**).

THE GATE OF THE DEAD. On the west side of the Second Court is a long portico at the far end of which is the Meyyit Kapısı – the Gate of the Dead (**7**). Funeral processions passed through this gate on their way to the cemeteries. The gate also leads down to the Imperial Stables, where the sultans' carriages and harnesses are now exhibited (**8**).

THE KITCHENS. The right side of the Second Court is mostly taken up by the kitchens (**9**) as well as the living quarters of those in service at the palace. The kitchens themselves are a suite of ten large chambers which are situated along the eastern wall of the Inner Palace; their lofty domes and tall, thin chimneys make them conspicuous landmarks when seen from the Sea of Marmara. The two southernmost domes date back to Fatih's time and the other eight to that of Beyazıt II (1481–1512). As for the chimneys in front, Sinan added them when he rebuilt much of the area following its destruction by fire in 1574. At present, the kitchens house an important collection of Chinese porcelain, celadon and silver, as well as kitchen utensils, notably the great cauldrons known as *kazans*.

THE TREASURY OF MINIATURES
Two buildings form a right angle at the north end of the Pavilion of Fatih. The one on the left – beyond a passage leading to the Fourth Court – is the former dormitory of the senior students of the Palace School. Today it houses one of the great treasures of Topkapı Sarayı: the manuscripts of calligraphy and

Persian as well as Turkish miniatures. A unique collection of 13,000 works, most of them are kept in albums and therefore only part of the collection is on view at any one time. Generally, the miniatures illustrate texts recounting the lives of great men and important historical events. Plans and maps were used for documentary or even strategic purposes.

THE GATE OF FELICITY
Also called Akağalar Kapısı, or the Gate of the White Eunuchs, this fortified gate leading to the Inner Palace dates mainly from the reign of Selim I (1512–20). The decoration dates from the 19th century. On either side are apartments once occupied by the head gatekeeper and the White Eunuchs.

155

16TH-CENTURY IZNIK CERAMIC PLATES

THE GATE OF FELICITY ● 83. At the bottom of the Second Court, the Bab-üs-Saadet (**10**), or Gate of Felicity, opens into the Third Court, the sultan's own private residential quarters and the heart of the Inner Palace – the House of Felicity. The great gateway, which has stood since the time of Fatih, was reconstructed in the 16th century and redecorated in the rococo style in the 18th. It was here that the Sultan received his subjects and heard their complaints on the eve of two important Muslim holidays: Şeker Bayramı, the Festival of Sugar, and Kurban Bayramı, the Festival of Sacrifice, commemorating the sacrifice of Abraham. Just inside the Gate of Felicity stands the Arz Odası, the Throne Room (**11**), a handsome pavilion with massive, projecting eves carried upon an arcade of ancient marble columns. It was here that the Sultan received ambassadors from abroad, as well as, and far more often, the Grand Vizier and other members of the Divan who came to report on their most recent decisions and to seek the sultan's consent. Here too, each newly installed sultan mounted the throne for the first time and accepted the homage of the empire's civil and religious dignitaries, beginning with the descendants of the Prophet Mohammed.

Several thrones are on display in the Treasury. The most sumptuous of them is surely the one the Ottomans brought back from their victory over the Persians at Çaldıran, which is fashioned in red and green enamel on gold leaf and encrusted with 25,000 pearls and precious stones. Although based on a plan designed during Fatih's reign, most of the structure dates from the time of Selim I (1512–20). Moreover, inscriptions on the building cite renovations carried out under Ahmet III (1703–30), Mahmut II (1808–39), and in 1856, the last following a fire that destroyed much of the furniture and decorations. Only the magnificent canopy over the throne, erected in 1596, and the bronze-gilt *ocak* (chimneypiece) escaped the flames. The building consists of a small antechamber on the right and, on the left, the audience hall itself.

THE THIRD COURT

THE PALACE SCHOOL AND IMPERIAL TREASURY. The buildings of the school for the pages were situated around the Third Court or ENDERUN (**12**). The purpose of this institution was to prepare the future civil, religious, and military leaders of the empire. The pupils entered the school at the age of twelve and left at eighteen; most of them were Christians taken from their families in the annual *devşirme* (levy) throughout the empire. Also in the Third Court were the quarters for the White Eunuchs and the *ağa*, the teachers

THE AĞALAR CAMI'I Situated in the Third Court, the Ağalar Mosque now houses the museum's new library. A great many Turkish and Persian manuscripts from various parts of the palace have been assembled in its collection. At the center of the Third Court stands the library of Ahmet III (**13**), founded in 1719.

responsible for administration and discipline at the school. The large building positioned diagonally in the northwest corner of the Third Court is the AĞALAR CAMI'I, the Mosque of the Ağa (**14**), where pages, pupils, teachers, and the White Eunuchs all attended services. Today, it shelters the NEW LIBRARY OF THE MUSEUM. On the right is the former Campaign Hall (**15**), where the pages chosen to accompany the sultan on his campaigns were trained. It is entered

through a dome-vaulted colonnade constructed from splendid Byzantine columns of verd antique. The building now serves as an exhibition hall for the Imperial Wardrobe, a collection of the sultans' ceremonial kaftans, masterpieces of weaving and decorative design.

THE APARTMENT OF FELICITY. In the far left corner of the Third Court is the HIRKA-I SAADET DAIRESI (**16**), which contains the relics of the Prophet Mohammed: his banner, saber, and, most sacred of all, his mantle. They were brought from Egypt by Selim I after he had captured Cairo in 1517 and made himself Caliph, a title that would also be taken by his successors. The pavilion comprises four domed rooms that together form a square. Its foundation and plan were established under Fatih Mehmet, but Murat III rebuilt and refurnished much of the structure.

THE EVERYDAY LUXURY OF THE SULTANS
Several parts of the Topkapı Museum are devoted to precious objects used regularly at the Ottoman court, among them the glass and ceramic pieces displayed in the former kitchens. Especially noteworthy are the dishes produced at the Iznik workshops. Together they reveal the entire evolution of the classic decorative style created by the Iznik artisans, from simple arabesques in blue and white, through floral motifs in five colors, to the brilliant polychromy of late works. Ewers and pitchers could be transformed into masterpieces of the silversmith's art, especially when inlaid with precious stones. The most important pieces, however, have been assigned to the Treasury, which is in the Third Court.

A TIGHTROPE SHOW FOR AHMET III
In 1720 Sultan Ahmet III commissioned a glorious illuminated manuscript to commemorate the circumcision of his four sons, which was celebrated by a two-week festival involving continuous entertainments arranged by the city's guilds. The shows involved magicians, acrobats, tightrope walkers, and dancers and musicians, who performed on the Okmeydanı and by the seaside pavilions.

157

THE HAREM

The most private quarters in the palace were in the Harem. The life led there was probably less like a garden of earthly delights, whose mysteries so fired the imagination of 19th-century Europe, than a gilded cage where hierarchy governed even the games of intrigue. Thus, every lady longed to become the Valide Sultan, mother of the reigning sovereign, a status that allowed almost total power over the Harem and, most of all, an influence strong enough to affect the public, artistic, and sometimes even political affairs of the empire. Among the 400-odd women who lived in the Topkapı Harem, only the elect few could become *haseki* – that is, favorites – and then, if they gave birth to a male child, *kadın*, or legitimate spouse. Those whom the Sultan actually wed left the common dormitory for a personal room. Only now would the beloved receive jewels and magnificent robes, all weapons with which to extend her powers of seduction.

THE FOURTH COURT

The next destination on the tour is the Fourth Court (**18**), also called the TULIP GARDEN with its terraces dotted with pavilions or kiosks. On the highest level, in the southwest corner, a flight of stairs leads to the L-shaped PORTICO OF COLUMNS, which was built as an extension to the PAVILION OF THE SACRED MANTLE. Here, in the axis of the angle, we find a marble pool. On one side stands the Rivan Köşkü (**19**), a kiosk erected by Murat IV in 1636 to commemorate the taking of Rivan in the Caucasus (present-day Yerevan). The cruciform room is completely clad in beautiful Iznik tiles and the exterior faced in rare, variously colored marbles.

THE CIRCUMCISION ROOM. On the other side of the pool is the sünnet Odası, the Circumcision Room (**20**) commissioned by the Sultan Ibrahim in 1642 to celebrate the circumcision rites of his first son, the future Mehmet IV. This rectangular building is also generously clad in Iznik faience, both inside and out ▲ *292*. It stands on the edge of a wide terrace paved in marble, bordered on the west by a curving, white-marble balustrade with a view over the gardens below and the Golden Horn beyond. Inserted at the center of the balustrade is a delightful little balcony with a domed, bronze-gilt canopy held aloft by four, thin bronze pillars. An inscription on the domed canopy gives the date of construction as 1640, the first year in the reign of Ibrahim I. It also names the balcony Iftariye, after Ibrahim's practice of taking Iftar on the balcony – that is, the festive meal consumed just after sunset during the holy month of Ramadan. Several miniatures in the Saray collection depict the scene. One of them portrays the Sultan watching his children at play on the terrace.

THE BAGHDAD KÖŞKÜ ● *83*. At the northern end of the terrace stands another pavilion, the cruciform Baghdad Köşkü (**22**) built by Murat IV in 1638 to mark his capture of Baghdad in the same year. Its broad-eaved roof, a masterpiece of the genre, is carried on an arcade of slender columns with lotus capitals and serrated voussoirs of alternating white and colored marble. Inside and out, the walls are clad in blue and white ceramic tiles. The sumptuously furnished interior includes a magnificent bronze fireplace, two tiers of stained-glass windows on one wall, carved tables and cabinets inlaid with mother-of-pearl, window recesses fitted with embroidered divans, and a domed canopy made of leather decorated with arabesques painted on a crimson ground. This pavilion also provides a

spectacular view over the lower Bosphorus.

THE SOFA KÖŞKÜ. The charming kiosk at the center of the garden, on the main terrace of the Fourth Court, is the SOFA KÖŞKÜ (**23**). Built at the beginning of the 18th century for Ahmet III, it was probably used as a private gallery for observing the famous Tulip Festival staged by the sultan in these gardens. In 1752, Mahmut I had the kiosk restyled in the rococo manner.

THE MECIDIYE KÖŞKÜ. At the bottom of the courtyard, on the right, we find a European-style pavilion upon a marble terrace. This is the MECIDIYE KÖŞKÜ (**24**), built in 1840 during the reign of Abdül Mecit. An excellent restaurant, the

THE "DINING ROOM" OF AHMET III (1705–06) A superbly decorated room, distinguished by a revived interest in still-life motifs from Europe's Renaissance. The main theme – simple trompe l'oeil bouquets in niches – is enhanced by the Oriental passion for geometry.

159

THE OTTOMAN SULTANS
From left to right, Selim II (1566–74), Murat III (1574–95), Süleyman I (1520–66), and Selim I (1512–20). Around 1579, Seyyid Loqman, historiographer to Selim II and then to Murat III, wrote an important work on the subject of the Ottoman sovereigns: *Kiyâfet al insaniye fi ğemaâ'il el'Osmaniye*. It is illustrated with a dozen portraits, all by the master Nakkaş Osman, the great miniaturist of the period. Here, Loqman recounts the events marking the reign of each Sultan and describes the subject's character and appearance in

great detail. Thanks to this writer, we have a description of Süleyman the Magnificent: ". . . a handsome round face, with knitted brows, blue eyes, the nose of a ram, a body like that of a graceful lion, a full beard, a long neck and great height, a fine-looking man with a broad chest and square shoulders, long fingers, strong arms and feet, a sovereign without fear or fault and glorious. . . ."

Murat III's ceremonial throne of pure gold studded with emeralds.

KONYALI now occupies the building. It is situated on the northwest extremity of the Saray and its hill, so there is a superb view looking out over the Bosphorus.

THE HAREM

To reach the entrance of the Harem (**26**), return to the northwest corner of the Second Court. This brings us to the CARRIAGE GATE (**6**), which was built in 1588 but had to be almost completely rebuilt after a fire in 1665. The Harem is open to visitors but it is necessary to make an appointment in advance.

THE GOLDEN WAY. From the gateway we enter a vestibule that opens into a guardroom clad in faience. The Black Eunuchs guarded this entranceway to prevent intruders from gaining access to the Altın Yolu, the Golden Way (**25**), a passage paved with pebble mosaics that runs along the eastern side of the Harem. The Golden Way begins on the left, with a portico of ten columns crowned by lotus capitals and hung with wrought-iron lamps, which, in the days of the sultans, lighted the way to the Carriage Gate.

THE EUNUCHS' QUARTERS. Built in 1668 to 1669, the tile-clad building behind the portico was once used as the dormitory of the Black Eunuchs. A passageway leads into the central courtyard of the dormitory, around which there are a dozen cells on each side of the building's three stories. Here the hundreds of eunuchs must have slept in relays, according to their round-the-clock watches. Elderly ones were

> "O Sultan, let your friends be joyful and happy
> and your enemies be full of woe."
>
> Cufic inscription, *Çesmeli Oda* (AD 1665–66)

in charge of the "inner services," under a chief known as
Kizlar Ağası, "Lord of the Women." He lived apart, in the
building on the left of the Golden Way which commanded the
approach to the Cümle Kapısı, the main entrance to the
Harem proper. Beyond this entrance is another
guardroom, strategically located at the principal
intersection of the Harem, which was designed
as a veritable gilded prison.

THE WOMEN'S QUARTERS. The corridor on the
right leads to the Kuşhane Kapısı – the Aviary
Gate (**27**) – which leads to a third courtyard. On
the left, a long and narrow passageway descends
towards the courtyard of the *cariyeler*, the
female servants of the Harem. From there,
straight ahead, a gateway opens onto the large
courtyard of the Valide Sultan (**28**) on the western
side of the Golden Way. The apartments of the
dowager sultana take up most of the two floors on the west
side of the courtyard, while those on the north side were
occupied by the first and second kadin, the highest ranking of
the sultan's four hasekis. The mounting block in the
northwest corner was used by the sultan when he arrived or
departed on horseback.

THE ROOM WITH A HEARTH. Behind the mounting block, the
Throne Door leads into the Ucaklı Oda, the magnificent
"Room with a Hearth" completely clad in faience and
dominated by a bronze fireplace. The door on the right leads
to the apartments of the *kadin*, and the one on the left to a
smaller chamber, the Çeşmelı Oda or "Fountain Room"
named after its wall fountain ● *66* dating from 1665.
These two rooms, like the next one, served as
antechambers between the Harem and the sultan's
own suite.

THE CHAMBERS OF THE VALIDE SULTAN. In the
southwest corner of the courtyard a passageway leads
into the salon of the dowager sultana. The Valide's
chambers also included an adjoining reception room,
an interior courtyard, a sitting room, a prayer room,
and a small suite upstairs. Leaving the Valide's salon,
we now make our way past the sultan's and Valide's
baths into the largest chamber of the Inner Palace.

**THE IMPERIAL
TREASURY**
The second building
on the right in the
Third Court is the
Pavilion of Fatih
or the Imperial
Treasury (**17**).
Mehmet the
Conqueror had it
built as the *selamlık*, a
suite of reception
rooms reserved for
the sultan, his sons,
and the court pages,
together with two
domed rooms for the
Treasury. Soon after
the apartments
became a repository
for precious objects
and the *selamlık* was
transferred to
another part of the
palace. Recently
restored, the Treasury
now displays a unique
collection of valuable
works that once
belonged to the
Sultan.

**THE HEAD
OF THE JANISSARIES**
Drawing by Joseph-
Marie Vien (18th
century).

The roofs of the
Topkapı Harem,
beyond which rises a
structure known as
the Tower of Justice,
situated in a corner of
the Divan.

161

▲ TOPKAPI SARAYI

The "Alexander Sarcophagus" (6th century BC).

THE SARCOPHAGUS OF AN IMPORTANT PERSON
This gentleman (right) is reclining on a couch, with his wife seated at its head. A serving boy prepares a rhyton of wine. The dog, sparrowhawk and helmet suggest he was a military hero.

EURIPIDES
The subject (right, below) brings the mask of tragedy towards his face. Although there are oriental elements, the style of this relief sculpture adheres closely to that of classical Greek art, in particular the way the figures are posed and the rendering of the folds of their clothing.

THE KIOSK OF FAIENCES
This is a distinctly characteristic example of Turkish architecture from Central Asia, in its structure as well as in its décor of tiles displaying calligraphy on a blue ground.

THE IMPERIAL CHAMBER. The HÜNKAR ODASI (**29**) is divided by an arch into two unequal parts. The larger part is dome-vaulted and the smaller, slightly raised one has a balcony for musicians. This splendid salon must have been built during the reign of Murat III, which would make it the work of Sinan. The dome, pendentives, and arches have been restored to their original state, but the lower sections still display the Baroque décor installed by Osman III (1754–7). The small chamber off the southwest corner of the Hünkar Odası functioned as a private sitting room for the sultan. A door in the northeast corner opens into the Room with a Hearth, which you cross in order to enter a small but sumptuously tiled antechamber, also probably by Sinan.

THE SALON OF MURAT III.
Although a bit smaller than the Hünkar Odası, this splendid chamber is more authentic since it retains the whole of its original décor. In addition to the gorgeous Iznik tiles covering the walls, an exquisite panel depicting plum blossoms surrounds the

elegant bronze fireplace, and graceful calligraphy forms a frieze all around the room. Opposite the fireplace there is a lovely three-tiered *selşebil*, or cascade fountain, carved of polychrome marble. The sheer perfection of the room's décor and proportions identify it as the work of Sinan.

THE LIBRARY OF AHMET I. Opening off the west side of the Salon of Murat III is the small chamber that Ahmet I had converted into a library and sitting room in 1608. It is one of the most charming chambers in the whole palace, a room of marble shelves, exquisite cabinets inlaid with ivory and tortoiseshell, and walls faced in beautiful green and blue

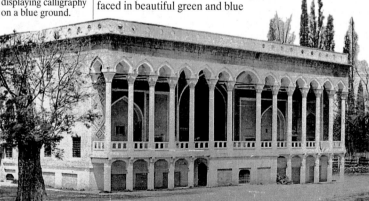

THE IONIC
SARCOPHAGUS OF
ALEXANDER ▲ *165*
This example of
Greek funerary art is
remarkable both for
its beauty and for its
superior state of
preservation.
Moreover, the
expression of the
figures and the
vitality of the forms
are of the greatest
refinement.
Originally, the sense
of life would have
been reinforced by
the use of vivid
colors, traces of which
are still visible. The
scenes carved in
marble represent a
battle between the
Persians and the
Greeks, as well as lion
and stag hunts.

faience. The north- and south-facing windows provide the library with light as well as stunning views across the Sea of Marmara, the Bosphorus, and the Golden Horn.

THE "DINING ROOM" OF AHMET III. A door in the south wall of the library leads into another wonderful chamber, the Dining Room of Ahmet III, also called the Yemiş Odası, the "Fruit Room". As this name would suggest, the décor features bowls of fruit and vases filled with flowers, painted in sparkling colors on laquered wood. This oriental interpretation of a European style is characteristic of the "Tulip Period" – Lâle Devri – which emerged in the first half of the 18th century.

THE PRINCES' APARTMENTS ● *83*. Returning through the Salon of Murat III and its anteroom, you now come to this stunning pair of chambers. The ceramic tiles decorating the Princes' Apartments are examples from the Iznik workshops in their prime, which dates the rooms to the end of the 16th century or the beginning of the 17th. The dome over the first room is decorated with a painting on canvas, as is the ceiling of the inner room with a bronze-gilt fireplace, flanked by some of the most beautiful tiles ever made. Until recently, the

ROMAN HEADS 2nd century, Pergamon.

SARCOPHAGUS OF THE WEEPERS Formed like an Ionic temple, this stone coffin from the 4th century BC was one of the first of its kind. The marble retains traces of the original bright colors.

The Archeological Museum in the First Court of Topkapı Palace.

A PHRYGIAN PERFUME BOTTLE, FROM THE END OF THE 7TH CENTURY BC
This small bottle was found in a tumulus at Gordion, the famous capital of Phrygia, about 60 miles from Ankara. The excavations there uncovered fortifications and houses as well as royal residences.

chambers were thought to have been the infamous *kafes*, in which the younger brothers of the sultan were interned to keep them from challenging the succession. The "cages" are now understood to be a cluster of dark cells situated beyond the Princes' Apartments along a corridor known as the "Consultation Place of the Jinns."

THE TERRACE OF THE FAVORITES. The Consultation Place of the Jinns also leads to the GÖZDELER TAŞLIĞI (**31**), a large courtyard overlooking the lower gardens of the palace. Here, on the eastern edge stands a long, two-story dormitory in which the sovereign's favorite women lived. On the ground floor the Sultan maintained a suite of rooms for his personal use.

THE MUSEUMS OF THE FIRST COURT

Leaving the Inner Palace, return to the First Court, pass through the Kiz Bekçiler Kapısı, and go to the terrace below the Saray. On the left is the MUSEUM OF THE ANCIENT ORIENT, on the right, the Archeological Museum, and, farther along on the left, the Çinili Köşkü.

THE ÇINILI KÖŞKÜ. Called the "Tiled Pavilion" in English, the Çinili Köşkü is one of the buildings that survive from the original Topkapı. It is also a masterpiece of Ottoman architecture, both its design and décor showing Persian influences. The façade is decorated with blue and white calligraphy, and turquoise ceramic tiles similar to those on the famous Green Mosque of Bursa. The pavilion was built in 1472 at the command of Fatih Mehmet, who used it as a hunting lodge, as well as a place from which to watch his pages play *cirit*, an early form of polo. From 1874 to 1891 it served as a repository for antiquities, which were subsequently transferred to the Archeological Museum. Restored in the 1950's, the Çinili Köşkü now houses the Museum of Turkish Tiles. This is a remarkable collection, which includes faiences from Iznik and Çanakkale, a mirhab from the Mosque of Ibrahim Bey from the pre-classical period, and a beautiful 19th-century Ottoman-Baroque ablution fountain.

THE ARCHEOLOGICAL MUSEUM. This institution was founded in 1881 by Hamdi Bey, Turkey's first archeologist of international status. In 1991, on the occasion of the one-hundreth anniversary of the museum's opening, a new wing was inaugurated at the southwest end of the old building. Here, pride of place in the collection

is taken by the so-called "Alexander Sarcophagus," ▲ 163 one of the funerary monuments discovered in 1887 by Hamdi Bey in the royal necropolis at Sidon in Syria. Because of its decorative bas-reliefs, depicting Alexander in battle and hunting scenes, the sarcophagus was long believed to have come from the tomb of the emperor. However, it has now been dated to the 4th century BC and identified as belonging to a sovereign of the Seleucid dynasty. Also among the important sepulchral monuments in the collection are the "Sarcophagus of the Weepers" ▲ 163 and the sarcophagi of Meleager, Phaedra and Hippolytus, Sidamara, a Satrap, and, finally, Tabnit. In addition, the museum owns a superb collection of Greek and Roman sculptures, the two most celebrated of which are the Ephebos of Tralles and a head of Alexander, the latter copied after the famous original by Lysippus. Both date from the 3rd century BC. Also on display is a superbly sculpted late-Roman head of the Emperor Arcadius, dated AD c. 400. Also not to be missed is the colossal statue of Bes, the Cypriot Heracles, a monstrous figure holding a decapitated lioness by her hind legs. In the new wing the floors are installed thematically, beginning with the ground floor devoted to classical sculpture found in Anatolia. In the vestibule there is also a scale model of the Temple of Athena in Assos. On the next floor up, we find "Istanbul through the Ages," an exhibition ranging from prehistoric times through the ancient Greek, Roman, Byzantine, Latin, and Ottoman periods. Above, on the third floor, the theme is "Neighboring Cultures of Anatolia": Cyprus, Syria, and Palestine. The great variety of exhibits and the quality of their presentation ranks the Archeological Museum among the best institutions of its kind.

THE MUSEUM OF THE ANCIENT ORIENT. Two great Hittite lions flank the door of this museum, which shelters an important collection of antiquities from all over Anatolia and the Middle Eastern dominions of the Ottoman Empire. The collection includes Egyptian, Sumerian, Akkadian, Babylonian, Hittite (see especially the "Treaty of Kadesh," the oldest known peace treaty, signed on clay tablets by Hittites and Egyptians ● 29), Urartian, and Assyrian artefacts, as well as unique objects from pre-Islamic Arabia and Nabatea. A visit here gives a complete picture of the archeological and artistic heritage of Turkey, heir to all the treasures of the ancient world acquired by the Ottomans when they conquered Byzantium and the Middle East.

THE JEWELRY ROOM IN THE ARCHEOLOGICAL MUSEUM
This collection of jewelry includes pieces from the ancient kingdoms of Mesopotamia, Sumer, Babylonia, and Assyria, as well as the Byzantine Empire. Illustrated above are gold ear pendants found at Troy and dating from the Bronze Age. Illustrated on the left is an earring from the 9th century and a Byzantine medal from the 6th.

HITTITE ART IN THE MUSEUM OF THE ANCIENT NEAR EAST
Among the Anatolian civilizations represented in this museum, that of the Hittites is one of the most important. A number of pieces came from the ruins of Hattuşaş, the ancient capital of the Hittite Empire and today known as Boğazkale (near Yozgat). Of particular interest are a guardian lion (c. 800 BC), a work carved in basalt and covered with hieroglyphs, a flared, beak-shaped pitcher (16th century BC), and several terra-cotta tablets (13th century BC), all covered with cuneiform script.

165

▲ OTTOMAN MINIATURES

THE ORIGINS OF OTTOMAN MINIATURES

For centuries the representation of the human form, either in sculpture or in painting, was forbidden in Islamic countries. Turkish artists, therefore, developed other areas of creativity, principally architecture but also various branches of the decorative arts. The degree of skill and sophistication that were attained in these arts deserves worldwide recognition and appreciation. The origins of the miniature go back to the Anatolian Selçuk period (11th to 13th centuries) and beyond to the pre-Islamic, central Asian Turko-Uygur period, but it is only with the reign of Mehmet II that new schools would develop in Istanbul. The Sultan surrounded himself with miniaturist painters, the most talented of whom was the portraitist Sinan of Bursa; his style shows the influence of the visits of Italian painters, like Gentile Bellini, who were invited to the seraglio by the Sultan.

ISTANBUL AND GALATA

Matrâki, 1536–37. Somewhere between a geographical map and a landscape, Matrâki's prints have a unique charm. Matrâki – warrior, wise man, and topographical painter – produced a series of pictures that show the cities conquered or visited by the sovereign, his armies, and his fleet.

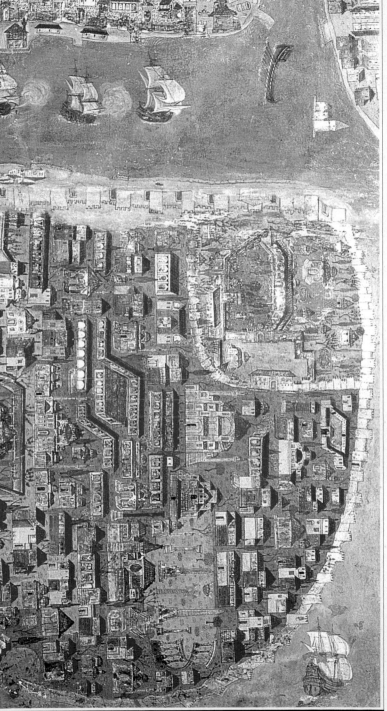

167

> "From now on painting, portraiture, calligraphy, and
> miniatures will meet with success and finery in Istanbul."
>
> Bâki

The celebration of the sultan himself, his military campaigns, and the feasts and parties of the palace, would constitute the principal inspiration of the Ottoman miniaturists. Their number, while modest under Mehmet II, would rise to 29 masters under Süleyman the Magnificent, reaching the respectable number of 1000 artists working in 100 studios in the 17th century. Despite a certain uniformity of style, a number of strong personalities would emerge in each reign. Under Beyazıt II, for example, there was Ahmet of Bursa, student of the painter Sinan, as well as Baba Mustafa. The painters recruited by the sultans were mostly of Turkish origin, but there were also many of Iranian or Balkan origin, and this merging of cultures created a style which can be appropriately called Ottoman. Among the host of artists of the reign of Murat III, it was undoubtedly the master Osman who was the most talented. His skill is shown at its best in a collection of exquisite images called *The Book of Accomplishments*, which describes the life of the seraglio and the military campaigns in a decorative light. Whether clean-shaven or bearded, the faces are almost all alike. The particular beauty of the two-dimensional images is due to his technique of using flat colors of equal density.

The prohibition of figurative art was not adhered to by the sovereigns, who appreciated and encouraged the art of the miniature, and even, as was the case during the reign of Mehmet II, portraiture. This art was expressed almost entirely in princely books of calligraphy. Turkish miniatures depict men and women in a formulaic, standardized manner, and as part of an erudite composition. The artists are not interested in capturing the personality of the subjects. In a social structure where the land and people are all part of the imperial domain, the quest for an artistic definition of the individual was unnecessary: the people are the servants of the sultan and are inter-changeable. The landscapes of the miniatures do not obey the constraints of perspective, with no distinction made between near and far, flattening the world as though it were all within reach of the great lord. This was an aesthetic bias that, by a curious twist, was often adopted by modern, especially abstract painters. On the left is shown the *devşirme*, or collection of the young Christian children in the *Süleymanahme*, commissioned by Süleyman in 1517. To the right, science is glorified in this representation of *Astronomers in their Observatory in Galatasaray*, an extract from *Sehinsehname*, 1581.

▲ THE MINIATURES OF SIYAH QUALEM

SIYAH QUALEM
The Selçuk Turks and the Ottomans, who came from the depths of Central Asia and converted late to Islam, remained faithful to their pre-Islamic heritage. The work of Siyah Qualem shows traces of Chinese painting and its development in Central Asia. The influence of the Uigur Turks, who had opted for the Manichean religion, was crucial, as iconography occupied a fundamental place in their religion.

Among the masterpieces of this Central-Asian period, the mysterious work of Siyah Qualem can be attributed to this pre-Islamic tradition.

The heros of the Central Asian epics are generally the chiefs of nomadic tribes who perform heroic deeds and do battle with demons from the underworld.

> "You could not cross the land of Karaman.
> There are no bridges: you would not make it
> across the torrents."
>
> Yunus Emre

THE ALBUM OF FATIH

In the art collections of Mehmet II (1451–81) there are some superb and unusual works of art from Siyah Qualem. These paintings, of wandering dervishes, warriors and mythic giants, constitute the most vivid and passionate account of this nomadic world which, wave after wave, came down from Central Asia to Asia Minor.

Siyah Qualem reconciled the supernatural world with all the naturalistic freshness of a nomadic society. These paintings of uncertain date and origin did not start a trend, however, because the élite of the seraglio, heavily influenced by the Arabo-Persian culture and æsthetic, were resistant to the shamanic vigor of Siyah Qualem and his disciples.

KÜÇÜK AYA SOFYA
SOKOLLU MEHMET PAŞA CAMI'I

THE FORUMS OF ANCIENT BYZANTIUM
In the 5th century, the new capital could boast several major forums or squares, which together gave the city a decidedly Roman appearance: the Augustaeum, whose site is now occupied by Haghia Sophia; the Forum Constantini, situated in what became the Çemberlitaş quarter; the Forum Tauri, later renamed the Forum of Theodosius I; the Forum Amastrianum, situated at the southern end of today's Şehzadebaşi quarter; the Forum Bovis, today covered by Aksaray Square; and the Forum of Arcadius which was south of the Millet Caddesi, where a massive base survives as the sole remnant of the 5th-century Column of Arcadius.

AYA SOFYA MEYDANI

This itinerary will take you around the First Hill, beginning in AYA SOFYA MEYDANI, the great square that lies between Haghia Sophia and Sultan Ahmet Cami'i, the "Blue Mosque." Aya Sofya Meydanı occupies the site of the Augustaeum, which was the focal point of public and cultural life in Constantinople as well as the forecourt to the Great Palace of Byzantium. On the northern side, it gave access to Haghia Sophia and the Patriarchal Palace. On the eastern side stood the Chalke – the Bronze House – which was the main gateway into the Great Palace and the Senate (re-established by Constantine in his New Rome). Completing this collection were, on the southwestern side, the Hippodrome and, on the south, the Baths of Zeuxippe, the largest in the city. In addition, there was the Stoa Basilica, an extension of the Augustaeum which led to the University of Constantinople, the imperial law courts, a public library, and an outdoor book market. It was in this area that the principal avenues of the capital converged and there were the houses of rich Byzantines and later the mosque complexes named after their Ottoman founders. (The Aya Sofya Meydanı is still the site of the university, the law courts, and an important book market). **THE HAMMAM OF ROXELANA.** The "Hasseki Hüssem" is also situated in the square ● *58*, on the northwest side between Haghia Sophia and Sultan Ahmet (the Blue Mosque). Süleyman commissioned Sinan to build it in honor of his wife. Completed in 1556, this splendid twin-domed structure lies outside the Haghia Sophia precincts. It has recently been restored as a hall for the display and sale of Turkish rugs and kilims ● *60*.

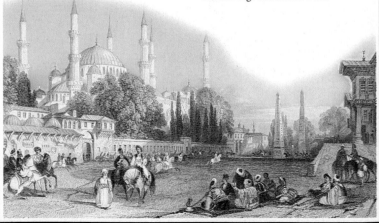

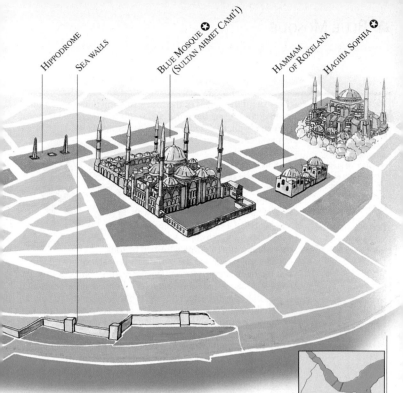

HIPPODROME SEA WALLS BLUE MOSQUE ✪ (SULTAN AHMET CAMI'I) HAMMAM OF ROXELANA HAGHIA SOPHIA ✪

BLUE MOSQUE

Its magnificent series of domes and semi-domes, its six slender minarets sprouting from the corners of the mosque, its spacious courtyard, and its grandiose yet elegant proportions, make Sultan Ahmet Cami'i (also known as the Blue Mosque) one of the architectural marvels of the world. Davut Ağa built it on the orders of Sultan Ahmet I (1603–17), hence its official name. The courtyard in front of it is on a scale equal to that of the enormous mosque itself. It can be entered through one of the large gateways located on each of the three sides. Within there is a peristyle with 26 columns forming a portico surmounted by a series of 30 small cupolas. A handsome octagonal *şadırvan* ● 66 stands in the center.

No other mosque in Istanbul has ever had six minarets. The four at the corners of the building have balconies. The cascade of domes begins with the vast main dome and continues with the four flanking semi-domes, each quite large and abutted by smaller semi-domes, which are further echoed in the smaller cupolas reinforced on either side by round turrets at the corners of the building. Adding to this symphony of spherical forms are the little cupolas atop the tall octagonal turrets

🕓 **Four hours**
◆ E C5

BLUE MOSQUE, "GARDEN OF PARADISE" ✪
Although no longer the starting point for the pilgrimage to Mecca, its 20,000 blue faïences from Iznik still offer a glimpse of paradise. Before going in by the north entrance, reserved for tourists, approach the mosque through the courtyard from the Hippodrome, in order to best appreciate the classical layout of the domes and cupolas.

BYZANTINE IVORY WORK
The finest pieces made by the capital's ivory carvers date from the late 5th century. A precious material, ivory was reserved for images of the emperor, who gave them to notables who had supported his bid for the throne.

175

▲ BLUE MOSQUE

RACES IN THE HIPPODROME
A race generally involved four chariots running seven laps around the track, a distance of some 2,700 yards. Each chariot driver wore the colors of one of Constantinople's socio-political factions, which was sponsoring him financially. The White and Blue parties consisted of aristocrats and landowners, all allied with the throne.

The Red and Green parties drew their members primarily from the artisan and merchant classes. The victor emerged as a great public hero; thus, Emperor Anastasius (451–518) had two bronze statues erected in honor of Porphyrus, one of the most famous of the Hippodrome stars. Members of the imperial court watched the races from a private enclosure, the *kathisma*, which was probably situated on the east side of the arena, where it could be entered through the wall of the Great Palace, now vanished. Between races, clowns, dwarves, acrobats, and wild animals performed for the assembled crowd.

that extend the height of the four structural pillars under the main dome. Along the north and south fronts are two floors of porticoed galleries, and the form is continued in the arcades around the walls of the courtyard below.

THE INTERIOR. Measuring 174 by 167 feet, the prayer hall is almost square, and above it rises the immense dome, reaching a height of 77 feet above the pavement and with a diameter of 141 feet. This heavenly vault rests upon the cubic base thanks to a circular rim or cornice formed by four ogival arches joined at the corners by four smooth pendentives. But the main support for the superstructure comes from four colossal pillars – 16 feet in diameter – banded at the waist and ribbed with convex fluting. Light floods into the building through 260 windows, which, alas, are modern imitations of the original ones installed in the 17th century. The painted tiles that sheath the great dome as well as the upper walls were also recently installed, and account for the mosque's popular name. However, the tiles on the lower walls and the galleries merit close attention. Indeed, they are from the Iznik workshops and are decorated with superb floral motifs in an exquisite blue-green palette. The white marble mirhab and mimbar are fine examples of 17th-century Ottoman sculpture. No less remarkable are the bronze gateways in the forecourt and, within the mosque, the doors and window shutters made of wood inlaid with ivory, mother-of-pearl, and tortoiseshell. On the ceiling under the Sultan's loge, found in the upper gallery to the left of the mihrab, there is a rare example of the first Ottoman style, an array of painted floral and geometric motifs. An exterior ramp on the mosque's northwest corner leads to the *hünkar kasrı*, the imperial pavilion, connected to the imperial loge by an internal corridor. The *hünkar kasrı* houses the KILIM MUSEUM ● *60*. At the east end of the mosque, the vaulted, subterranean storerooms and stables have now been restored to house the CARPET MUSEUM.

THE COMPLEX OF THE BLUE MOSQUE. The mosque and its forecourt were in turn surrounded by an outer precinct wall, of which only the northern section remains. This rampart isolated the mosque from the other buildings within the complex: the *medrese*, *türbe*, hospital, caravanserai, primary school, and *imaret*. All of these structures still exist today except the hostel and the hospital. The *medrese* lies outside the walls on the northeast side, near the large square *türbe* or mausoleum, which has now been renovated and opened to the public. Here lie the remains of Ahmet I, his wife Kösem, and three of his sons, Osman II (1618–22), Murat IV, and Prince Beyazıt.

THE HIPPODROME. The AT MEYDANI, the vast, tree-shaded esplanade spread out before the Blue Mosque is on the site of the ancient Roman Hippodrome. The street encircling it corresponds to the course of the original racetrack. Built in AD 198 by the Emperor Septimius Severus, the Hippodrome was reconstructed on a much grander scale by Constantine the Great once he had decided to make Byzantium his new capital. Thereafter, the Hippodrome became the scene of many a Byzantine drama, beginning with the official birth of the New Rome on May 11, 330. It was here the court and public acclaimed victorious emperors and generals; some were also executed here, as were several heretical patriarchs. It was also to the Hippodrome that the people came to vent their frustrations, as when the Nika Revolt broke out on January 13,

THE EGYPTIAN OBELISK
First erected by Pharaoh Tutmosis III (16th c. BC), this obelisk once stood 195 feet tall. It broke apart while being unloaded in Constantinople,

leaving only the top third to be mounted on the spine of the Hippodrome by Theodosius the Great in 390.

SOKOLLU
MEHMET PAŞA
One of the most
capable bureaucrats
in the whole of
Ottoman history,
Sokollu Mehmet
entered the Janissary
Corps at a very early
age and was educated
in the Palace School
at Topkapı Sarayı.
By 1565 he had
become Grand
Vizier under
Süleyman the
Magnificent, a post
he continued to hold
during the reign of
Selim II, whose
daughter, Princess
Esma, he married.

He built the mosque
that bears his name in
her honor. After the
death of the drunken
Selim in 1574, Sokollu
Mehmet Paşa became
Grand Vizier to
Murat III; he was
assassinated in 1579
by a demented soldier
in the Divan.

532 ● 32, only to be crushed five days later by General
Belisarius, who ordered Justinian's troops to block the exits and
massacre the 30,000 insurgents trapped inside the arena.
During the Roman occupation of Constantinople (1204–61)
the Hippodrome was plundered, and by the time the Turks
arrived in 1453, it had fallen into ruins.
From 1609 to 1616 the once-glorious
Hippodrome served as a quarry for the
construction of the Blue Mosque. The site
then became known as At Meydanı (Place of
Horses), for the game of *cirit*, a forerunner
of polo, that the Topkapı pages played. In
1890, the French architect Bouvier drew up
plans for converting the square into a park.

THE EGYPTIAN OBELISK. The Obelisk of Theodosius –
Dikilitaş in Turkish – is mounted on four bronze cubes set upon
a marble base, which is decorated with bas-reliefs portraying
Theodosius and his family in their enclosure at the
Hippodrome. On the southern face, the Emperor observes the
races depicted in the lower part of the relief; on the east, he
places a laurel crown on the head of the winning charioteer; on
the north, he oversees the erection of the obelisk; and on the
west, he receives the homage of his vanquished enemies.

THE SERPENT COLUMN. The central feature of the square is
the Serpent Column (Yılanlı Sütun in Turkish), a twisting shaft
of three entwined snakes, which once served as a base for the
trophy of thanksgiving offered by thirty-one Greek cities whose
conscripts had helped defeat the Persians at Platea in 479 BC.
Constantine the Great had it brought from the Temple of
Apollo at Delphi. The beasts' heads disappeared following the
Conquest, although the upper part of one head was found in

178

1847 and is now exhibited in the Archaeological Museum.
THE COLUMN OF CONSTANTINE. Örme Sütun, as the Turks call
the third column which stands on what was the spine of the
Hippodrome, is situated at the southwest extremity of At
Meydanı. Petrus Gillius referred to it as the "Colossus," but
most modern commentators speak, incorrectly, of the
"Column of Constantine Porphyrogenitus." Both names derive
from Greek inscription on the base, which
compare it to the Colossus of Rhodes, and
also indicate that the column had been
badly damaged but then repaired and clad
in bronze by Emperor Constantine VII
Porphyrogenitus (913–59). The original
column dates from a much earlier period,
perhaps that of Constantine the Great.
THE PALACE OF IBRAHIM PAŞA. On the west
side of At Meydanı is the Ibrahim Paşa
Sarayı, built by Ibrahim Paşa in 1523
shortly after Süleyman named him Grand
Vizier. The restored structure now houses
the MUSEUM OF TURKISH AND ISLAMIC
ARTS, which has a fine collection. Part of
the lower floor in the northern wing has
been turned into an old-fashioned Istanbul
coffee house, a perfect place to relax after
visiting the museum. On the right, a stone
lion from the Selçuk period guards the
stairway to the upper floor of the north
wing, where the exhibition begins.

The brilliant
polychromy of the
finest Iznik tiles
decorating the
Sokollu Mehmet Paşa
Cami'i is accentuated
by the stained-glass
windows.

THE MUSEUM OF TURKISH AND ISLAMIC ART ★. Objects
dating from the 7th to the 19th century are exhibited in the
nineteen cells of the north and east wings. They represent
every period of Turkish and Islamic art: Ummayid,
Abbasid, Mameluk, Selçuk,
Beylik, and Ottoman. The
superbly organized displays
embrace everything from
kilims, manuscripts,
calligraphy, miniatures,
carved wood, ironwork,
and stone sculpture to
faience, stained glass,
and folk art. In the south
wing, on the garden level,
we find the Ethnological
Collection, devoted
mainly to the Yürük,
the nomads of Anatolia,
whose way of life has
scarcely changed since
the first Türkmen swept
across Asia Minor following
their victory over the
Byzantines at Mantzikert in
1071. The objects on
display, in black tents
made of lamb skins, are
still used by the wandering
tribes.

**THE BYZANTINE
PALACE**
Constantinople had
few links with the
ancient Byzantium
that preceded it. In
place of the old city's
unity arose several
diverse quarters. The
11th-century
miniature seen here
depicts a Byzantine
palace encircled by a
wall, set within a
garden, whose
fountain fed cistern
water through a
complex network of
pipes ● 76. In the
areas around these
aristocratic dwellings
were comfortable
houses of up to three
stories tall, or more
modest houses
containing artisan
workshops.

SOKOLLU MEHMET PAŞA CAMI'I

Returning to At Meydanı and continuing along the western side to the end of the square, you come to a narrow street called Şehit Mehmet Paşa Yokuşu, which makes its circuitous way downhill towards the Sea of Marmara. The second turning on the left brings us to the main entrance of the Sokollu Mehmet Paşa Cami'i, an exceptionally beautiful mosque erected by Sinan in 1571–72. The entrance is most unusual, following a flight of stairs under the vaulted chamber of the former lecture hall of the *medrese* ● *78*. It leads to the courtyard, at the center of which stands the *şadırvan* ● *66*, an ablution fountain surmounted by a cupola with wide projecting eves. Three sides of the courtyard are bordered by the sixteen cells of the *medrese* and the fourth side, opposite the *dershane*, is given over to the dome-vaulted bays of a portico that opens onto the prayer hall. Calligraphic inscriptions in blue and white faience decorate the lunettes of the mosque windows. The prayer hall is a hexagon inscribed within a rectangle, vaulted by a dome buttressed at the corners by four small half-domes. There are no side aisles, but around three sides runs a lower gallery supported by marble columns with lozenge capitals – a typical feature of Ottoman architecture. Characteristic of the period is the vivid color of the ogival arches, with their alternating green and red marble voussoirs.

TILES AND STAINED-GLASS WINDOWS. The décor of the Sokollu Mehmet Paşa Cami'i is especially refined; the sober walls are brightened only by tiles sheathing the pendentives, a floral frieze, and the beautiful frame around the mihrab on the east wall. This frame is made of faience glazed with turquoise vine and flower motifs on a pale green ground, interspersed with white calligraphy on a deep blue field. The mimbar, finely carved from white marble, is capped by a tall conical hood with the same turquoise tiles as those surrounding the mihrab. There are two tiers of stained-glass windows in the wall above the mihrab. Above the entrance door,

This wood relief comes from the imaret of Karaman Ibrahim Bey at Konya. It constitutes a rare example of a Beylik work in which figurative elements are used. The central medallion is composed of six- or twelve-pointed stars and twelve-sided polygons. Winged lions and a pair of griffins occupy the corners, while an interlace of palmettes and leaves frames the entire shutter. A calligraphic inscription fills the headband, leaving the octagons of the lower band to be embellished with spirals and palmettes.

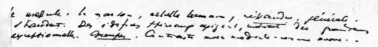
ketch (below) and manuscript (above) by Le Corbusier.

ne can still see a fragment of the painted decorations that
riginally covered the wall in elaborate multicolored designs.
A fragment of black basaltic stone from the Kaaba in Mecca
survives over the door, and there are other pieces of sacred
stone set in the mimbar and mihrab.

Sts Sergius and Bacchus. Leaving the Sokollu Mehmet
Paşa Cami'i, proceed through one of the most picturesque
parts of the city, towards the Sea of Marmara as far as Küçük
Ayasofya Caddesi. On the right stands the Küçük Aya Sofya
Cami'i, the Little Mosque of Haghia Sophia, so called
because it resembles the famous basilica. In fact, it was
originally the church of Sts Sergius and Bacchus ● 74, one of
the most beautiful in Constantinople and one of the most
important churches in the history of the capital. Justinian
commissioned the building in 527, the first year of his reign,
and it remained a place of Christian worship for almost a
thousand years. Early in the 17th century, the church was
converted into a mosque by
the head of the black
eunuchs under Sultan
Beyazıt II, Hüseyin Ağa,
whose remains lie in a *türbe*
north of the apse. The shape
of the building is an irregular
octagon within an
even more irregular
rectangle. The
transition from the
rectangular to the
circular has been
accomplished in the most astonishing manner, with the dome
divided into sixteen alternating flat and concave sections so
that the latter end precisely at the corners. The dome is
supported by eight polygonal pillars, one on either side of
the four interior angles, separated by pairs of alternate
red and green marble columns which follow the curve
of the exedra at each corner. The space between
this colorful, vibrant screen and the exterior
walls becomes a walkway below and a
capacious gallery above, the latter
reached by a stairway at the southern
end of the narthex. The column
capitals and the classic
entablatures, with their
intricate, deeply undercut
carving, exemplify the
lapidary style of
the 6th century.
The arcaded
epistyle or
architrave
would become
more or less
standard in later
Byzantine
architecture, most
notably in Haghia Sophia.
However, the trabeated
rather than arcuated

**Little
Haghia Sophia**
This was the first of
many churches
founded by Justinian
which were dedicated
to Saints Sergius and
Bacchus. Martyred
for their faith, they
were the patron
saints of Christian
centurions in the
Roman army.

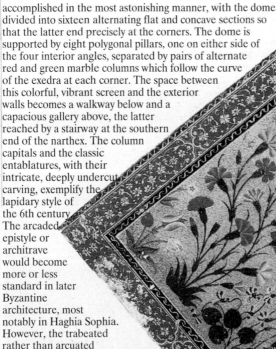

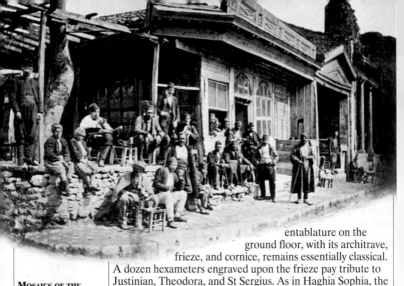

entablature on the ground floor, with its architrave, frieze, and cornice, remains essentially classical. A dozen hexameters engraved upon the frieze pay tribute to Justinian, Theodora, and St Sergius. As in Haghia Sophia, the interior walls have been clad in variegated marble revetments. The south doors open onto a narrow, winding street that runs under a railway and on to the shore of the Marmara.

THE SEA WALLS

Originally, the walls that Constantine the Great had constructed along the Sea of Marmara coastline extended as far as Samatya, where his land walls descended to the shore below the Seventh Hill. In the following century they were extended still further, all the way to the Theodosian walls, which had just been completed. Four hundred years later, the ramparts would be almost entirely rebuilt by the Emperor Theophilus (829–842), eager to reinforce the capital's defenses against Arab attacks. Theophilus' name can still be made out among the inscriptions on the gigantic towers. Altogether, the sea walls constituted a continuous line of defense 40 to 50 feet high, with 13 gateways and 88 towers at regular intervals. These fortifications extended for some 5 miles, beginning at Saray Burnu, where they intersected those along the Golden Horn,

MOSAICS OF THE GREAT PALACE OF BYZANTIUM
The Mosaic Museum was established to house a remnant of the paving of the peristyle in one of the Great Palace's vast courtyards, which was excavated between 1935 and 1954. Although dating from the 6th century, these mosaics had been covered in the 7th century with marble flagstones, and then lost under buildings constructed on the site between the 7th and 9th centuries. They depict human figures and various motifs in vivid colors: red, blue, yellow, green, brown, and black. The images appear against a background of square white tesserae set in a "fish-scale" pattern. The subjects come from the Hellenistic repertoire of decorative themes: hunting scenes, mythological beings, vignettes of everyday life. Alongside them appear realistic and fantastic animals. Of particular interest is a lion being strangled by an elephant, an eagle doing battle with a serpent, a griffin and a chimera, a tiger hunt, a centaur and a satyr, and a superb Dionysus with a beard of fresh leaves and fruit.

and continuing to the Marble Towers, where they connected with the old Theodosian walls. Constantinople was thus completely surrounded and protected by a barrier of ramparts some 15 miles long. Although a good part of the sea walls, together with their towers and gates, were destroyed in the 19th century, the sections that remain show how formidable they were, particularly the walls at the foot of the First Hill.

THE PALACE OF BUCOLEON. Not far away are the ruins of a very grand Byzantine gateway, which the Turks call Çatladı Kapı, meaning "Cracked Gate." The marble arch and its supporting posts are decorated with bas-reliefs of acanthus leaves and a large monogram of Justinian ● *32*. It is very likely that this was the Imperial Marine Gate, one of the entrances to the Bucoleon port, an exclusive harbor serving the Great Palace. The Bucoleon, or Palace of the Bull and the Lion, took its name from a sculpture of a lion overcoming a bull, which has long since disappeared. Anyone arriving at the port entered the palace by a stairway in the massive tower just beyond the Çatladı Kapı, where all that remains of the Bucoleon can be seen – a loggia with three marble-framed windows opening onto a vaulted hall.

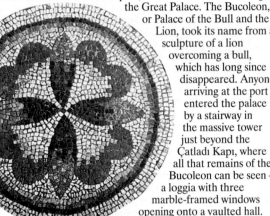

THE GREAT PALACE OF BYZANTIUM.
The fragments described above are all that survive from the Great Palace of Byzantium whose pavilions, gardens, and courtyards once spread over the slopes of the First Hill facing the Sea of Marmara. Constantine the Great commissioned the first buildings, which suffered grave damage during the Nika Revolt of 532. Justinian had them reconstructed and enlarged. Later, other emperors, especially Basil I of Macedonia, renovated, expanded, and decorated them. The wonder of the medieval world, the Great Palace remained the imperial residence until the sack of Constantinople by the Venetians and Crusaders in 1204 ● *32*. However, after the restoration of the empire in 1261, the immense, sprawling palace had decayed into such a state that the Palaeologus emperors preferred to live in the Palace of the Blachernae which was in the northwest of the capital overlooking the Golden Horn.

THE STABLE GATE. The next tower in the defensive walls beyond the Bucoleon was used as Constantinople's *pharos* or lighthouse. A little further along we come to the Ahır Kapı or "Stable Gate," the only sea-wall gateway still standing on the shores of the Marmara. During the Ottoman period, it opened into the sultan's stables, which accounts for its popular name.

THE GREAT PALACE
The imperial residence in Constantinople was actually a collection of different structures: the Sacred Palace and the Palace of Daphne, both near the present site of the Blue Mosque; the Chalke Palace, or the House of Bronze, abutting the south side of the Forum Augustaeum; the Palaces of Magnaura and Mangana, on the slope of the First Hill facing the Sea of Marmara, slightly to the east of the present Topkapı Palace; and the seaside Palace of Bucoleon. Here stood the famous Pavilion of the Porphyrogenitus, the *gynaeceum,* or women's quarters, reigned over by the empresses; its walls were covered with splendid purple marbles brought from Rome by the first emperors. This décor is behind the saying "born to the purple," which is the meaning of *Porphyrogenitus.* By the time the Turks occupied the city, the Great Palace was little more than ruins. Shortly after the Conquest, Mehmet II surveyed the wasted halls and found them so depressing that he recited a sorrowful distich by the Persian poet Saadi: "The spider weaves the curtains of the Palace of the Caesars. The owl hoots its nocturnal call on the Tower of Aphrasiab."

THE SMALL TRADERS OF ISTANBUL
A striking feature of the city is the number and diversity of the small trades that figure so prominently in everyday life. Strung out along the streets are tiny refreshment stalls stands selling döner kebab, barber shops, and public scribes. Also at work in the open are bootblacks and itinerant vendors of such items as cigarettes and newspapers, indeed everything that can be consumed on the run or can satisfy a sudden need. The first drop of rain brings out a rush of umbrella peddlers, only to be replaced by peddlers of dark glasses and cool drinks as soon as the sun reappears.

THE WHITE MUSTACHE QUARTER

Pass through the Ahir Kapı, turn left onto Ahir Kapı Sokağı and then right into Heresteci Hakki Sokağı, and you will soon come to Ak Bıyık Meydanı, the Square of the White Mustache, which lies at the heart of Ak Bıyık, one of Istanbul's oldest and most picturesque quarters. It is a veritable maze of alleyways with such colorful names as Street of the Bushy Beard, of the Sweating Whiskers, and of the Shame-Faced. In the center of the Square of the White Mustache there are two Ottoman fountains. The old city boasts more than 400 Ottoman *çeşme* ● 66, ranging from simple wall fountains to great domed and arcaded street fountains. Formerly, these facilities provided the citizens with their only source of drinking water, and they remain indispensable, particularly in older quarters.

THE MOSAIC MUSEUM

From Ak Bıyık Sokağı, turn right into Mimar Mehmet Ağa Caddesi, and then left into Torun Sokağı or the Street of the Little Child. In this street is the main entrance to the Mosaic Museum, the repository for fragments of columns, antique marble capitals, and various other remains of the Great Palace of Byzantium. Most important of all, the museum exhibits mosaics salvaged from the Great Palace, all restored and mounted on panels. On this very site, they once adorned the Mosaic Peristyle, a colonnaded passage thought to have led to the *kathisma*, the imperial enclosure in the Hippodrome. The subjects depicted in the mosaics include pastoral landscapes, scenes of hunting and animal combat, and various events in the Hippodrome, some of which are very amusing, for example the efforts of two inebriated spectators to play horse and charioteer.

> "A blue light spread more and more; gradually it bathed the wise, devout smokers, but the deserted square remained in the shadow of the massive sacred walls."
>
> Pierre Loti

The mosaics date from the first half of the 6th century and must have been installed when Justinian rebuilt the Great Palace.

THE STREET OF THE BUSHY BEARD.

From the upper doorway of the Mosaic Museum, turn right into Kaba Sakal Sokağı – the Street of the Bushy Beard – which passes behind the Blue Mosque. This traditional *arasta*, or bazaar street, underwent reconstruction in the 1970's. Since then its arcaded shops have catered largely to the tourist trade. At the end of the street on the left there is an entrance to the Carpet Museum housed in the Blue Mosque. Continuing uphill towards the left, we pass the HAMMAM OF ROXELANA. On the east side of Kaba Sakal Sokağı there are two old buildings, the first of which is the MEHMET EFENDI MEDRESESI, built in the 17th century and restored by

the TTOK. This one-time educational building now shelters the Istanbul Fine Arts Market, and its workshops occupy the little stalls bordering the courtyard, each of them dedicated to one of the old Ottoman crafts, such as bookbinding, paper marbling, embroidery, miniature painting, engraving, and doll-making. The other structure, a fine old *konak* (mansion) has also been restored by the TTOK. Called the Yeşil Ev, or Green House, it is now a deluxe hotel and restaurant, and in good weather tables are set outside in the very attractive courtyard. This is a perfect place to stop for lunch after a stroll about the First Hill.

THE MUSEUM OF CARPETS AND KILIMS

In the 13th century, Marco Polo extolled the beauty of Turkish carpets. The thousand-year-old craft is the fruit of several ancient traditions: those of the Anatolian nomads on the one hand and those of the Türkmen tribes of Central Asia on the other, both of whom passed their skills to the Selçuks.

THE KAISER'S FOUNTAIN

At the northeast extremity of the Hippodrome stands the fountain given by Kaiser Wilhelm II to Sultan Abdül Hamit II. At the end of the 19th century the Ottoman Empire represented a key piece on the geopolitical chessboard of Europe. In the midst of Franco-German and Austro-Russian tensions stood the Balkans, strategically located at the gates to Asia and the eastern Mediterranean. The Balkan wars proved to be a prelude to world conflict. In November 1914 the Ottoman Empire entered World War One on the side of Germany and Austro-Hungary.

185

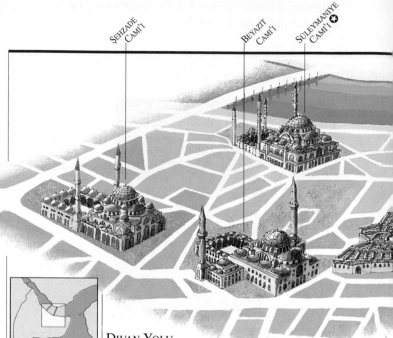

ŞEHZADE
CAMI'I

BEYAZIT
CAMI'I

SÜLEYMANIYE
CAMI'I ✪

🏃 One day

◆ D

**EXIT FROM THE
GRAND BAZAAR**
Customers leaving the
Grand Bazaar near
the Nuruosmaniye
Mosque (below).
The houses on the
ground floor have
been converted into
grocery shops and
stalls for a wide
variety of craftsmen.

DIVAN YOLU

Byzantine Constantinople's main thoroughfare was the Mese,
or Middle Way, which ran from the Forum Augustaeum to the
Adrianople Gate on the Sixth Hill. The first stretch of the
Mese followed the same course as today's avenue, which
connects the summits of the First and Third Hills. Between
the summits of the First and Second Hills the route is known
as Divan Yolu, the Road of the Divan, and the
section to the top of the Third Hill as
Yeniçeriler Caddesi, the Avenue of the
Janissaries. Both names derive from
Ottoman times, when the Janissaries
paraded along here for the thrice-
weekly meetings of the Divan.

THE MILION

At the beginning of Divan Yolu on the right we see an
Ottoman *suterazi*, or water-control tower, one of the very
few that survive. The ancient marble stele at its base has
been identified as the Milion, a triumphal archway of the
late Roman period crowning the route between the Forum
Augustaeum and the Mese. Modeled on the Miliarium
Aureum erected in Rome by Augustus as the reference
point for all road distances in the empire,
the Milion served a similar purpose – the
zero point for the milestones on the roads
between Byzantium and the Adriatic.
According to Petrus Gillius (1545),
the Milion was surmounted by statues
of Constantine the Great and his
mother, Helena, together holding a
large cross. The first street on the
right leads to the entrance to the
Yerebatan Sarnıcı.

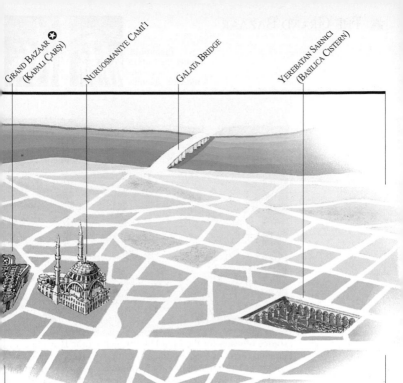

GRAND BAZAAR
(KAPALI ÇARŞI)

NURUOSMANIYE CAMİ'İ

GALATA BRIDGE

YEREBATAN SARNICI
(BASILICA CISTERN)

YEREBATAN SARAYI

The so-called Underground Palace is better known to
foreigners as the Basilica Cistern ● 76. Until the 1980s only a
small part of the vast subterranean reservoir could be viewed,
from the landing at the bottom of the stairs. In 1987, however,
the Yerebatan Sarayı was reopened to the public after years of
restoration, and
there is now a *son-
et-lumière* show too.
The water level had
scarcely fallen and
walkways were
built throughout
its labyrinthine
expanse. The
Basilica Cistern is
by far the largest
and grandest of the
ancient Byzantine
reservoirs in the
city. It gets its
English name
because it was built
under the Stoa
Basilica, or Imperial
Portico, on the west

YEREBATAN SARAYI
Since the Byzantine
era, the abundant
springs in the
Belgrade Forest near
the Black Sea have
been tapped and
their waters stored in
reservoirs called *bent*.

side of the Forum Augustaeum. The Stoa Basilica, probably
commissioned by Constantine the Great, was destroyed by
fire in c. 475. Justinian rebuilt it after the Nika Revolt of 532
and reconstructed the cistern below, using material from
older buildings. The Basilica Cistern provided the main

Formerly, the waters
flowed into the city's
cisterns by means of
pipes and a number
of monumental
aqueducts.

Binbirdirek
Sarnıcı, the Cistern
of a Thousand-
and-One Columns

source of water for the First Hill throughout the Byzantine era and on into Ottoman times, when every street corner and square in Istanbul had its own fountain, or *sebil,* making water freely available to all who passed. It arrived through porcelain conduits from sources such as the Yerabatan Sarayı. Originally, the cistern comprised 336 26-feet columns set at intervals of 13 feet in 12 rows of 218 each. However, 90 of them have now disappeared behind a wall built at the end of the 19th century. Most of the columns are capped by Byzantine Corinthian capitals, whose impost blocks support small domes of brick structured herring-bone fashion. In the far left corner of the cistern there seems to have been a *nymphaion,* or ornamental fountain. When first installed, it would have been accessible from the Stoa Basilica.

FIRUZ AĞA CAMI'I

This little mosque was erected in 1491 for Firuz Ağa, Chief Treasurer in the reign of Sultan Beyazıt II. It constitutes one of the few examples in Istanbul of a pre-classical mosque ● *78* – that is, a mosque built before 1500. Austerely elegant in its simplicity, the building belongs to the "single-unit" type, and consisted merely of a square domed room entered through a small, three-bay porch with a minaret placed, atypically, on the left.

THE REMAINS OF TWO ROMAN PALACES. Beyond the Firuz Ağa Cami'i there is an archeological site which was first excavated in the 1960's. The incomplete ruins that were uncovered are thought to be of two small palaces which were owned by two patricians of the late Roman period named Antiochus and Lausus. The somewhat grander palace belonged to Antiochus and was a hexagonal structure constructed with paired, semicircular apses which alternated with circular rooms. Early in the 7th century the palace was converted into a martyry dedicated to St Euphemia, who had died for her faith in Chalcedon in AD 303. In the 13th century it was decorated with frescoes, but these have been moved in order to preserve them and are kept in a shelter situated next to the Law Courts.

THE MEDUSA HEAD
After dismantling the walls of Chalcedon, the city on the Asian side of the Bosphorus overlooking the entrance to the Euxine Sea, or Black Sea, Justinian had much of the building material brought to Constantinople and re-used in the aqueducts (among them the Valens Aqueduct) and the covered cisterns. Therefore, it is quite likely that the splendid Gorgon's head turned on its side and employed as a column base in the Basilica Cistern came originally from the city of Chalcedon.

> "You may linger a whole day in one bazaar.
> you walk in the midst of towering heaps of brocades
> from Baghdad, silks from Bursa..."

Edmondo de Amicis

THE CISTERN OF A THOUSAND-AND-ONE COLUMNS

At the first corner of Divan Yolu turn left onto Işık Sokağı, which leads uphill to a small park. At the south end of this park there is a shed which is the entrance to Binbirdirek Sarnıcı, the Cistern of a Thousand-and-One Columns. The cistern has not been restored, but the caretaker, if available, will admit visitors in exchange for a modest gratuity. Binbirdirek is the second largest of the city's ancient cisterns, though only a third the size

of Yerebatan Sarnıcı. Though rather muddy it is worth exploring. The cistern was originally about 60 feet high, from the floor to the crown of the small brick vaults built in a herring-bone pattern, but it is now reduced in size because of a 15-foot layer of mud. The structure is supported on 224 two-tiered columns bound together by stone rings and arranged in 16 rows of 14, though 12 of the columns have long been walled up. The impost capitals are plain except for monograms inscribed by the stone masons. It was traditionally believed that Philoxenus, a Roman senator who accompanied Constantine in his move to Byzantium, commissioned Binbirdirek, but investigations have shown that it was probably built in either the 5th or 6th century.

THE MAUSOLEUM OF MAHMUT II. On returning to Divan Yolu you will see on your right the domed *türbe* (mausoleum) of Mahmut II, a large tomb built in the French Empire style and completed in 1839, the year of Mahmut's death. Buried with him are his son Abdül Aziz and his grandson Abdül Hamit II.

THE KÖPRÜLÜ KÜLLIYE

On the left side of Divan Yolu stands a handsome little brick-and-stone structure housing an Ottoman library which is still used as a research center. The building, with its colonnaded portico and domed reading room, forms part of the Köprülü Cami'i, constructed between 1659 and 1660 by Mehmet Paşa and his son Fazil Ahmet Paşa, two members of the distinguished Köprülü family who both served as Grand Vizier. Along the same side of the avenue there are two other buildings of the Köprülü complex, the open *türbe* of Mehmet Paşa and the mosque of the foundation, the latter, a few steps beyond the tomb, jutting onto the sidewalk of the avenue. This building once served as the lecture hall of the *medrese*.

THE ÇEMBERLİTAŞ HAMMAM. The Turkish bath on the opposite side of Divan Yolu is one of the finest examples of the classical period. Founded in 1583 by Valide Sultan Nur Banu, the widow of Selim II and the mother of Murat III, it was originally used by both women and men, but only the men's section survived after the avenue

THE COLUMN OF CONSTANTINE

Also known as Çemberlitaş, the "hooped" Column of Constantine stands in Divan Yolu next to the baths of the same name. It has stood there since May 11, 330, the day the Emperor renamed the city Constantinople and simultaneously inaugurated this monument. It is also called the "Burnt Column" for the damage wrought during a fire of 1779. When new, the column had a square, five-step pedestal and a porphyry plinth, above which rose the seven cylinders of the shaft. Shaken by an earthquake in 416, the column was reinforced with iron hoops, now replaced by steel rings. At first it was crowned by a Corinthian capital supporting a colossal statue of Constantine, and then, after c. 1150, an immense cross resting upon a marble block and brick courses. The cross disappeared after the Conquest. Following the fire, Sultan Abdül Hamit I had encased the base in masonry up to the top of the first porphyry cylinder.

189

▲ THE GRAND BAZAAR

Birds-eye view of
the Grand Bazaar.

The Grand Bazaar consists of a vast network of covered streets and buildings. At its center rises the Old Bedestan – the secure place for valuable goods – with its little domes.

was widened in modern times. The plan, like the rest, is paradigmatic, consisting as it does of a large domed *camekan*, or reception room, which leads into a small triple-domed *soğukluk* (chamber of moderate temperature), which in turn leads to a square *hararet* (steam room).

NURUOSMANIYE CAMI'I

THE CISTERN OF YEREBATAN

From the Column of Constantine, Vezir Hanı Caddesi leads to the Nuruosmaniye Cami'i, the Mosque of the Sacred Light (*Nur*) of Osman. The *külliye*, or complex, which includes a *medrese*, library, *türbe*, and *sebil*, was commissioned in 1748 by Mahmut I and completed in 1755 under his successor, Osman III. Like most mosques influenced by the European Baroque, this one is essentially a cubic prayer hall with an arch in each of the four sides, which all support a large domed vault. The arches are round-headed, rather than ogival or pointed as in classical Ottoman architecture, and are dramatically accentuated, particularly on the exterior.

MAHMUT PAŞA CAMI'I

Early in the 20th century, when the photograph below was produced, the Grand Bazaar had just been restored after an earthquake. Looming high above the scene is Nuruosmaniye Cami'i, its style clearly influenced by the European Baroque which held sway over Turkish art during the second half of the 18th century.

The Mosque of Mahmut Paşa is situated a short distance along the same street. It was constructed in 1462 and is the oldest vizierial mosque in Istanbul. Mahmut Paşa, who commissioned it, was born into the Byzantine nobility, but before the Conquest he converted to Islam and rose in Ottoman service to become Grand Vizier under Mehmet Fatih. However, he fell from grace and was dismissed from his post and in 1474 was decapitated. The prayer hall of the mosque is a long rectangle divided at the center by an arch, which creates two square chambers each vaulted by a dome of the same size. A barrel-vaulted passage, on either side of the prayer hall, provides access to a suite of three small rooms as well as to the body of the mosque. The entrance to the building is through a porch and a narthex, or vestibule, both with five bays that run the width of the building. **THE MAUSOLEUM OF MAHMUT PAŞA.** Mahmut Paşa lies at rest in his *türbe* situated in the mosque garden. A tall octagonal structure, it is illuminated by two tiers of windows but capped by a blind dome. The upper façades are decorated with mosaics of blue and turquoise faience tiles set in wheel patterns.

> "We have drunk the Lord's sherbet, glory to the Lord
> We have crossed the sea of might, glory to the Lord."

Yunus Emre

A MOSQUE DOOR,
IN A PAINTING
BY ŞEVRET DAĞ
A pupil of Osman
Hamdi, who had
studied in the Paris
atelier of Gustave
Boulanger, Şevret
Dağ (1876–1944) is
best known for his
pictures of the
interiors of mosques.
Arguably the most
famous of these
works is the one seen
here, painted in 1911.
It shows one of the
heavy leather door-
curtains that, when
rolled down for a
religious service,
insulate the interior
from outside noise
and also prevent
unwelcome intrusions
which may disturb
the prayers within.
These curtains also
symbolize the
invisible frontier
separating the outer,
profane world from
the sacred, exclusive
world accessible
only to the faithful.
In appearance,
moreover, they
resemble the
sumptuous tapestries
of gold-embroidered
velvet that may be
hung from the
portico of the
mimbar.

THE COMPLEXES OF THE YENI ÇERILER CADDESI

THE ATIK ALI PAŞA CAMI'I. The Mosque of Atik Ali Paşa
occupies a corner of the Yeni Çeriler Caddesi slightly beyond
the Column of Constantine. Built in 1496 for Hadim Atik Ali
Paşa, eunuch and then Grand Vizier to Beyazıt II, the mosque
presents a vast basilican hall oddly divided into two unequal
parts. The larger western section is dome-vaulted and flanked
on either side by a pair of small rooms capped by cupolas.
The smaller eastern section, with its semi-dome, becomes an
apsidal space terminating in the mihrab. As in most of the
early Ottoman mosques, the corner pendentives supporting
the semidome and the four little cupolas are embellished with
stone-carved stalactites ● *78*.

THE KÜLLIYE OF KOCA SINAN PAŞA. A short distance beyond
the Atik Ali Paşa Mosque are the marble wall and iron grilles
enclosing the complex of Koca Sinan Paşa, Grand Vizier
under both Murat III and Mehmet III. This beautiful
Ottoman *külliye*, with its *medrese*, *sebil*, and *türbe*, was
completed in 1593 by Davut Ağa, who succeeded the great
Sinan as Chief Architect of the Empire. The most interesting
building is the polygonal mausoleum, its sixteen sides built of
white- and rose-colored stones surmounted by an exuberant

A street of shops
in the Spice Bazaar.

191

stalactite cornice and pierced by windows with elegant
moldings. From an entrance through a gate in the side alley, the
medrese opens onto an enchanting courtyard with a portico in
the form of an ogival arcade. The equally handsome *sebil*, or
public fountain, boasts bronze grilles which alternate with small
columns and has a deeply overhung roof.

**THE KÜLLIYE OF ÇORLULU ALI
PAŞA.** Across the alleyway from
the Koca Sinan Paşa fountain is
the Çorlulu Ali Paşa complex,
which is also surrounded by a
marble wall. Built in 1708 the
little mosque and the *medrese*
are largely classical in style,
though the capitals of the porch colonnade already show the
influence of the European Baroque. In 1711, Ali Paşa, the son-
in-law of Mustafa II, was beheaded at Mytilene on the orders of
Ahmet III, for whom he had been Grand Vizier.

THE KÜLLIYE OF KARA MUSTAFA PAŞA. Opposite Yeni Çeriler
Caddesi is the complex of Kara Mustafa Paşa of Merzifon. Its
construction had barely begun in 1663 when it came to a halt
because of the execution of its patron the Grand Vizier to
Mehmet IV, following his failure to take Vienna despite the
long Turkish siege ● *40*. The son of the executed vizier
oversaw the completion of the complex in 1690, after
which he buried Kara Mustafa Paşa's remains in the
mosque's cemetery. Stylistically its architecture is
transitional, from the classical to the Baroque, and the
complex is mainly of interest because of its octagonal
mosque, a shape rarely used for such a building. Today the
medrese houses a research institute dedicated to the poet
Yahya Kemal (1884–1958).

"The Great Bazaar has nothing on the exterior to attract the eye, or give an idea of its contents. It is an immense stone edifice of Byzantine architecture, surrounded by gray walls."

Edmondo de Amicis

THE GRAND BAZAAR

On returning to Yeni Çeriler Caddesi, cross the avenue and continue straight ahead on Çarşıkapı Sokağı, the Street of the Market Gate. This takes its name from the Kapalı Çarşı or Covered Bazaar – more commonly known in English as the Grand Bazaar – one of the most famous markets in the world, the entrance to which is at the end of Çarşıkapı Sokağı.

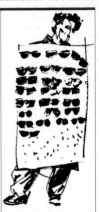

HISTORY. The Grand Bazaar was built at the command of Fatih Mehmet shortly after the Conquest. At first, it consisted merely of two *bedesten* (warehouses); merchants began setting up stores and workshops around it, thereby creating a whole warren of lanes sheltered under canvas. Dignitaries built *hans,* or caravanserais, at its edges and through them riches from all over the empire were imported. After the installation of gates and doors the bazaar became a medieval city within a city, securely locked up each night. In the course of time, the makeshift arrangements were replaced by the ogive-vaulted arcades that we know today. Gradually, the network of galleries expanded until it incorporated the two *bedesten* at the center of an immense labyrinth. From the 16th century until the 19th, the Grand Bazaar was restored and rebuilt on several occasions following earthquakes and numerous fires that ravaged that area of the city.

THE STRUCTURE OF THE GRAND BAZAAR. An 1880 census reveals the Kapalı Çarşı to have contained 4,399 shops, 2,195 workshops, 497 stalls, 20 *hans*, 12 storehouses, 18 fountains, a primary school, a tomb, and a *mescit*, or small mosque. Among the 1,742 businesses counted in 1976, there were 472 jewelers, 181 shoemakers, 154 tailors or dressmakers, 131 tourist shops, 129 dealers in furniture and decorations, 116 rug merchants, and 56 restaurants, cafés, and tearooms. Also present are public toilets, two banks, and a tourist information office. On first entering, the great market resembles a bewildering maze, but closer acquaintance

THE GRAND BAZAAR, A CITY WITHIN A CITY ✪
This comprises 75 acres of alleyways spreading out from the old city center. The vaulted *Şark Kahvesi*, at the end of Fesçiler Cad., is thronged with traders and their customers. Further to the north, do not miss the old *han*: take a look round the workshops and get a guide to take you up to the cupolas in their roofs.

THE WOMEN OF THE GRAND BAZAAR
Watercolor by A. Preziosi (1816–82). In the 19th century the Grand Bazaar was still one of the very few places where women appeared in public; certainly it was a place they frequented often and with enthusiasm. Invariably they would be accompanied by a servant or a eunuch, and they would always be fully veiled. Théophile Gautier wrote that "their apple-green or sky-blue feredges, their dense and carefully closed yashmaks, their little boots of soft yellow morocco shod in street clogs of the same color have Muslim written all over them."

▲ THE GRAND BAZAAR

BOOTBLACKS' BOXES
These boxes, made of wood covered with sheets of engraved brass and often embellished with photographs, hold shoe polishes of every color. In Istanbul, bootblacks show up almost everywhere, especially in or around hotels and the Grand Bazaar.

Evliya Çelebi dates the beginning of the gem market to the period of Mehmet the Conqueror. "The Old Bedesten," he wrote, in the mid-17th century,

"held the entire wealth of the Ottomans, and the assets of the high and mighty of the Empire were hoarded there. In its basement were hundreds of storerooms with iron gates." The Old Bedesten had been constructed to house goldsmiths and jewelers. The goldsmiths worked in silver as well as gold, while the jewelers cut and sold emeralds, brilliants, diamonds, rubies, and other precious stones.

reveals it to be a fairly orderly, gridlike arrangement of streets and squares. Traditionally, shopkeepers clustered together according to the kind of goods or services they offered, and the names of the Bazaar's arcades – such as the Street of the Turban-Makers and the Street of the Sword-Cutlers – bear this out, even when the colorful trades they evoke have vanished. Today jewelers, silversmiths, shoemakers, and ironmongers, among others, still occupy the arcades named for them.

THE OLD AND THE NEW BEDESTEN

The Iç Bedesten, which is also known as the Jewelers' Bedesten, or Cevahir Bedesteni, constitutes the very heart of the Grand Bazaar. It is made up of 15 dome-vaulted halls arranged in rows of 3 units each, supported by 8 fat pillars called "elephants' feet." Intended for the sale of the most valuable merchandise, its shops and warehouses were from the beginning fitted with heavy iron gates that could be locked at night, when 70 soldiers stood watch. During the period witnessed by Evliya Çelebi (mid-17th century), the Old Bedesten housed merchants of luxurious fabrics such as silks and velvets, turban-makers, armorers, booksellers, jewelers specializing in precious stones, money changers, and rug merchants. Today the Old Bedesten is dominated by antiquarians dealing in old coins and brass or copper trays and utensils, weaponry and other valuable items from the Ottoman era. Of course, rug dealers also proliferate, as do tourist shops offering a range of objects handcrafted from copper or pewter. The four gates to the Old Bedesten (one on each side) bear the names of the businesses operating there and in neighboring galleries. Over the Gate of the Goldsmiths appears a bas-relief representing the imperial eagle of the Comnenus dynasty that ruled Byzantium in the 11th and 12th centuries. (The Palaeologus dynasty, who held power during the last two centuries of the Byzantine Empire took the two-headed eagle as their emblem ● 32). Since the Old Bedesten was very likely commissioned by Fatih himself, the Byzantine sculpture must have been salvaged from some other monument and set into the Ottoman structure, a common occurrence in Istanbul.

THE NEW BEDESTEN. Called Sandal Bedesteni in Turkish, after a fabric with a particular motif woven in Bursa, the New Bedesten is situated in the southeast corner of the

Grand Bazaar. Fatih Mehmet had it constructed towards the end of his reign, as the rapid expansion of Ottoman commerce outstripped the capacity of the Old Bedesten. The immense roof of this building comprises 20 brick domes resting on 12 massive pillars arranged in 3 rows of 4 each. In Ottoman times, the New Bedesten was the center of the silk business, and it eventually accepted commerce in other fabrics, in mirrors, and, as in the Old Bedesten, in arms embellished with precious stones. The principal activity of this Bedesten suffered from the profound changes that occurred in textile manufacture after the Industrial Revolution, which caused one stall and shop after another to close. In 1913, the municipality created in their place a variety of public services, as well

as an auction hall, which is particularly lively on Monday and Thursday afternoons, the times reserved for the sale of carpets.

The stores in the Grand Bazaar are owned and operated by individuals, but the New or Sandal Bedesten belongs to the municipality of Istanbul which restored the structure, taking great care to keep its traditional seats and cupboards. Auctions are held twice a week.

SHOPPING IN THE GRAND BAZAAR

CARPETS AND KILIMS. Those eager to take home a Turkish carpet ● *60* will be able to choose from a huge variety in the many carpet shops of the Grand Bazaar, particularly in Sahaflar Caddesi, the first arcade north of the Old Bedesten. Buying a carpet involves a certain amount of ritual, and given the length of the negotiations it is considered poor taste to begin them if the interest in buying is only half-hearted. Indeed, the ritual of taking tea signifies that one is dealing in good faith.

JEWELRY. Jewelers own the greatest number of shops in the Grand Bazaar. In addition to gold jewelry set with precious stones, they also sell handcrafted pieces in silver based on traditional designs.

COPPER AND LEATHER. In Turkey, leather work has always been an important craft, and today it is an industry. The Grand Bazaar offers leather garments in the latest fashion as well as pelisses of the Mongol type made of pigskin.

PIPES AND NARGHILES. Pipe-smoking is rare in Turkey, even though the country is

ÇAY ! ÇAY !...
Every week the merchants of the Grand Bazaar purchase tokens at a stall that only sells tea. Around ten merchants are linked to this shop by telephone; they place their orders and the shop delivers tea to their stalls, where they in turn serve it to their clients.

195

▲ THE GRAND BAZAAR

Seals of the Ottoman
Sultans

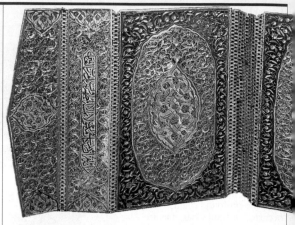

In the mid-19th century, Théophile Gautier wrote of the Grand Bazaar: "There are jewelers whose gemstones are put away in safes or in glass cases placed beyond the reach of thieves. In these dark boutiques, rather like cobbler's workshops, riches of the most incredible sort abound." Today the treasures of the Ottoman Empire are in the Topkapı Museum, and the Grand Bazaar no longer yields up superb 16th-century Korans transcribed by calligraphers, bound in guilloched leather, decoratively engraved, and bound.

THE GRAND BAZAAR TODAY
Since the devastating fire of 1954, the Bazaar has been modernized, the lighting of its walls, arcades, and cupolas improved and glass showcases added. Some of the names still indicate the kind of merchandise offered there: The Street of the Jewelers, of Carpets, of Leather, even of Jeans! They all remain busy throughout the day.

extremely rich in meerschaum, a tender, light calcareous stone much favored for making tobacco pipes with bowls. It softens the harshness of the tobacco and absorbs the nicotine, gradually coloring the pipe bowl in a rich array of tones, from ivory to deep black. The Grand Bazaar boasts two or three serious pipe merchants in whose stock one can find not only an important selection of traditional pipes, but also intricately sculpted ones, representing everything from the head of a bearded, beturbanned Turk to an eagle's claw and a sleigh drawn by reindeer. In the Egyptian Bazaar, the prices are lower, but so is the quality of both the work and the meerschaum. For centuries the Turks have made an art of smoking, especially in their use of the narghile. However, the time has long passed when young harem women indulged themselves with precious objects of engraved crystal covered with rose petals. Today, the cigarette has become a tough competitor to the elaborate narghile, an impressive instrument that can be as high as 4 feet, not to mention the 6-feet-long copper tube through which the smoke is drawn after being cooled in the water. Nevertheless, there are still two or three public places in Istanbul where one can smoke the water pipe using flavorsome *tömkı*, a tobacco grown on the shores of the Black Sea. Dry and rough-cut, the substance releases its powerful aroma once it has been humidified, rolled into a compact ball, placed in a small terra-cotta bowl, and then burned under a hot coal. The Nargileci on Çorlulu Pasajı is an excellent place to experiment with the narghile. Almost invisible from the street, this café occupies the courtyard of a former *medrese*. After taking a seat at one of the wrought-iron table, you can smoke, talk, and play *tavla* while drinking Rize tea from little balloon-shaped glasses, or *elma çay* ("apple tea") made from a chemical powder, which the people of Istanbul are especially partial to.

THE CARAVANSERAIS

The Grand Bazaar was once surrounded on all four sides, even in adjacent neighborhoods, by some thirty *hans*, or warehouses, in which merchants and craftsmen stored their goods. Following the earthquake of 1894, which destroyed much of the area, many of the warehouses were moved farther away, with the result that only thirteen remain next to the Grand Bazaar. A number of these continue to serve their original purpose, while the rest house a wide range of workshops and stores. Among the latter, the finest may be the ZINCIRLI HANI, situated near the northeast corner of the Grand Bazaar, which

houses carpet merchants and antique dealers. Many of the *hans* outside the Grand Bazaar line the streets leading from the Bazaar to the Golden Horn. Two of them worth special notice are the Valide Han, built in 1651 by the dowager Sultana Kösem, and the Büyük Yeni Han, commissioned by Mustafa III in 1764.

THE HANS
A number of traditional *hans*, or warehouses, cluster all about the Grand Bazaar. It is in their shops that many of the goods sold in the Grand Bazaar are made. Thus, at the Kalcılar Han, which specializes in silver, the craftsmen are busily at work upstairs. The Büyük Yeni Han is entered on the third floor, and there, near the entrance, one can buy the little bird houses that the people of Istanbul like to place on their balconies.

AROUND THE GRAND BAZAAR

A gate in the northeast corner of the market opens onto the Mahmut Paşa Yokuşu.

THE HAMMAM OF MAHMUT PAŞA. About a hundred yards down the street is an imposing hammam within the Mahmut Paşa complex. Completed in 1476, two years after the death of Mahmut Paşa, this bathhouse is the oldest in Istanbul after that of Gedik Ahmet Paşa. Like most of the large Ottoman public baths, this one originally served both women and men. However, the women's section was demolished to make way for the *han* next door.

THE ÇUHACILAR HANI QUARTER. Turning back on Mahmut Paşa Yokuşu and then left along Çuhacılar Hanı Sokağı, you will encounter the gateway to the *han* from which the street takes its name, at the edge of a quarter whose labyrinthine lanes date from the 18th century. As Çuhacılar Hanı Sokağı becomes Çarşıkapı Nuruosmaniye Caddesi, the street runs along the east flank of the Grand Bazaar. On the left we come to Nuruosmaniye Sokağı, entering it through the courtyard just opposite the main gateway to the Grand Bazaar. At

THE BOOK MARKET
From the Nuruosmaniye gate, Kalpakçılar Caddesi runs across the Grand Bazaar to the Bayazıt gate, where, turning to the right and crossing Çardırçılar

Caddesi, is the entrance to the Sahaflar Çarşısı, the ancient and still busy book market of Istanbul. Once built of wood, the shops and stalls that line the charming old square were reconstructed in the 1960's. On display are a vast number of secondhand books in every language, rare Korans, works of history, and cheap, recently published paperbacks. Refreshment is available at the tree-shaded Çay Bahçesi, a tea and coffee house popular with students from the university nearby.

the next corner we turn right onto Kalpakçılar Başı Caddesi, the main artery through the Bazaar that continues along the south side of the market to the upper end, concluding at the gateway in the southwest corner. Turning right at the exit, go along Çadırçılar Caddesi a little way and then make a left turn through Hakkaklar Kapısı, an ancient stone gateway known in English as the "Gate of the Engravers".

THE SAHAFLAR ÇARŞISI

A flight of steps leads us to an ancient vine-shaded courtyard. This is the Sahaflar Çarşısı, a picturesque and noisy market in whose shops bibliophiles can find not only secondhand books but also new editions. One of the oldest markets in Istanbul, the Sahaflar Çarşısı occupies the site of the Chartoprateia, which was the book and paper market of Byzantium. Following the Conquest, turban-makers and metal-engravers set up shop there, the latter trade accounting for the name of the stone portal leading to the market: Hakkaklar Kapısı. Not until the 18th century did booksellers begin to abandon the Covered or Grand Bazaar (where a street is still named after them) and make their headquarters in the courtyard. Shortly thereafter, the legislation controlling printing and publishing allowed the trade to expand its activity enormously, and thus take over the entire market, henceforth known as the Sahaflar Çarşısı. Throughout the 19th century and into the 20th it would dominate the sale and distribution of books in the Ottoman Empire. During the last fifty years, however, the Sahaflar Çarşısı has suffered from the spread of

modern bookshops and libraries elsewhere in the city. However, it still takes pride of place as the world's oldest market for publications on Turkey. A bust of Ibrahim Mütererrika, the first printer of books in the Turkish language (1732), has recently been installed in the garden at the center of the square.

Beyazit Meydani

Passing through Sahaflar Çarşısı brings you into the outer courtyard of the *külliye* of the Beyazıt Mosque. This complex virtually dominates the vast and somewhat irregular square that sprawls over the Third Hill. A delightful open-air café provides a good place to have lunch. Originally, this was a coffeehouse frequented by the Janissaries – that formidable élite corps of the Imperial Army – who had their main barracks in this district. The old coffeehouse survived until the 1960's, shaded by an enormous *çınar* or plane tree – the "tree of idleness" as the poet said – under which intellectuals loved to while away their time. Since the construction of the Beyazıt *külliye* in the early 16th century the complex has been the favorite outdoor market among the people of Istanbul. Recently the throngs of noisy local pedlars and hawkers have been joined by similar groups of tradesmen from Eastern Europe.

The Mosque of the Beyazit complex. This *külliye* has scarcely changed since Evliya Çelebi, writing in the mid-17th century, described it in his *Book of Travels*: "The inner and outer courts of the Beyazıt Cami'i are ringed about by stalls offering every kind of goods or service. There is also a public kitchen, a refectory, and a hostel for travelers, as well as a school for instruction in the Koran. The courtyard, which can be entered through six different gateways, is planted with majestic trees in whose shade thousands of people earn their livelihood by selling merchandise of the greatest variety."

The Hammam of Gedik Paşa. On the other side of Yeni Çeriler Caddesi, in the Gedik Paşa Caddesi, stands the oldest hammam in Istanbul, dating from 1475. The man whose name it bears, Gedik Ahmet Paşa, was Chief Vizier under Süleyman the Magnificent. He was also commander of the fleet that captured Azov, the Greek island of Lefkada, and the Italian port of Otranto. The *soğukluk* of this hammam – which is a monumental dome-vaulted space flanked by alcoves and cubicles – is considerably larger than most. A feature worth special attention is the alcove on the right, which has an elaborate vault with numerous carved-stone stalactites.

The Grand Bazaar in the 19th century
In Julia Pardoe's *Beauties of the Bosphorus*, published in the 19th century, the Bazaar was illustrated with the above engraving by W.H. Bartlett.

The arcaded streets of the Bazaar
Along every lane of the Grand Bazaar, tourists are assailed from all sides in an array of languages babbled by zealous vendors touting every conceivable sort of merchandise. Scores of shops display jumbled masses of junk jewelry next to fine gems, piles of rugs, sumptuous fabrics, and gleaming copper objects.

199

▲ THE BEYAZIDIYE AND THE SÜLEYMANIYE

THE BEYAZIDIYE

The Beyazıdiye Cami'i was built in 1501–6 by the architect Yakub-şah bin Sultan; his only other known work is the caravanserai at Bursa. The Beyazıdiye marks the beginning of the classical period of Ottoman architecture, which would continue for more than two centuries. Two minarets decorated with geometric motifs are off-center on the outer corners, reinforcing the originality and architectural power of this mosque. In front of the mosque is an attractive courtyard, with magnificent entrances on three sides. A peristyle of twenty ancient columns – porphyry, verd antique, and Syenitic granite – forms an arcade picked out by alternating red-and-white or black-and-white voussoirs and a portico covered by twenty-four small domes. At the center stands a beautifully ornamented ablution fountain. Stalactite moldings bring

The Beyazıdiye was founded by Sultan Beyazıt II, Mehmet the Conqueror's son and successor, and the mosque complex was the second of its kind to be built in Istanbul. The first *külliye*, constructed by Sultan Mehmet II shortly after the capture of Byzantine Constantinople, was destroyed by an earthquake in 1766, and the mosque that took its place dates from 1771. The Beyazıt Cami'i is therefore Istanbul's oldest imperial mosque still in existence.

drama to the capitals, cornices, and niches. The harmonious proportions, the wealth of restrained decoration, and the brilliance of the variegated marbles combine to give the

> "He whose feet have been covered with dust
> from the paths of the Lord will be saved by Him
> from the fires of Hell."
>
> Beyazit II

courtyard a charm unlike anything else in Istanbul.

THE INTERIOR.
There is a grandiose entrance to the prayer hall. The basic plan of its interior is a smaller, simplified version of the one already seen at Haghia Sophia ● 74. As in the basilica, the central dome of the Beyazıdiye (55 feet in diameter) and its two flanking semi-domes on the east and west define the space of the nave, the latter supplemented by side aisles on the south and north. Free of upper galleries, the aisles open directly onto the central space, the division between them marked only by the four corner pillars supporting the great cupola. The sultan's loge, raised upon columns of rare, precious marbles, is atypically placed on the right of the mimbar rather than on the left. Along the west side of the interior runs a broad corridor divided into bays that, even while domeless, project from the mass of the building to form a kind of narthex. At the southern end of the corridor there is a small library, which was an 18th-century addition by Şeyh-ül Islam Veliyüttin Efendi.

THE OLD WOODEN HOUSES OF THE BEYAZIT QUARTER
The shape of the traditional Ottoman house is characterized by the *çikma*, similar to a bay-window, which extends from the main wall. It is an extension of the *başoda* or main living room of the house, invariably on an upper story. The design of the façade is almost always the same – two-tiered bays of three windows each, plus one on either side. Conservationists nostalgic for the past and conscious of the historical value of the houses have attempted to restore them in the true spirit of their time.

THE BEYAZIDIYE COMPLEX

In addition to the mosque, the *külliye* includes a *medrese*, an *imaret*, a hammam, an elementary school, and several mausoleums ● 79.

THE MAUSOLEUM OF BEYAZIT II. The cemetery lies behind the mosque, and here the remains of Beyazıt II rest in a simple, well-proportioned *türbe* constructed of limestone accented in verd antique. The nearby tomb of Selçuk Hatun, the Sultan's daughter, is even simpler, particularly by comparison with the French Empire structure erected not far away for Koca Mustafa Reşit Paşa, the Grand Vizier to Abdül Mecit and Tanzimat reform leader who died in 1858 ● 41. Sinan's long-demolished shopping arcade, installed below the cemetery, has now been reconstructed precisely in keeping with the original plan.

THE FORUM OF THEODOSIUS

Embedded in the base of the wall bordering Ordu Caddesi are ancient bas-reliefs from the late Roman period, one of which is upside down and carved with a series of centurions. These remains are all that survive from a Roman column that once stood in the Forum

Theodosius, which extended to the top of the Third Hill. Traces of it can be found more or less everywhere along Ordu Caddesi on the far west side of Beyazıt Meydanı.

THE MEKTEP. Behind the bazaar is the double *sıbyan mektebi*, or primary school, a building with two domes and a porch that is the oldest Koran school in Istanbul.

THE IMARET. The Beyazıdiye *imaret*, a public kitchen that also included a caravanserai, still stands in the outer courtyard facing the northern minaret. Restored in 1852, at the command of Abdül Hamit II, the Beyazıt *imaret* now houses a research library for journalists.

BEYAZIT SQUARE. The main entrance to the University of Istanbul can be found on the northern edge of Beyazıt or Hürriyet Meydanı, where the institution has been situated since the early years of the Turkish Republic. Dominating the university courtyard is a 100-feet-high tower, erected by Mahmut II as a lookout tower for fires. It remained in service until the 1960's. Some thirty years ago one could still climb to the summit and enjoy the breathtaking panoramic view of Istanbul. Today the tower is closed to the public.

THE CALLIGRAPHY MUSEUM ▲ *206*. The Beyazıdiye *medrese* occupies the western edge of the square. Here, as in all classical *medrese*, the students' cubby-holes completely line the four sides of the courtyard, while the *dershane*, or lecture hall, stands directly opposite the main entrance. Now restored, the building shelters the municipal library and the Calligraphy Museum. In one of the cells a calligraphy workshop has been reconstructed, complete with wax figures representing a master teaching his pupils this profoundly Islamic art.

THE THIRD HILL

The Beyazıdiye hammam lies a little farther along the main avenue, here called Ordu Caddesi. Directly opposite the hammam are two Ottoman *hans*. The one on the left, built during the reign of Fatih Mehmet, is the newly rebuilt Şimkeş Hanı – Han of the Silver-Thread Spinners – while that on the right, dating from c. 1740, was commissioned by Seyyit Hasan Paşa, Grand Vizier to Mahmut I. A further 350 yards or so along Ordu Caddesi is the *külliye* of Ragip Paşa, Grand Vizier under

Mustafa III (1757–74). Erected in 1762, this small complex is probably the work of the architect Mehmet Tahir Ağa. Its main building is a lending library. There is a *mektep* over the gates. Two blocks farther along Ordu Caddesi you come to the Lâleli Cami'i – the Tulip Mosque – which is arguably the most beautiful Baroque mosque in Istanbul.

THE TULIP MOSQUE

The Lâleli Cami'i – popularly known as the Tulip or Lily Mosque – was built between 1759 and 1763 at the command of Mustafa III. The architect, Mehmet Tahi Ağa, built it on a high terrace overlooking a maze of small shops and serpentine lanes. In the middle of the complex there is a large hall with a fountain at the center and four enormous piers. The plan of the mosque itself is an octagon inscribed within a rectangle. The walls are load-bearing, except on the west side, where columns support a gallery. On this side as well, the wall is decorated with *opus sectile* medallions made of rare marbles and such semi-precious stones as onyx, jasper, and lapis lazuli.

CALLIGRAPHY
Handwriting is considered to be one of the major art forms of Ottoman and Islamic cultures, intimately linked as it is with the copying of the Koran. Moreover, Arabic script lends itself quite naturally to a number of stylistic variations.
▲ 206.

Itinerant pedlars proliferate along the main streets and squares of Istanbul, among them watermelon vendors like the one here.

Galata port at the end of the 19th century.

A lid from a box of Turkish delight.

AHMET III, THE TULIP KING
By the time Ahmet III ascended the throne in 1703, the empire was already in decline. Tired of war, the new Sultan very quickly became known as an aesthete dedicated

to a pursuit of the finer pleasures. Ahmet III sponsored many fêtes, and patronized art, music, poetry, and literature. During his reign, five libraries were founded, as well as Turkey's first printing house, established in 1724. The Sultan's infatuation with tulips went to such extremes that the second half of his reign, beginning in 1717, has come to be known as Lâle Devri, meaning the "Tulip Period." The craze for this flower, which was traded like gold, had started a century earlier in the Netherlands, where the first tulips had been imported from Anatolia in 1559. The Janissaries forced Ahmet III to abdicate in 1730, because they were fed up with his Western tastes and his weakness in military matters. His son, Sultan Mustafa III, who ascended the throne in 1757, commissioned the Tulip Mosque.

Elsewhere, extravagantly colored, variegated marbles clad every wall with vibrant effect. The *külliye* includes a *medrese*, an *imaret*, a *han*, and a hammam, as well as a *türbe* in which Mustafa III and his son Selim III (1789–1807) are buried.

THE MOSQUE OF THE PRINCE

Fethiye Bey Caddesi opens into Fevziye Caddesi, which in turn leads to Şehzade Başı Caddesi. Follow it to the left. On the right is the monument that gives the avenue its name: the Şehzade Cami'i, or the Mosque of the Prince. This great complex was commissioned by Süleyman the Magnificent in memory of his eldest son, Prince Mehmet, who died of smallpox in 1543 at the age of twenty-one. The commission went to Sinan ▲ *314*, who completed it in 1548. It was the first of his large-scale, imperial *külliye*. The mosque is entered through an elegant *avlu* with a portico running entirely around the four sides and, naturally, a *şadırvan* at the center. The forecourt ranks among Sinan's greatest triumphs, and incorporates a brilliant innovation by the architect: colonnaded galleries the full length of the north and south façades in order to conceal the buttressing.

THE INTERIOR. All but unique among imperial mosques, the Şehzade Cami'i has a vast and empty prayer hall, with neither columns nor galleries. Sinan was determined to centralize the plan, and so took the bold step of extending the enclosed space not with two half-domes, as at Haghia Sophia, but instead with four. The resulting symmetry along both axes produces a somewhat bland, uninspiring effect. Moreover, the four pillars supporting the dome look a bit stranded in the middle of such an enormous empty space, and their inevitable monumentality appears rather out of place. However, the austere simplicity of the interior is impressive.

THE TÜRBE GARDEN. In the walled garden behind the mosque there are half a dozen tombs, the largest of which is the sumptuous monument to Prince Mehmet, built by Sinan in 1543 to 1544. The interior is remarkably beautiful, even by Istanbul standards. However, it is not always open to the public, and neither are the other mausoleums in the garden, two of which merit close attention: that of Süleyman's son-in-law, the Grand Vizier Rüstem Paşa, built by Sinan in 1561, and the other in 1603 by Dalgiç Ahmet, for Ibrahim Paşa,

> "This temple has been constructed for true believers by the glorious deputy of Allah, the tenth of the Ottoman Emperors, in accordance with the sacred laws of the Koran."

Tomb of Süleyman

Murat III's son-in-law and Grand Vizier. Both are embellished with superb Iznik tiles. The complex's *medrese* is situated in the northwest corner of the *avlu*. The *imaret* and *mektep* are found in Dede Efendi Sokağı, the street leading off Şehzadebaşı Caddesi just beyond the *türbe* garden.

THE MEDRESE OF DAMAT IBRAHIM PAŞA.
Opposite the garden of the Prince's Mosque, at the intersection of Dede Efendi Sokağı and Şehzade Başı Caddesi, is a *medrese* with a charming *sebil* at the corner. The elegant complex was constructed in 1720 at the command of Nevşehirli Damat Ibrahim Paşa, son-in-law of Ahmet III and Grand Vizier (1718–30) during the golden era of Lâle Devri – "the Tulip Period."

THE KALENDERHANE CAMI'I

In the 1970's, the Dumbarton Oaks Society, under the directorship of C. Lee Striker, established that the building now known as the Kalenderhane Mosque was originally the Church of Theotokos Kyriotissa – Our Lady, Mother of God – a structure dating from the 12th century ● *75*. Its conversion into an Islamic place of worhip took place shortly after the Conquest ● *34*, when it was assigned to an order of dervishes, which gave it the present Turkish name.

THE MARKET OF ADDICTS. A vaulted passage alongside the Kalenderhane Cami'i runs under the Valens Aqueduct. From there turn right and then left into Süleymaniye Caddesi. At the end of this street looms the mighty Süleymaniye Cami'i.

THE RÜSTEM PAŞA
The interior of the Mosque of the Prince is decorated with white calligraphy on a blue background.

POETRY AND GEOMETRY
The two minarets rising from the two western corners of the Şehzade Cami'i are justly famous for their bas-reliefs carved with geometric motifs, and for their *şerife,* or balconies, whose complex fretwork is inlaid here and there with terra-cotta. As a symbol of Islam, the minaret was seen as competing with the bell towers of churches, particularly in a city like Istanbul, where mosques appeared at the same time as a new empire. This explains the concern for their

embellishment. The most beautiful of them reflect the high-art status of geometry in Islam. This aesthetic is a profoundly original one in which the very logic of the forms lends itself to infinite variation according to the principles of geometric symmetry. The crowning cupolas and semi-domes, with their accentuated ribs and openwork cornices, cascade through a series of contrasts and repetitions that is breathtaking in its virtuosity.

The development of oriental calligraphy is closely linked to the celebration of the verses of the Koran and the word (*hadis* in Turkish) of the prophet Mohammed. The calligraphers Ibn Mukle in the 10th century, Ibn Bervah in the 11th century, and Yakut in the 13th century are the main reference sources for sacred writing. In Turkey it is only under Beyazıt II that an innovative master appeared in the person of Sheik Hamdullah (1429–1520). He would later be considered the founder of Ottoman calligraphy. Hamdullah was a great master of the *nesih* style. The writing presented, *sülüs-nesih*, interprets an aphorism of Ali, the son-in-law of the prophet: "It is through uprightness that man gains access to the richness of the great men."

AHMET KARAHISARI
Originally from the Anatolian city of Afyo-Kara-Hisar (The Black Opium Fortress), Ahmet Karahısarı (who died in 1556) was soon nicknamed "Light of Writing" for the perfection of his compositions. The greatness of Karahısarı is due to the epic audacity of his large, alluring horizontal and vertical strokes. In the style exercise presented here, the author has added in the margin: "Each letter is like another ocean, each line like another wave, and each punctuation mark like another pearl."

ANONYMOUS CALLIGRAPHY FROM THE 19TH CENTURY

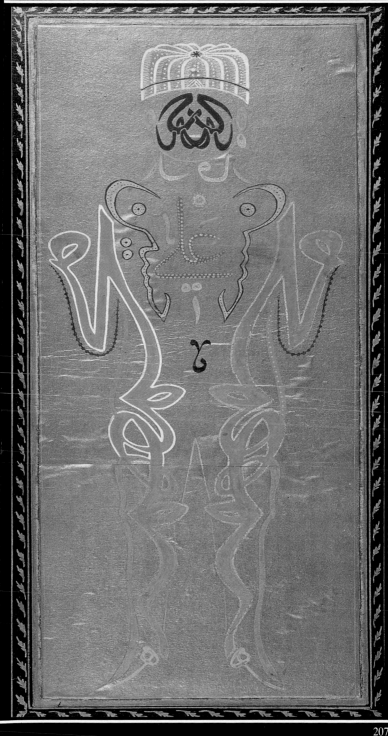

Among the many different styles, which encourage reflection and thought, the anthropomorphic writing developed at the

Bektachis school is perhaps the most interesting. The aim of their skilled calligraphers is to celebrate the divine nature of the human body through their style and the interlacing of letters, in the name of Ali and his martyred sons. Ali, the son-in-law of the prophet, symbolizes the martyr for many Muslim congregations because he was murdered along with his two sons in the city of Karbelâ.

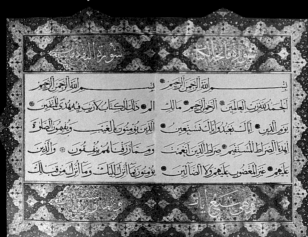

CALLIGRAPHY FROM THE 16TH CENTURY

PORTRAIT OF A PAINTER (C. 1480)
Painters, calligraphers, and illuminators worked in the *Nakkashane* (imperial workshop) created by Mehmet II after the Conquest.

NECMEDDIN OKYAY (1883–1976)
Of the contemporary calligraphers, Okyay and Tugrakes Hakki are among the last exponents of the Istanbul school. Like Hamdullah, his 15th-century predecessor, Okyay excels in writing techniques. He has cultivated 400 varieties of roses which are as dear to him as his writing.

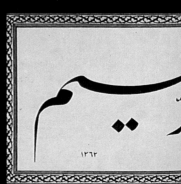

MÜSENNA CALLIGRAPHY OF THE 19TH CENTURY

Hurufism lived on in handwriting. Braving the orthodox ban on the figurative representation of human beings, a distinct calligraphic art was born in the hurufi drawings which combine letters to produce drawings of human faces or sacred animals. A game of mirrors in which images are multiplied, results in a knotting together of Man, God, and the Word.

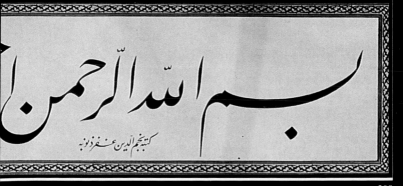

Sultan Ahmet III (1673–1736) was a renowned calligrapher who became a master in the art of *tugra*. Sultans practiced this art from a very young age, and it was considered to be a written emanation of their power. Learned calligraphers were on good terms with the sultans, and they held a privileged position in the seraglio hierarchy.

The calligrapher sits cross-legged and uses his left hand as a support, holding a felt pad on which he places his paper, while in his right hand he uses a reed dipped in a traditional ink well, the *divit*. The writing action involves a double movement of the hands, requiring the calligrapher to control his breathing so as not to upset the line. Success depends upon the perfect co-ordination of all of these factors at the same time. The calligrapher keeps his hands in shape like a musician, with hours of repeated exercises. The accuracy of each piece of work is checked against a drafting system consisting of a lozenge shape traced using the inked reed in order to calculate vertically or horizontally the size of each of the letters.

The manufacture of black or colored inks, both dense and smooth, involves a fairly complicated process using tallow, grenadine blossoms, vine sap, and various other ingredients, heated and mixed in the correct proportions. The quality of the ink is tested by dipping a hedgehog spine into it. Of the fourteen types of paper used, that from Samarkand is the best. If the calligrapher so desires, he might dye his chosen paper with mixtures prepared from ingredients such as linden, tea, saffron, tobacco, straw, onion skins, and bitter pomegranate skin. The perfect sheen of the ink on the paper is due to egg, as well as different types of polishing materials, such as marble, shells, glass, and ivory.

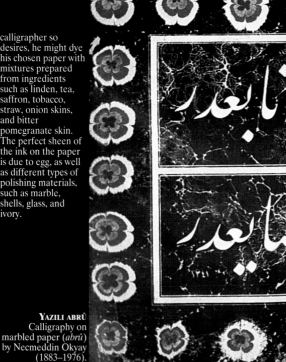

YAZILI ABRÛ
Calligraphy on marbled paper (*abrû*) by Necmeddin Okyay (1883–1976).

> "Muhamet is a man, but as different from his peers,
> as the ruby is different from the stones."

Calligraphy by Mehmet Celaleddin

Calligraphers use a range of shades of color, from light to dark, in their compositions. The masterpieces of calligraphy are more than equal to the magnificent settings they may decorate, whether palaces, mosques, tombs and fountains, or whether they are incorporated into paintings or sculpture. Calligraphy is a distinct art form, with its own masters and fervent admirers. In the past as today the most famous works fetched considerable prices.

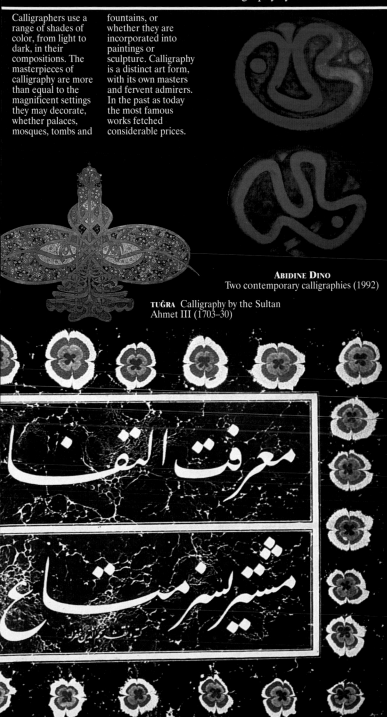

ABIDINE DINO
Two contemporary calligraphies (1992)

TUĞRA Calligraphy by the Sultan
Ahmet III (1703–30)

MOSQUES AND TÜRBE

The Ottoman calligraphers used
their superb writing to decorate
the beautiful blue faience of the
mosques and the *türbe* of the
princes or viziers. In the 19th and
20th centuries the calligraphers
made signs on wood or
calligraphic paintings on slabs of
glass which decorated the walls of
houses and occasionally the
windows of shops and cafés.

BEKTACHI CALLIGRAPHY
This inscription of Bektachi inspiration unites the names of the prophet Mohammed and Ali, his son-in-law. They are superimposed here to form a visual and spiritual unity which constitutes an act of faith.

In the Ottoman Empire a popular type of imagery, often based on the letters of the alphabet, developed parallel to the work of the calligraphic scholar, which was destined for an élite or for the requirements of a monumental art. This imagery allows for all types of caprice and charm. In this way prayers can be transformed into mosques, ewers, lions, or swans, or sometimes into a sacred character. This tradition has not completely disappeared today and one can still find inexpensive examples of the style in the Istanbul markets, in the form of paintings on glass or lithographic reproductions.

Because of the adaptablity of its shape, writing composed in a circular fashion was used to decorate swords, ceramics, and talismans.

AH! LOVE According to a popular tradition, the union of the Arab letters "A" and "H" form the exclamation "Ah!" These two letters express pain or regret and are almost always accompanied by the word "love". In the two cells of the letter "H" nest eyes that cry over their disappointments in love.

The image of the headgear of a brotherhood master is pictured on a ceremonial stool. The turbans and the various ways of covering the head define the hierarchies and functions in Ottoman society, and accompany each person to the grave, which is itself "hatted" according to the rank and function of the deceased.

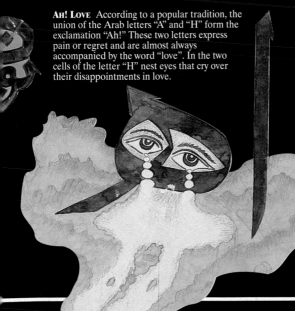

▲ THE BEYAZIDIYE AND THE SÜLEYMANIYE

THE SÜLEYMANIYE, SINAN'S MASTERPIECE ✪
This is one of the biggest and most beautiful of all the great Imperial architect's buildings (after the Selimiye in Edirne). The pyramidal structure, the interplay of lines and forms and the interior's architectural unity all make it a classic symbol of Ottoman religious art. The four minarets and their ten balconies signify that Süleyman was the 4th Sultan of Istanbul and the 10th of the Ottoman dynasty.

THE CITY AND ITS INHABITANTS
The reign of Süleyman saw the construction of numerous mosques throughout the new quarters. The city was organized so that each quarter had its own mosque and market square. Several quarters together made up a municipality. With the arrival of the Muslims, many churches were converted into mosques. The population of Stamboul grew steadily throughout the 16th century. In 1554, there were 40,000 Christians, 4,000 Jews, and 60,000 Turks, with 10,000 more Turks in the suburbs.

Entering on the south side of the Süleymaniye Cami'i, you proceed through the Tiryaki Çarşısı – the Street of the Addicts. And indeed it appears that in Ottoman times the tea shops of the *medrese*, on the sidewalk to the left, dispensed not only tea, coffee, and tobacco but also opium.

THE MOSQUE OF SÜLEYMAN THE MAGNIFICENT

The complex of the Süleymaniye Cami'i was the fourth imperial *külliye* constructed in Istanbul. Although not as vast as Sultan Fatih Mehmet's complex, it surpasses all three of its precedessors in splendor and majesty. Indeed, the Süleymaniye is without question one of the greatest works of its architect, Sinan. Begun in 1550, the mosque was completed in 1557, with two more years required in order to finish the entire *külliye*. The mosque itself is surrounded by a vast precinct, enclosed by a wall. Arranged around it, in neighboring streets, are the other parts of the complex. Four slender minarets stand like sentinels at the corners of the forecourt. The two taller ones, abutting the mosque, are furnished with three *şerefe* each, while the two shorter ones have only two balconies each. The magnificent dome is flanked on the east and west by two semi-domes and, on the north and south, by arches with tympana pierced by windows. Within the mosque, the central cupola is borne by four gigantic pillars reinforced by thick buttresses, which Sinan cleverly embedded in the north and south walls so that they project equally both inside and out. To mask this projection he constructed an arcaded gallery between the buttresses. The gallery has two tiers on both the outside and inside, with twice as many columns on the upper level. All in all, the design of the building was distinctly innovative and quite magnificent.

THE INTERIOR. The prayer hall, a 230 by 200-feet rectangle, is vaulted by a central dome

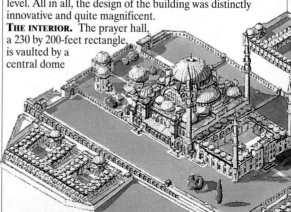

THE ANCIENT CHURCH OF THEOTOKOS KYRIOTISSA

Excavations carried out in the Kalenderhane Cami'i have brought to light a series of frescoes on the life of St Francis of Assisi, painted in the small chapel to the right of the nave. The full-length portrait of the Saint and the ten related scenes were executed around 1250, during the Latin occupation of Constantinople.

THE AVLU OF THE SÜLEYMANIYE
The Süleymaniye is approached through the usual colonnaded forecourt, or *avlu;* this particular one is exceptionally grand, with columns of porphyry, marble and granite. At the center is an ablution fountain.

with a diameter of 86 feet and its keystone is 162 feet above the floor. Semi-domes and corner exedrae extend the central space along its main axis, while five domed spaces flanked by galleries extend its width. The only elements separating the nave from the side aisles are the four structural piers under the heroic dome and the two pairs of porphyry columns supporting the tympanum walls pierced by three tiers of arcaded windows. Two other pairs of porphyry monoliths, north and south of those between the pillars, support the intermediate dome-vaulted spaces on either side, with the columns linked together as well as to the engaged buttresses by the gallery arcades. The discreetly decorative tiles from Iznik ▲ *292* are among the finest ever produced, reflecting the new techniques pioneered in the mid-16th century by the Iznik craftsmen. They depict flowers and foliage and are fired in turquoise, sapphire, and red on a pure white ground. The white-marble mimbar and mihrab are sumptuous but simple, as are the doors, shutters, and *kuran kürsü* inlaid with ivory and mother-of-pearl. The inscriptions, which are everywhere in the building, were executed by Ottoman calligraphers who copied Ahmet Karahisari's style ▲ *206* at Iznik for the tiles. Elsewhere the restored inscriptions are unremarkable and certainly not in his style.

THE MAUSOLEUMS OF SÜLEYMAN AND ROXELANA. The great Sultan and his wife lie at rest in their *türbes* located in the garden behind the mosque. The tomb of Süleyman the Magnificent is, not surprisingly, the grandest *türbe* ever created by Sinan. Finished in 1566, the structure is an octagon in shape surrounded by a colonnade, and, like

PLAN OF THE SÜLEYMANIYE COMPLEX
The various parts of the *külliye* are arranged about the terrace and in the streets bordering the enclosure: five *medrese,* one of which served as a preparatory school; a *tip medrese* (medical school); a hospital/ asylum; an *imaret* or public kitchen; a caravanserai; a *darü'l-hadis* (Koranic college); a *darü'l-kurra* (school for instruction in the various ways to read the Koran); a hammam; and a shopping street. The *darü'l-kurra* is built into the cemetery wall, with its vast, domed, harmoniously proportioned space erected over a small four-column cistern.

The Golden Horn viewed from the Süleymaniye.

THE MAUSOLEUM OF SINAN ▲ *314*
Sinan was the greatest architect in the service of Süleyman and two of his successors, Selim II and Murat III. In the course of his long career, Sinan provided Istanbul with twenty mosques and various other monuments. He worked right up to his

death in 1588, at the age of 90. The tomb in which he rests is close to the magnificent masterpiece that he created for Süleyman the Magnificent, whose reign he so brilliantly glorified.

THE WINDOWS OF THE SÜLEYMANIYE
In the 16th century, windows were assembled from pieces of stained glass joined by gesso mullions and mounted in a frame. They were decorated with the motifs most common in the so-called "minor" arts and crafts, especially ceramics and court carpets. Here the motifs are *saz* leaves, arabesques and "four flowers".

some of Sinan's other mausoleums, this one has a double dome. The interior of the cupola, which is supported by columns, has splendid decorations painted in black, gold, and wine-dark red. The walls are entirely clad in Iznik tiles, twice as many of them in this small chamber as in the whole of the enormous mosque. The imposing cenotaph stands like a throne at the center of the room, together with the Sultan's great white turban. The majestic size of this turban clearly indicates the importance of the person who wore it. Süleyman was sultan from 1520, when he ascended the throne at the age of twenty-five, until his death in 1566. His rule, the longest and most illustrious in Ottoman history, was summarized in the mid-17th century by Evliya Çelebi: "In the forty-six years of his reign, he conquered the world and made eighteen monarchs his tributaries. He established order and justice throughout his lands, marched victoriously through seven sectors of the globe, embellished every country vanquished by his arms, and succeeded in all his undertakings." The *türbe* of Roxelana, to the east of her husband's, may be smaller, but its tiles are even more beautiful. The cylindrical base of the cupola, set back somewhat from the building's octagonal cornice, bears an inscription carved in relief like a frieze. The mausoleum dates from 1558, the year of the Sultana's death.

THE SÜLEYMANIYE COMPLEX

Beyond the cemetery, the terrace ends in a triangular area due to the layout of the streets below. It was known in Süleyman's time as the "Wrestling Ground," after the weekly contests held there. To the left of this area,

216

approached from the cemetery, is the *darü'l-hadis*, an unusually built *medrese*, whose twenty-six compartments are arranged in a single, straight row instead of around a courtyard. They face a simple wall, with grilled openings, that encloses the long strip of a garden. The terrace gives us a view of the street below that borders the northern edge of the complex. This old *arasta* – shopping street or bazaar – is still commercially active, though somewhat dilapidated and the subject of plans for restoration. Right across the street are two of the Süleymaniye's five *medrese*. To find the other buildings of the *külliye*, you must retrace your steps to the eastern end of Tiryaki Çarşısı, where the small building at the corner of the street east of the esplanade once served as the *mektep* for the children of the Süleymaniye staff. Now renovated, the little school building houses a children's library. Next to the *mektep* are the *medrese* Evvel and Sani, which today contain the celebrated Süleymaniye library, one of the most impotant in Istanbul. On the other side of the street, to the west, is the *imaret* that was converted to a restaurant in 1991. A few steps beyond the Sani *medrese* brings you to the *tip medrese*, once the site of the empire's foremost medical college. All that remains of this building is a row of compartments along the Tiryaki Çarşısı. Turning right off Tiryaki Çarşısı, we move to the western end of the precinct wall to the complex's *imaret*, which once dispensed food to thousands of beneficiaries, both the poor of the quarter and many others directly dependent upon the Süleymaniye. Today the hospital is home to a fundamentalist girls' boarding school. The interior courtyard, with its ancient plane trees, young palms, and pretty marble fountain, is a pleasant, relaxing haven from the roar of the city.

ROXELANA AND SÜLEYMAN
Roxelana is known to the Turks under the name Haseki Hürrem – "the Joyous Favorite." Westerners call her Roxelana, literally "the Russian," because of her presumed origins. At the beginning of his reign, Süleyman fell madly in love with Roxelana and married her. The Italian Bassano, who was a page at Topkapı Sarayı during the period, left this account of the Sultan's passion: "He displays such love and trust that his astonished subjects all say that she has bewitched him, and call her *Cadi* – that is, the Sorceress."

SÜLEYMAN AND SINAN

Sultan Süleyman the Magnificent and his gifted architect, Sinan, were two of the greatest personalities associated with the apogee of Ottoman art in the 16th century. Between the sovereign and the artist there developed a special and mutually rewarding relationship. The architect depended upon the good will of the Sultan for the financing of his ambitious projects. Reciprocally, Süleyman relied entirely upon the genius of Sinan in order to realize his dreams of eternity – to leave the imprint of his power on the works that would survive him.

SINAN'S MAUSOLEUM

At the western end of the Market of the Addicts Street, facing the northern corner of the wall surrounding the Süleymaniye complex, is a domed *sebil* in a small triangular cemetery. This was once the garden surrounding the house in which Sinan lived during the time he worked on Süleyman's mosque. Within the garden the elderly master built his own *türbe*, an open structure composed of an ogival arcade in six sections, supporting a marble roof with a tiny cupola, above a marble sarcophagus surmounted by a large turban similar to the one worn by the deceased in his role as chief architect. The south wall of the garden is inscribed with a long verse composed by the poet Mustafa Sa'i in praise of the great works created by his friend Sinan. Mustafa Sa'i also wrote about Sinan in his *Tezkere-ül Ebniye*, where he compiled a complete list of the numerous achievements of the famous architect.

THE CARAVANSERAI

The next building along is the caravanserai. This grandly proportioned building included rooms for guests, stables for horses and dromedaries, and a place where travelers could safely leave their baggage. There was also an *imaret*, complete with its own refectory, pantry, bakery, and an olive press, which provided free food. There was an age-old Ottoman custom that all accredited merchants should be given lodging and food free of charge in any hostel within the empire. Evliya Çelebi has left this record of the traditional hospitality practised at the Süleymaniye: "The caravanserai is a splendid establishment in which all travelers receive twice a day a bowl of rice, a dish of groats and some bread, every night a candle, and fodder for each horse, but the welcome is good for only three days." The coherently and thoughtfully planned complex, with its wide range of institutions and services – mosques, hospitals, inns, schools, and a library – inevitably became the very heart of the quarter's religious and social life. Because of the layout and the beauty of the various buildings in the complex, the Süleymaniye remains, even today, unquestionably one of the supreme examples of Islamic architecture.

THE ARCHITECT SINAN AT SÜLEYMAN'S FUNERAL
Süleyman died during the Hungarian campaign and his body was returned to Istanbul for burial.

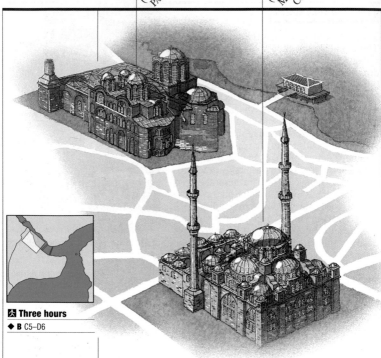

FETHIYE CAMI'I (THEOTOKOS PAMMAKARISTOS)

FATIH CAMI'I (MOSQUE OF MEHMET THE CONQUEROR)

⚐ Three hours
◆ **B** C5–D6

THE BURMALI CAMI'I
A hundred yards
before the Valens
Aqueduct, a little
beyond the western
wall of the Şehzade
Cami'i, stands the
Burmalı Minare
Cami'i, the Mosque
of the Spiral
Minaret. Founded in
1550 by Emin
Nurettin Osman
Efendi, the *kadi*
(judge) of Egypt, this
Muslim place of
worship takes its
name from the spiral
ribs on the brick-
built minaret, a
traditional form
unique in Istanbul
although known in
Anatolia. Another
peculiarity of this
edifice is the
domeless porch,
whose pitched roof is
supported by four
columns with capitals
in the Byzantine
Corinthian style.

THE VALENS AQUEDUCT

The Atatürk Bulvarı, running between the Third and Fourth
Hills, is spanned by the immense Valens Aqueduct ● *76,*

which in Turkish is known as *Bozdoğan
Kemeri*, the "Arcade of the Gray
Falcon." Built in 378 during the reign of
Emperor Valens, it was part of the vast
system supplying water for the New
Rome, Constantinople ▲ *356.* It has been damaged by several
earthquakes, the last in 1967, but restored after each of them.

THE MAIDEN'S COLUMN. Turning left off Macar Kardeşler
Caddesi into Kız Taşı Sokağı, you come to a small square in
which stands the Kız Taşı, or Maiden's Column. This Roman
commemorative column is constructed with a
three-step pedestal made of Corinthian
marble and a granite column surmounted by
a Corinthian capital and, above that, a plinth
with eagles. These probably supported a
statue of the Emperor Marcian, as a Latin
verse on the plinth states that the
monument was erected in honor of Marcian
(450–457) ● *31.* Its Turkish
name arises from
the broken
Nike, or
Winged
Victory, on
the base.

> "Soon there appeared the high arches of the Valens Aqueduct, their immense stone structure overwhelming the humble houses of the Turks built entirely of wood."

Nerval

THE COMPLEX OF MEHMET II

Higher up, on the right of the main avenue, you turn into Aslanhane Sokağı, a name that means "Street of the Lion," after the menagerie that Mehmet II installed here. Turning left, halfway along Aslanhane Sokağı, you arrive at a vast esplanade laid out before the *külliye* ● *79* founded by Fatih Mehmet, with a mosque at the center, an *avlu* in front and a cemetery alongside. The rest of the complex stretches both north and south. Built between 1463 and 1470 by the architect Atik Sinan, the Fatih Cami'i was in its time the largest and most sumptuous Ottoman *külliye* ever built. The forecourt, the main entrance, the mirhab, the minarets up to the level of the *şerefe*, the southern wall of the cemetery, and the adjoining gate are no doubt part of the original complex. All else dates from the reign of Mustafa II, who rebuilt the mosque and other elements destroyed by the 1766 earthquake. Among these, the eight *medrese* and the *tabhane* have recently been restored. Little remains of the public kitchen, and the caravanserai no longer exists.

MEHMET II, THE BUILDER
By 1453, the capital of the dying Byzantine Empire was little more than a ghost of what it had been. Inside the walls, vegetation grew in abandoned quarters, Roman ruins, and the dilapidated palaces. The population, which had shrunk to some 40,000 Greeks, huddled ever-closer about the Basilica of Haghia Sophia. Mehmet II the Conqueror revitalized the legendary city. Within a few years, a new population, come from all over the Ottoman Empire, took up residence there, building mosques, bazaars, and caravanserais.

THE MOSQUE OF MEHMET THE CONQUEROR.
In 1766, an earthquake demolished the FATIH MEHMET CAMI'I. Mustafa III immediately had it rebuilt, but in a Baroque style quite unlike the original. The new mosque, completed in 1771, is constructed to the plan devised by Sinan for the Şehzade Cami, the Sultan Ahmet Cami'i, and the Yeni Cami'i, which consisted of a central dome flanked by four half-domes. While the exterior remains agreeably classical, the interior is weak and over-elaborate. Indeed, the lower walls are revetted in white tiles of such mediocre quality that they have turned dark with damp. Still, the mirhab, saved from the old mosque, is handsome, even if supplemented with gilt-edged Baroque panels. Its style resembles that of the entrance. Equally Baroque yet attractive is the elaborate mimbar made of polychrome marble.

ITINERANT PEDDLER

THE TÜRBE GARDEN. The tombs of Fatih Mehmet and his wife, Gülbahar, the mother of Beyazıt II, were reconstructed following the earthquake. The interior of the conqueror's Baroque *türbe* is lavishly decorated. Outside Fatih Mehmet's *tabhane*, or hospice for dervishes, stands the *türbe* built in 1817–18 for the dowager Sultana Naksidil, the wife of Abdül Hamit I and mother of Mahmet II. This splendid example of the Ottoman Baroque style ● *84* contrasts with the classical austerity of the *külliye*.

▲ THE FETHIYE CAMI'I

OTTOMAN COINS
Mehmet II initiated the standardization of the Ottoman monetary system. Most coins have only calligraphic inscriptions on both sides, sometimes accompanied by

braided motifs. Coins with portraits are extremely rare. Unlike the gold coins, called *altin*, the silver ones were used mainly in commercial transactions.

THE MOSQUE OF SELIM I

On the right of Fevzi Paşa Caddesi, Yavuz Selim Caddesi brings you to the Sultan Selim Cami'i, or SELIMIYE CAMI, and an ancient open cistern, the immense Cistern of Aspar, today the site of a municipal market. The Mosque of Selim I, one of the most beautiful buildings in Istanbul, is situated upon a high terrace at the summit of the Fifth Hill, overlooking the Golden Horn. At its completion in 1522, Süleyman the Magnificent dedicated the mosque to his father. The shallow main dome, with its collection of little domes on either side, looks like an enormous crown. The courtyard is one of the most colorful and charming in the city, its space defined by marble and granite columns, arches built of multicolored voussoirs, a very pretty ablution fountain encircled by cypress trees, and magnificent early Iznik tiles decorating the lunettes above windows. The interior furnishings are superb, especially the mirhab, the mimbar, and the Sultan's loge. The border around the ceiling under the loge provides a stunning example of Ottoman painted and gilded woodwork from the 16th century.

THE MAUSOLEUMS.
The cemetery is situated directly behind the mosque. The large octagonal *türbe* capped by a cupola is that of Selim I. The tile panels decorating the porch are presumed to have come from Iznik, although their color and design do not resemble any other known examples. There is another mausoleum opposite, attributed to Sinan; it houses the remains of four of Süleyman the Magnificent's children who died in infancy. Also standing near the Sultan's tomb is the mausoleum of Abdül Mecit, who died in 1861.

> "Venerate and adore the true conception
> in the paintings and images of Christ. . . .
> If you do not, you take in vain the name of Christian."
>
> The Life of Saint Iônnikios

FETHIYE CAMI'I

Leaving the Selimiye Cami'i by Sultan Selim Caddesi, turn right into Manyasizade Caddesi, which leads to the mosque. This was the Byzantine church known as the *Theotokos Pammakaristos* or "Joyous Mother of God", a building splendidly restored in the 1960's by the Byzantine Institute of America. The main body of the church was constructed in the 12th century by two members of the nobility, John Comnenus and his wife Anna Doukaina. At the end of the 13th century, General Michael Doukas Glabas Tarchaniotes, commander of cavalry under Andronicus II Palaeologus (1282–1328), had it reconstructed. Around 1310, a paracclesion (side sanctuary) was added by the general's widow as a chapel for her husband. Following the Conquest, the church served as the Patriarchate of the Greek Orthodox Church from 1456 to 1586. In 1591, Murat III converted the building into an Islamic place of worship, naming it Fethiye Cami'i – the Mosque of the Conquest – to commemorate his victory over the Persians and the annexation of Georgia and Azerbaijan by the Ottoman Empire. However, the conversion had a number of damaging effects. Since the restoration carried out by the Byzantine Institute, the large prayer hall continues to function as a mosque, while the paracclesion, set apart from the nave and with its missing columns restored, has become a museum devoted to the mosaics that survive intact, now cleared and cleaned. Those covering the dome, previously neglected, have now been restored to their original beauty. Although fewer in number, the mosaics in this chapel join those in the Kariye Cami'i as evidence of the brilliance of the last Byzantine renaissance that blazed during the reign of the Palaeologus dynasty.

MOSAICS IN THE PARACCLESION OF THE THEOTOKOS PAMMAKARISTOS
A Christ Pantocrator is depicted on the ceiling, surrounded by the Twelve Apostles of the New Testament. On the conch vault over the apse there is the

Christ Hyperagathos; on the left wall, the Virgin facing St John the Baptist on the right wall. Above each of the latter hover four angels. Elsewhere, on the conches, on the soffits of arches, and on the pilasters figure twenty-seven saints. A long inscription in gold letters on a blue background unfolds between the marble-clad lower wall and the mosaics on the upper wall. It is a threnody written by the poet Philes to commemorate the love that Maria Blachena, the chapel's foundress, bore her deceased husband, General Michael Tarchaniotes.

THE CONQUEROR
Today the only land walls that survive are those left intact by Mehmet II after he took the city of Constantinople in May 1453.

THE LAND WALLS

The land walls, for the most part, date from the reign of Emperor Theodosius II (408–450). The initial phase of construction, which produced one long high wall punctuated at regular intervals by some hundred bastions or defense towers, was completed in 413 under the supervision of Anthemius, Prefect of the Eastern Empire. In 447, an earthquake destroyed most of this fortified rampart, toppling fifty-seven towers just when Attila the Hun and his Golden Horde were advancing upon Constantinople. Reconstruction began immediately, this time under Constantine, the new Prefect of the Eastern Empire, who, aided by all factions of the Hippodrome, got the new walls built within two months, reinforcing them with both a moat and a second, outer wall. These formidable defenses stopped Attila, the Scourge of God, who, having given up the idea of taking Constantinople, turned around and ravaged the Western Empire. The Theodosian system of defense rested primarily on the

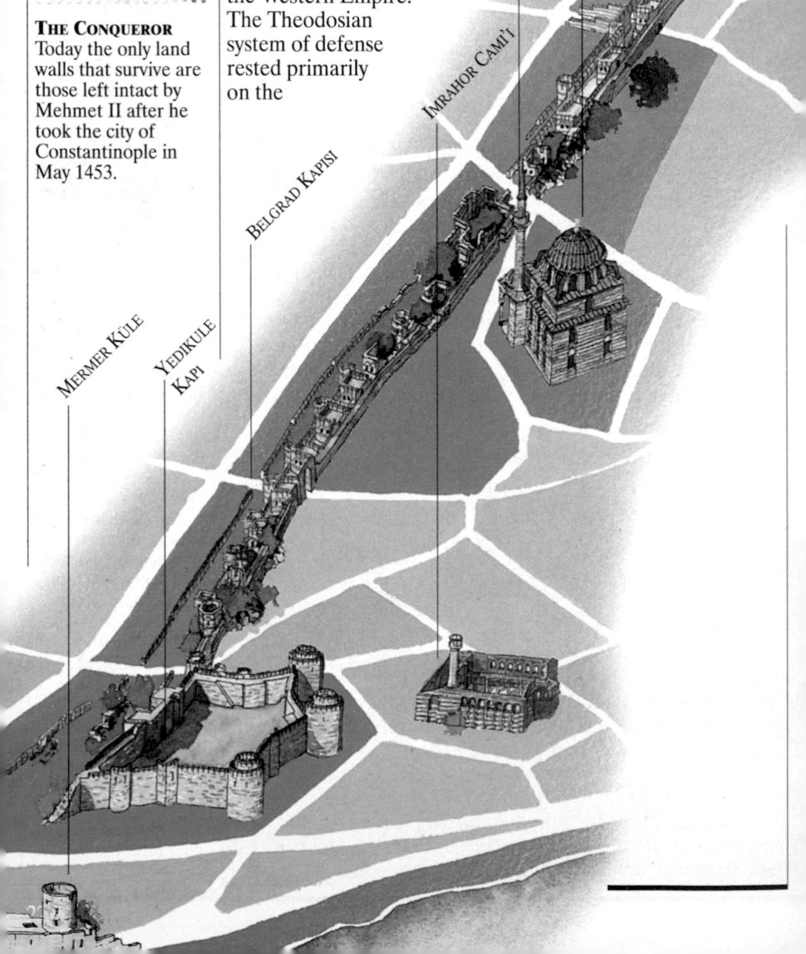

TOP KAPI

İBRAHIM PAŞA CAMI'I

SILIVRI KAPISI

İMRAHOR CAMI'I

BELGRAD KAPISI

MERMER KÜLE

YEDIKULE KAPI

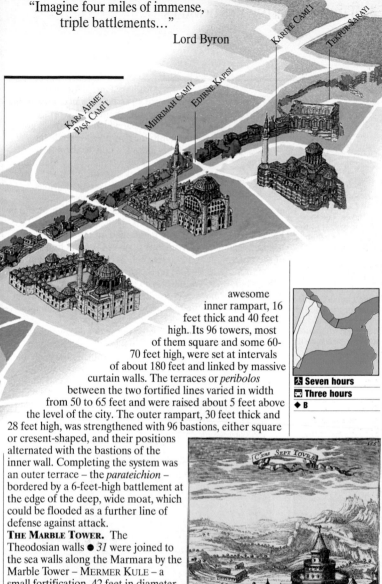

> "Imagine four miles of immense, triple battlements…"
>
> Lord Byron

KARA AHMET PAŞA CAMİ'İ

MİHRİMAH CAMİ'İ

EDİRNE KAPISI

KARİYE CAMİ'İ

TEKFUR SARAYI

⚔ Seven hours
🚶 Three hours
◆ B

awesome inner rampart, 16 feet thick and 40 feet high. Its 96 towers, most of them square and some 60-70 feet high, were set at intervals of about 180 feet and linked by massive curtain walls. The terraces or *peribolos* between the two fortified lines varied in width from 50 to 65 feet and were raised about 5 feet above the level of the city. The outer rampart, 30 feet thick and 28 feet high, was strengthened with 96 bastions, either square or cresent-shaped, and their positions alternated with the bastions of the inner wall. Completing the system was an outer terrace – the *parateichion* – bordered by a 6-feet-high battlement at the edge of the deep, wide moat, which could be flooded as a further line of defense against attack.

THE MARBLE TOWER. The Theodosian walls ● *31* were joined to the sea walls along the Marmara by the Marble Tower – MERMER KULE – a small fortification, 42 feet in diameter and 100 feet high, that still dominates the northwest quarter of the old city. Built on a promontory, the bastion is now isolated from the wall by the shore highway. The Marble Tower – named for the revetment on its lower half – may have begun as a beach house for the emperor to use when he went for a trip on the Marmara.

THE GATE OF CHRIST. Moving slightly away from the shore highway is the first of the ancient gates, just beyond the first tower of the inner wall. It is surmounted by the monogram XP crowned in laurel, which accounts for its name: the Gate of Christ. In addition to several small posterns, the Theodosian walls had ten gates, five of them for the public and five reserved for the military. The Gate of Christ counted among the latter, and so it was also known as

VIEW FROM THE CASTLE OF SEVEN TOWERS
Along the castle walls facing the water is the Marble Tower, built on a promontory right next to the sea.

225

THE CASTLE OF SEVEN TOWERS
"At the corner of the city facing Gallipoli, at the edge of the sea, there is, as mentioned earlier, a castle composed of seven huge towers linked into a fortified enclosure by high, strong walls and equipped with much artillery, which castle is called Iadicula."
Nicolas de Nicolay

THE CANNON GATE
For the Byzantines, this was the Gate of St Romanus. On May 29, 1453, when Mehmet II launched the Turks' final assault upon Constantinople, he focused his attack upon the land walls at this point. The sultan sacrificed the first waves of infantry so that their corpses would fill in the moat. Then a great cannon began bombarding the gate with 270-pound cannonballs, which soon broke through the wall. The portal is called Top Kapı ("Cannon Gate"), to commemorate the episode.

the First Military Gate. However, the gates were all essentially alike except that the public ones opened onto bridges across the moat which led to roads going deep into the countryside, while the military gates led only to the outer defenses. Between the Sea of Marmara and the railway line, the great walls are remarkably well preserved. Various inscriptions cite the names of the emperors who, over the centuries, ordered major repairs to be carried out upon the fortifications. Thus, we find John VIII Palaeologus (1425–48) ● *33* mentioned on the first outer bastion; Romanus I Lecapenus (919–944) on the fourth tower of the inner wall; and Leo III (717–741) as well as his son Constantine V (741–775) on the seventh inner tower. Altogether, there are thirty such inscriptions, which cover a period lasting more than a millennium, providing clear proof of the importance the Byzantine emperors attached to the defenses of their capital.

Between the sixth and seventh towers of the inner wall, take the main road outside the walls and cross the bridge over the railway line that cuts through the ramparts at this point. Some distance farther along, you will come to the Yediküle Gate.

THE CASTLE OF SEVEN TOWERS

The Yediküle Kapı is a small Byzantine gateway with an imperial eagle, emblem of the Comnenus dynasty, carved in marble above the arch on the interior. Passing through the gateway, turn right to find the entrance to the YEDIKÜLE itself – the Castle of Seven Towers – a curious

This 15th-century engraving shows the sea wall that ran along both shores of the Golden Horn.

structure containing both Byzantine and Ottoman features. The whole building projects inward from the Theodosian walls just beyond the railway line. While four of the towers are integrated with the high wall, the other three, built much later by Fatih, stand inside the enclosure, linked together and to the outer defenses by four thick curtain walls, thereby forming a pentagon-shaped enclosure. At the northwest and southwest corners are two of the polygonal bastions of the main Theodosian wall, between which stand the two other towers – actually marble pylons flanking the famous Golden Gate. Two of the towers – particularly the one on the left – served as prisons for foreign diplomats and prisoners of war, and the other towers were depositories for part of the national treasure. A stairway in the so-called Tower of the Ambassadors gives access to the top of the keep and thence to the ramparts along which you can walk as far as the Golden Gate.

THE GOLDEN GATE ▲ *234.* This structure originated around 388 as a Roman triumphal arch erected on the route to the Great Palace by Theodosius I, before he began work on his own defense walls. Like all

THE LAND WALLS
"I have travelled through a great deal of Turkey, many another country of Europe and some Asiatic countries, but I have never come across a work of nature or of art that has made such a strong impression on me as the panorama that unfolds on both sides of the Seven Towers to the Golden Horn."

Lord Byron

triumphal arches, the Porta Aurea stood apart. Its classic form – a triple arch composed of a large, central arch flanked by two smaller ones – stood astride the part of the highway that ran along the Marmara coast and then out of Constantinople. A quarter of a century later the Golden Gate would be integrated within the defense system when Theodosius had Constantine's wall rebuilt. The pylon north of the Golden Gate served as a prison, as well as one of the city's principal places for dispatching the condemned. Instruments of torture and death from that period can still be seen there, along with the sinister "well of blood" into which the heads of the executed were tossed for flushing out to sea. Leaving the Castle of Seven Towers, follow Yediküle Caddesi and take Imrahor Ilyras Bey Caddesi.

THE CHURCH OF SAINT JOHN OF STUDIUS

About 500 yards in front of the Yediküle, on the right, is an enormous but dilapidated and roofless building. This is the IMRAHOR CAMI'I, converted from the ancient Ayios Ioannis Prodomos, St John the Forerunner, which is extremely difficult to get into. The foundation dates from the years 454–63, and its related monastery a bit later, both of them under the patronage of the Roman patrician Studius, consul during the reign of Marcian. In the first quarter of the 9th century, the monastery acquired an immense reputation while Theodore the Studite was abbot. An old iron gate leads to the church's walled garden which, in place of the original atrium, spreads before the three-bayed narthex, whose handsome central entrance is composed of four magnificent Corinthian columns *in antis* supporting a sumptuously carved architrave, frieze, and cornice. Also still in place are two of the marble door frames. From the narthex, three portals and two side doors open into the church, a basilican structure ending in an apse and separated from its side aisles by flanking rows of seven columns each. The six surviving columns on the north are verd-antique monoliths with capitals and

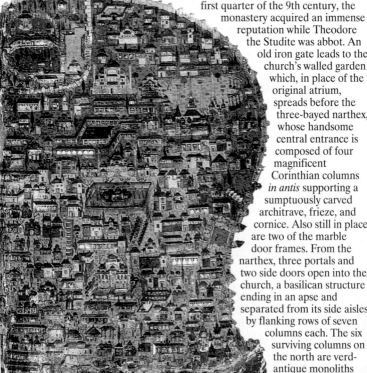

> "The surrounding countryside
> was spangled with cypresses in whose shade
> huddled thousands of sepulchers."

Pierre Loti

**CEMETERIES
AND WALLS**
It was in the first
half of the 18th
century that a law
was promulgated
forbidding all further
burial within the city.
Thereafter a number
of cemeteries were
developed outside the
land walls. Known as
"fields of the dead."
these graveyards
were composed of a
thronging mass of
stelae planted in the
midst of sweet,
luxuriant vegation.
But times change,
and now the urban
sprawl nibbles away at
the old fields of the
dead, which are left
to deteriorate slowly.

entablature similar to those in the narthex. The entablatures
over the lateral colonnades each supported an upper
colonnade upon which rested the timber roof. All of this,
along with the main colonnade to the south, was shattered by
an earthquake in 1894, which left it in its present ruined state.

TOWARD THE GATE OF EDIRNE

THE BELGRAD KAPI. Returning to
the Yediküle Kapı, walk
approximately 600 yards
along the walls to the
Second Military Gate.
This was renamed
Belgrad Kapı when
Süleyman I reinstalled
nearby the artisans he had
brought back from Belgrade
following his capture of the
Balkan city in 1521.

THE SILIVRI KAPI. Along the 680-yard
stretch from the Belgrade Gate to the Silivri Kapi, the line of
fortifications is well preserved, including all thirteen of the
inner bastions. The Byzantines called the Silver Gate the
"Porta ton Pigi" because of its proximity to the pilgrimage site
known as the PANANYIA ZOODOCHUS PIGI – "Our Lady of the
Life-Giving Spring" – located 500 yards outside the walls. As
with all the large gates, the Silivri Kapı is double, opening
through both inner and outer walls. It was
here that the Byzantines broke through
when they recaptured Constantinople
from its Latin occupiers in 1261.

THE MEVLÂNA KAPI. From the Silver
Gate to the Mevlâna Gate, the land walls
retain all their original elements, including
the fifteen stout towers. This stretch
concludes at the Mevlâna Kapı, named for
the founder of an ancient order of
dervishes. The Byzantines called it the
"Gate of the Reds," for the Hippodrome
faction that built it, according to an
inscription in both Greek and Latin on the
south corbel above the outer gateway.

**THE NORTHERN
WALLS, A BRIEF
HISTORICAL TOUR ○**
Go to the Edirne Kapı.
The Mihrimah Sultan
Cami'i (▲ 231) and its
two hundred windows
crown the highest
point of the old town.
Cross the Fevzi cad.,
following the walls,
then go down the
Kariye Cami'i Sok to
the right of the mosque
of the same name
(▲ 232). Its mosaics are
the most beautiful in
the whole city. Go
north, toward the
palaces of Tefkur and
Blachernae (▲ 236),
the last remnants of
Byzantine civil art.
Finally, visit the areas
of Balat and Fener
(▲ 242).

229

THE MOSQUE OF TWO HUNDRED WINDOWS
The space inside the Mosque of Princess Mihrimah is magically enhanced by the abundant light pouring in from some two hundred windows, half of them in the huge tympana and around the base of the vast central dome. But the windows are relatively lightly colored, at least by comparison with those in the Süleymaniye or the mosque dedicated to Mihrimah at Üsküdar and Edirne. In the Istanbul mosque, the effect is exquisite, its clarity serving to dramatize the purity of the surrounding space.

TOP KAPI. Along the 900-yard stretch from the Mevlâna Gate to the Cannon Gate, only one of the original fifteen towers has disappeared. However, the ramparts themselves were demolished between the tenth and eleventh towers to make way for Millet Caddesi, punched through in the 1960's. Top Kapı, situated at the summit of the Seventh Hill, takes its name from the mighty cannon aimed at it by the Ottoman forces during the final siege of Constantinople in 1453.

THE MESOTEICHION. The line extending from Top Kapı to Edirne Kapı is about 1,300 yards long, interrupted between the sixth and seventh towers by Vatan Caddesi. This avenue and the Istanbul Metro beneath it follow the course of the old Lycus River. Called the Mesoteichion, meaning "middle of the walls," this part of the fortifications is midway in the defense system between the Sea of Marmara and the Golden Horn. It is also the most vulnerable part of the defenses, since the terrain dips into the Lycus Valley, allowing an enemy to attack from the hills on either side. Thus, in 1453, the Byzantine defenders found themselves caught in the crossfire of the bombardments which finally breached the walls, allowing the Turks to enter the city and leaving these ramparts the most damaged of all.

THE GATE OF THE ASSAULT. Called the Murus Bacchatureus by the Byzantines, the northern portion of the Mesoteichion, between the Lycus and the Edirne Kapı, was pierced by only one gate, the Pyli ton Pempton, or the Fifth Military Gate. Constantine XI transferred his command post here in the final hours of the Turkish siege in May 1453. Even as the walls gave way, he continued to fight valiantly, together with his cousins, Theophilus Palaeologus and Don Francisco of

Toledo, and his faithful companion, John Dalmata. The body of the Emperor is said to have been discovered near the Pempton Gate during the evening of the city's capture and then secretly buried in a church. The Turks would call the gate Hücum Kapı, meaning the Gate of the Assault.

THE MIHRIMAH SULTAN CAMI'I

Just inside the walls north of Hücum Kapı stands the Mihrimah Sultan Cami'i, a major Istanbul landmark that dominates the city's old quarter from atop the Sixth Hill ▲ 265. It is in fact one of the masterpieces of the great Sinan, a foundation dedicated to Süleyman the Magnificent's favorite daughter.

THE MOSQUE COMPLEX. Constructed between 1562 1565, the *külliye* includes a *medrese* or college, a *mektep* or primary school, a double hammam, the mausoleum of the Grand Vizier Semiz Ali Paşa, Mihrimah's son-in-law, and an *arasta*, or street bazaar, installed in the substructure under the terrace on which the complex was built. We enter through a gate which leads to a flight of stairs that go up to the terrace above. On the right is the *avlu* or courtyard, enclosed by colonnades and the cells of the *medrese* on three sides and an ablution fountain (*şadırvan*) at the center. The entrance to the mosque is through a porch composed of seven domed bays supported by eight marble and granite columns, a structure that was originally preceded by a "foreporch," probably with a sloping timber roof borne upon twelve columns, traces of which remain on the ground.

THE MOSQUE. Its prominent position reinforces the already imposing nature of the building, with its main dome resting upon a massive cubical structure anchored at the corners by four stout towers buttressing the great arches. The tympana are each pierced by fifteen ogival windows and four round

CROSS-SECTION AND PROFILE OF THE MIHRIMAH SULTAN CAMI'I (ABOVE)
"The plan of the baldachin with a projection of the cupola inscribed. In red, the remains of the supporting structures: the four granite columns and pilasters. Above: Diagonal section of the cupola and its square baldachin, showing the large spherical pendentives."
Augusto Romano Burelli,
La Moschea di Sinan.

231

MOSAICS IN THE CHRIST PANTOCRATOR CHURCH
The mosaic tondo on the south cupola of the narthex at St Savior-in-Chora is à pendant of the Virgin and Child tondo on the north cupola. These two medalions are each surrounded by twenty-eight figures represented on the ribs of the dome: patriarchs, prophets, leaders of the twelve tribes, and the sixteen kings of Israel.

THE DEATH OF THE VIRGIN MOSAIC
Called Koimesis in Greek, the figure appears in the nave of St Savior-in-Chora (Kariye Cami'i). The Virgin, laid out on her bier, is surrounded by the Apostles. At the center, a haloed Christ cradles a babe in swaddling clothes symbolizing the soul of Mary reborn in Paradise.

ones, all glazed with stained glass. On the interior, the square nave constitutes the central space of the mosque, which is crowned by the vast cupola, 65 feet in diameter and 120 feet high, resting upon a rim base formed by alternating arches and pendentives. On the north and south, the prayer hall opens into triple arcades, each supported by granite columns, while the upper galleries on either side each have three domed bays.

THE EDIRNE GATE. Situated at the point where the main road to Adrianople left the city, the Byzantines' Porta Adrianople became the Turks' EDIRNE KAPI after Adrianople was renamed Edirne ● *308*. Its other name, Porta Polyandriou, or "Cemetery Gate," comes from the presence of a huge necropolis just outside the fortifications. It was through this gate, on top of the Sixth Hill – the highest terrain in the old city – that Mehmet II made his triumphal entrance into Constantinople in the early afternoon of May 29, 1453, a historic moment commemorated by a plaque on the south side of the gateway.

THE KARIYE CAMI'I

At the right of the Edirne Kapı, take Fevzi Paşa Caddesi and turn left at the next corner into Vaiz Sokağı. At the third intersection Kariye Cami'i Sokağı appears on the right, leading directly into the square in front of Kariye Cami'i, the former Church of St Savior-in-Chora, situated only a short distance from the Theodosian walls and near the summit of the Sixth Hill.

THE HISTORY OF THE CHURCH. St Savior-in-Chora could very well be translated into "St Savior-in-the-Country," since, as the name implies, the church and its monastery originally stood outside the Constantinian wall. Later, they were integrated into the expanded city enclosed by the Theodosian fortifications. Still, the name stuck, even if used merely in a symbolic sense, reinforced by old inscriptions in the church referring to Christ as the "Country" or "Land of the Living." The actual building dates from between 1077–1081, when it was erected at the behest of Maria Doukas, the mother-in-law

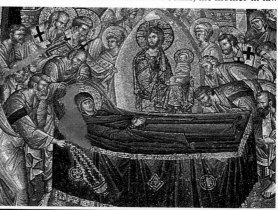

of Alexis I Comnenus. It probably began as the four-column type much esteemed during this period. At the beginning of the 12th century, Isaac Comnenus, grandson of the foundress and the third son of Alexis I, commissioned a rather elaborate remodeling of the church. Two centuries later, between 1315 and 1321, Theodore Metochites, prime minister and first lord of the treasury during the reign of Andronicus II Palaeologus, undertook to renovate the church yet again, giving it the appearance we know today. This makes the works of art in Kariye Cami'i contemporary with those in the Fethiye Cami'i (Pammakaristos), also produced during the Palaeologian renaissance. St Savior-in-Chora would remain a Christian sanctuary for more than fifty years after the Conquest, until Atik Ali Paşa, Grand Vizier to Beyazıt II, had it converted into a mosque. However, over the centuries, some of the mosaics and frescoes were shaken loose by earthquakes, while the others gradually disappeared under plaster, paint, and grime. Finally, in 1948, Thomas Whittemore and Paul A. Underwood, sponsored by the Byzantine Institute of America and the Dumbarton Oaks Center for Byzantine Studies, launched a major program of restoration.

THE STRUCTURE OF THE CHURCH ● *74*.
We enter the sanctuary through an exonarthex followed by a narthex, to find a nave flanked by a paracclesion on the right and a two-story corridor on the left. The central space is capped by a cupola resting upon a tall cylinder, and this superstructure is supported by four enormous pilasters at the corners of the nave. From them spring the arches and the linking pendentives that make the transition from a square base to a circular one for the cylinder and dome. The present dome is Turkish, but the cylinder dates from the reconstruction of 1315 to 1321.

THE DÉCOR OF THE CHURCH. The mosaics and frescoes ● *64* in St Savior are by far the most important works of Byzantine pictorial art known today, in terms of both their beauty and their number. It is fascinating to realize that they are coeval with the frescoes of Giotto in Italy. And while different in certain particulars, they nonetheless appear

THE LAST JUDGMENT FRESCO
In the paracclesion at St Savior-in-Chora, Christ is presented as the Supreme Judge, accompanied by the Virgin Mary, St John the Baptist, and a choir of prophets.

TESSERAE
In this detail from a mosaic, the tesserae are delicate enough to capture the subtle play of light and dark.

THE MARRIAGE AT CANA MOSAIC
This treatment of a scene from the New Testament also reflects everyday life in Byzantium. Vineyards and wine-making were actually the main industry around Constantinople, and the wine was stored in great earthenware jars.

CONSTANTINOPLE IN 1422, MAPPED BY CRISTOFORO BUONDELMONTI
In this depiction, executed just a few years before the Conquest, the capital of the Byzantine Empire can be seen completely ringed by its sea and land walls. Only the principal monuments are shown, among them, and easily recognized, the Great Palace, the Basilica of Haghia Sophia, the Hippodrome, the Senate, St John the Studite, the Palace of the Porphyrogenitus, and the many commemorative columns dotted about the city. To the north, on the opposite side of the Golden Horn, stand the walls of Galata, the thriving Genoese concession dominated by its famous tower.

THE GOLDEN GATE
This is a classic Roman triumphal arch, with a large central arcade flanked

by two pylons faced in marble. It was through this gate that the emperors made their triumphal entries into Constantinople following successful campaigns abroad.

to radiate the same sense of living, breathing reality so characteristic of the Early Renaissance. Certainly, they exist in a world well removed from the iconic, static, rigorously stylized painting of the old Byzantine tradition. The movement of the figures, with their graceful gestures, endow many of the scenes represented with an air of lightness and gentle beatitude. The almost painterly vitality of these works is reinforced by clear, luminous colors – blue, green, red, and gold – blended into a harmony of more delicate tones such as gray, mauve, and rose. Finally, the sheer variety of the biblical scenes depicted demonstrates the breadth and power of Byzantine art in this late period.

THE MOSAICS. Iconographically, the mosaics unfold in a very precise order, which can be divided into seven great cycles: the six large Dedicatory panels in the narthex and exonarthex, one of which portrays Theodore Metochites offering his church to Christ; the Ancestry of Christ in the domes of the narthex; the Life of the Blessed Virgin in the first three bays of the narthex; the Infancy of Christ in the lunettes of the exonarthex; the Ministry of Christ on the vaults of the exonarthex and the fourth bay in the narthex; the Portraits of Saints on the arches and pilasters of the narthex; and, finally, the nave panels.

THE MOSAICS. The superb frescoes in the paracclesion, the last commission by Theodore Metochites, probably date from 1320 to 1321. The anonymous author of these masterpieces is

> "You made me wander in the lands of Rumelia and Damascus: They will not understand you, the ignoramuses; they will abandon you. . . ."
>
> Karaca Oğlan

undoubtedly the person who also executed the mosaics in the church. The themes are those generally found in mortuary chapels: Resurrection, Last Judgment, Heaven and Hell, and the Mother of God as Mediator between Earth and Heaven. Below the cornice, between the four tombs, there is a procession of saints and martyrs. The greatest scene of all is the Anastasis – the Resurrection, or the Harrowing of Hell – represented on the conch vault over the apse in the funerary chapel. This extraordinary work is Byzantine art at its very zenith. Indeed, many consider it to be one of the most sublime paintings ever executed. At the center of the grandly spacious composition, Christ triumphant has trampled the gates of Hell beneath his feet, where Satan lies writhing in chains. With his right hand the Savior lifts Adam from his tomb, while with his left he plucks Eve from hers. Behind the First Man comes John the Baptist, David, and Solomon, while Abel stands with another group of the just next to Eve's tomb. The four tombs in the paracclesion occupy deep niches, each of which originally held a sarcophagus with mosaics and frescoes above, fragments of which survive.

THEODORE METOCHITES. The tomb located at the rear of the paracclesion rests under a richly carved and decorated archivolt. Although the inscription has vanished, the sepulcher is probably that of Theodore Metochites: a true Renaissance man, he was a diplomat, high government official, theologian, astronomer, poet, patron of the arts, and major force behind the artistic and intellectual renewal of the Palaeologian era. After Andronicus III seized the throne in 1328, he banished Metochites and other members of the old regime. Late in life, Metochites was permitted to re-enter Constantinople on condition he retire to the St Savior monastery, where he died on May 13, 1331.

THE CAMEL TRAINS
The last emperor to make a triumphal entry into Constantinople through the Golden Gate was Michael VIII Palaeologus (1261–82) on August 15, 1261. Today the Golden Gate is no more than one gate among many others. At the beginning of the century, it was still possible to see fully loaded camel trains passing in single file through certain gates on their way to Edirne. Within Istanbul, they stopped at the *han*, hostelries known to Europeans by the Persian term caravanserai.

THE TEFKUR SARAYI
Located on the Sixth
Hill, this was one of
the residences of the
first Byzantine
Emperors, and it
remain occupied until
the end of the
Byzantine Empire.
Following the
Conquest, the palace
served a variety of
purposes. During the
16th and 17th
centuries, it was the
imperial menagerie,
housing a variety of
animals, such as
elephants and
giraffes, which
astonished European
travelers. In 1597,
Fynes Moryson,
described a giraffe
thus: "[It was] a wild
animal recently
imported from
Africa, the mother of
Monsters. . . . Its fur
was red with many
black and white spots
Even with stretched

arms I could barely
reach the hind end of
its spine, which
climbed higher and
higher towards the
shoulders. Its neck –
very thin and of a
prodigious length –
permitted the beast to
extend its head to any
part of whatever
room it was held in."

THE TEFKUR SARAYI

At the end of the Theodosian ramparts, between the inner
and outer barriers, stands one of the most remarkable
remnants of the Byzantine Empire ● *74*. This is the Tefkur
Sarayı, or the Palace of the Sovereign, more popularly called
the Palace of the Porphyrogenitus. It is thought to date from
the end of the 13th century, and it may have
served as an annex to the nearby Blachernae
Palace, which was the main imperial
residence during the last two centuries
of the Byzantine Empire. A huge
rectangular building with three stories, it
had a vaulted ground floor, which
contained a grand hall 55 feet long and
with four large arcades opening onto a
courtyard preceded by a propyleum. On
the next floor up, another vast room, 75
feet long and 32 wide, had six large
windows, the last providing access to the
rampart's sentry path on top of the
defense walls. The top story, which rose
above the Theodosian ramparts, was
windowed on all sides, with seven
openings onto the courtyard. On the south side the wall
curiously curves out like an apse, and on the east side there
remain traces of a balconied window. Everywhere, but
particularly on the couryard façade, the palace displays a
geometric décor composed of red
brick and white marble, all
entirely characteristic of late
Byzantine architecture.
THE WALL OF MANUEL I COMNENUS. The
Theodosian walls stop abruptly just after
the Tefkur Palace, where the defenses are
of a later construction, carried out during
Manuel I Comnenus' reign in the mid-11th
century. The architecture represents a

> "If you see beauty you stop. Oh my heart,
> I cannot bear your pain."
>
> Anonymous

significant departure from that of the Theodosian sections. The new barrier, which runs from the Tefkur Sarayı to the Golden Horn, does not, for the most part, include either an outer wall or a moat; their absence is justified by the greater height and thickness of the wall, as well as by its taller, more massive towers, which were built close together, eight of them square and one round. Structurally, the Manuel wall is composed of a high arcade closed in on its outer face. These defenses contain only one gate, which the Turks call the EĞRI KAPI or Crooked Gate, because a *türbe* just outside the gateway causes the narrow road entering the city to bend around it. The remaining stretch of fortification, from the third tower to the retaining wall of the Blachernae terrace, seems to have been constructed still later.

THE BLACHERNAE PALACE

The Blachernae Palace is approached by way of the terrace that once supported the upper part of the building. Its substructures are almost completely intact, and go all the way down to ground level outside the walls. The ruined towers at the outer edge of the terrace are all that remain of the superstructure of the Blachernae Palace, the rest undoubtedly destroyed during the siege of 1453. The fortifications from the north corner of the Blachernae terrace to the Golden Horn consist of two parallel walls joined at either end to form a citadel. The inner wall was built by the Emperor Heraclius (610–641) in 627, apparently replacing the original Theodosian walls in this very vulnerable area where the barbarian Avars had almost succeeded in breaking into the city in 626. The three hexagonal towers are perhaps the finest bastions in the whole system of fortifications. In 813, Leo V (813–820), believing a single wall inadequate, had the outer wall with four towers constructed, though on a less massive scale and to a poorer standard. The "citadel" is entered through the Gate of the Blachernae, situated between the first and second towers of the Heraclian wall. This then brings you to Toplu Dede Sokağı, a winding lane that leads to the ancient Porta Kiliomene, at the west end of the sea wall on the Golden Horn. Here, the land fortifications come to an end, and from there on the sea defenses, when they were still standing, completed the defenses from the Golden Horn to the Sea of Marmara 7 to 8 miles away.

TURKISH WOMEN
Mustafa Kemal, the father of the Turkish Republic, longed to transform his country into a modern, secular state closely modeled on the nations of Europe. He granted women the right to vote in 1934, and since then more and more of them have gone out to work and reached positions of great responsibility, such as the former prime minister Tansu Ciller. However, Muslim traditions are undergoing a revival and the wearing of veils is once more as widespread in Istanbul as it is in the countryside.

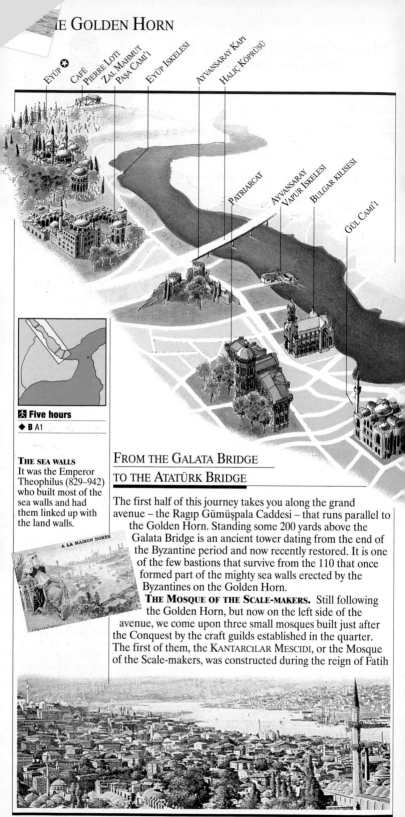

EYÜP ✪ — CAFÉ — PIERRE LOTI — ZAL MAHMUT PAŞA CAMI'I — EYÜP İSKELESI — AYVANSARAY KAPI — HALIÇ KÖPRÜSÜ

PATRIARCAT — AYVANSARAY VAPUR İSKELESI — BULGAR KILISESI — GÜL CAMI'I

🏃 **Five hours**
◆ **B** A1

THE SEA WALLS
It was the Emperor Theophilus (829–942) who built most of the sea walls and had them linked up with the land walls.

A LA MAISON DORÉE

FROM THE GALATA BRIDGE
TO THE ATATÜRK BRIDGE

The first half of this journey takes you along the grand avenue – the Ragıp Gümüşpala Caddesi – that runs parallel to the Golden Horn. Standing some 200 yards above the Galata Bridge is an ancient tower dating from the end of the Byzantine period and now recently restored. It is one of the few bastions that survive from the 110 that once formed part of the mighty sea walls erected by the Byzantines on the Golden Horn.

THE MOSQUE OF THE SCALE-MAKERS. Still following the Golden Horn, but now on the left side of the avenue, we come upon three small mosques built just after the Conquest by the craft guilds established in the quarter. The first of them, the KANTARCILAR MESCIDI, or the Mosque of the Scale-makers, was constructed during the reign of Fatih

> "The landscape, the entire length of the Golden Horn, is captivating, all the way to the landings at Hasköy and Eyüp."
>
> A. T'Serstevens

Mehmet by Sarı Demirci Mevlâna Mehmet Muhittin. Muhittin appears to have been a member of the guild of scale-makers, whose still have shops in Kantarcılar Caddesi.

THE MOSQUE OF THE CAULDRON-MAKERS. About 250 yards farther along is the KAZANCILAR CAMI'I, or the Mosque of the Cauldron-makers, which is also known as the Üç Mihrablı Cami'i, the Mosque of the Three Mihrabs. Founded in 1475 by Hoca Hayrettin, the temple was subsequently enlarged by Fatih Mehmet himself and then again by Hayrettin's daughter-in-law, each of whom added a mihrab ● *81*, which accounts for its more popular Turkish name.

THE MOSQUE OF THE LEATHER-WORKERS. The third of these extremely old mosques, the SAĞRICILAR CAMI'I, or Mosque of the Leather-workers, is situated about 150 yards farther along, just before you come to the Atatürk Bridge. It is probably the oldest mosque in Istanbul, founded in

FENER VAPUR İSKELESI

ATATÜRK KÖPRÜSÜ

GALATA KÖPRÜSÜ

1455 by Yavuz Ersinan – who was Fatih Mehmet's standard-bearer during the siege of Constantinople in 1453. Yavuz Ersinan was an ancestor of Evliya Çelebi, the famous writer and chronicler, who was born in 1611 in a house next door to Sağrıcılar Cami'i.

THE HARBOR OF THE GOLDEN HORN

A CAIQUE ON THE GOLDEN HORN

THE PRISON TOWER
A few remnants of the sea walls can still be found along the upper reaches of the Golden Horn, usually surrounded by more modern structures. Only two of the walls' monumental gateways have survived, but the ghosts of others linger in the names of the sites where they stood: Aya Kapı and Cibali Kapı. The huge defense tower, standing just beyond the Galata Bridge, served as a prison under both the Byzantines and the Ottomans. Indeed, the Romans called it "the Prison". Inside is the tomb of a Muslim saint, Cafer Baba, the peaceful emissary from Haroun al-Rachid to Constantinople, who was nonetheless imprisoned in the tower. Found after the Conquest, his tomb remains, even today, a popular pilgrimage site.

239

Zeyrek Cami'i

A POSTER OF THE COMPAGNIE FRANÇAISE DES MESSAGERIES MARITIMES
Until the outbreak of World War One, large passenger steamships made regular calls at Istanbul, which had become a popular tourist destination, attracting between 40,000 and 65,000 visitors a year.

THE MOSQUE OF THE ROSES
In 1453 the feast of St Theodosia, which falls on May 28, was celebrated in the Church of St Theodosia on the very eve of Constantinople's capture by the Turks. According to tradition, the building was still decorated with roses when the first Turkish troops stormed it. When the church was converted into a mosque it was called the Gül Cami'i, meaning the Mosque of the Roses, in memory of this event. Meanwhile, the Greeks call it the Church of the Immortal Rose, and some of them believe that Constantine XI was secretly buried there on the day Constantinople fell to the Turks.

THE CHURCH OF CHRIST PANTOCRATOR

At the end of Atatürk Boulevard, approximately 400 yards from the intersection, stands a church known in Turkish as the Zeyrek Cami'i. This is the ancient Church of the Pantocrator, one of the most famous buildings in Constantinople. In fact, it consisted of two churches with a chapel wedged in between, as well as a large, elaborate, and renowned monastery, which has long since disappeared, except for a few ruins.

Around 1120, the Empress Eirene, the wife of John II Comnenus (1118–43), founded the monastery as well as the church to the south and dedicated both to Christ Pantocrator – "Christ the Almighty." After

240

> "The caïque is to Istanbul as the gondola is to Venice:
> a rather short boat, with a shallow draft and a rower who faces you."
>
> A. T'Serstevens

her death in 1124, Emperor John II had a second church constructed a few yards away, which was almost identical to the first, and dedicated it to Panayia Eleousa – "Our Lady of Mercy." Next, the Emperor joined the two churches together by building a small chapel of rest between them. This was the place he chose for the burial of the Empress and, in 1143, himself. Three other Byzantine emperors would also be

Constantinople. Corne d'or: Eglise bulgare à Phanar

entombed in the chapel: Manuel I Comnenus (1143–80), Manuel II Palaeologus (1391–1425), and John VIII Palaeologus (1425–48), together with his third and final wife, Maria of Trebizond. She was the last Empress of Byzantium, since the widower Constantine XI did not remarry after he ascended the throne.

A view of the Golden Horn from Pera.

THE GREAT SCHOOL Looming above the Fener Quarter, and clearly visible from a distance, is a large red-brick building. Built in 1881, it is now occupied by a high school serving the Greek community. This was formerly the Megali Scholea, or Grand School, a secular institution of higher education, many of whose graduates went on to fill high positions in the Ottoman Empire. They included some of the most illustrious Feneriotes of the post-Byzantine Empire, from such families as the Palaeologues, Cantacuzenos, Cantemirs, Mavrocordatos, and Ypsilantis.

FROM THE ATATÜRK BRIDGE TO THE FENER

THE CIBALI GATE. On the other side of Atatürk Boulevard, continue along the Golden Horn through a park laid out on the water's edge. About 450 yards from Atatürk Bridge, on the left, there is one of the two surviving gates from the Byzantine sea walls. This is the Cibali Kapı, known in antiquity as the Porta Putea. An inscribed plaque states that Fatih's troops broke through the gateway on May 29, 1453 ● 35, the day that Constantinople finally fell to the Turks.

Here too the Byzantines had taken the full force of the bombardment from the Venetian fleet when the Romans made their assault upon Constantinople in 1203, an attack they renewed successfully in 1204. On the opposite bank, in the Kasımpaşa quarter, we see the Aynalıkavak Kasrı, the Palace of the Arsenal, also known as the Palace of Mirrors. Built during the reign of Ahmet III (1703–30) and renovated by Selim III (1789–1807), the building takes its name from the large Venetian mirrors that decorate the salons, all gifts from the Venetian Republic following the Treaty of Passarowitz, signed in 1718. Today it is a music museum.

THE CHURCH OF ST NICHOLAS. Another 250 yards beyond Cibali Kapı there is a Greek church built just inside the sea walls. Dating from 1720, it is dedicated to St Nicholas, the patron saint of sailors. The sanctuary remains open to the faithful, though today there are relatively few.

THE CHURCH OF ST STEPHEN OF THE BULGARS A cast-iron neo-Gothic monument erected in 1871.

THE MOSQUE OF THE ROSES. Aya Kapı, the Holy Gate, is the second of the two gateways from the sea walls still standing on the Golden Horn. In the Byzantine era, it was also known as the Gate of St Theodosia, because of the celebrated

SMALL TRADES
This itinerant pedlar, near the Blue Mosque, sells his seeds to feed the pigeons. In front of the Mosque of Eyüp a great variety of religious souvenirs are for sale, mainly to tourists: they include amber prayer beads, handkerchiefs, and talismans against the evil eye.

FRIDAY PRAYERS
Before prayers, the Muslim faithful stop at the ablution fountain in the Mosque of Eyüp. On Friday, they listen to an imam who preaches from the top of the mimbar.

church it led to, a Christian place of worship subsequently converted into a mosque. Continue for 50 yards beyond Aya Kapı, then turn left into Kara Sarıklı Sokağı and you arrive at the Gül Cami'i, the ancient Church of St Theodosia, founded in the first half of the 9th century and originally dedicated to St Euphemia. It became known as St Theodosia after the remains of that venerated saint were buried there. The building is in the shape of a Greek cross, with side aisles supporting galleries. The disengaged pillars allow for two-story corner alcoves, but the arches and domes they support date from Ottoman times ● 78. Following its conversion in the early seventeenth century, the church became known as the Mosque of the Roses in memory of the fact that when the Turkish conquerors stormed the church on May 29, 1453, they found the inside decorated with roses to commemorate the feast day of St Theodosia.

THE CASTLE OF THE PETRION. Past Aya Kapı, about 100 yards farther along, is the Yeni Aya Kapı. However, the "New Gate" was not built in the Byzantine era but in 1582, possibly by the great Sinan ▲ 314. Another 100 yards farther along is the Sadrazam Ali Paşa Caddesi, which runs next to, but veering away from, the Golden Horn. There was once a gateway here that the Turks called Petri Kapı, which led to a fortified site known as the Castle of Petrion, an enclosure built during Justinian's reign. It played an important role during the Venetian sieges of 1203 and 1204. On May 29, 1453, the stronghold stood fast against the Turkish fleet, and its defenders did not give up until they learned that the capital had been taken. Hearing this, Mehmet II ordered that the houses and churches within the enclave be spared the general pillaging unleashed elsewhere.

THE FENER QUARTER

By the beginning of the 16th century, the Greek merchants and traders of the quarter – the Feneriotes – had amassed substantial fortunes while enjoying the protection of the Sublime Porte, and some of them had even achieved high standing within the Ottoman Empire. An enormously lucrative post traditionally reserved for the Feneriotes was that of *hospodar* – viceroy – to Moldavia and Walachia, Danubian principalities that remained vassal states of the Ottomans until the 19th century.

A camel train left every year from Eyüp on a pilgrimage to Mecca.

THE GOLDEN HORN
Its Turkish name – Haliç – means "Channel." It is a gulf 4 miles long and 870 yards across at its widest point; it has an average depth of 115 feet. It came to be known as the Golden Horn at a time when its banks were places of recreation for the sultans and the great Ottoman families, who lived there in palaces and those charming seaside villas known as *yalı*, all with attractive gardens. Alas, industrialization has made devastating inroads. Recently a program of rehabilitation has been undertaken in the hope of restoring the Golden Horn to something of its former glory.

THE GREEK ORTHODOX PATRIARCHATE. Leaving the main, waterside avenue and turning left into Sadrazam Ali Paşa Caddesi, you soon arrive at the Greek Orthodox Patriarchate, transferred here in 1601 after the church it had occupied – the Pammakaristos – was converted into the Fethiye Cami'i. The present Patriarchal Church of St George, which dates from 1720, replaced a much older one of the same name. The ivory-inlaid Patriarchal throne stands in the side aisles on the right. The administrative headquarters of the Greek Orthodox Patriarchate are opposite the church. During the Ottoman period, the Patriarch of Constantinople, although under the suzerainty of the sultan, functioned as the spiritual leader of all orthodox christians within the Empire. Today the Patriarch of Istanbul is the nominal head of the Greek Orthodox Church, but in fact his flock is the Greeks living in the city and on a few islands off the Turkish coast.

THE GATE OF THE LIGHTHOUSE. The street corner just beyond the entrance to the Patriarchate is the site of the famous Porta Phanari, the "Gate of the Lighthouse", which the Turks call the Fener Kapı. Long after the structure disappeared its name survives in that of the Fener Quarter, once famous for its great mansions.

BALAT-DRAMAN-FENER, POPULAR ISTANBUL ✪
The squat, colored houses of Balat were home to a significant Jewish community after the Spanish Inquisition. The Fener was inhabited by the Greeks of Istanbul, and Draman by the Armenians. These days, they are colorful neighborhoods that contrast with the austerity of nearby Fatih. Explore the narrow streets in the morning, but make sure you have a detailed map and sturdy shoes. The simplest route runs from the top of the sixth hill (Kariye Cami'i, ▲ 232) down the slope to the Golden Horn.

EYÜP İSKELESI
These boats carry passengers from one bank to the other.

THE MOSQUE OF EYÜP
This is the most frequented and venerated of Istanbul's mosques, thanks to its mausoleum, which contains the bones of Eyüp Ensari, the friend and standard-bearer of the Prophet Mohammed.

THE TOMBS OF THE GRAND VIZIERS
They stand at the head of Cami Kebir Caddesi, leading to the Mosque of Eyüp.

OUR LADY OF THE MONGOLS. High on the hill overlooking the Patriarchate there is a small rose-colored church dedicated to Our Lady of the Mongols. This is the only Byzantine church in the city that has remained continuously under the control of the Greek Orthodox Patriarchate, even during the Ottoman era. Although services continue, the congregation has dwindled considerably. The church is dedicated to the Theotokos Panayiotissa – Mother of God – but is generally known as Mouchliotissa, or Our Lady of the Mongols. Recent investigations indicate that the original church was built as early as the 10th century. Princess Maria, the illegitimate daughter of Michael VIII Palaeologus, ordered its reconstruction around 1282. In 1265, she had married Abagu, the Great Khan of the Mongols, as a result of which she lived at the Mongol court in Persia for about fifteen years. Under her influence, the Khan and his subjects converted to Christianity. Following the assassination of Abagu by his brother, Ahmet, in 1281, Maria found it necessary to return to Constantinople. Shortly afterwards, her father proposed that she be married to another Mongol Khan, but this time she refused, having decided to take up life in a convent. Thus came into being the actual church, to which Maria also added a convent, both dedicated to Theotokos Panayiotissa. The fame of the foundress, as the one-time Queen of the Mongols, meant that the church quickly became known by its more popular name.
THE CHURCH OF ST STEPHEN OF THE BULGARS. Continuing along the shore, you soon come upon the Church of St Stephen of the Bulgars. This sanctuary and the building opposite, the former Exarchate, date from 1871, a time when the Bulgarian Church was declaring its

> "Oh my friends, I caused a palace to be erected, and it is
> I who was the first to bring its beams crashing down."
>
> Karaca-Oğlan

independence from the Greek Orthodox Patriarchate. Dedicated to St Stephen, the patron saint of Bulgaria, it is a neo-Gothic building made entirely of cast iron, all of it prefabricated in Vienna and shipped in sections down the Danube and across the Black Sea. In the cemetery of this unusual yet impressive church are buried several local leaders of the Bulgarian Orthodox Church.

THE CHURCH OF ST JOHN THE BAPTIST. A further 250 yards along the Golden Horn brings you to the Greek Church of St John the Baptist. Although a Byzantine sanctuary is thought to have stood here originally, the present building only dates from 1830. The somewhat dilapidated old mansion near the church courtyard is the former Metochion of the Monastery

of St Catherine on Mount Sinai. From 1686 until as recently as the 1960's, the Metochion served as the residence of a prelate representing the St Catherine Monastery.

THE BALAT QUARTER

Some 150 yards or so farther along is the Balat Kapı, the site of one of the former gates in the sea walls. The Turkish name Balat, which also applies to the neighboring quarter, derives from the Greek word *palation,* "palace." Here it also relates to the nearby site of the Blachernae Palace, the last residence of the Byzantine emperors. For centuries Balat was home to an important Jewish community, Greek-speaking Jews and then the more dominant Latin-speaking Sephardim from Spain. Several of the synagogues still in use date from the Byzantine period, though the buildings appear to be late-Ottoman. The most remarkable of the synagogues is the OKRIDA SYNAGOGUE. Meanwhile, Balat and the neighboring Ayvansaray boast many old Greek and Armenian churches, some founded in the Byzantine era. Beyond the Balat Kapı, on the right, there is a small mosque designed by Sinan. A long, elegantly calligraphed inscription over the entranceway states that it was Ferrah Ağa, the *kethüda* or "steward" to the Grand Vizier Semiz Ali Paşa, who had it built between 1562 and 1563. The mihrab is clad in faience that dates from the period of the Tekfur Saray's construction (11th century). On the east of the mosque stands an old hammam.

The double portico of the Mosque of Eyüp and the entranceway to its courtyard are both surmounted by cartouches inscribed with calligraphy of verses taken from the Koran.

A YOUNG BOY IN FESTIVE COSTUME FOR HIS CIRCUMCISION DAY For young Muslim boys, circumcision is comparable to Christian baptism, symbolizing their admission into the community of believers. The day also constitutes a family holiday.

THE AYVANSARAY QUARTER

THE MOSQUE OF ATIK MUSTAFA PAŞA. The last of the old Byzantine sea gates on the Golden Horn is the Ayvansaray Kapı, approximately 500 yards beyond the Balat Kapı. Another 100 yards before the gate, on the left, is a narrow street leading to the Atik Mustafa Paşa Cami'i, another Byzantine church converted into a mosque at the end of the 15th century, this one by Atik Mustafa Paşa, grand vizier to the sultan Beyazıt II. The apse, on the south side, houses the supposed tomb of Eyüp Ensari, discovered after the Conquest. He was a companion of the Prophet Mohammed, and died during the siege of Constantinople in 670.

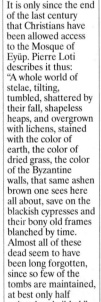

THE CEMETERY OF EYÜP
It is only since the end of the last century that Christians have been allowed access to the Mosque of Eyüp. Pierre Loti describes it thus: "A whole world of stelae, tilting, tumbled, shattered by their fall, shapeless heaps, and overgrown with lichens, stained with the color of earth, the color of dried grass, the color of the Byzantine walls, that same ashen brown one sees here all about, save on the blackish cypresses and their bony old frames blanched by time. Almost all of these dead seem to have been long forgotten, since so few of the tombs are maintained, at best only half painted and gilded."

THE SACRED SPRING OF THE BLACHERNAE. Turning left into Ayvansaray Sokağı, you come to the *ayazma* of the Blachernae, a "sacred spring" in a little church surrounded by a pretty garden. The church dates from 451, when Empress Pulcheria, the sister of Theodosius II and wife of Marcian, had the sacred spring enclosed in a great church, dedicating it to the Blacherniotissa – Our Lady of Blachernae – who, according to tradition, saved Constantinople from the Avars in 627. The church burned in 1434 and has since been replaced several times, the last time in the 19th century. Returning to the shore – the *iskele* of Ayvansaray – you can then take the ferry as far as Eyüp, about one mile away on the Golden Horn.

AN ORNAMENTAL DETAIL ON A MAUSOLEUM
Above, trellis-screened windows of a birdhouse
designed like a miniature ablution fountain.

THE EYÜP QUARTER

Eyüp takes its name from Eyüp (Job) Ensari, the companion
and standard-bearer of the Prophet Mohammed killed during
the first siege of Constantinople (670). Fatih Mehmet, after
his own siege of 1453, made the miraculous discovery of the
supposed burial place of Eyüp, a site surrounded by hills
covered with cypress groves. In less than five years the
grateful conqueror had the site endowed with a large *külliye*,
including a mosque and a mausoleum for the remains of the
disciple. In the Ottoman period, many important people of
the empire chose to be interred here, often in splendid *türbe*.
Several of the mausoleums are surrounded by large
complexes where once all manner of pious
activity took place. The structures turn
Eyüp into a romantic, open-air museum of
Ottoman architecture, especially of
funerary monuments ● 79. Many other
Ottomans of more modest means
arranged to be buried on the side of the
hill above the shrine, thereby making the
cemetery the second largest in Turkey,
surpassed only by the Karaca Ahmet
cemetery above Üsküdar.

THE MAUSOLEUM OF EYÜP. From the landing stage at Eyüp,
follow Eyüp Iskele Caddesi to the intersection with Boyacı
Feshane Caddesi, where the classical, octagonal *türbe* of
Ferhat Paşa, dating from 1595, is situated. A further 100 yards
or so, in Caddesi Kebir Cami'i, is the tomb of the Grand
Vizier Sokollu Mehmet Paşa. This severe yet elegant
structure, with blue and green stained-glass
windows, was designed by Sinan around 1572. On
the opposite side of the street is the austere
mausoleum of Siyavuş Paşa, another
building built by Sinan sometime
around 1583. This "street of tombs"
leads to the quarter's main square,
a place constantly busy with
itinerant pedlars selling all kinds
of food and religious objects to
the hosts of pilgrims who come
to visit the *türbe* of Eyüp.

EYÜP, THE "SAINT DENNIS BASILICA" OF THE OTTOMAN DYNASTY ✪
Every new Sultan was enthroned in the Eyüp mosque with elaborate ceremony. The mausoleum, another pilgrimage sight, contains a footprint of the Prophet. Go through the cemetery when the sun sets to refresh yourself in Pierre Loti café (▲ 248–249).

A TALISMAN AGAINST THE EVIL EYE
Shops specializing in religious articles also sell talismans against the evil eye, such as this one above made of turquoise stones.

The Mausoleum of Eyüp is hidden away among bushes and trees at the center of cypress gardens. Grass grows wild all around the old tombstones covered with lichens. Until 1926 stones for men had a fez on top and those for women had bouquets of flowers.

THE MOSQUE OF EYÜP COMPLEX. On the right can be seen
the entrance gate to the enclosure around the Mosque of
Eyüp. In addition to the mausoleum and the mosque, the
külliye originally included a *medrese*, a hammam, an *imaret*, a
caravanserai, and a covered market, which was constructed in
1458 on the orders of Fatih Mehmet. Thereafter, his
successors, beginning with Beyazıt II, would all mark their
accession to the throne by coming to Eyüp for the ceremony
of having themselves girt in the sword of Osman. At the end
of the 18th century, the mosque had fallen into ruin, which
prompted Selim III to order its complete reconstruction
between 1798 and 1800, except for two minarets replaced
earlier by Ahmet III. The mosque is entered through an outer
court shaded by enormous old plane trees populated by lame
storks and, in spring, gray herons ■ *18*. From the outer
courtyard, you enter the inner courtyard, which is bordered

on three sides by an unusually imposing colonnade, and it too is shaded by venerable plane trees.

THE MOSQUE OF EYÜP. In plan the Eyüp Cami'i – the holiest Muslim shrine in Istanbul – is an octagon inscribed within a rectangle. Even though of recent construction, the mosque is a remarkably attractive one, with its clear, honey-colored stone, its decorations highlighted in gold, its elegant chandeliers suspended from the center of the dome, and its magnificent turquoise carpet covering the floor from wall to wall. (The former Prime Minister Adnan Menderes gave the carpet to the mosque in gratitude for having been saved from an airplane accident.) The blind wall facing the shrine is clad in a patternless mix of tiles from every period, some of which are extremely beautiful. A gate in the wall opens onto the *türbe* of Eyüp Ensari, an octagonal monument three sides of which project into the vestibule. Meanwhile, the vestibule itself is revetted in faience dating in part from the high period of Iznik production. The decoration of the *türbe* is lavish, but mostly in the Turkish Baroque manner.

THE GREAT CEMETERY OF EYÜP ● *250*. This enormous cemetery spreads across the hillside overlooking the mosque. It is one of the most attractive and picturesque sites in all of Istanbul, dotted with thousands of tombs and tombstones scattered among the cypress groves. The oldest stones are beautifully carved and crowned with some kind of representative headdress, often a turban for the men, or a shawl for women, together with a diadem if the deceased had been a princess. The women's tombstones are decorated with floral motifs, usually roses, the number of flowers signifying the number of children borne. Those of men are typically engraved with epitaphs in old Turkish script, some of which have a jocular tone: "Visitor, deny me your prayers, but please do not steal my tombstone."

THE CAFÉ PIERRE LOTI. The path running across the cemetery leads to the small teahouse or café that Pierre Loti frequented during his days as a naval officer living in Eyüp. Several episodes in his novel *Aziyadé* take place in this ancient cemetery, whose appearance has hardly changed since then. The view from the café is particularly romantic at sunset, when the Golden Horn is flooded with the fading glow of twilight. While smoking his narghile, Loti could see all the way to the source of the Golden Horn, where legend holds that Cereossa gave birth to the child sired by Poseidon, a boy who grew up to be Byzas the Megarian, eponymous founder of Byzantium.

EXCURSIONS UPON THE SWEET WATERS OF EUROPE IN THE 19TH CENTURY

"If, instead of leaving the Golden Horn by its mouth, we turn back into the past across the sea lanes in a city of vessels; if we pass under a floating bridge that closes off the arsenal of the Imperial Navy, then we see the banks of the Golden Horn slowly converging and thus arrive, by following the narrow neck of the gulf, at a small, clear, calm river that runs through the most beautiful meadows. This is the little valley of the Sweet Waters of Europe."

Charles Reynaud

"Disembarking at the Sweet Waters, one experiences that pleasure which always comes with a harmonious ensemble of verdure, shade, and limpid waters spread over a variable terrain. Here the river is squeezed into a channel some one hundred feet wide, whose rocky banks are shaded by rows of beautiful trees. The channel runs through a series of falls that, while shallow, extend completely across the flood. Between the cascades one sees the kiosks dressed in color and picked out in gold."

Castellan

▲ CEMETERIES

The Muslim cemeteries, or "fields of the dead," are an important part in the life of everyone in Istanbul. They are like immense forests situated on the outskirts of the city, by the land walls, at the top of Üsküdar, around the mosques or sometimes along the streets, and are far from melancholy places. People come to stroll or have picnics, enjoying the peaceful freshness beneath the shade of the cypress trees. Flowers, milk and perfume are offered to the deceased, demonstrating the intimacy the living feel with death. The Turkish cemeteries are remarkable for their apparent disorder: the unkempt vegetation which expresses the vitality of nature, and the sense of abandonment that signifies a gentle resignation to the passage of time.

The tombstones of men and women can be distinguished by their decoration. For the men there is a cylindrical stone topped with a turban, the sophistication of which is in relation to the importance of the deceased. For women a flat stone ends in a crown of flowers or fruit sculpted in relief.

Columns and stelae with epitaphs in ancient Turkish writing.

A small basin is dug in the center of the tombstone to collect the offerings made by friends and family of the deceased.

The dead are celebrated on the second day of the Festival of Delicacies, the *Şeker Bayramı,* which is part of Ramadan. On this occasion cake and candy sellers used to gather at the entrance to the cemetery.

"Hurry to bury your dead, so that they might rejoice in the eternal beatitude."

The Koran

Tombs from the 18th and 19th centuries can still be seen in the old Turkish cemeteries. During this era Ottoman funereal art reached its height, taking advantage of an abundant supply of marble.

The atmosphere of a garden gone wild reigns in these "fields of the dead". Grasses and flowers besiege the tombstones that lie scattered among the trees.

Laid bare little by little, the stones and stelae tip over in all directions; others, broken, lie on the ground. The lichen-covered stones take on the shiny color of the walls, and are hard to distinguish from those on the ground.

251

▲ GALATA AND BEYOĞLU

AZAPKAPI CAMI'I

GALATA TOWER ✪

GALATASARAY SCHOOL

ÇIÇEK PASAJI

⚄ Half a day
◆ C

THE GALATA TOWER
High above the modern houses of Galata towers the ancient bastion of the fortified wall which enclosed the Genoese concession. The view from the top, at about 170 feet, is spectacular.

THE GALATA BRIDGE
This watercolor (right) by Hawizy Hvanson, painted in 1908, shows the old wooden bridge before it was rebuilt between 1910 and 1912 with a metal span, which in turn was replaced in 1992.

The two oldest quarters on the north shore of the Golden Horn are Galata and Beyoğlu. Pera, the ancient name of Beyoğlu, means "beyond" or "over there" in Greek. At first it signified the northern side of the Golden Horn; then, in the Byzantine era, the village opposite Constantinople; and, still later, the elegant suburb overlooking Galata.

HISTORY

THE BYZANTINE PERIOD ● 32. Galata, a fortified town in the Greco-Byzantine period and thus older than Constantinople, grew tremendously after the Genoese took control in the 13th century. Beginning in the 11th century, the Byzantine emperors allowed Venice, Genoa, and other city-states to establish trading posts in Constantinople. When the Venetians and their allies, the knights of the Fourth Crusade, took possession of the Byzantine capital in 1204, the Genoese found themselves evicted and forced to make do on the other side of the gulf. They settled in Galata and seized its port. In the last year of the Roman occupation, the Genoese allied themselves with the Byzantines, formalizing the relationship in the Treaty of Nymphaeum, signed at Nicaea on March 12, 1261 by the exiled Michael VIII Palaeologus. By the terms of this agreement, the men from Genoa gained important trading and commercial

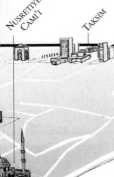

concessions in the empire. After recovering Constantinople four months later, the Byzantine emperor authorized the Genoese to make maximum use of their concession in Galata, which would soon become an independent city-state under the protection of Genoa. Power rested with an Italian-style *podesta* (governor) appointed annually by the Genoese Senate and aided by a council. When the Ottoman Turks laid siege to Constantinople in 1453 ● *34*, Genoese Galata attempted to secure its own interests by remaining neutral, even though many of its Italian inhabitants decided to fight on the Greek side. A year later, the sultan integrated the Galata concession into the Ottoman Empire and appointed a *voivode* (mayor) to govern the new possession.

THE OTTOMAN PERIOD. Even after the Conquest, the Genoese retained a degree of independence in Galata, up to the middle of the 17th century, during which time they went on managing their civic affairs through a council known as the "Magnificent Community of Pera." Little by little, however, their power drained away, until by the end of the 19th century it had disappeared entirely.

A CHURCH IN OLD PERA AND A MOSQUE IN GALATA
The heavily Europeanized Pera quarter lay next door to Galata, where, following the Conquest, several mosques were constructed. Istanbul long provided the civilized world with a model of religious tolerance.

▲ GALATA AND BEYOĞLU

GALATA AND PERA
A map drawn in
c. 1536 by the painter
Matrakçı Nasuh
representing the
Genoese concession
on the banks of the
Golden Horn.
Virtually an
independent city-
state, the concession is
encircled by defensive
walls with numerous
towers, including the
great keep to the
north. Pera can be
seen on the vine-
planted hills situated
above Galata.

**GALATA'S
EUROPEAN SCHOOLS
IN THE 19TH CENTURY**
Each foreign embassy
surrounded itself with
the institutions
necessary to its well-
being: church, post
office, shops, and
religious schools. The
schools enjoyed such
a reputation for
excellence that the
great Ottoman
families sent their
children to study at
them alongside the
Europeans.

**THE UNDERGROUND
FUNICULAR**
This subway links
Istiklal Caddesi, near
Karaköy Square, with
the Galata Bridge.

THE ARSENAL. After the Conquest, Fatih Mehmet had the gigantic *tersane*, or Marine Arsenal, constructed on the Golden Horn just above Galata, and the shipyard is still in operation today. Thanks to its infrastructure and its extremely busy port, Galata soon developed into the center of Istanbul's maritime industry, where a host of Italian, Greek, Jewish, and Armenian merchants worked as suppliers to both the ships in port and their multinational crews.

PERA. Within a century after the Conquest, the richest merchants began moving outside the overcrowded, wall-encircled town and taking up residence among the vineyards on the hills above Galata, an area that came to be known as Pera and then Beyoğlu. Here, as well as foreign embassies, they built great mansions surrounded by gardens along what would become the main street of Pera, which in its time was both fashionable and famous.

THE MOSQUE OF THE ARABS. After crossing the Atatürk Bridge from Istanbul, you come to the shipyard on the left and, on the right, the Sokollu Mehmet Paşa Cami'i, which has an exceptionally beautiful Baroque fountain. Going towards the Galata Bridge, it is best to avoid the highway which runs along the shore, and instead follow Tersane Caddesi through the maze of tiny streets that border it. Just beyond the Yanık Kapı Sokağı there is a large building with an imposing campanile, which, on first sight, could be taken for an Italian church. It is, however, the ARAP CAMI'I, or the Mosque of the Arabs. A vaulted passage beneath the campanile leads to the mosque's main entrance and courtyard.

THE STREET OF THE THURSDAY MARKET. Some 50 yards beyond the Arap Cami'i turn left into PERŞEMBE PAZARI SOKAĞI, or the Street of the Thursday Market; this runs uphill to the old quarters that the Genoese enclosed within a circuit of defensive walls in 1304. The street is flanked by enormous old buildings with façades of stone and brick set in alternating courses and with corbeled upper stories thrusting outwards at odd, irregular angles and intervals. The buildings were long thought to have been constructed by the Genoese during the Byzantine era. However, the discovery of the dates 1735–6 inscribed on one of them in Arabic indicates that all the houses in the street were built in the 18th century.

> "Whole clans of Periot families move into and occupy space
> left free by idle consumers dressed in European attire."
>
> Pierre Loti

THE OLD PODESTAT

Perşembe Pazarı Sokağı ends in Bankalar Caddesi, where, on the opposite side of the avenue, in Eski Banka Sokağı (the "Street of the Old Bank"), a flight of stairs takes us down to Galata Kulesi Sokağı. On the right stands the old Podestat, the Town Hall erected in 1316 to house the podesta dispatched annually from Genoa to govern Galata. Substantially rebuilt in 1939, the building has lost much of its medieval character.

THE CARAVANSERAI OF ST PETER

Take the little street on the left to the top of the stairs; the right side is almost entirely taken up by an old European-style building. This is the *han*, or caravanserai, of St Peter, built in

1771 at the behest of the Count of Saint-Priest for the purpose of establishing "the residence and the bank of the French nation," as he wrote in his will. A plaque on the façade bears the arms of the Bourbon dynasty as well as those of the Count. Another plaque informs us that the French poet André Chénier was born here on October 30, 1762, in a house that pre-dated the present *han*.

SAN PIETRO. Halfway along Galata Kulesı Sokağı, where the street bends to the right, you come to the Roman Catholic Church of Sts Peter and Paul. Better known by its Italian variant, San Pietro, it was founded at the end of the 15th century by the Dominican order, to which it still belongs. During the Ottoman era, San Pietro came under the protection of

TOBACCO
During the period when Istanbul seemed enveloped in a cloud of romantic smoke from the Orient Express, Turkish cigarettes were all the rage. To protect the legitimacy of Turkish tobacco and assert its distinction relative to foreign imitations then undercutting the product in the marketplace, the Ottoman Office of Tobacco stamped the origin of the contents on every box it sold: "the only authentic Turkish cigarettes."

The entrance to the Tünel in the late 1950's.

GALATA AND BEYOĞLU

The entrance to one of the many commercial arcades in Beyoğlu and the stairs in Eski Banka Sokağı – the "Street of the Old Bank".

GALATA TOWER, LEGACY OF THE GENOESE ✪

The banishment of the Europeans to the other bank of the Golden Horn dates back to the Byzantine Emperors, anxious to protect their power from any Western influences. At the height of this relative autonomy, Galata even won itself the status of a completely separate town. Climb the Galata Tower in the late afternoon to revel in its unique 360° vantage point, with particularly striking views of the old town with its jungle of domes and minarets.

France, serving as the parish church for the French community. Later, it administered to the Maltese in Pera. The present structure was erected in 1841 by the Fossati brothers, who restored Haghia Sophia between 1847 and 1849.

THE GALATA TOWER

The Galata Tower rears up at the top of Galata Kulesı Sokağı. This massive, cone-capped structure, built at 115 feet above sea level and rising to a height of 220 feet above its base, overlooks the entire northern side of the Golden Horn. An elevator goes to the penultimate floor, after which you must take the stairs to reach the top, where a restaurant and observation deck 174 feet above ground level provides an unrivaled view over the whole of Istanbul. The Galata Tower is generally thought to have been constructed by the Genoese around 1348 as a great bastion reinforcing the defensive walls designed to protect them in the event of an attack by the

Byzantines. After the Conquest, Sultan Fatih Mehmet II had its height shortened by 22 feet. The Turks eventually used it to incarcerate prisoners of war. Under Murat III (1574–95), the tower was converted into an observatory, and then, towards the end of the Ottoman period, a lookout for fires, which it remained until the 1960s. After being closed for several years, the old Galata Tower was reopened and became one of Istanbul's major tourist attractions. A plaque near the elevator stop at the summit tells of an extraordinary feat that was performed in the

17th century by Hezarfen Ahmet Çelebi: equipped with wings of his own design, he flew from the top of the Galata Tower all the way across the Bosphorus before landing safely in Üsküdar on the far side.

Modern paintings representing Beyoğlu and the Golden Horn.

THE MONASTERY OF THE WHIRLING DERVISHES

At the upper end of Galip Dede Caddesi, we find a *tekke*, or monastery, of the Mevlevi dervishes on the left next to a charming *sebil*, or fountain, built at the beginning of the 19th century by Halil Efendi. The monastery was established in 1492 by Şeyh Muhammad Semai Sultan Divani, a direct descendant of Mevlâna Rumi, the 13th-century saint and mystic poet who founded the Mevlevi Brotherhood, best known in the West as the "Whirling Dervishes." At the bottom of the courtyard we find the *semahane*, the building in which the dervishes performed their dances. Since its restoration in the 1970's, the structure houses the Museum of Literature of the Divan, devoted to the works of mystic poets of the Ottoman era, the most famous of them being Galip Dede. The collection also includes manuscripts and objects once owned by the Whirling Dervishes, who occupied the monastery until the dissolution of their order in 1924. From time to time performances of Mevlevi dances are given here, mainly during the Istanbul Summer Festival.

DERVISHES (CENTER)
These Whirling Dervishes from the Galata *tekke*, all disciples of the Mevlevi Brotherhood, perform a dance that symbolizes the planets rotating about the sun and is supposed to induce a state of ecstasy.

THE OLD MAIN STREET OF PERA

Galip Dede Caddesi leads to Istiklal Caddesi, which begins immediately on the left, near the terminus of the Tünel, the underground funicular. The tramway service on the former main street of Pera has recently been restored between the Tünel station and Taksim Meydanı, the square at the other end of Istiklal Caddesi. It makes only one midway stop at Galatasaray Square. Save for the tramway, Istiklal Caddesi is closed to all motorized traffic, with the result that a stroll along the avenue is as pleasant as it must have been in former times, when this was still the main street of Pera.

VIEW FROM THE TOP OF THE GALATA TOWER
Galata spreads out at the foot of the old Genoese tower. From the summit of this medieval bastion, one can see old Istanbul from Seraglio Point to the Eminönü quarter, bristling with the minarets of the large mosques: Sultan Ahmet Cami'i, Aya Sofya Cami'i, and Süleymaniye Cami'i.

...

Istiklal Caddesi can boast a glittering past, dating back to the arrival of the big European embassies, beginning in the 16th century. Each legation, installed within its own little palace and compound, became a kind of separate nation, complete with the ambassador's residence, a church, a post office, and other institutions, all functioning more or less independently of Ottoman authority. The advent of the Turkish Republic in 1923 meant that the embassies moved to the new capital, Ankara, leaving the old ones in Istanbul to become consulates. At the first intersection stands the former Russian Embassy; built in 1837 it was the first building completed in Istanbul by the Fossatis. On the right is the elegant old Swedish Embassy, which probably dates from the late 17th century.

THE PROTESTANT CHURCH

At the next intersection, on the right, is the Kumbaracı Yokuşu, a street that derives its name from the mansion at its upper end once owned and occupied by Kumbaracı Ahmet Paşa. Some 200 yards down this street on the right is the recently restored Crimean Memorial Church, the only large building

of Protestant Christian worship ever built in Istanbul, and one of the most attractive of the city's Western churches. Its principal patron, Lord Stratford of Redcliffe, Britain's influential Ambassador, laid the cornerstone on October 18, 1858, the year the Crimean War ended. Designed by C.E. Street, the architect of the London Law Courts, the Crimean Memorial Church was Istanbul's first neo-Gothic building, the style so esteemed in the West during the Victorian era.

THE CHURCH OF ST MARY DRAPERIS. A little farther along Istiklal Caddesi is the Franciscan Church of St Mary Draperis. In 1453, the Franciscans had built a sanctuary of the same name in Constantinople on a site near the present Sirkeci Station. After the Conquest deprived them of these premises, the monks had to make do with various temporary quarters in Galata, until Clara Bartola Draperis provided a building near today's Customs House. The new Church of St Mary, whose name the Franciscans expanded to include that of their benefactress, was once again displaced in 1660 and then reconstructed several times following fires and an earthquake. The present church dates from 1769.

Early-20th-century cabaret beauties.

NIGHTLIFE AND THEATER
Nightclubs have long been a feature of the old European quarter of Pera, now called Beyoğlu. They are especially evident along Cumhuriyet Caddesi, between Taksim Square and the Hilton Hotel. The performances include everything from folk music to all kinds of singers and orchestras, as well as a plenitude of Oriental dancing.

THE PERA PALACE HOTEL

The grand hotel created in 1892 by the Compagnie des Wagons-lits to house Orient Express passengers still exists at 98-100 Mesrutiyet Caddesi in the Tepebaşı quarter. The room occupied by Mustafa Kemal Atatürk (no. 101) has been turned into a museum. But one can also request room no. 103, where Garbo slept, no. 104, which was Mata Hari's room, or no. 304, the accommodation taken by Sarah Bernhardt. Agatha Christie wrote a good part of *Murder on the Orient Express* in no. 411, which has retained an air of mystery ever since. Without having to stay at the hotel, one can still enjoy a cocktail in the elegant Orient Bar and enjoy the magic of this celebrated place.

THE EMBASSIES

Next, on the right, Istiklal Caddesi crosses a steep, narrow lane, Postacılar Sokağı, or the "Street of the Postmen", which leads downhill past, on the left, the former embassies of Holland and France, whose entrances are on Istiklal Caddesi. At the bottom, Postacılar Sokağı opens into a small square flanked by two large European buildings. The one on the left, a 19th-century structure, is the old French Law Court, or Palais de Justice, in which the legal affairs of the European "nations" in Constantinople were processed. The building on the right, the Palazzo di Venezia, served as the embassy of the Serene Republic of Venice from the end of the 16th century to 1797, before becoming the Italian Embassy.

A melodrama at the Pera Theater, some time between 1850 and 1870.

THE FRENCH RESIDENCE

France became the first European nation to establish diplomatic relations with the Ottoman Empire when, in 1535, François I sent an emissary to Süleyman the Magnificent. France was also the

THE ORIENT EXPRESS
On the day in 1883 when the Orient Express was being prepared to leave the Gare de l'Est in Paris for the first time, no one could have imagined that this superb piece of heavy machinery, some 230 feet long, would become a myth capable of enchanting several generations and inspiring works of fiction. Its destination was Istanbul, the "pearl of the Orient." Inside this mother of all the great *trains de luxe* was exquisite wood paneling, fine china, immaculate linens, Lalique crystal, and oceans of champagne.

first to build an embassy in the Grand-Rue de Pera. The 1581 building and its attendant church, Saint-Louis-des-Français, were burned down in 1831 and replaced by the structures there today.

THE CHURCH OF ST ANTHONY. Beyond the second turning on the right, we arrive at the Franciscan Church of St Anthony of Padua; built in 1913 it is a fine example of the Italian neo-Gothic. This Roman Catholic parish was originally served by a much older church dedicated to St Francis, built on the main street in 1725.

GALATASARAY SQUARE

A major intersection halfway along Istiklal Caddesi, Galatasaray Square, like the rest of the quarter, takes its name from the school whose name can be seen on the gateway to the right. Although the buildings only date from 1908, the institution has existed since the late 15th century, when Beyazıt II established it as an extension to the Campaign Hall at Topkapı Sarayı. In 1868 Sultan Abdül Aziz had it reorganized along the lines of French lycées. Since that time the Lycée Galatasaray has educated the political and intellectual élite of Turkey, thus playing an important role in the country's modernization.

THE BRITISH EMBASSY. The British Embassy is on Hamalbaşı Caddesi, the avenue heading off to the left of the square. The relationship between England and the Sublime Porte began when Elizabeth I and Murat III signed an agreement which allowed English merchants to establish the Levant Company in 1580. Around 1800, Lord Elgin had the first British Embassy

Galatasaray Lycée and Square.

> "Under walls frescoed by a Russian artist,
> *le tout-Moscou*, absurdly capped in fezzes,
> wandered among the palm trees."
>
> Paul Morand

THE RUSSIAN RESTAURANT IN THE AYAPAŞA QUARTER IN THE 1940s
This restaurant is situated near the Park Hotel (a modern building which replaced the old hotel of the same name demolished in 1979) and not far from Taksim Square. In the 1940's, it was one of the most famous restaurants in Istanbul, and the whole of the city's artistic and intellectual community went there for borscht and beef stroganoff. This was still the period of Bugattis and the first tramway. Women, obligingly decolletées, tended to imitate Hollywood starlets. Even now, the restaurant continues to evoke the charm and cordiality of yesteryear.

built on this site, but it was destroyed by fire in 1831. Parts of the present building were designed by Sir Charles Barry, one of the architects of the Houses of Parliament in London. W.J. Smith completed it in 1845 along somewhat different lines.

THE PERA PALACE HOTEL. The romantic Pera Palace Hotel, opened in 1892 to serve the passengers on the Orient Express,

still exists in Meşrutiyet Caddesi, left of Hamalbaşı Caddesi. Although the whole of the Tepebaşı quarter, once so elegant, has fallen on hard times, the Pera Palace still maintains its original splendor.

THE GALATASARAY MARKETS

The first street on the left, after Galatasaray Square, is Sahne Sokağı, or "Theater Street". Here and in neighboring lanes, is the picturesque Galatasaray Balık Pazar – the local fish market. Its maze of tiny streets is lined with stalls and barrows selling a wide variety of fish, meat, fruit, and vegetables. A short distance along Sahne Sokağı is a gate opening into the famous Çiçek Pasajı, or "Passage of Flowers", whose entrance lies on Istiklal Caddesi. Some twenty years ago Çiçek Pasajı still had a few of its old flower stalls, but the market has since moved to Sahne Sokağı. The L-shaped alleyway passes through a once-elegant apartment block built in 1871 and called the Cité de Pera. For the last fifty years this passage has been taken over by *meyhane*, or beer taverns, which, though formerly notorious for their raffishness, now seem fairly tame. Those nostalgic for the past miss the colorful mob of wandering minstrels, real or phony beggars, sword-swallowers, and other such exotic denizens of Beyoğlu, who have long since been banished from their old haunts.

A street in Pera at the turn of the 20th century.

The Galatasaray
Jesuit College

THE MAIN STREET OF PERA
At the turn of the
20th century, Istiklal
Caddesi was the most
modern avenue in
Istanbul; some of its
elegance can be seen
in this little, five-story
neo-classical building.

The façade of a
19th-century building
in Beyoğlu.

MONUMENT TO THE WAR OF INDEPENDENCE
This monument
commemorating the
heroes of the War of
Independence, which
liberated Turkey from
the occupying armies,
stands in the center of
Taksim Square.

THE CAFÉS. Meanwhile, the area between Galatasaray
Square and Taksim Square remains a popular rendezvous for
intellectuals, idlers, and celebrities of Istanbul, who often
gather in the early evening at the Café Pub, the Kulis, or the
Papyrus, all three of which are located on Istiklal Caddesi.

TAKSIM SQUARE

On the left, at the upper end of Istiklul Caddesi, is the old
French Consulate. Constructed in 1719, the building
originally served as a hospital for plague victims. Beyond this,
we find the octagonal *taksim* (reservoir), from which both the
square and the quarter take their name. In 1732 Mahmut I
had the reservoir built to collect
water from the Belgrade Forest to
supply the modern districts on the
north bank of the Golden Horn.
On the right stands an imposing
neo-Byzantine building crowned by
a tall tympanum and with a pair of
towering campaniles in front. This
is the Aya Trianda, the Greek
Orthodox Church of the Holy
Trinity, which dates from 1882. The
group of sculptures standing on the
western edge of the square are of
Atatürk and other nationalist
heroes. On the east side of the
square is the glass-walled Atatürk
Cultural Center, which is also the
home of the Istanbul Opera. The
Center is also the main venue for
most performances of music,
theater, and dance, including the
events of the Summer Festival.

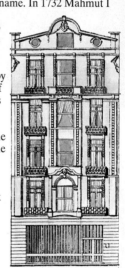

THE HARBIYE QUARTER

Cumhuriyet Caddesi, on the north side of Taksim Square,
leads into the more modern quarters of the city: Harbiye,
Maçka, Şişli, and Nişantaşı. Harbiye boasts not only two
important museums but also the Sports and Exhibition
Palace (Spor ve Sergi Sarayı) and the Istanbul Concert
Hall, both used for performances during the Istanbul
Summer Festival. The first, and larger, of the museums is
the Askerı Müzesi, or Military Museum, in whose
remarkable collection of objects can be found the whole of
Turkey's martial history. Here too the famous Mektar
Band gives concerts of Ottoman military music. At 25
Halaskargazi Caddesi there is a small
museum devoted to Mustafa Kemal
Atatürk, the father of modern Turkey,
who lived in this house from
1918 to 1919 during the last
days of the old Pera, just
prior to his departure for
Anatolia, where he would
organize the nationalist
movement ● *44*.

▲ ÜSKÜDAR AND THE PRINCES' ISLANDS

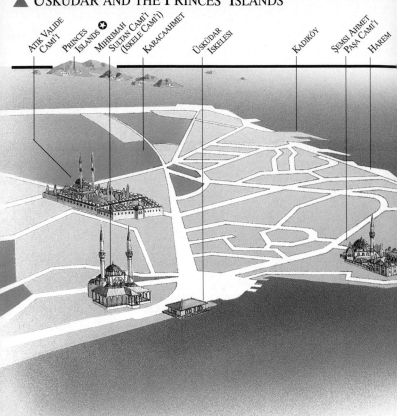

ATIK VALIDE CAMİ'İ   PRINCES ISLANDS ✪   MIHRIMAH SULTAN CAMİ'İ (İSKELE CAMİ'İ)   KARACAAHMET   ÜSKÜDAR İSKELESİ   KADIKÖY   ŞEMSİ AHMET PAŞA CAMİ'İ   HAREM

🏃 One day

◆ **F** and **A** D6–E6

ÜSKÜDAR
This is the Asian quarter of Istanbul and, as such, it retains a certain oriental feel. Amongst the maze of narrow streets there are picturesque old wooden houses, but also some great Ottoman buildings, among them several mosques designed by Sinan ▲ 314. There is also the immense Karacaahmet Cemetery, with many fine examples of Ottoman funerary art.

HISTORY

Üsküdar, the largest and most historic of Istanbul's Anatolian suburbs, is situated on the Asian shore of the lower Bosphorus, directly opposite the Constantinople peninsula. The town or quarter was known in antiquity as Chrysopolis – "City of Gold" – and was founded at about the same time as Byzantium. Given its proximity to Constantinople, Chrysopolis inevitably had much the same history as the capital itself. However, the community could not be so well defended and thus suffered the disasters of several invasions and occupations, while Constantinople remained protected by its great walls until the sack by the Crusaders in 1204 and the Turkish siege of 1453 ● 32. Finally, in the mid-14th century, Chrysopolis – by then known as Scutari – succumbed to the Turks and was never recovered by the Byzantines. During the long Ottoman era that followed some of the great men and women of the realm endowed Üsküdar with splendid mosque complexes and other pious foundations, all of which still adorn the town.

KIZ KULESI

THE ÜSKÜDAR ISKELESI.

Ferries leave from both Eminönü and Kabataş on the European shore of the lower Bosphorus. The great square by the ferry landing pier (*iskelesi*) in Üsküdar is known as Hakimiyeti Milliye Meydanı, the former destination of Anatolian commercial routes. It was also the mustering place for the Sürre-i-Hümayun, the "Sacred Caravan" that departed for Mecca and Medina every year with its long train of pilgrims and its sacred white camels bearing gifts from the sultan to the Şerif of Mecca.

From Eminönü or Kabataş, on the European shore, ferries cross the lower Bosphorus to the port of Üsküdar. In antiquity, this was the port of Chalcedonia, today's Kadıköy, though a bit farther south on the Sea of Marmara. Like the villages of the Bosphorus, Üsküdar preserves its fishing industry, with tiny vessels working alongside the big oil tankers. At lunchtime, local people throng the quays to buy fish sandwiches.

MIHRIMAH SULTAN CAMI'I

The square has a majestic Baroque fountain in the center, and is dominated by a graceful *külliye* at its northern end built upon a high terrace close to the shore. This imperial mosque complex, which the Turks call the Iskele Cami'i ("Mosque of the Landing"), was built by the great Sinan between 1547 and 1548 for Sultana Mihrimah ▲ 231, the daughter of Süleyman the Magnificent and the wife of the Grand Vizier Rüstem Paşa. This was the first of two *külliye* that Sinan built for Princess Mihrimah, the second one being the imperial complex already seen on the other side of the Bosphorus, at the top of Istanbul's Sixth Hill. The mosque was given its imposing raised position because it had previously been flooded by the sea. It has a double portico with a belvedere which shelters a charming ablution fountain. The interior, however, is disappointing, as the central dome is supported by three instead of the usual two or four half-domes, giving it a somewhat awkward and truncated appearance.

THE ELEMENTS OF THE COMPLEX. The *külliye* of Mihrimah Sultan included an *imaret*, a *medrese*, and a *mektep*, but only the last two survive. The former *medrese*, or college, to the north of the mosque, is a rectangular building and now used as a clinic.

ÇAMLIKA
From the top of Çamlıka Hill, northeast of Üsküdar, there is a splendid view of the Bosphorus below. On the opposite European shore stands the Palace of Dolmabahçe clad in glistening white marble.

265

A small birdhouse under the entablature of the Mihrimah Sultan Cami'i.

KIZ KULESI
This symbol of the Bosphorus appears on boxes of candy and Turkish delight.

The old *mektep*, or primary school, stands behind the mosque on such steeply rising ground that its supporting arches are revealed. The building is now used as a children's library. Passing the fountain and entering Hakimiyeti Milliye Caddesi – Üsküdar's busy main street, where on weekends a number of antique dealers set up shop in a small street bazaar– you come to a new supermarket housed in an old but recently restored hammam on the corner of Büyük Haman Sokağı. The sign identifies it as Sinan Hamam Çarşısı a bold attempt at claiming the baths as the work of Sinan, the great architect who worked for Süleyman the Magnificent. Although no sure evidence supports this attribution, the structure certainly dates from Sinan's era, which was the 16th century. Farther along on the same side of the street is the 15th-century Nişancı Kara Davut Paşa Cami'i, a religious building preceded by a forecourt and garden. Inside the mosque, the prayer hall is a long, narrow room divided into three sections by arches, with each section having a dome, a design that is unique in Istanbul.

THE MOSQUE OF PRINCESS MIHRIMAH, AS DEPICTED BY AHMET ZIYA AKBULUT
At the foot of the stairs leading down from the terrace of the Mihrimah Sultan Cami'i there is an elegant Baroque fountain, constructed in 1726 and dedicated to Ahmet III. Théophile Gautier described it thus: "Bordered all about in arabesques, foliage, and flowers, colorful Turkish inscriptions relief-carved in marble, surmounted by one of those charming, deeply overhung roofs, whose Top-Hané fountain modern *good taste* has seen fit to remove, a fountain graciously occupies the center of the little quay-like square to which the main street of Scutari leads."

YENI VALIDE CAMI'I

Across the street and opening into Hakimiyeti Milliye
Meydanı is the large mosque complex known as the Yeni
Valide Cami'i, or the "New Mosque of the Dowager Sultana,"
built between 1708 and 1710 for Ahmet III ● *204* and
dedicated to his mother, the Valide Sultan Gülnûş
Ümmetullah. At the corner is her open *türbe*, which looks like
a large aviary, and next to it a large *sebil*, or public fountain.
The mosque itself, whose plan adheres to the octagon-within-
a-square theme, is one of the last to be built in the classical
Ottoman style. The *mektep* of the *külliye* ● *79* is over the main
gate, and outside this gateway stands the *imaret* (public
kitchen), at one corner of which is a Baroque fountain added
at a later date ● *66*.

ŞEMSI PAŞA CAMI'I. Returning to the shore of the Bosphorus,
by Şemsipaşa Caddesi, west of Hakimiyeti
Millieye Meydanı, you come to the
Şemsi Ahmet Paşa Cami'i, which
Evilya Çelebi described as "a small
pearl of a mosque on the lip
of the sea." Sinan built it in
1580 for Şemsi Ahmet
Paşa, a famous
Vizier descended
from the dynasty
of Selçuks who
reigned over
Anatolia
before the
Ottomans
● *33*. The Şemsi Ahmet Paşa Cami'i
is sober in style, with a prayer hall crowned by a cupola
supported upon a pair of flanking conch vaults. The Vizier's
türbe is separated from the mosque by nothing more than a
green grille. The *medrese* takes up two sides of the forecourt,
leaving the fourth side to be formed by a wall with windows
opening directly upon the quay along the Bosphorus.

LEANDER'S TOWER

South of the quay is a fortified islet off the Asian shore at the
mouth of the Bosphorus. This is Kız
Kulesı, or "Maiden's Tower," so named
after the legend of the sultan's daughter
who was locked in a tower to protect her
from a prophetess' prediction that she
would die from a snake bite. The bastion
is known in English as Leander's Tower.
According to the Byzantine chronicler
Nicetas Choniates, Manuel I Comnenus
was the first to fortify the islet, in the
mid-12th century, using it to anchor one
end of the great chain that was stretched across the
Bosphorus in time of siege. Since then the islet has been used
as the site of a lighthouse, a semaphore station, a quarantine
post, a customs control point, and now an inspection station
for the Turkish Navy. The present quaint structure dates from
the late 18th century.

RUM MEHMET PAŞA CAMI'I

On the hill behind Şemsi Paşa Cami'i we see Rum Mehmet
Paşa Cami'i, the oldest mosque in Üsküdar, dating from 1471.
Perched on a hill behind the Şemsi Ahmet Paşa Cami'i, the
mosque appears Byzantine on the exterior. The high
cylindrical drum of the dome, the exterior cornice following
the curve of the round-headed windows and the square base
broken by the great dome arches suggest a Byzantine
influence. This is perhaps connected with the fact
that Mehmet Paşa was Greek (Rum means
European, hence the name), a renegade,
who, following the Conquest of 1453,
became one of the viziers to Fatih
Mehmet, serving between 1467
and 1470. In the interior, the
prayer hall is vaulted by the
usual central cupola, here
borne upon smooth
pendentives and one half-dome
to the east, with side chambers
that are completely cut off from
the nave. Behind the mosque is
Rum Mehmet Paşa's *türbe*.

AYAZMA CAMI'I

Leaving the mosque precinct by the back gate and
following the winding Eşretsaat Sokağı outside, while
keeping to the right, you come to a Baroque mosque of the
same name. Built 1760–1 by Mustafa III and dedicated to
his mother, the Ayazma Cami'i – "Mosque of the Sacred
Fountain" –is one of the more successful of the
Ottomans' Baroque mosques, particularly the
exterior. A handsome entrance opens onto a
courtyard from which a pretty flight of semicircular steps leads up to the mosque porch. On
the left is a large cistern, and beyond that an
elaborate two-story colonnade providing access
to the imperial loge. The upper structure is also
decorated with little domes and turrets.
Numerous windows allow light into the interior,
which, however, is of little interest beyond the gray-marble
gallery supported by a colonnade running the length of the
entrance wall.

ATIK VALIDE CAMI'I

The most important Ottoman monument in Üsküdar is
the Atik Valide Cami'i,
which stands in a
dominant position
in the hills above
the lower town. This
great mosque
complex was built by
Sinan in 1583 for the
Valide Sultan Nur
Banu, wife of Selim II

and mother of Murat III. This is the most splendid and extensive of all of Sinan's constructions in Istanbul with the sole exception of the Süleymaniye.

THE MOSQUE COURTYARD. You enter the precincts through an alley beside a graveyard and find one of the most beautiful of all the mosque *avlu* in the city, a grandly proportioned cloister with domed porticoes supported on marble columns. In the center the *şadırvan*, or ablution fountain, is shaded by ancient plane trees and cypresses. The mosque is entered by way of an elaborate double porch; the outer one has a penthouse roof, while the inner is domed and has attractive tiled inscriptions over the windows. The facade, above the windows, is sheathed in tiles decorated with calligraphic motifs.

THE MOSQUE.
The prayer hall is a rectangular room with a central dome supported by a hexagonal arrangement of pillars and columns. The side aisles on the north and south are composed of domed bays. Along three sides of the nave run galleries, under which the wooden ceilings retain their rich painted decorations, all quite typical of the period: floral and arabesque designs in black, red, and gold. The mihrab is in a square, projecting apse entirely clad in the best Iznik tiles ▲ *292*. The window frames are also worthy of attention, made of deep-red marble mosaic, and their shutters are richly inlaid with mother-of-pearl. The mihrab and mimbar are pale, carved marble.

THE KÜLLIYE. The complex of the Atik Valide Cami'i consists of a *medrese*, or college, a hospital, a hammam, and a public kitchen, which included several refectories meant for the *medrese*'s students and faculty, as well as patients in the hospital. Even today the kitchens serve meals to the poor of Üsküdar. All the buildings survive, most of them in a good state of preservation. The *medrese*, situated at a lower level than the mosque, is reached by a staircase in the western wall of the courtyard. The courtyard of the *medrese* is almost as pretty as that of the mosque itself. It is oddly irregular, having five domed bays to the south but only three to the north. The *dershane* is in the center of the west side in the axis of the mosque, though at an obtuse angle to it; the lecture hall projects over the street below, which passes under it through an archway. At the next corner beyond the *medrese* stands the huge hospital, which is also irregular in plan. The remaining buildings of the complex are today either part of a prison or in a poor state of repair.

THE COASTLINE AND BEACHES OF THE PRINCES' ISLANDS
The beaches of Sedef Odasi, famous for their relatively clear waters, are increasingly popular among those who love to swim in the sea. On the shore and around the central square modern construction has made some inroads but the government takes care not to sell land except at a prohibitive price. One can only hope that the islands will long remain like rare pearls, even while, not far away, the yalı along the Bosphorus are left to decay and collapse, just as the Beyoğlu quarter is violated by wide modern boulevards.

BÜYÜK ADA
The island of Büyük Ada is covered

with dwarf pines and has sandy beaches. Beautiful gardens surround the town, which is situated on the northern coast. The port is an excellent anchorage.

269

▲ ÜSKÜDAR AND THE PRINCES' ISLANDS

THE BYZANTINE MONASTERIES
The spread of Christianity to Constantinople coincided with the reign of Theodosius I (379–95) and the development of monasticism. The monasteries, which

numbered all of 23 during the reign of Theodosius II (408–450), increased over the centuries until there were some 300 of them. The religious communities, which shunned the everyday world and its populated areas, tended to settle on the outskirts of Constantinople and on the islands in the Sea of Marmara. Because their principles inclined them towards becoming hermits, they sought the isolation of hilltops. Dressed in black homespun, the monks lived by the most ascetic rules and their religion was in dramatic contrast to that of the patriarchs and other ecclesiastical dignitaries closely linked to the imperial court, whose quasi-functionaries they were.

ÇINILI CAMI'I

The street east of Atîk Valide Cami'i leads, after about a mile, to the Çinili Cami'i – the "Tiled Mosque" – which is surrounded by a garden filled with flowers and trees. This small complex was built in 1640 for the Valide Sultan Kösem, wife of Ahmet I and the mother of the Sultans Murat IV and Ibrahim the Mad.

THE MOSQUE. Constructed by the architect Koca Kasım in 1640, the mosque is small and simple, just a square prayer room vaulted by a circular dome. It takes its name from the Iznik tiles ▲ *292* that cover both the façade and the interior. Even if from a period later than the Iznik's golden age of craftmanship, the faiences – pale blue and turquoise on a white background – are quite superb. The conical roof of the mimbar is decorated with tiles of white marble picked out in gold, red, and green. The mosque's Baroque porch is a later addition, as is the minaret. Here the *şerefe*, or balcony, from which the muezzin calls the faithful to prayer, has a corbel of folded-back acanthus leaves, apparently unique in Ottoman architecture. Within the precinct there is *sardırvan* with a huge witch's cap for a roof, as well as a tiny, triangular-shaped *medrese* sloping headlong downhill. Just outside the precinct stands the *mektep* of the *külliye*, and the hammam can be found a short way along the main street beyond the mosque.

THE GREAT MOUNTAIN OF PINES

A popular excursion from Üsküdar leads to Büyük Çamlıca – the "Great Mountain of Pines" – which is 875 feet above sea level, the highest point in the immediate vicinity of the Bosphorus ■ *16*. The Turkish Touring and Automobile Club (TTOC) has recently built a pleasant

> "Those crystal streams of paradise
> Flow. the name of God repeating,
> The nightingales of Islam there
> Sing, the name of God repeating."
> Yunus Emre

café and a teahouse on the summit, from which there are stunning views over the lower Bosphorus and the imperial city between the Golden Horn and the Sea of Marmara ▲ 274. The scene clearly explains the phrase "city ringed about by a diadem of water," used by Procopius, the chronicler at the court of Justinian and Theodora, to describe the sight that greets those who journey to the hilltop.

THE PRINCES' ISLANDS

Ferries leave from both Eminönü and Üsküdar for the Princes' Islands (Kızıl Adalar in Turkish), an archipelago off the Asian coast in the southwest of the Sea of Marmara some 20 miles from Istanbul. For those on a tight schedule, a more rapid service is available on motorboats that make frequent trips to and from the port of Kabataş. Arriving at the islands in summer, one cannot avoid being struck by the contrast between the noisy bustle of a fashionable seaside resort and the surviving remains of a bygone era. The group consists of nine islands, four of them fairly large, listed here with their Greek names in brackets: Kınalı (Proti), Burgaz (Antigone), Heybeli (Chalki), and Büyük Ada (Prinkipo). In Byzantine times, Prinkipo, the largest and most populated island, gave its name to the entire group.

HISTORY. In the Byzantine era, the islands were also called Panadanisia, meaning the "Priests' Isles," because of the monasteries built there. Those on Kınalı Ada and Burgaz Ada are now in ruins, but Heybal Ada has a monastery on every hilltop. Holy Trinity was founded in 850 and then rebuilt in 1844 by the Patriarch Germain IV, who transformed it into a seminary.

MOVING ABOUT ON THE ISLANDS
Carriages drawn by ponies or donkeys, and bicycles are the only means of transportation on the islands, where cars have been outlawed since 1928 except for ambulances and fire engines.

OTTOMAN HOUSES
The Princes' Islands have preserved several of the old wooden Ottoman houses, which require constant upkeep.

THE PRINCES' ISLANDS ✪
The copper miners and pirates have long gone; the two main islands now welcome Istanbul's moneyed classes at the weekend. Choose the longest route to get there (50 mins) and take the quick shuttle back. Have just the one drink on the terrace of one of the (expensive and unexceptional) seaside restaurants and instead sample the small snacks on offer in the center. You will need your identity papers to hire a bicycle.

GARDENS
Large houses are surrounded by gardens flowering with magnolia, lilac, mimosa, honeysuckle, and jasmine. One can buy necklaces of jasmine from little street stalls. Under the boughs of pine trees grow arbutus, lentisks, myrtle, and rock roses, which fill the air with their scent in spring.

THE WOODEN PALACES OF BÜYÜK ADA

The former mansion of Izzet Paşa, chief of police under Abdül Hamit II (1876–1909), is one of the most beautiful yalı on Büyük Ada, located at 55 Çankaya Caddesi. One of its celebrated guests was Leon Trotsky during the first years of his exile, from 1929 to 1933. Also well worth a visit is the palace of the papal nuncio outside the city. The future Pope John XXIII lived there during his long tenure as the pope's emissary to Greek and Islamic Turkey from 1933 to 1944.

Panaghia Camariotissa, to the east, was founded in the 14th century by John V Palaeologus. In 1942, after being used as an orphanage for a long time, it became the Turkish Naval College. Another peculiarity of the Princes' Islands is the concentration, in a small area, of the country's entire ethnic and religious diversity. Greeks, Armenians, and Jews of Spanish origin – whose ancestors fled persecution by Queen Isabella the Catholic – all converge upon the islands once summer arrives. Princes' Islands take their name from one of

the more sinister practices of the Byzantine Empire, for it was here that each new monarch relegated fallen patriarchs and princes plotting against him.

The prisoners, with their wives and children, were even blinded or otherwise mutilated to take away their will to return to Constantinople. The Turks also speak of the *kızıl adalar* – the "red islands" – because the nine small land masses were once famous for the wealth generated from the local copper mines, which made them vulnerable to repeated lootings, such as by Crusaders bound for the Holy Land, Genoese pirates, and all manner of sea rovers. However, only an informed visitor would discern the traces of this past, especially when distracted by the spectacle of the Belle Epoque relived before their very eyes.

THE YALI. Today, the Princes' Islands derive much of their charm from the old wooden houses, the numerous examples of which testify to the prosperity the islands in the 19th century. Fortunately, their façades are protected by law, and any renovation must be in keeping with the original plans. However, unless it is a recognized historic monument, a house can easily fall apart. But even now, the old yalı evoke the light-hearted, carefree spirit of the Belle Epoque.

THE ANADOLU CLUB. Mustafa Kemal Atatürk, the "father of modern Turkey," took over the Anadolu Club, founded in the last century at Büyük Ada by the English, and made it a resort for his cabinet as well as for himself. Even today, every Turkish deputy becomes a lifetime member of this very exclusive club, with its luxurious salons and gaming room – the only one on the island. Its park is studded with statues of more or less antique origin and below it has a private beach. The Hotel Splendid, opposite, is also a place favored by the country's old ruling élite and well-off, who appreciate the refined and somewhat old-fashioned atmosphere of the paneled salon. However, for all its propriety, the hotel can boast that Edward VIII and Mrs. Simpson have stayed there.

WOODEN MANSIONS
These dwellings were constructed in the 18th and 19th centuries by the merchants of Istanbul. They usually have two and sometimes three stories, as well as fairly large rooms and salons. Balconies extend from the façades and look out over the bay or the nearby woods.

THE MONASTERIES OF BÜYÜK ADA

A sanctum of orthodox Catholicism until the fall of Byzantium, Büyük Ada continues to be very much the home of monasteries. The Monastery of Jesus Christ, built in 1597, stands among the pines on top of the Hill of Jesus. The island's convent, which served as a place of retreat for several Byzantine princesses, houses the tomb of the Empress Eirene (1066–1123). The Franciscan mission from Ancona and the Eastern Orthodox rites observed in San Pacifico, an ecumenical Christian church where Armenians also worship, attract regular attendance during the summer months, even in this Islamic land.

THE MONASTERY OF AYOS YORGIOS.
The Monastery of St George on Ayios Yorgios, constructed in the 10th century high on the hill of the same name, still attracts many pilgrims. The bushes along the road to the monastery are bedecked with little strips of white cloth, symbols of the prayers addressed to St George, who, according to the faithful, has the power to make young people fall in love. The steep and uneven path winds its way through the pine forest that grows across some two-thirds of the island. On several occasions the government has attempted to improve the surface of the path, in order to encourage tourism, but just as often devotees of St George remove the paving stones to preserve the penitential way. Although the path is in almost constant use, it becomes most crowded on April 23, the saint's feast day, when thousands of pilgrims, of all persuasions, climb the hill to attend the first mass at dawn. Afterwards most of them retire to the terrace of a local restaurant to celebrate the day and enjoy the local wine, which the monks of Ayios Yorgios have been making for centuries.

Motor yachts and large sailing ships worthy of the most famous ports in the Mediterranean are anchored in deep water. During summer, little coastal vessels make regular trips between the large island of Büyük Ada and the most inhabited of the Princes' Islands: Kınalı, Burgaz, and Heybeli.

▲ THE BOSPHORUS

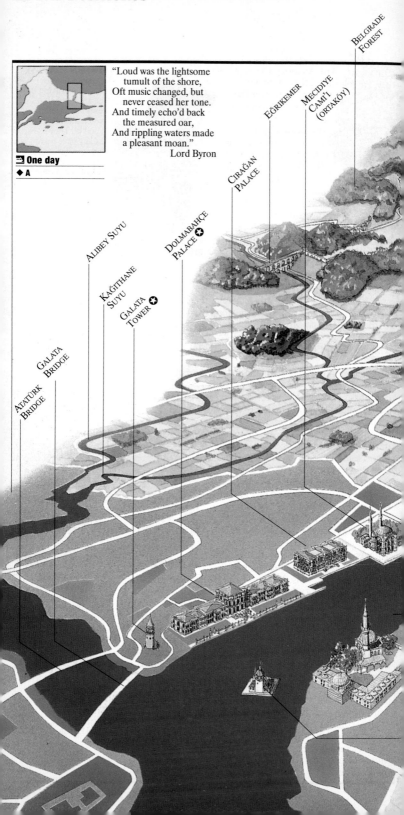

"Loud was the lightsome
tumult of the shore,
Oft music changed, but
never ceased her tone.
And timely echo'd back
the measured oar,
And rippling waters made
a pleasant moan."
Lord Byron

One day

◆ A

BELGRADE FOREST

EĞRİKEMER

MECIDIYE CAMI'I (ORTAKÖY)

ÇIRAĞAN PALACE

DOLMABAHÇE PALACE ✪

ALIBEY SUYU

KAĞITHANE SUYU

GALATA TOWER ✪

GALATA BRIDGE

ATATÜRK BRIDGE

YENİKÖY TARABYA BÜYÜKDERE SARIYER BLACK SEA BEYKOZ ANADOLU KAVAĞI RUMELİ FENERİ ANADOLU FENERİ

FATİH SULTAN MEHMET BRIDGE

ANADOLU HİSARI

RUMELİ HİSARI

ARNAVUTKÖY

BEYLERBEY

BOĞAZİÇİ BRIDGE

BOSPHORUS ✪

ŞEMSİ PAŞA CAMİ'İ

KIZ KULESİ

THE BOSPHORUS: MYTHOLOGY TO MYTH ✪
The river owes its name to its crossing by the god Io in the form of a heifer (in ancient Greek, *bous* means cow and *poros* is ford). It was reputedly sailed down by Ulysses and Jason. There are boat trips down the river (Boğaziçi Özel Gezi Seferleri) from Eminönü. Ask about departure times in advance (2–5 trips per day). Arrive early and take a wind-cheater.

275

THE EUROPEAN SHORE

EMINÖNÜ. Ferries sail from Eminönü for the villages along both shores of the Bosphorus, or Boğaziçi in Turkish, meaning "strait". The villages along the Bosphorus, some of which date back to the period of the ancient city of Byzantium, have in the past fifty years been, for the most part, amalgamated into the urban sprawl of Istanbul. Nevertheless, they still retain a village-like quality, particularly on the upper Bosphorus, where many of the men continue to earn their living as fishermen. Any description of the Bosphorus involves the names Rumeli and Anadolu, for these are used in referring to the opposing continental shores of the strait, the first to the European side and the second to the Anatolian or Asian side. The Bosphorus is usually serene, though even on the calmest of days one can feel its power as the mass of water surges between the continents. It is beautiful at any time, day or night and in all seasons, but particularly under a full moon, which rises out of the hills on the Asian side and casts a silver path across the strait to the European shore, a phenomenon that the Turks call *mehtap*. The first full moon in autumn usually marks the beginning of the season for the Bosphorus fishermen, for it is then that great schools of *lüfer*, a small bluefish, make their way down the strait. The fishermen use a rowboat called a *sandal*, derived from the Venetian word *sandalo*. Most of the vessels are now equipped with outboard motors, and they all have a bright lamp which is used to shine down into the water to attract the fish. As the Bosphorus ferry heads up along the European shore it passes the docks at Galata ▲ 252–6, after which can be seen a collection of monuments in Tophane, a village which surrounds the old marine arsenal of the same name.

DOLMABAHÇE SARAYI
Lamartine, during a visit to Istanbul in 1833, had this to say about Dolmabahçe: "It could be a palace of amphibians, for however slight the wind on the Bosphorus, it stirs up waves that sheet the windows and fling their foam into the ground-floor apartments. Even the steps leading into the palace tread water. Grillework gates open onto the sea from both the courtyard and the gardens. Here there are sheds for the caiques and baths for the sultans, who can swim in the sea sheltered by the slatted shutters of their salon."

DOLMABAHÇE CAMI'I. Designed by Nikoğos Balyan, grandson of Kirkor Balyan, the Dolmabahçe Mosque was completed in 1853. A year later, Nikoğos added the cut-stone clock tower to the north. The tower is 88 feet tall, making it one of the most prominent landmarks on the European shore of the lower Bosphorus.

DOLMABAHÇE SARAYI. The Dolmabahçe palace is by far the largest and grandest of the imperial Ottoman residences on the Bosphorus. In Byzantine times the site of Dolmabahçe, which means "filled-in garden," was an inlet on the strait. Fatih Mehmet II had the little harbor filled in and a garden laid out ● *50*. In 1842, Abdül Mecit decided to construct a huge new palace on the site, giving the task to the architect Karabet Balyan and his son Nikoğos, who completed the work in 1853. The main entrance to Dolmabahçe Sarayı is through the gardens at its southern end. The palace faces the Bosphorus, which reflects the entire length of its 814-feet gleaming white marble façade. The quay itself is about 650 yards long. Inside, the palace consists mainly of a great hall flanked by two main wings containing the state rooms and royal apartments, with the *selamık* on the south side and the harem on the north. The complex also includes quarters for the staff who lived in, bringing the total number of rooms to 285, among them 43 salons and 6 hammams. It is at Dolmabahçe that Mustafa Kemal Atatürk ● *42* died on November 10, 1938 at 9.05am. In memory of his death all the clocks in the palace are set at this time.

BEŞIKTAŞ ISKELE. About 300 yards beyond Dolmabahçe Sarayı the ferry stops at the Beşiktaş Iskele. In the park behind this landing stands a statue of the famous Ottoman Admiral Hayrettin Paşa, known in the West as Barbarossa. The Admiral's *türbe*, or tomb, is opposite the sculpture.

DENIZ MÜZESI. South of the Beşiktaş Iskele we come to the Deniz Müzesi or Naval Museum. The most famous item in the collection is a chart of the Atlantic coast of North America drawn in the 16th century by Piri Reis, the great Ottoman navigator. The museum houses a collection of *pazar* caiques, the beautiful rowing barges that ferried the sultans to and from their palaces and yalı on the Bosphorus and the Golden Horn.

In the 18th century, Princess Hatice had a summer palace built at Beşiktaş, from designs by the painter Melling.

DOLMABAHÇE, THE DYING EMBERS OF THE EMPIRE ✪
It was in this creek that Mehmet assembled his fleet before the final assault on Constantinople. The palace's exceptionally luxurious decoration was the work of the Frenchman Sechan, also responsible for the Palais Garnier (the Paris Opera House). The chandelier in the throne room, a gift from Queen Victoria, is the biggest in the world. Get there early in summer to avoid the queues. Your visit will be not be complete until you have seen the 820-foot high façade from a boat on the Bosphorus.

277

▲ THE DOLMABAHÇE PALACE

Cupola from the great
Muayede reception hall

The design of the Dolmabahçe
palace is an amalgamation of two
styles – half-occidental, half-oriental –
a singular and baroque mix of classical
orders with ornamentation evocative of the far off Indies. The
285 rooms and the 46 salons are in keeping with the overall mix
of styles. The extravagant decorations include mural paintings
by Russian and Italian artists, enormous candelabra in
Bohemian or Baccarat crystal, and the sumptuous furniture.

THE RED SALON
Divan and armchairs are
upholstered in red silk,
matching the drapes. On
the table is a red Bohemian
crystal chandelier.

**BACCARAT CRYSTAL
CHANDELIER AND
FURNITURE IN THE ROCOCO
STYLE**

**PALACE ENTRANCE
PORTAL, GARDEN
SIDE**
The entrance is
flanked by two curved
wings which give
access to the upper
level. The door is
framed with Greek
columns, and topped
by an extremely
ornate balustrade.

VASES FROM THE DOLMABAHÇE PALACE
Going through the rooms one notices numerous vases: Chinese vases, painted vases made in the Yıldız porcelain factory (left and center) and Sèvre vases (right).

THE GREAT STAIRS OF HONOR
The balusters that support the banister are made of crystal incrusted with gold. There are marble columns on both sides of the landing, which is lit by a large glass dome.

MAYBEN OR COURT ROOM The roof is enhanced with gilding and decorated with paintings of flowers. At the four corners hang pendanted candelabra and consoles crowned with large mirrors.

A Yalı in Yeniköy

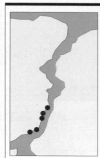

NAVIGATION ON THE BOSPHORUS
High-speed tankers on the Bosphorus constitute a major threat to the houses and palaces along the waterfront. During the last twenty years, a dozen "classified" yalı have been destroyed by such shipping. The powerful waves and wake they generate eventually damage both the quays and the foundations of the palatial old dwellings.

YENIKÖY
This is one of the Bosphorus villages least touched by urbanization. Here, many of the beautiful 19th-century Ottoman houses were influenced by Art Nouveau. The repair and maintenance of these seaside villas are demanding tasks, even when undertaken by specialists. The Greek Church of St George in Yeniköy shelters not only the tombs of three patriarchs but also an ancient icon of the Blessed Virgin.

ÇIRAĞAN SARAYI ● 84. Some 550 yards beyond the Beşiktaş Iskele the ferry passes Çırağan Palace, recently rebuilt as a casino attached to the new Çırağan Hotel. Abdül Aziz commissioned the palace, which Sarkis Balyran designed and then completed in 1874. In 1910, Çırağan was destroyed by fire, which left only the smoke-blackened shell of the façade standing by the Bosphorus until the recent reconstruction of the building.

YILDIZ PARK ● 50. A short distance beyond Çırağan Sarayı on the shore highway is the entrance to Yıldız Park, a place originally known as the "Gardens of Çırağan," after the various pavilions of Yıldız Sarayı. On the right of the entrance there is also a mosque built by the Sultan Abdül Mecit in 1848. A few yards beyond the entrance to the park, a steep but short lane leads up to the charming little complex of Yahya Efendi, who was one of Istanbul's most celebrated Muslim saints. He was born in Trebizond on the same day as Süleyman the Magnificent, also at Trebizond, and Yahya's mother even served as wet nurse to the future sultan. When Süleyman succeeded to the throne in 1520, Yahya Efendi accompanied him and became one of the most renowned divines of his age. The little *külliye*, built by the great Sinan shortly before Yahya Efendi's death in 1570, is a popular shrine attracting a constant stream of pilgrims.

ORTAKÖY. The next ferry stop is Ortaköy, or the "Middle Village." In recent years Ortaköy has become an arts-and-crafts center. In addition to its many recently restored old houses, Ortaköy boasts an abundance of restaurants and cafés around the ferry slip, where in summer craftsmen and secondhand booksellers set up their stalls. On the promontory beyond the *iskele* or landing is the charming Mecidiye Cami'i, a mosque built in 1854 for Abdül Mecit by Nikoğos Balyan. On either side of the main street, in what still remains a fishing village, stand three monuments that deserve notice: a synagogue built at the beginning of the 20th century; a 19th-century Greek Orthodox church; and a hammam ● 58 built in 1570 by Sinan for Hürsev Kethüda, head steward to the Grand Vizier Sokollu Mehmet Paşa.

> "After Dolmabahçe there begins an unbroken string of palaces, mansions, and gardens. All slumber beside the sea in order to breath the freshness of the air."
>
> Lamartine

THE BOSPHORUS BRIDGE. Just beyond Ortaköy the ferry passes under Boğaziçi Köprüsü, the Bosphorus Bridge. Its graceful span arcs across to the hills south of the village of Beylerbey on the Asian shore. Opened on October 27, 1973, the Boğaziçi Köprüsü is the sixth longest suspension bridge in the world, measuring 3,524 feet from tower to tower and 210 feet above the water at its mid-point.

ARNAVUTKÖY. This "Albanian Village" has one of the most colorful landing stages on the Bosphorus, with a row of pretty yalı along the shore south of the *iskele*. The streets of the equally picturesque inner village are lined with old wooden houses festooned with vines, a scene straight out of Ottoman times.

BEBEK BAY. Rounding Akıntı Burnu, the ferry enters the calm waters of Bebek Bay, a very beautiful inlet on the Bosphorus. The hillside above still retains its original woods, mainly umbrella pines and tall cypresses ■ 26. Just before reaching the *iskele*,

the ferry passes the former Egyptian Embassy, a splendid example of Art Nouveau architecture constructed in 1912 by Raimondo d'Aronco. Situated just beyond the landing stage there is a charming little mosque which was built in 1913 by the Turkish architect Kemalettin Bey.

THE UNIVERSITY OF THE BOSPHORUS. A few hundred yards beyond the *iskele* the shore road passes the lower entrance to the Boğaziçi Universitesi. The university campus occupies a hilltop site between Bebek and Rumeli Hisarı, the next village to the north. This Turkish university was founded in 1971, taking over the buildings and grounds of the former ROBERT COLLEGE, which, during the 108 years of its existence, numbered among its faculty and graduates many important and influential figures, including several people who played leading roles in the cultural and political life of Turkey.

RUMELI HISARI AND ANADOLU HISARI. On either side of the strait there are two Ottoman fortresses, Rumeli Hisarı and Anadolu Hisarı – the Fortresses of Europe and Asia – both surrounded by charming old villages. After the Conquest in 1453 ● *34* the two fortresses were no longer of any military importance. Anadolu Hisarı gradually fell into ruins, but Rumeli Hisarı survived and was used to hold prisoners of war, as well as ambassadors from unfriendly powers. Since 1953 this "Fortress of Europe" has become a museum and is open to the public; on summer evenings it is also used for theatrical performances during the Istanbul Festival.

GUILLOTINE OR SASH WINDOWS IN THE TURKISH BAROQUE STYLE

The Sadberk Hanim Museum.

281

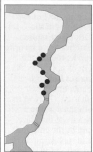

YILDIZ PARK
Here, both the Malta Köşkü, or Pavilion, and the Pembe Köşkü have been restored and transformed into elegant cafés.

THE FATIH MEHMET BRIDGE. The ferry now passes under the Fatih Sultan Mehmet Köprüsü, the new bridge over the Bosphorus. It is 33 feet longer than the bridge between Ortaköy and Beylerbey, and spans the strait between the hills above the two fortresses. Fatih Köprüsü opened in 1988, exactly 2,500 years after Mandrocles built his bridge of boats for Darius across this same stretch of the Bosphorus.

EMIRĞAN. The next village on the European shore is Emirğan. The village square is pleasantly shaded by plane trees and beneath them people gather to drink tea, which is particularly delicious because of the quality of the local water.

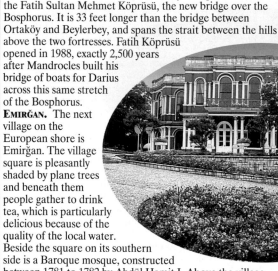

Beside the square on its southern side is a Baroque mosque, constructed between 1781 to 1782 by Abdül Hamit I. Above the village are the famous tulip gardens of Emirğan, well worth a visit in spring. The Turkish Touring and Automobile Club has restored a number of Ottoman kiosks in the gardens, among them the Beyaz Köşk, or White Pavilion, which has been converted into a concert hall. The others now serve as cafés.

ISTINIYE. After Emirğan, still on the European side, is Istiniye, which has a deeply indented bay that up until 1990 contained a floating dock. Istiniye is still an active fishing port, and the local fishermen sell their daily catch at a colorful market along the quay.

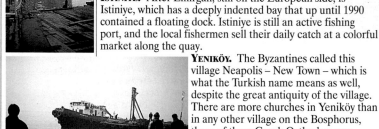

YENIKÖY. The Byzantines called this village Neapolis – New Town – which is what the Turkish name means as well, despite the great antiquity of the village. There are more churches in Yeniköy than in any other village on the Bosphorus, three of them Greek Orthodox, one Armenian Catholic, and another Roman Catholic. Yeniköy is famous for its row of terraced houses by the water's edge. At the northern end of the village there is a stone-built mansion that was once used as the summer embassy of Austria-Hungary, and today is still Austria's summer consulate. Beyond that lies Kalender, a hamlet named after the order of mendicant dervishes who had a *tekke*, or monastery, there. A bit farther along is a huge wooden yalı ● 88 that serves as Germany's summer embassy.

Fishing port and trawler at Ortaköy.

At Arnavutköy, a number of bars, including the Café Siné, feature concerts by young musicians.

TARABYA. The next village on the European shore is Tarabya, long celebrated for the beauty of its crescent bay. During the 18th and 19th centuries, Tarabya was a favorite resort of prominent Greeks from the Fener, as well as the affluent of Pera. Originally named Therapia, meaning "cure," by the Greek Patriarch Atticus, the village now bears the Turkish version of the same name and for the same reason – the beneficial climate.

BÜYÜKDERE. The next ferry stop brings us to Büyükdere, which means "Great Valley." The Byzantines called the village Kalos Agros or "Beautiful Meadow." It was here that the knights of the First Crusade camped in 1096, before they crossed the Bosphorus on their long arduous march across Asia Minor to recover the Holy Land for Christianity.

THE SADBERK HANIM MUSEUM. In its splendidly restored yalı, this museum houses a rich collection of antiquities, ranging from the Bronze Age ● *28* up to the Greco-Roman era ● *30*, along with Ottoman arts, crafts, and costumes, all beautifully displayed. The museum is dedicated to the memory of Sadberk Hanim, the late wife of Vehbi Koç, a leading Turkish industrialist.

KILYOS. Roads lead from both Büyükdere and Sariyer through the Belgrade Forest to Kilyos, a fishing village on the Black Sea which has a sandy beach, hotels, pensione, and restaurants. The road from Büyükdere passes through one of the arches of Eğrikemer, the "Bent Aqueduct" ● *76*, built by Mahmut I and completed in 1732.

SARIYER. This is the largest village on the European shore of the upper Bosphorus, and the principal fishing port on the strait. The port and the fish market around it are delightful, particularly when the fishermen of Sariyer return after voyages that take them not only to the upper Bosphorus and the Black Sea but also to the Marmara, the Dardanelles ▲ *322*, and the Aegean. Some of their catch is served in restaurants around the port, with tables set out on the quay in good weather.

RUMELI KAVAĞI. The last ferry stop on the European shore is Rumeli Kavağı. From there most ferries cross the strait to Anadolu Kavağı, the last *iskele* on the Asian side. There are numerous seafood restaurants all about the landings in both villages, which are popular places to have lunch during a journey along the Bosphorus.

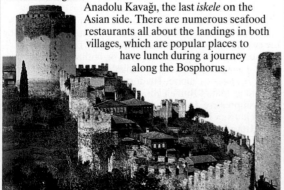

YALI AT BEBEK
Since the 18th century Bebek has been a residential village where rich Istanbuli built summer houses, such as the superb Yılanlı Yalı, now restored. Today, there is also an attractive marina.

THE VILLAGE OF RUMELI HISARI
Nestling in the green countryside, the houses of this little village rise in tiers on the hillside, with cobblestone lanes that descend towards the Bosphorus.

RUMELI HISARI
In 1452, Mehmet II prepared to besiege Constantinople by constructing a fortress at Rumeli Hisarı. It took less than four months to build, thanks to 3,000 laborers and master masons assigned to the task. Around the turn of the 20th century, wooden houses were built within the walls of the ruined fortress. They disappeared when the site was restored in 1953.

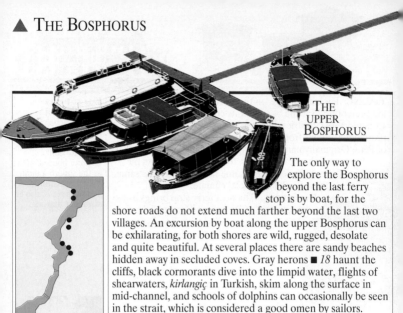

THE
UPPER
BOSPHORUS

The only way to explore the Bosphorus beyond the last ferry stop is by boat, for the shore roads do not extend much farther beyond the last two villages. An excursion by boat along the upper Bosphorus can be exhilarating, for both shores are wild, rugged, desolate and quite beautiful. At several places there are sandy beaches hidden away in secluded coves. Gray herons ■ *18* haunt the cliffs, black cormorants dive into the limpid water, flights of shearwaters, *kirlangiç* in Turkish, skim along the surface in mid-channel, and schools of dolphins can occasionally be seen in the strait, which is considered a good omen by sailors.

GARIPÇE. Three nautical miles beyond Rumeli Kavağı we pass a very craggy promontory on the European shore named Garipçe, meaning "strange," or "curious," probably because of its very contorted features. The Blue Rocks were also called Cyanean, or the Symplegades, and Gillius identified them as a striking feature at the mouth of the Bosphorus on the European side, 100 yards offshore at Rumeli Feneri.

RUMELI FENERI. Called the "Lighthouse of Europe," this huge rock still has the remains of a fort built in 1769 by a Greek military engineer in the Ottoman army. There was a similar fortress on the Asian side – a Byzantine toll station known as the "Lighthouse of Asia" – but this has not survived, probably worn away by the pounding waves of the Black Sea, which the Greeks called "Hospitable" only to placate it.

AN AERIAL VIEW OF RUMELI KAVAĞI AND ITS MOSQUE (right)

The balconies which extended from the façades of old Turkish houses were held up by wrought-iron corbels or brackets.

THE ASIAN SHORE

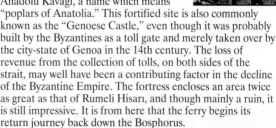

ANADOLU KAVAĞI. Travelling down the Asian shore of the Bosphorus you will come to the most prominent monument of the upper Bosphorus, a great fortress whose ruins are on the heights north of Anadolu Kavağı, a name which means "poplars of Anatolia." This fortified site is also commonly known as the "Genoese Castle," even though it was probably built by the Byzantines as a toll gate and merely taken over by the city-state of Genoa in the 14th century. The loss of revenue from the collection of tolls, on both sides of the strait, may well have been a contributing factor in the decline of the Byzantine Empire. The fortress encloses an area twice as great as that of Rumeli Hisarı, and though mainly a ruin, it is still impressive. It is from here that the ferry begins its return journey back down the Bosphorus.

THE HILL OF JOSHUA. Opposite Sariyer we pass the Yuşa Tepesi – Hill of Joshua – the second highest peak on the Bosphorus, reaching a height of 660 feet above sea level. On the summit is a shrine to a Muslim saint named Yuşa Baba, whose grave, marked by green pillars at the head and feet, is 40 feet long. His tomb, which Europeans call the "Giant's Grave," was known in antiquity as the "Bed of Hercules."

> "The channel, along its entire length . . . looks the same at every point; it is bordered by palaces, kiosks, country houses, and villages."

Castellan

SELVI BURNU. Opposite Büyükdere is a long shallow bay with a rugged and forbidding shoreline. At Selvi Burnu – "Poplar Point" – the coast turns east to the valley of Tokat Deresi. It was here Fatih built a villa, as did Süleyman. Gillius described the place as a "royal villa shaded by woods of various trees, especially planes," before going on to mention the landing stairs, "by which the King, crossing the shallow shore of the sea, disembarks into his gardens," hence the modern name of the site, Hünkar Iskelesi, or the "Emperor's Landing Place." The present little palace ● *84* was built in the mid-19th century for Abdül Mecit by Sarkis Balyan, a brother of Nikoğos Balyan. It is still shaded by a lovely grove of plane trees, but it is now used as a hospital.

BEYKOZ. The ferry stops at Beykoz, the largest fishing village on the Asian shore of the Bosphorus above Üsküdar. At weekends during the summer its seafood restaurants and small cafés are packed with visitors from the city. The principal monument in Beykoz is a beautiful street fountain ● *66* in the village square. Ishak Ağa, a customs inspector, had it designed and installed in 1746.

ŞILE AND INCIR KÖYÜ. A road leads from Beykoz to the picturesque village of Şile on the Black Sea, where there is a splendid sandy beach, with hotels and restaurants. Since antiquity the women of this village have woven a particularly light and silken cotton called *şile bezi*. Much of the cloth is exported. The French-built lighthouse just east of the village is now a registered historic monument. The Kumbaba Motel, which is on the beach east of Şile, occupies the site of ancient Calpe, a number of ruins of which have been uncovered by archeologists. South of Beykoz at Incir Köyü, or "Figtree Village," is the charming valley of Sultaniye Deresi, where Beyazıt II had extensive gardens laid out.

PAŞABAHÇE. A little farther on is Paşabahçe – the Paşa's Garden ● *50* – so called because of the palace and garden established here by Hezarpara Ahmet Paşa, who was grand vizier under Murat IV. Its renowned glass works produce the finest

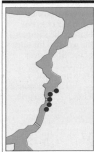

**THE BOSPHORUS
AT PAŞABAHÇE**
In this watercolor, by
Hoca Ali Riza, from
the beginning of this
century, the wooden
yalı is painted in a
traditional color –
rose-red. Yet nothing
could be more
modern than the
numerous bay
windows, all large
enough to permit the
rooms within to be
viewed from the
garden. The garden
surrounding the yalı
is planted with pines,
plane trees, and
climbers, such as
wisteria and sweetly
fragrant honeysuckle.

glassware in Turkey. Paşabahçe also has a large *rakı* factory
with a cascading fountain not of fresh water but of *rakı*, a
Turkish alcoholic drink derived from aniseed.

ÇUBUKLU. The ferry stops next at Çubuklu, which means
"with a cane" (in Turkish *çubuk*). Evliya Çelebi, writing in the
mid-16th century, tells an amusing story about it: "Beyazıt II,
having brought his son Selim, the future Selim I, from
Trebizond to Constantinople, gave him in this place, in a fit of
anger, eight strokes with a cane, which eight strokes were

prophetic of the years of his reign. At the same time, he said
to him, 'Boy, don't be angry, these eight strokes shall fructify
during the eight years of your reign.' Selim stuck the dry cane
into the ground, praying to heaven that it might strike root
and bear fruit. The Seyh Kara Beyazit and Beyazıt himself
said, 'Amen,' after which the cane began to grow and even
now bears cornels, five of which weigh a drachma." On a
hilltop between Çubuklu and Kanlıca, the next village along
the Bosphorus is the former palace of the Khedives, the
viceroys of Egypt. Its distinctive tower makes it one of the
most distinctive landmarks on this stretch of the strait. It was
built in c. 1900 by Abbas Hilmi Paşa, the last Khedive. The
western façade, overlooking the Bosphorus, is semi-circular,
with a marble-columned porch and a semi-circular hall within.
The upper floor, especially the tower room and a loggia on
the roof, commands some of the finest views of the
Bosphorus. The Turkish Touring and Automobile Club has
recently restored and redecorated the palace to its original
Art Nouveau splendor. The structure now serves as a deluxe
hotel and restaurant.

KANLICA. The village of Kanlıca has long been famous for its
delicious yogurt, which is served in restaurants around the
iskele and the little square behind it. The mosque at the rear
of the square was built by Sinan between 1559 and 1560 for
Iskender Paşa, a grand vizier under Süleyman the
Magnificent. The mosque is of the simplest type, with a
wooden porch and a prayer room covered by a flat ceiling.

Yalı of Sefik Bey at
Kanıca.

AMCAZADE HÜSEYIN PAŞA KÖPRÜLÜ YALI. Between Kanlıca
and Anadolu Hisarı, the next ferry stop, we pass once
again under Fatih Köprüsü, the bridge spanning the upper
Bosphorus. Just along here, on the Asian shore, you can
see the oldest of all the surviving yalı on the Bosphorus, a
rose-red wooden ruin suspended over the water on rotting
stilts and corbels. The yalı, which is being restored, was
built in 1698 by Amcazade Hüseyin Paşa Köprülü, grand

Yalı of Rutiye Sultan.

vizier to Mustafa II. The Peace of Carlowitz was signed here on January 26, 1699, which concluded one of the several wars between Tsarist Russia and the Ottoman Empire.

THE FORTRESS OF ASIA. The old fortress of Anadolu Hisarı lies just downstream from the *iskele* of the same name. Beyazıt I had the site fortified in 1394 as a base from which to keep Constantinople under siege. This lasted until 1402, when Tamerlane defeated the Turks at the Battle of Ankara, thereby granting the Byzantines a reprieve until 1453. A relatively small fortress, Anadolu Hisarı comprises a donjon or keep encircled by stout walls with barbican outworks, now partly demolished, and three bastions. According to the French scholar Gabriel, only the keep and its walls date from the reign of Beyazıt I. The barbican wall and the three bastions would have been added by Fatih Mehmet ● *34* when he built the fortress of Rumeli Hisarı on the opposite shore, in order to control the Bosphorus and thus strangle Constantinople. The village itself is very picturesque, with old wooden houses clustered around the castle on its promontory, where the Bosphorus is joined by a little river known as Göksu – the "Heavenly Stream".

THE PALACE OF KÜÇÜKSU. This pretty little rococo building ● *84* on the Bosphorus was built for Abdül Mecit 1856–7 by Nikoğos Balyan. The sultans used the palace as a pied-à-terre when they visited the Sweet Waters of Asia. Later, under the Turkish Republic, it was used as a presidential residence and also as a guest house for visiting dignitaries. Restored in the 1970's, it is now a museum. Beside the palace to its south stands the Küçüksu Çesmesi, an exceptionally beautiful Baroque fountain, built for Selim III in 1806. A 32-line calligraphic chronogram inscribed on the fountain gives the Sultan's name and the date of construction. The text is by the poet Hatif, who refers to the *çeşme* as a "soul-caressing fountain . . . a fragile beauty in the meadow."

The Ostrorog yalı at Küçüksu.

THE LITTLE PALACE OF KÜÇÜKSU
The palace's marble façade is reflected in the waters of the strait. The beautifully maintained garden around the palace is planted with rare trees, magnolias, and pines. The terraces behind the residence spread over the side of the hill.

THE YALI OF KÜÇÜKSU. South of the *iskele* at Küçüksu are two of the oldest of the surviving yalı on the Bosphorus. The one next to the beach at Küçüksu is the Kibrisli (or Cypriot) Mustafa Emin Paşa Yalısı, built originally c. 1760 but expanded and redecorated later on. It is still inhabited by the descendants of Mustafa Emin Paşa. A little further downstream we see the Ostrorog Yalısı, a very handsome wooden mansion painted rust-red. This dates from c. 1790, when it became the residence of the Counts Ostrorog, Polish aristocrats ennobled by the King of France, who enlisted in the Ottoman service in the late 18th century.

KANDILLI. The ferry stops next at Kandilli, adjacent to the promontory opposite Bebek Bay. The waters at Kandilli are known as the Devil's Current, the strongest on the Asian side of the strait, with a speed of over 5 knots when the prevailing wind blows from the north. The deepest point in the Bosphorus is some 300 yards off the Kandilli promontory, where the water reaches a depth of 360 feet.

VANIKÖY. Next is Vaniköy, opposite Arnavutköy. On the hilltop above this village we see the tower and telescope dome of the Istanbul Rasatname, a meteorological station and astronomical observatory. The Rasatname preserves the instruments used by the great mid-16th-century Turkish astronomer Takiuddin.

The yalı of Sadullah Paşa.

THE KULELI NAVAL STATION. The ferry continues on to Çengelköy, some 1,600 yards down the strait. About halfway between Vaniköy and Çengelköy we pass the Kuleli Military College, a large building flanked by cone-capped towers. The original training school and barracks were built in c. 1800 by Selim III, as part of his attempted reform of the Ottoman armed forces. The present structure dates from 1860 when an extensive rebuilding program, ordered by Abdül Mecit, was completed. The original building was used as a military hospital from 1855 to 1856, during the Crimean War. This was one of two hospitals in Istanbul directed by Florence Nightingale, the other being

in the much larger Selimiye Barracks in Üsküdar.

ÇENGELKÖY. According to Evliya Çelebi, the name of this village, which means "Village of Hooks," probably came from the ships' anchors discovered there after the Conquest. Despite the rather sinister tag, the village is a pretty one, with a number of waterfront restaurants offering a view of the Bosphorus and the skyline of old Istanbul. Downstream from the *iskele* we see the Sadullah Paşa Yalısı, a handsome seaside mansion dating from c. 1790.

BEYLERBEY. The next ferry stop is at Beylerbey, where, near the port, we see the Imperial Beylerbey Cami'i ● *84.* An inscription gives the date of construction as 1778 and the architect as Mehmet Tahir Ağa. The mosque is an attractive example of the Ottoman Baroque, with a dome sectioned by its prominent structural ribs into an octagon, a mihrab set into a deep apse, and a profusion of decorative tiles dating from the 16th to the 18th century. The mimbar and the *Kuran kürsü* (the lectern for reading the Koran) are particularly fine, elegantly fashioned of ivory-inlaid wood.

BEYLERBEY PALACE. Beyond the village we come to Beylerbey Sarayı, the far end of which is almost underneath the Bosphorus Bridge. The name of the village and the palace – Beylerbey – means provincial governor, in memory of Mehmet Paşa, who administered Rumeli in the reign of Murat III. Mehmet Paşa built a *konak* (mansion) here in the last quarter of the 16th century. Sarkis Balyan constructed the present sarayı between 1861 and 1865 for Abdül Aziz. For the

exterior the architect adopted European neo-classicism, but left the interior to be completed in the traditional Ottoman manner.

KUZGUNCUK. Passing under the lower Bosphorus bridge, the ferry then stops at Kuzguncuk, a lovely village that has retained its character despite the proximity of a rapidly expanding Üsküdar. The next call is at Üsküdar, after which the ferry crosses the strait to the terminus on the shore of Eminönü on the Golden Horn, which was the start of this journey along the Bosphorus.

THE PALACE OF BEYLERBEY
This palace was used both as a summer lodge and as a

residence for visiting royalty, the first of whom was the Empress Eugénie of France. The anti-reformist and overthrown Abdül Hamit II was confined at Beylerbey after his return from exile in Thessalonica, and he died here in

1918. The palace was splendidly restored in the 1970's and converted into a museum.

THE VILLAGE AND BAY OF BEYLERBEY
Here, as in all the Bosphorus villages, the most agreeable place is the quay at the port where both fishermen and tourists find shade and comfort at the little bowered cafés.

Toward the
Dardanelles Strait

IZNIK LAKE

ROMAN AMPHITHEATER

ISTANBUL KAPISI

⚘ Half a day

THE RAMPARTS
Even though partially
ruined, Iznik's ancient
defense walls remain
an imposing presence,
surrounding almost
the whole of the city.
An earlier wall,
Hellenistic in origin,
was replaced by the
Emperor Gallienus
following the sack of
the town by the Goths
in 256. Claudius II
Gothicus completed
the project in 268–9,
which is known from
inscriptions still
visible on the
Yenişehir and Lefke
Gates. Other
inscriptions cite major
programs of
reconstruction

carried out during the
reign of Michael III
in 858, after one of
the many earthquakes
that periodically
devastated Nicaea.
The last restoration
came during the reign
of John III Vatatzes
(1222–54), who added
an outer fortification
and increased the
height of the inner
walls and their
towers.

HISTORY

The walls enclosing Nicaea were
constructed during the Hellenistic era, at
the time of the wars that broke out
following the death of Alexander the
Great in 323 BC. Despite
the fortifications, the
first city, Antigonia,
fell in c. 300 BC to
Lysimachus, who renamed it Nicaea in
memory of his first wife. The city
served as the capital of the
kingdom of Nicomedia and then of
Bithynia from the 3rd century to
the 1st century BC. Still later,
Pompey made Nicaea the capital of
the Roman province of Bithynium,
and it would play a similar role
during the Byzantine Empire.
Diocletian resided there for a while,
as did both Constantine the Great
and Justinian. In the Middle Ages,

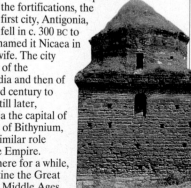

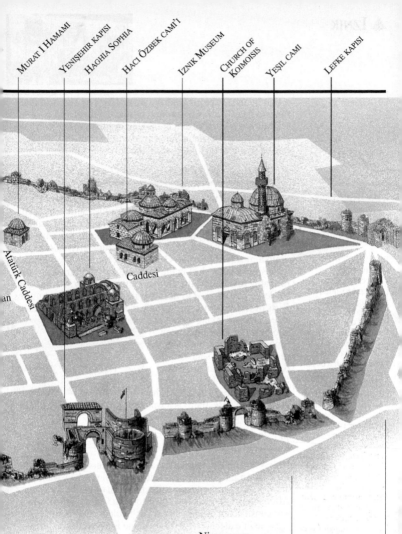

MURAT I HAMAMI
YENIŞEHIR KAPISI
HAGHIA SOPHIA
HACI ÖZBEK CAMI'I
IZNIK MUSEUM
CHURCH OF KOIMOISIS
YEŞIL CAMI
LEFKE KAPISI

Atatürk Caddesi

an

Caddesi

Nicaea was conquered in turn by Goths, Arabs, Persians, Selçuks, Crusaders, Byzantines, Ottomans, Mongols, and again by Ottomans in 1331. After this last conquest, Nicaea entered a new era altogether, a period named after the Sultan Orhan Gazi. From the 15th to the 17th century, the city enjoyed great fame for the magnificent faience tiles produced by its workshops.

THE ISTANBUL GATE

You enter the town through an opening in the walls beside the Istanbul Kapısı, one of the four main gateways in the defense system. Like the other entranceways, this is a double gate because the city was surrounded by two concentric walls, each guarded by more than a hundred towers. Between the two gates there is a triumphal arch, constructed to commemorate

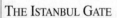

AN OTTOMAN CARAVANSERAI IN THE 17TH CENTURY The dining room reserved for travelers opened onto the central courtyard.

293

AYASOFYA
4. YÜZYILDA İNŞA EDİLMİŞ
AİH BAZİLKADIR. M.S. 787.
YILINDA II İZNİK KONSÜLÜ
BURADA TOPLANMIŞTIR.
1331 YILINDA CAMİ OLARAK
AÇILMIŞTIR.

IT IS AKIND OF BASILICA
WHICH WAS BUILT IN THE 4 t h
CENTURY. THE SECOND IZNIK'S
CONSUL MET HERE IN 787 A.D.
IT WAS OPENED AS A MOSQUE
IN 1331.

a visit by the Emperor Hadrian in AD 123. The lintels of the innermost gate are surmounted by ancient theatrical masks, taken from Nicaea's Roman theater. A little farther along, on the left, is the hammam built for Murat I (1359–89), which makes it one of the oldest of all the surviving Ottoman baths.

THE FORMER BASILICA OF HAGHIA SOPHIA

In the town center, at the southeast corner of the intersection where Atatürk Caddesi and Kiliçaslan Caddesi meet, are the ruins of the ancient Basilica of Haghia Sophia, Iznik's most important Byzantine monument ● 74 after its great ramparts. Converted into a mosque by Orhan Gazi in 1331, the building suffered extensive damage during the 15th and 16th centuries. It was probably restored by the great architect Sinan ● 314, but was subsequently allowed to disintegrate slowly over the centuries. Parts of the structure, principally the apse, the pair of domed side chapels flanking it, and the lateral walls, have since been renovated. A glass covering protects the nave's mosaic pavement. All that survives of the frescoes is a Deisis under an arch on the north side of the

nave. In the apse, there is a *synanthron*, a semicircular tier of seats for the clergy.

HACI ÖZBEK CAMI'I

Iznik's most important Ottoman monuments are situated in the eastern part of the city, which you can reach by walking along Kılıçaslan Caddesi in the direction of the Lefke Kapı. After some 380 yards you come to Hacı Özbek Cami'i, which was constructed in 1333 and so is the oldest Ottoman mosque in existence. The brick dome is covered with terra-cotta tiles curved to fit the spherical surface, a typical feature of early Ottoman mosques. The Hacı Özbek Cami'i is unusual in that it is too small to have a minaret. The original three-bay porch was removed when the road was widened in 1959. The vestibule that replaced it mars the external appearance of the structure. Fortunately, the interior has scarcely been altered, save for the galleries and a few minor renovations made in 1959. Hacı Özbek Cami'i is a single-unit type of mosque, with a 25-feet square room, covered by a hemispherical dome which is supported on a belt of Turkish triangles.

THE GREEN MOSQUE ★

Farther still, on the left in Müze Sokağı, is the Yeşil Cami – the Green Mosque, so called for the color of the glazed brick that originally sheathed the minaret. This revetment has subsequently been replaced by tiles of a much inferior quality from Kütahya, the

YEŞIL CAMI
The entrance to the Green Mosque is through a three-bay porch. The small, ribbed dome over the central bay porch is supported by an octagonal drum resting upon a band of Turkish triangles. The prayer hall, capped by a large cupola, is preceded by an antechamber, a sort of narthex with three bays whose arches spring from two massive columns. The principal dome, measuring 36 feet in diameter, and which at its crown is 57 feet above the floor, rests upon a circle of Turkish triangles very similar to those in the Hacı Ozbek Cami'i. The brick minaret is clad in a geometric pattern of red, black, and, most of all, blue-green tiles.

> "Half-hidden by greenery, the little village of Iznik, a bit lost within the walls of the ancient city, huddled among its solemn ruins and its too enormous past."
>
> André Gide

capital of Phrygia. Commissioned by the Grand Vizier Çandarlı Kara Halil Hayrettin Paşa, the Green Mosque was built between 1378 and 1392 by Hacı ben Musa.

THE IMARET OF NILÜFER HATUN

Continuing along Müze Sokağı, you arrive at the *imaret* of Nilüfer Hatun, built in 1388 by Murat I, who dedicated it to his mother Nilüfer Hatun, wife of Orhan Gazi. The *imaret* is constructed of stone courses alternating with four courses of brick. Square tiles cover both vaults and domes. The building is fronted by a five-bay porch open at either end and topped by a small cupola over the central bay. A large dome resting on a band of Turkish triangles crowns the main room within. On either side there are large shallow-domed rooms, each with a generous *ocak*, or hearth, which could be used as a kitchen or a dormitory. Before the principal room another chamber of comparable size, divided into two lateral sections by a great arch, served as a small mosque.

THE LEFKE KAPISI. This gate has a triumphal arch between its inner and outer gates, also constructed to mark Hadrian's visit in 123. Two panels of ancient reliefs have been built into the façade of the outer gate. They show Roman centurions in battle against tribesmen, perhaps the Goths who were defeated by Claudius II Gothicus.

A small ceramic lamp (Iznik Museum).

THE CHURCH OF THE KOIMOISIS

Returning along Kılıçaslan Caddesi, you will see the ruins of a Byzantine church at the end of the fourth block of houses on the right. This is the Koimoisis, or Assumption of the Virgin, dating from the 7th or 8th century. Unfortunately only a few sections of wall and a bit of the mosaic pavement survive. The church served as an imperial chapel for the first Byzantine Emperor from Nicaea, Theodore I Lascaris, who was buried here in 1222. The chapel was damaged during the Greco-Turkish wars of 1913.

A GREEK SARCOPHAGUS IN THE IZNIK MUSEUM

THE AYAZMA

East of the Koimoisis we come to the remnants of a sacred Byzantine fountain or spring – an *ayazma* – which may have been the baptistery for the

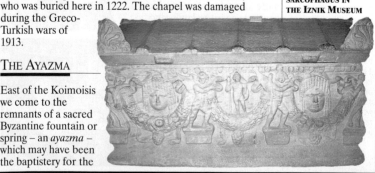

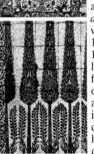

From the 15th to the 17th century, Iznik faience became well known and was used to decorate palaces, mosques, tombs, and other sumptuous buildings of the Ottoman Empire. The tiles made in the city of Iznik constituted a major

contribution to Islamic art during the Golden Age of Ottoman culture. The Iznik workshops reached the peak of their craftsmanship towards the end of the 16th century, a period in which the great architect Sinan used their products for the embellishment of all his important buildings. After 1620, the quality of the faience went into rapid decline, and the ceramicists seem to have lost their skill. The kilns were kept in operation until the middle of the 18th century, but they would never again match their past achievements.

imperial chapel. One of the stones still bears a low relief depicting the Jewish *menorah*, the eight-branched candelabrum used in Jewish worship, together with an inscription in Hebrew, which suggests that an ancient synagogue once stood in the vicinity. Certainly, Nicaea had a substantial Jewish community during the late Roman and early Byzantine eras.

THE ROMAN AMPHITHEATER

Some distance farther along Yakup Sokağı, cross Atatürk Caddesi and continue for another 300 yards or so, until you come to Nicaea's Roman amphitheater. The excavations now under way have revealed parts of the stage building and its side exits, as well as the proscenium, orchestra, *cavea*, and *diazoma*. It seems that, in its heyday, this vast theater could accommodate around 15,000 spectators. The remains of a 13th-century Byzantine church and a large burial ground have also been found above the *cavea*. The excavation of the stage area revealed many ancient architectural and sculptural remains, including a relief depicting Roman charioteers in action. Archeologists have also uncovered on the site large quantities of pottery from the Roman, Byzantine, Selçuk, and Ottoman periods. The theater was commissioned by Pliny the Younger during his tenure as the Roman governor of Bithynium from AD 111 to 113.

IZNIK LAKE

Kılıçaslan Caddesi leads westward, all the way to the Göl Kapı – the "Lake Gate" – which opens on to the waterfront, lined with restaurants and attractive picnic sites. Indeed, there could not be a more agreeable place in which to conclude a visit to Iznik, since there is a magnificent view from here of the Bithynian countryside that surrounds the lake as well as the massive ramparts, which are a reminder of the old and once-powerful city of Nicaea.

▲ BURSA

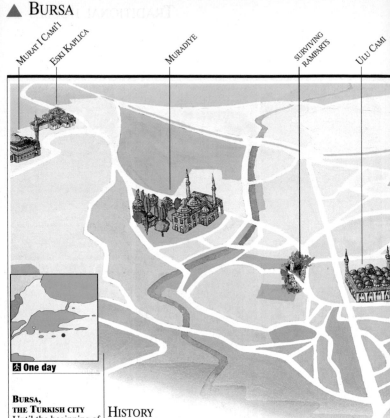

MURAT I CAMI'I · ESKI KAPLICA · MURADIYE · SURVIVING RAMPARTS · ULU CAMI

☉ One day

Bursa, **the Turkish city**
Until the beginning of the 15th century Bursa was the capital of the Ottoman Empire ● *36*, which was then expanding rapidly. When the central government moved to Edirne, Bursa continued to hold pride of place as the former capital and the burial site of Osman Gazi and the first five sultans. Their imperial mosques, mausoleums, and religious foundations continue to adorn the venerable city, which the Turks call Yeşil Bursa – "Bursa the Green."

HISTORY

Bursa, or *Prusa* in Greek, was founded by Prusias I in 183 BC. The letters of Pliny the Elder confirm that the city was a prosperous one with a number of impressive public buildings. Its most prominent feature was the citadel, and remnants of its defensive walls can be seen on the acropolis, which the Turks call Hisar. Otherwise, nothing remains of ancient Prusa apart from a few exhibits in the Archeological Museum. All evidence of the Greek city disappeared after it was captured in 1326 by Orhan Gazi ● *36*, the first sultan of the Ottoman Turks, and the son and successor of Osman Gazi, the eponymous founder of the imperial Osmanli line.

THE OLD MARKET QUARTER

ULU CAMI. At the center of Bursa, in Cumhuriyet Meydanı, take Atatürk Caddesi, which leads westward towards Ulu Cami (the "Great Mosque"). The mosque is situated in the old market quarter at the base of the citadel hill. Ulu Cami was built between 1396 and 1399 by Beyazıt I (1389–1403), known to the Turks as Yıldırım, "Lightning," because of the speed with which he moved his armies back and forth between campaigns in Europe and Asia. The Sultan financed the construction of Bursa's Ulu Cami with the loot from his victory at the Battle of Nicopolis on September 24, 1396. It is the most ambitious of all the great mosques constructed in Anatolia during the two centuries prior to the Turkish Conquest of Constantinople. The exterior of Ulu

298

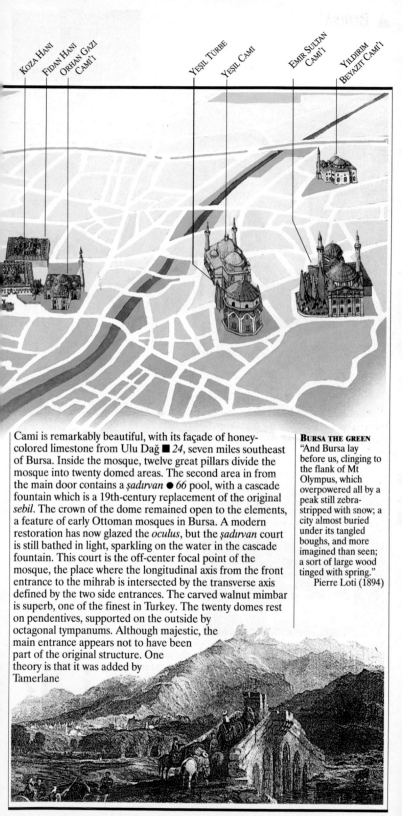

KOZA HANI   FIDAN HANI   ORHAN GAZI CAMI'I   YEŞIL TÜRBE   YEŞIL CAMI   EMIR SULTAN CAMI'I   YILDIRIM BEYAZIT CAMI'I

Cami is remarkably beautiful, with its façade of honey-colored limestone from Ulu Dağ ■ 24, seven miles southeast of Bursa. Inside the mosque, twelve great pillars divide the mosque into twenty domed areas. The second area in from the main door contains a *şadırvan* ● 66 pool, with a cascade fountain which is a 19th-century replacement of the original *sebil*. The crown of the dome remained open to the elements, a feature of early Ottoman mosques in Bursa. A modern restoration has now glazed the *oculus*, but the *şadırvan* court is still bathed in light, sparkling on the water in the cascade fountain. This court is the off-center focal point of the mosque, the place where the longitudinal axis from the front entrance to the mihrab is intersected by the transverse axis defined by the two side entrances. The carved walnut mimbar is superb, one of the finest in Turkey. The twenty domes rest on pendentives, supported on the outside by octagonal tympanums. Although majestic, the main entrance appears not to have been part of the original structure. One theory is that it was added by Tamerlane

299

A view of Bursa
from the hillside.

BASHIBAZOUKS
Part-time soldiers, or
Ziebek, near Bursa in
the 19th century.

THE BAZAAR In
Bursa, as in Istanbul,
the heart of the
covered market is the
bedestan, formerly
reserved for valuable
merchandise. It was
rebuilt during the
reign of Beyazıt I.
North of the *bedestan*
is the horse bazaar,
an open market built
in Mehmet I's reign.

Above, an aerial view
of the Ulu Cami.

during his occupation of Bursa from 1402 to 1403.

ORHAN GAZI CAMI'I. Retrace your steps a short distance back
along Atatürk Caddesi, and you come to the oldest of Bursa's
imperial mosques, the Orhan Gazi Cami'i built in 1339. It
has twice been destroyed, first by the Karamanid Türkoman
tribe in the interregnum that followed
the battle of Ankara in 1402, and then by
an earthquake in 1855; it was repaired
after both catastrophes, presumably with
some changes in structure. The essential
plan of the mosque is the same as the
original, which was the first example of a
mosque formed like an upside-down "T".
The five-bay porch is supported on the
façade by six pillars, with a slender
column separating the two arches at
either end; the three central bays are
domed and those at the ends cross-
vaulted and flat-topped. You pass through a domed
antechamber to reach the central hall, a rectangle with a
deep arch on the north that creates a
square base on the upper level for the
hemispherical dome. In the south, the
main prayer hall is raised up on three
steps from the central chamber.
Because the design is rectangular
at both lower and upper levels,
the dome is ellipsoidal rather
than spherical, with a niche in
its southern wall containing
the mihrab. The central space is
flanked by two other rectangular

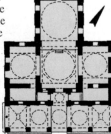

> "A simple round orifice, from deep within the chill pool, brought forth a surge of quivering water, the silent birth of a spring into which I long peered. . . ."
>
> André Gide

rooms, with back-to-back arches on the north and south forming a square base at a higher level for the hemispherical domes. The height of the domes over the central hall and the three rooms varies, as does the system of transition from the square base to the circular or elliptical cornice. On the exterior, however, all the cupolas rest upon octagonal drums.

THE COVERED MARKET. The principal market of Bursa lies behind the two mosques. The entire area was gutted by fire in 1955, but since then most of the quarter has been restored to its original appearance. Something of the former oriental atmosphere has unfortunately been lost in the process of restoration, but one is still able to experience the sense of what it must have been like in an old Ottoman market town.

THE CARAVANSERAI. Within the market complex are four caravanserai and two hammams. The Koza, or "Silk Cocoon," Hanı was built in 1490 by Beyazıt II to accommodate the silk trade, a function it still performs. At the center of its porticoed courtyard is an octagonal şadırvan surmounted by a *mescit* (a small mosque), a feature derived from the imperial Selçuk caravanserai of the 13th century. The two baths are the Sengul Hammam and the Bey Hamamı, both part of the *külliye* of Orhan Gazi Cami'i.

AROUND THE CITADEL

West of the Ulu Cami, Atatürk Caddesi divides into two avenues, one running around the hill and the other climbing steeply along the ramparts of the citadel, or Hisar. These are the massive remnants of the citadel's ancient defensive wall, constructed in the Hellenistic era and then rebuilt in both the Byzantine and Ottoman periods. This is all that remains above ground of the Greek city of Prusa. At the top of the acropolis are the tombs of Osman and Orhan Gazi. Osman Gazi died in the nearby town of Soğut in 1324, but his body was reinterred here following the capture of Prusa two years later, in what had originally been the baptistery of the Byzantine Church of St Prophitis Elias, which was converted into a mosque. When Orhan Gazi died in 1359, he was buried in the former nave of St Prophitis Elias. Today all that remains of the original church are a few fragments of mosaic pavement around the catafalque of Orhan Gazi, whose wife Nilüfer Hatun is also buried beside him.

HAMMAMS ● 58
"The sonority of the word contains all the sensuality of a purification rite. Haloed in mist that softens the harshness of reality, ghostly silhouettes wander from room to room with the demeanor of penitents, then kneel at the base of marble fountains to rest near those horns of plenty atrickle with scalding water. Under beams of light issuing from occuli set into the cupolas or the spectral glimmer of

neon tubes, bodies are kneaded, joints crack, thighs slap against wet marble, and spirits give up to long hours of moist languor."

E.P.

OSMAN GAZI
Founder of the Osmanli dynasty.

301

▲ BURSA

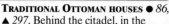

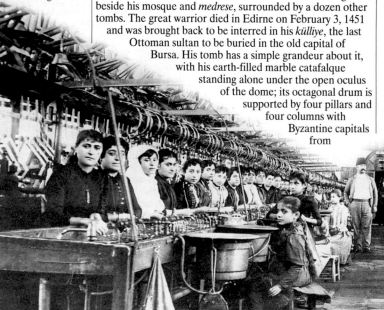

A traditional wooden house with overhanging upper stories and a little painted shop on the ground floor.

BURSA, THE CAPITAL OF A PROVINCE
The city of Bursa is renowned for its fruit trees, agricultural products, olive oil, wine, honey, tobacco, and cotton. Since antiquity,

Bursa's prosperity has depended on the production of silk-worm cocoons. Until the 20th century, the Ottoman government supplied peasants with mulberry seedlings free of charge.

TRADITIONAL OTTOMAN HOUSES ● *86,* ▲ *297.* Behind the citadel, in the picturesque back streets of Bursa, a few old, wooden Ottoman houses still survive, although they are fast disappearing.

THE MURADIYE

The Muradiye was built between 1424 and 1426 by Murat II (1421–51), father of Mehmet the Conqueror. This was the last imperial mosque complex to be constructed in Bursa. Besides the mosque itself, it included a *medrese*, an *imaret*, the *türbe* of the founder, and many other tombs, some built in later times.

THE MOSQUE AND MEDRESE OF MURAT II. Like the Orhan Gazi Cami'i, the Muradiye Cami'i was built following a cross-axial upside-down "T" plan ● *78,* with a five-bay porch, and it too has a pair of *zaviye* (shelters for pilgrims or dervishes) flanking its main chamber. The *medrese* is the most beautiful in Bursa. The courtyard forms a perfect square with five *hücres* (studies for students) each on the east and west sides, larger rooms in the corners, and a pair of rooms on either side of the entranceway. The little *dershane* (lecture hall) opposite the entrance has brilliant tile decoration. The *medrese* serves as a dispensary, its courtyard converted into a pretty garden with a fountain at its center. Little now remains of the *imaret* that once served food to the students and the staff of the complex.

THE MAUSOLEUMS. The *türbe* of Murat II stands in the garden beside his mosque and *medrese*, surrounded by a dozen other tombs. The great warrior died in Edirne on February 3, 1451 and was brought back to be interred in his *külliye*, the last Ottoman sultan to be buried in the old capital of Bursa. His tomb has a simple grandeur about it, with his earth-filled marble catafalque standing alone under the open oculus of the dome; its octagonal drum is supported by four pillars and four columns with Byzantine capitals from

> "... Bury me directly in the ground.
> May the rain, sign of the benediction of God,
> fall upon me. ..."
>
> Sultan Murat II

which rise eight ogival arches. Murat's tomb was left open to the elements according to the terms of his last will and testament. The next *türbe* to the west is that of Prince Mustafa, the eldest son of Süleyman the Magnificent ● *36*. Mustafa was heir apparent until he was executed in 1551 by Süleyman, who had been persuaded by Roxelana that his son was plotting to usurp the throne. Thereby Roxelana's son, Selim "the Sot," succeeded to the throne when Süleyman died in 1566, and with his reign began the long decline of the Ottoman Empire. The next *türbe* to the southwest contains the graves of two sons of Fatih, Princes Mustafa and Cem. Mustafa was killed in action in 1474 at the age of 25, and Fatih brought his body to Bursa for burial next to his grandfather Murat. Cem died in 1495 in Italy, having spent fourteen years in exile after being defeated by his brother Beyazıt II in a war of succession. The deceased Prince was not brought back to Bursa for burial until 1499, for even after his death he continued to be the subject of negotiations between Beyazıt and the European powers that had held him captive. Evilya Çelebi, in his *Seyahatname*, spins a fable about the body's return to Bursa: "The remains of Cem, and the possessions of the departed, among which figured a magic cup (which refilled itself whenever it was taken in hand by a drinker), a white parrot,

A SILK FACTORY IN 1900
"We expected to find one of those sad interiors dominated by machines. We entered a room, populated by young people, handsome and happy. On the right, Greek and Armenian girls, their huge eyes glued to us. On the left, Turkish women, their yaşmak slightly lowered, their noses sharp, a bit long, the mouth delicate, timid but graceful, modest."
Comtesse de Gasparin, 1867

An unglazed
ceramic jug and
a bronze candlestick
from the 18th century.

and thousands of splendid works, were entrusted to Saïd Çelebi and Haydar Çelebi for delivery to the Sultan. Just as his grave was being dug, there came such a clap of thunder followed by such confusion in the funerary chapel that everyone present took flight, and no one could cross the threshhold for the next six days. When the Sultan learned of these events, he ordered that the body of Cem be interred near his grandfather. . . ."

THE HÜDAVENDIGAR COMPLEX

The oldest of Bursa's three other mosque complexes is the Hüdavendigar *külliye.* Hüdavendigar was the pompous imperial title assumed by Murat I (1359–89), the only sultan who ever styled himself "Creator of the World." The *külliye*, built by Murat I between 1365 and 1385, is situated in the pleasant suburb of Çekirğe, in the heights west of the city. The Hüdavendigar *külliye* is less a complex of the familiar type than a two-story building with a mosque-cum-hospice on the ground floor and a *medrese*

THE MURADIYE KONAK
The grandest of Bursa's old Ottoman mansions, the Muradiye Konak, stands in the square in front of the Mosque of Murat II. Built in the early 18th century, the *konak* has been restored and is now open to the public, with some of its rooms furnished as they were in Ottoman times.

above. The mosque is fronted by a five-bay porch with a gallery of five bays above, now walled in, the two floors connected by a pair of stairways flanking the vestibule. The interior of the ground floor comprises four *eyvans* around a central fountain court, as well as six other rooms. The two-story central hall is a square surmounted by a dome 36 feet in diameter and 72 feet high, with an oculus at the apex of its crown. A flight of steps leads up from there to the prayer hall, a rectangular room covered by a barrel vault, with the mihrab placed inside a niche at the back of the building. The *medrese*, or college, on the second floor has a large room between the staircases, eight studies for students on either

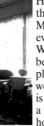

side of the central hall and the prayer hall, as well as a small room above the mihrab. The Hüdavendigar is an extraordinary building, and nothing like it would ever again be built by the Ottomans. Murat I is buried in a *türbe* in front of his complex.

THE THERMAL BATHS

Bursa has been famous for its thermal baths ● *58* since Roman times, and the oldest of its bathing establishments, the ESKI KAPLICA, stands at the foot of the Çekirğe hill, a short distance below the Hüdavendigar. According to tradition,

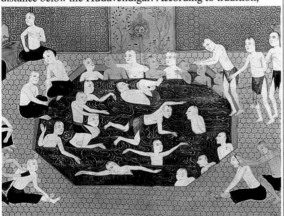

these baths were first built by Justinian and Theodora. They were constructed in their present form during Murat I's reign, but the ancient columns and capitals incorporated into the building indicate that the original structure dates back to late Roman or early Byzantine times. Returning toward the city center, you see in the fields below the road the Yeni Kaplica, built in the 1550's by Rüstem Paşa.

THE KÜLTÜR PARKI. Next on the left is the Kültür Parki, where the people of Bursa come in the summer to enjoy themselves at outdoor cafés and an amusement park. Within the park is the ARCHEOLOGICAL MUSEUM, which exhibits antiquities found in Bursa and the surrounding region, including a number of funerary stelae from the late Roman and early Byzantine eras.

YEŞIL CAMI

Yeşil Cami ● *78* – the Green Mosque – was commissioned by Mehmet I in 1412, the year before he became sultan. Designed by the architect Haci Ivaz Paşa, the mosque was not finished when Mehmet died in 1421. Although work continued for another three years, the building was never completed, and lacks its entrance portico. Nevertheless, Yeşil Cami is the most beautiful of the imperial mosques in Bursa, both in the harmony of its design and the opulence of its interior decoration. The plan is yet another variation of the upside-down T, or

PANORAMA
The postcard above, from the beginning of the century, gives an idea of the beautiful countryside around Bursa. Seen here is a mosque with its cemetery in the foreground.

A HOLIDAY RESORT
Since the beginning of the 20th century, Bursa has become an important holiday and tourist resort, where visitors can enjoy the hot springs. This 16th-century miniature depicts the steam room in a hammam.

A MINIATURE FROM THE 17TH CENTURY
This dancer, painted by the miniaturist Levni, wears an elegant costume made of silk from Bursa.

**TOMBS OF OSMAN
AND ORHAN GAZI**
Erected shortly after
the conquest of
Byzantine Bursa, the
mausoleums were
destroyed by an
earthquake, but they
were rebuilt in the
19th century.

**A GENERAL VIEW
OF BURSA IN
THE 19TH CENTURY**
Behind the 14th-
century Mosque of
Emir Sultan, the
Beyazıt Cami'i can be
seen on the horizon.

**THE MOSQUE WITHIN
THE BEYAZIT COMPLEX**
An aerial view that
includes the *medrese*
and *türbe* rebuilt in
the 19th century.

cross-axial *eyvan* type. Beyond the vestibule you pass through
a small barrel-vaulted *eyvan* into the central court, in the
middle of which is a *şadırvan* pool. On the left and right there
are side *eyvans* raised above the central court by a single step,
while the main *eyvan* – the prayer hall – is raised by four steps.
Each of the side *eyvans* is flanked by a pair of rooms of
comparable size. The dome over the central court, slightly
higher than the one over the prayer hall, is surmounted by a
lantern, replacing the original open oculus. From the central
court you can see the beautifully tiled imperial loge, and to
either side of it the screened balconies reserved for the royal
family. This is the most beautiful mosque interior in Bursa,
with the magnificent mihrab framed in the
great arch of the prayer hall,
and the still water of the
şadırvan pool mirroring the
colors of the stained-glass
windows in the kiblah wall.

YEŞİL TÜRBE ★

Yeşil Türbe, the "Green Tomb", the mausoleum of Mehmet I,
stands at the top of the hill across the street from the mosque.
Originally its exterior walls were revetted in the turquoise tiles
from which the *türbe* and the mosque took their names, but
these were destroyed by the 1855 earthquake and replaced by
Kütahya tiles. The interior decoration of the *türbe* rivals that
of the mosque, particularly the finely carved doors, the tile
revetment of the walls, the beautifully decorated mihrab, and
the Sultan's sarcophagus, with its epitaph in golden
calligraphy on a blue ground.

THE MUSEUM OF TURKISH AND ISLAMIC ART. The *külliye* of
Mehmet I also included a *medrese*, an *imaret*, and a hammam,
but of these only the *imaret* has survived. It now houses the
Museum of Turkish and Islamic Art, whose collections
include Ottoman weapons, kitchen utensils, jewelry,
calligraphy, and antique books in Arabic and Osmanli script.

THE COMPLEX AND MOSQUE OF BEYAZIT I

The fourth of Bursa's imperial mosque complexes is that of
Beyazıt I, located on a hilltop site northeast of Yeşil Cami and

reached by Yeşil
Caddesi. The
complex was begun
in 1390 and
completed in 1395.
It suffered severe
damage in the 1855
earthquake ■ 16,
since which it has
been restored twice,
in 1878 and in 1948.
Nevertheless, the
külliye appears to
have retained most
of its original
character. When
finished, the

complex consisted of the mosque with its dervish hospice, along with two *medreses*, a hospital, a palace, and the *türbe* of the founder. Today all that remains are the mosque, the *türbe*, and one of the *medreses*, which now serves as a dispensary.

THE MOSQUE OF BEYAZIT I. The mosque is entered through a five-bay porch and then a domed vestibule, which leads into the large central prayer hall. The interior plan is of the familiar reversed-T or cross-axial *evyan* type, with pairs of *zaviye* – hospices for pilgrims or dervishes – flanking each of the side *eyvans*. The three rooms are raised three steps higher than the central hall. All are domed, with the cupola of the main space being only slightly higher than that of the central court, while those of the side *eyvans* are considerably lower.

THE YEŞIL TÜRBE
The "Green Tomb" takes its name from the green faience with which its façades are decorated (above left).

The two minarets were destroyed by earthquakes, one of them in 1855 and the other in 1949, and they have never been rebuilt. The exterior of the mosque is particularly handsome, with its impressive portico of five arches and its shining façade of marble and cut stone.

THE ULU DAĞ NATIONAL PARK ★

The best time to visit Bursa is in spring, when the broad plain below Ulu Dağ turns a verdant green and the hillsides are bright with wild flowers and blossoming trees. And of course no visit to Bursa is complete without an ascent of the Great Mountain, which in winter becomes a popular ski resort. One approach is to take the cable car that starts from the hillside east of town, not far from Yeşil Cami; another is to drive or

take a taxi up the mountain road that ascends from Çekirğe. This leads to the Ulu Dağ massif and from there it is a three-hour walk to the summit, 8,343 feet above sea level, by far the highest peak in northwestern Anatolia. In the resort village there are numerous hotels and restaurants, and thermal facilities remain open throughout the year. The mountain is now part of the Ulu Dağ National Park, more than 27,000 acres of woodland, which includes olive groves and clumps of bay, chestnut, elm, oak, plane, beech, pine, juniper, and aspen trees ■ *24*. A sizeable bird population nests here, and this includes a number of rare species ■ *18*. The summit offers an unforgettable view over the whole of Bythnia. On a clear day you can see the domes and minarets of Istanbul sparkling on the northern horizon.

In the vast garden of the Muradiye there are several mausoleums of the princes of the Ottoman dynasty as well as for Sultan Murat himself.

A mountain stream in the Ulu Dağ National Park.

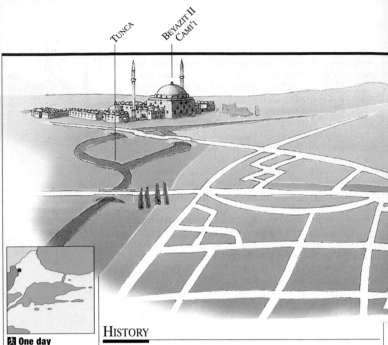

TUNCA

BEYAZIT II CAMI'İ

🚶 One day

THE CITADEL QUARTER
The old quarter of Kale İç spreads out west of the Semiz Ali Paşa bazaar. Its name means "inside the citadel" and comes from the Byzantine era when the ramparts of the citadel did indeed surround it. The streets of the quarter, which extends to Saraçlar Caddesi to the west and to Salat Paşa Caddesi to the south, form a regular grid-pattern square. To the southwest flows the Tunca, near which the remains of the ancient Byzantine defense walls can still be seen.

HISTORY

Edirne, ancient Hadrianopolis, is situated near the confluence of the rivers Meriç and Tunca, known in antiquity as Hebrus and Tonsus. The original settlement on this site was a Thracian market town founded in the 7th century BC. It bore the name Odrysia, for the Odryses, the Thracian tribe then in control of the region. The Odryses would be supplanted by the Orestes, a Hellenic tribe from Epirus, who established themselves nearby and called their city Orestia. In AD 125, the Roman Emperor Hadrian joined the two cities under the common name Hadrianopolis, which in Greek became Adrianopolis and thus in English Adrianople. Diocletian (284–305) made Hadrianopolis the capital of one of the four provinces of Thrace. When Constantine the Great transferred his capital to Constantinople in 330, Adrianople developed rapidly and grew into the most prosperous as well as the most populous city in Thrace. And so it would remain to the end of the Byzantine era. During the following five and a half centuries Adrianople was fought over and captured in turn by the Byzantines, Avars, Bulgars, Romans, and Turks, finally succumbing to Murat I in 1361, after which it would be called Edirne ● *33*. Edirne became the capital of the expanding Ottoman Empire, a position it held until a few months after the Conquest of Constantinople. Nonetheless, Edirne remained prominent long after Istanbul replaced it as the principal seat of government. Indeed, several of the sultans and their grand viziers looked upon the city as their second home, continuing to adorn it with splendid buildings. Its status did not begin to dim until the Ottoman Empire itself fell into decline. During the

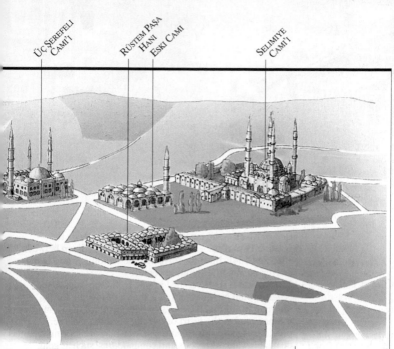

ÜÇ ŞEREFELİ CAMİ'İ   RÜSTEM PAŞA HANI   ESKİ CAMİ   SELİMİYE CAMİ'İ

19th century Edirne suffered
terribly at the hands of various invading armies: the Russians in
1829 and 1878, the Bulgars in 1913, and the Greeks between
1919 and 1923, after which the Treaty of Lausanne granted it to
Turkey in 1923. Today Edirne is a lively market town, made
glorious by its numerous imperial Ottoman monuments.

THE ESKI CAMI

The Eski Cami, or "Old Mosque,"
was begun by the Emir Süleyman
Çelebi, son of Beyazıt I, shortly
after his father's defeat at the
Battle of Ankara in 1402.
Construction then ceased while
Süleyman fought a war of succession
with his brothers Musa Çelebi and Mehmet
Çelebi. After Musa defeated Süleyman in 1411, he himself
suffered defeat at the hands of his only surviving brother. As
Mehmet I, the victor ordered Eski Cami to be completed,
which the dedicatory inscription on the mosque confirms.
This also cites Ömer ibn Ibrahim as master mason and Hacı
Alaettin of Konya as architect. Damaged by a fire in 1749 and
an earthquake in 1752 ■ *16*, the Old Mosque was restored
during the reign of Mahmut I and then again as
recently as 1932 and 1944. The interior is a
perfect 162 feet on each side, divided into
nine equal sections covered by nine
domes supported on the inside by
four massive pillars.

RÜSTEM PAŞA'S CARAVANSERAI

Southwest of the Eski Cami is the
bazaar quarter, which boasts three old
Ottoman buildings of great interest, the

THE SULTANIYE
Edirne can count
more than fifty
historic monuments,
including Ottoman
mosques, *medrese*,
hammams, fountains,
and bridges, as well as
the scattered remains
of Roman and
Byzantine walls and
an ancient synagogue.

**THE FOUNTAIN
OF HACI ADIL BEY**

309

A STREET IN EDIRNE
Watercolor by Murat
Çakan, 1991.

**MINARETS OF THE
ÜÇ ŞEREFELI CAMI'I**
The first Ottoman
mosque to have four
minarets. Those on
the east are decorated
with lozenges, while
on the southwest the
three-balcony minaret
is embellished with
zigzagging geometric
patterns. The most
original of all is the
minaret on the
northwest, with its
distinctive spiral form.

first of which is the caravanserai of Rüstem Paşa – the
Rüstem Paşa Hanı – constructed by the great Sinan between
1560 and 1561. Built for travelers, the building is now being
converted into an exhibition center.

THE COVERED MARKET. Just beside Eski Cami we see the
bedesten built by Mehmet I as a source of income for the
mosque. In Edirne, the *bedesten* became more than a market;
it functioned as the heart of the city's commercial life,
providing secure storage and a safe display area for merchants
dealing in valuable goods and commodities, such as gold,
jewelry, armor, brocade, and fine carpets.
Only major trade centers like Istanbul,
Edirne, and Bursa would have such a
facility.

THE SEMIZ ALI PAŞA ARASTA. An old
Ottoman street-market flanks the west
side of Saraçlar Caddesi, the first main
street west of Eski Cami. This is the
Semiz Ali Paşa Arasta, built by Sinan in
1568 to 1569, four years after the death
of the Grand Vizier whose name it bears.
The *arasta* is a long (320 yards) and
narrow structure with 126 vaulted shops on either side.

THE MOSQUE OF THREE BALCONIES

A water tower.

The Üç Şerefeli Cami'i – the Mosque of Three
Balconies – stands to the right of the *arasta*, in
a little street that crosses Hükümet Caddesi.
The Üç Şerefeli is an imperial mosque, built
by Murat II between 1437 and 1447 to be the
most monumental building in the Ottoman
Empire, which it remained until the conquest
of Constantinople. Architectural
historians view it as a turning point
in the history of Ottoman
architecture, as it was the first
central dome to have a
diameter of 79 feet, which was
only surpassed by the mosques
of Süleyman and Selim in the
16th century ● 78. Like
the Eski Cami, the
Mosque of Three
Balconies was restored by
Mahmut I after it was badly

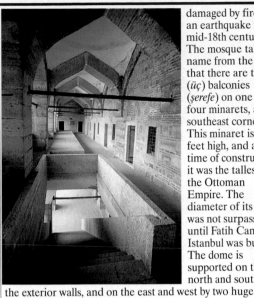

damaged by fire and an earthquake in the mid-18th century. The mosque takes its name from the fact that there are three (*üç*) balconies (*şerefe*) on one of its four minarets, at the southeast corner. This minaret is 222 feet high, and at the time of construction it was the tallest in the Ottoman Empire. The diameter of its dome was not surpassed until Fatih Cami'i in Istanbul was built. The dome is supported on the north and south by the exterior walls, and on the east and west by two huge hexagonal pillars, 19 feet in diameter, which obstruct the view of the mihrab and mimbar from the side areas.

THE RÜSTEM PAŞA KERVANSARAYI
Divided into two sections, each with its own plan and function, the caravanserai accommodated the merchants of Edirne and travelers. The former were housed in the Büyük Han (Big Caravanserai) and the latter in the Küçük Han (Small Caravanserai). The whole has been recently restored and transformed into a deluxe hotel called the Rüstem Paşa Kervansarayi. The renovation won the Agha Khan Prize for Architecture in 1980.

THE SELIMIYE IMPERIAL COMPLEX

The culmination of classical Ottoman architecture came with the Selimiye Cami'i● *80*, which stands only a few hundred yards away down Mimar Sinan Caddesi, named after the great architect who built this magnificent mosque complex. Sinan built the Selimiye for Selim II during the years 1569 to 1575, completing it when he was at least 79 years old, and to the end of his life he regarded the mosque as the masterpiece of his career, surpassing even the Süleymaniye in grandeur. The Selimiye dominates Edirne from its prominent position on the east side of town, built on a platform called Kavak Meydanı, where Beyazıt I had built a palace in the last quarter of the 14th century. The mosque and its *avlu*, or forecourt, which are both identical rectangles, each 196 feet wide and 144 feet long, are situated toward the northern end of this platform.

Grape-gathering in the village of Soufli near Edirne.

Fontaine dans la cour de Sultan Selim

Interieur de Sultan Selim

Interieur de Sultan Selim

THE COBBLERS' ARCADE. The west side of the precinct is occupied by the Kavaflar Arasta, which used to contain 124 shops once used by the guild of shoemakers, with a *dar-ül kura* projecting from the middle of its outer side. The arcade has been severely damaged by fire. These buildings seem to have been added by the architect Davut Ağa, on commission from Murat III, but the *külliye* contains few elements comparable with the grandeur of Selimiye, the greatest Ottoman mosque ever built.

THE PRAYER HALL IN THE SELIMIYE CAMI
The dome, with its crown at 143 feet above the floor, is supported by eight elegant pillars, two of which flank the main entrance, while two others frame the mihrab set in the recess of a vaulted apse. The tribune of the muezzin stands at the center of the prayer hall, directly under the keystone of the dome. It consists of a marble platform supported by rectangular pillars and surmounting a patio with a pretty fountain at the center, an arrangement which is unique in Ottoman architecture.

Detail of a minaret in the Selimiye Cami.

THE EXTERIOR. The Selimiye dome is ringed by eight buttresses topped with turrets and framed by its four slender minarets, which at 232 feet are among the tallest in the Islamic world. The buttresses are the projections of the eight octagonal piers that provide the main internal support for the dome, which is flanked at the corners by semicircular exedrae, with a rectangular apse on the south containing the mihrab.

THE INTERIOR. The dome of the Selimiye is 143 feet from floor to crown, whereas that of Haghia Sophia is 182 feet high. However, the important thing is not whether Sinan could build a dome higher and wider than that constructed by Justinian's architects, but that in developing classical Ottoman architecture to its logical conclusion, he could design and

construct a building that compares in grandeur with Haghia Sophia. Two of the Selimiye's huge dome pillars flank the main entrance from the *avlu* and two others flank the mihrab. Meanwhile, the lower walls of the mihrab apse are revetted in beautiful Iznik tiles above which there is a calligraphic inscription with flowing white letters on a blue background. At the southwest corner of the prayer hall, the imperial loge partly rests upon the arcade of a portico linked to the east gallery. The loge is particularly splendid, with its decoration of superb Iznik tiles. The mihrab of the imperial loge is also beautiful, with two wooden shutters opening on to a view over Edirne and the surrounding countryside.

THE MUSEUMS. The Selimiye *medrese* now serves as the Archeological Museum, while the *dar-ül hadis* (college for the study of the Haditks) houses the Museum of Turkish and Islamic Works. The ethnographic collection includes Turkish embroideries, kilims, antique armaments, Ottoman coins, and beautiful Thracian folk costumes. In the archeological

collection there is ancient jewelry, pottery, ceramics, coins, architectural fragments, and sculpture. The *dar-ül hadis* contains inscriptions from demolished Ottoman monuments, kitchen utensils, glass, tiles, and embroideries, as well as handwritten Korans and various objects that once belonged to a local monastery of Mevlevi dervishes.

THE MOSQUE OF MURAT II

The Muradiye Cami'i stands on a hill to the northeast of Edirne, and is best approached along Mimar Sinan Caddesi. Murat II had the building constructed in 1435 as a *zaviye*, or hostel, for Mevlevi dervishes, whose founder, Celalettin Rumi, appeared to the Sultan in a dream and requested that he build such a facility for his brotherhood. Later Murat converted the *zaviye* into a mosque and rehoused the dervishes in a separate *tekke*, or monastery, in the garden. The mosque is of the cross-*eyvan* or upside-down-T variety, comprising a five-bayed porch, a minaret, and four interior units. The largest unit is the one just inside the entrance, its dome resting on Turkish triangles and culminating in a lantern which is on top of the originally open oculus. The main *eyvan*, or room, is richly decorated with ceramic tiles and frescoes, especially the mihrab.

THE MOSQUE OF SELIM II

DECORATIVE CALLIGRAPHY IN ESKI CAMI
Calligraphy plays a major role in the decoration of mosques. Allah could not be represented other than by his name, as here.

SURRENDER OF EDIRNE TO TSAR FERDINAND OF BULGARIA
The Bulgarians' capture of the Turkish fort at Edirne occurred during the Balkan War of 1912–13. It cost many lives on both sides.

▲ SINAN, IMPERIAL ARCHITECT

Sinan's real name is not known, but it is known that he was born into a Turkish-speaking Christian family in the village Aghrianos (today called Agurnas) in Cappadocia, in the final years of the 15th century. During Selim I's reign (1512–1520) he was enrolled by imperial agents as a *devşirme* in the sultan's service. From the beginning of Süleyman I's reign (1520–1566) he joined the Janissaries and participated in the Belgrade (1521), Rhodes (1522), Hungary (1526), Vienna (1529), Baghdad (1534), Corfu (1537), and Moldavia (1538) campaigns, after which he was named imperial architect. For half a century until his death in 1588 he exercised an unlimited power over Ottoman architecture.

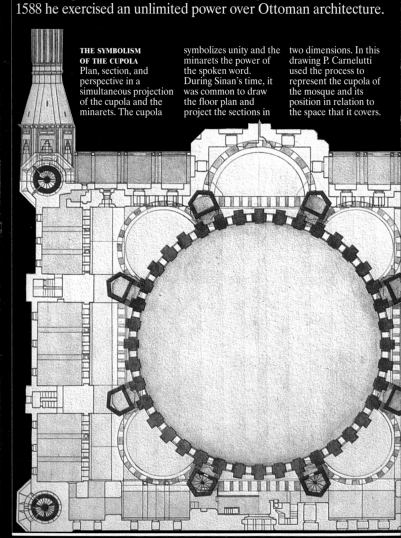

THE SYMBOLISM OF THE CUPOLA
Plan, section, and perspective in a simultaneous projection of the cupola and the minarets. The cupola symbolizes unity and the minarets the power of the spoken word. During Sinan's time, it was common to draw the floor plan and project the sections in two dimensions. In this drawing P. Carnelutti used the process to represent the cupola of the mosque and its position in relation to the space that it covers.

MIHRIMAH MOSQUE, ISTANBUL (1562–5)
Sinan constructed this mosque with 200 windows:

"God is the light of the heavens and the earth" (Koran, *Sourate* XXI).

RÜSTEM PAŞA CAMI'ı(1561–62)
View from the prayer room decorated with Iznik ceramics.

THE CUPOLA OF THE SELIMIYE MOSQUE IN EDIRNE
The size, height, and elegant architecture of this magnificent cupola seem to signify the unity of the empire under Sultan Selim II – a unity that is further emphasized by the four cardinal points symbolized in the four minarets.

THE SELIMIYE OF EDIRNE (1569–75)
The prayer room and gallery, situated in the center of the mosque.

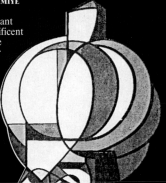

SÜLEYMANIYE
The architects present a model of the mosque. *Sûrnâme*, 1582.

"Architects of any importance in Christian countries consider themselves far superior to Muslims, because until now the latter haven't accomplished anything comparable to the cupola of Sainte Sophia. Thanks to the All Powerful and the favour of the sultan, I have succeeded in building a cupola for Sultan Selim's mosque that surpasses that of Sainte Sophia, one that is four zira (alders) in diameter, and six in height."
Sinan,
Autobiography

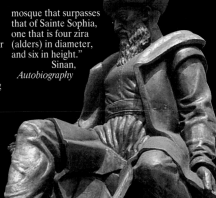

315

Sinan inherited the already well-established tradition of Ottoman architecture and was able to rely on the guilds of builders, whose members came from all over the empire to work on imperial construction sites. Sinan said that the Süleymaniye was the creation of a good worker, Şehzade his work of apprenticeship and Selimiye his masterpiece.

The gypsum stained glass played an important decorative role in the architecture. The most remarkable examples are the tinted stained glass of the mirhab wall of the Süleymaniye, the Mihrimah stained glass, and that of the Rüstem Paşa. Opposite, the stained glass of the Piyale Paşa mosque and of the *türbe* of Süleyman in Istanbul.

PLAN, SECTION, AND FAÇADE OF SOKOLLU MOSQUE BY ROBERTO PETRUZZI
Color plays an important part in this mosque. It is used to distinguish different sections, and to highlight symbolic functions, masking pendentives, and softening the planes of the free-standing walls.

The entrance and the mihrab of the mosque are oriented in the direction of Mecca. The cornices highlighted with white and the oblique arches accentuate the liveliness and originality of the hexagonal baldaquin.

MINBAR The marble pulpit of the Edirne Selimiye is very airy. It is decorated with geometric patterns; interlacings of hexagons, stars, and circles that are of *seljukide* inspiration.

Without abandoning the rectangular prayer room, the architect tests all of the spaces with square-plan cupolas like those at Selimiye (above).

At least 477 buildings are attributed to Sinan, including 107 mosques (*cami*), 52 small mosques (*mescit*), 45 türbe, 74 *medrese*, 56 hammams, 38 palaces, and 31 caravanserais (*han*). Of these, 204 survive today, most of them in Istanbul and Edirne.

▲ SINAN, IMPERIAL ARCHITECT

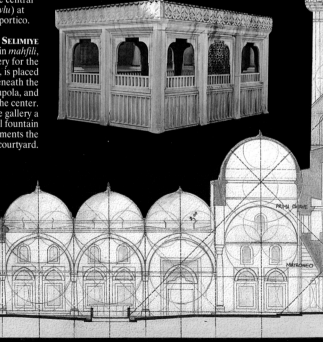

Whereas many other monuments were the work of a group of architects, those commissioned by the imperial family and great dignitaries were seen to be the personal creations of Sinan and they demonstrate his genius. He invented numerous variations on the basic task of covering a rectangular area with a dome. Haghia Sophia represented the standard to be surpassed, and Sinan's desire to improve on previous sucesses led him to create variations on half-domes (two at the Süleyman mosque, four at Şehzade's), galleries (the mosque at Kılıç Ali Paşa), and tympani (the Mihrimah).

Sinan's inventiveness is evident in his attempts to mount a dome on a hexagonal (Sokollu mosque) or octagonal plan (Rüstem Paşa mosque), and in the judicious layouts of the schools (Şemsi Paşa mosque in Üsküdar, and Sal Mahmut Paşa's in Eyüp). Sinan also distinguished himself with his search for new forms (the Rüstem Paşa *medrese*) and with a certain decorative exuberance (Süleyman and Selim II *türbes*), as well as with his special effects on façades (Süleyman mosque).

SÜLEYMANIYE
Ablution fountain in marble in the central courtyard (*avlu*) at the mosque portico.

SELIMIYE
The muezzin *mahfili*, or gallery for the singers, is placed directly beneath the key of the cupola, and marks the center. Beneath the gallery a small fountain complements the one in the courtyard.

PRIMA CHIAVE

MATRONEO

LONGITUDINAL SECTION OF THE SELIMIYE COMPLEX
This section shows the interior space, and outlines in blue the arches and the cupola that rests on eight pillars. For the first time Sinan introduces an arcade with alternating large and small arches on pairs of columns. The weight of the cupola is absorbed by eight buttresses which create the exterior rhythm of the façade, designed around pairs of windows. The four minarets, one measuring 232 feet in height, are positioned at the four corners of the mosque. The two minarets close to the courtyard (*avlu*) have triple spiral staircases, and each one leads to a balcony or *şerefe*. Drawing by Pietro Carnelutti, in Burelli's *The Mosque of Sinan*.

▲ EDIRNE

Bass drum and clarinet set the pace for contenders in the Kirkpinar wrestling match.

THE KÜLLIYE OF BEYAZIT II

The River Tunca divides into two branches, the first of which is spanned by a stone bridge constructed during the reign of Süleyman the Magnificent which leads to Sarayıcı Island. Leaving the island by the Fatih Mehmet Bridge, you cross the second branch of the Tunca, where, on the opposite bank, a highway runs along the river and towards the *külliye* of Beyazıt II. This is the most extensive and elaborate of the imperial mosque complexes in Edirne, designed and built for the sultan by the architect Hayrettin between 1484 and 1488.The religious foundations line the vast outer courtyard, where the horses and camels of the caravans that stopped at the caravanserai were once tethered. Along the east side of the courtyard are the *imaret* and the food store. Both served the needs of travelers, while also supplying food for the patients and staff of the hospital, the various buildings of which are on the west side of the courtyard. Just beside the mosque is the domed structure that served as the hospital proper, with the asylum for the insane (*timarhane*) adjoining it and the medical school (*tip medrese*) set back at the end.

THE SÜLEYMAN BRIDGE
Built in 1554 by Süleyman, the bridge leads to Tunca Island, the site of the famous but long-gone Edirne Sarayı, a palace begun by Murat II in 1450 and finished by Fatih Mehmet. Unfortunately, the structure went up in flames in 1878 during the Russian occupation and not a trace of it remains.

THE MOSQUE OF MURAT I. The oldest of Edirne's imperial mosques stands to the southwest of the Beyazıt II complex. Once attributed to Beyazıt I and dated to the period of his reign, this mosque is now believed to date from Murat I Hüdavendigar's reign, probably built soon after his capture of Hadrianopolis in 1361. It was undoubtedly built upon the ruins of a Greek church, since the foundations and the lower courses are obviously of Byzantine construction. This is the oldest mosque in Turkey's European region, and though badly in need of repair, it is still serving the faithful of Edirne.

THE KIRKPINAR WRESTLING MATCHES. Back on Sarayıçı Island, you will see the site of the mid-June Kirkpinar ("Forty Springs") wrestling matches. Although held annually only since the beginning of the Republic, the festival goes back to the mid-14th century, when the Ottomans first penetrated Thrace under Süleyman Paşa, the son of Orhan Gazi. The matches commemorate those organized by the leader among his forty favorite companions, for their amusement in camp between campaigns. As heroes died in battle each supposedly gave rise to a spring, hence the name. Today, the festival

attracts at least 100,000 spectators. Some 800 contestants, well oiled and clad only in leather pants, advance slowly, clap their hands with extended arms, and finally make body contact, each one striving to pin down his adversary in less than thirty minutes. The contest lasts for three days and then the victor receives a Golden Belt. Meanwhile, the public enjoys other aspects of the festival – children's competitions, horse races, and the election of Miss Edirne.

PAINTING BY L-F. CASSAT (1756–1827)
The captain attends a wrestling match.

OIL WRESTLING
Ottoman soldiers used to smear themselves with grease and wrestle with one another before departing on a military campaign. The tradition of wrestling survives, and the annual champion is acclaimed throughout Turkey.

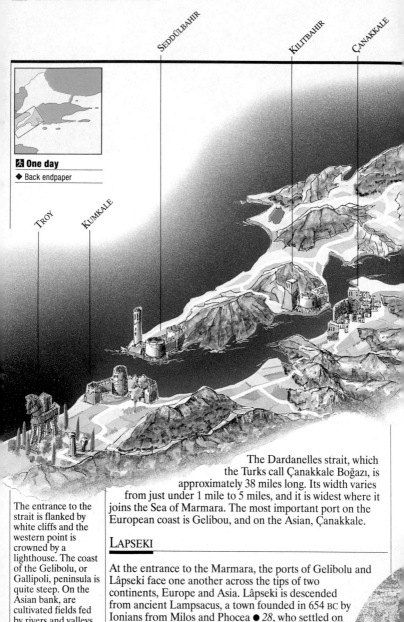

SEDDÜLBAHIR

KILITBAHIR

ÇANAKKALE

One day

◆ Back endpaper

TROY

KUMKALE

The Dardanelles strait, which the Turks call Çanakkale Boğazı, is approximately 38 miles long. Its width varies from just under 1 mile to 5 miles, and it is widest where it joins the Sea of Marmara. The most important port on the European coast is Gelibou, and on the Asian, Çanakkale.

The entrance to the strait is flanked by white cliffs and the western point is crowned by a lighthouse. The coast of the Gelibolu, or Gallipoli, peninsula is quite steep. On the Asian bank, are cultivated fields fed by rivers and valleys covered with forest.

A VIEW OF THE PORT OF GELIBOLU

LAPSEKI

At the entrance to the Marmara, the ports of Gelibolu and Lâpseki face one another across the tips of two continents, Europe and Asia. Lâpseki is descended from ancient Lampsacus, a town founded in 654 BC by Ionians from Milos and Phocea ● 28, who settled on this fertile strait. However, modern Lâpseki retains not one trace of its antique past. During the Greco-Roman era, the port, together with Abydos near Cape Nagara, controlled all maritime commerce on the Hellespont, where the Dardanelles join the Sea of Marmara. Lampsacus was well known for its wine, which the inhabitants believed to have been blessed by the gods. After his banishment from Athens in 450 BC, for impiety and "Medeism" (pro-Persian sympathies), the great philosopher Anaxagorus, the teacher of Pericles, came to end his days at Lampsacus, where he founded a school of

GELIBOLU

A PIRATE SHIP IN THE DARDANELLES
Painting by
L. Garneray
(1783–1857)

philosophy. At the death of Anaxagorus, in 428 BC, the local population built an altar in his memory, dedicated to the Spirit and to Truth.

GELIBOLU

Gelibolu, known to Westerners as Gallipoli, was the Greeks' Callipolis – the "Beautiful City." In antiquity it was less important than Lampsacus, but this position was reversed during the Byzantine era, when it became the stronghold of the Hellespont. Justinian fortified the site, and it was further strengthened by Emperor Philippicus Bardanes (711–713), since by controlling the Hellespont the Byzantines could secure the western maritime approaches to Constantinople. It was here that Frederick Barbarossa led his army from Europe to Asia in 1190 during the Third Crusade.

GELIBOLU CASTLE. The principal monument in Gelibolu is its Byzantine castle, the ruins of which form part of the inner harbor. As Callipolis Castle, it constituted the key to the maritime route giving access to Constantinople. In 1303, the site was occupied by the Grand Army of Catalonia,

HERO AND LEANDER
The crossing between Sestus and Abydus is the site of the romantic legend of Hero and Leander. Leander, a youth of Abydus, fell in love with Hero, a priestess of Aphrodite in Sestus, and each night he swam the Hellespont to see her, guided by a lamp that she placed on the European shore. But one night the lamp was extinguished in a gale, and Leander lost his way, and drowned in the Hellespont. When his body was washed ashore in Sestus, Hero threw herself into the water in despair and was also drowned.

▲ THE DARDANELLES

ΚΑΛΛΙΠΟΛΙΣ ·

An auction of the water tanks from a shipwrecked yacht.

THE FORTRESSES ON THE DARDANELLES, AN ENGRAVING OF 1711
When Mehmet II mounted the throne in 1451, he began to prepare for the Conquest by constructing forts on the Dardanelles, in order to isolate Constantinople from the West: the Kale-i-Sultaniye on the Asian side (near Çanakkale) and Kilitbahir on the European side (near Eceabat). A century later, during the war between Venice and the Ottoman Empire, the Turks built two more fortresses, at the Aegean end of the strait: Kumkale and Seddülbahir.

which was composed of mercenaries raised by Andronicus II to help the Byzantines fight against the Turks. However, the Catalans, under the command of Roger de Flor, seized the fortress, from which they proceeded to launch raids across Thrace. For seven years they withstood repeated attempts from the Byzantines and their Genoese allies to drive them out, before giving up the castle in 1310 and moving south to conquer Athens. Then, in 1354, came Süleyman Paşa, who in his turn seized the fortified site, which allowed the Ottomans to gain a foothold in Europe. Even so, the Byzantines managed, on rare occasions and only briefly, to retake the territory.

THE GELIBOLU CEMETERY. After the Conquest of 1453, the Ottoman navy made Gelibolu one of their bases, staying there between campaigns in the Mediterranean. Often the ships' captains returned, after a life of adventure, to end their days at Gelibolu. In the old cemeteries outside the city there are several *türbe* of ships' captains. The most famous of these is the tomb of the navigator Piri Reis (1465–1554) whose *Katibe Bahriye* (*Book of the Sea*) was the first treatise on navigation ever written by a Turk. His statue still looks out over the sea, while a small museum in the town commemorates his career. Apart from several other tombs of local celebrities, the most interesting funeral monument is a small open-air mosque (a *namazgah* or

324

mescit) dating from 1407. Built of marble blocks and panels taken from an ancient structure, the mausoleum is unique with a mihrab flanked by a pair of mimbars. Gelibolu also boasts an important *bedesten*, although it is more modest than the covered markets of Istanbul, Bursa, and Edirne, with six domes in two rows of three each, all supported by paired columns.

THE EUROPEAN SHORE OF THE DARDANELLES

About eight miles beyond Gelibolu the road follows the European coast of the Dardanelles near the little cove known as Inci Lımanı, the "Port of the Pearl," at the confluence of the Dardanelles and the Cumali Çayı, which the Greeks called Aegospotami, the "River of the Goat."

SESTUS AND ABYDUS. Eleven miles further, you come to a bay, the site of ancient Sestus, at the beginning of the narrows opposite Cape Nagara, the site of ancient Abydus. Both were Greek colonies founded in the 7th century BC, Sestus by Aeolians from the northern Aegean coast of Asia Minor and Abydus by Ionians from Miletus. As the main crossing point of the strait, Sestus and Abydus were the two most important cities on the Hellespont in Classical times. The armies of Alexander the Great traversed the Hellespont in 334 BC on their way to conquer Asia. Meanwhile, Alexander himself crossed at the Aegean end in order to make a pilgrimage to Troy.

ECEABAT. Following the European coast of the Dardanelles for a further four miles you come to Eceabat, where there is a ferry service across the strait to Çanakkale. Eceabat, which was known to the Greeks as Madytos, was founded in the 7th century BC by Greeks from the Aeolian coast of Asia Minor.

THE PREFECTURE AND COURTHOUSE IN GALLIPOLI

GREEK SCULPTURE IN THE ÇANAKKALE MUSEUM (LEFT)

THE KILITBAHIR FORTRESS
The Turks built new forts in the second half of the 18th century, during the war between the Ottomans and the Russians. The fortresses from the 14th and 15th centuries, such as Kilitbahir, were modernized as well as re-equipped, and later played a decisive role during World War One.

THE GOEBEN AND THE BRESLAU
When the Russian fleet threatened Istanbul, Germany, Turkey's ally, sent two powerful battleships, the *Goeben* and the *Breslau*, which entered the Dardanelles on August 10, 1914.

THE TRIPLE ALLIANCE
The Alliance leaders – Wilhelm II (Germany), Franz Joseph (Austria), and President Giolitti (Italy) – are depicted in this emblem with their Ottoman ally, Sultan Mehmet V.

KILITBAHIR AND KALE-I-SULTANIYE. Three miles from Eceabat is Kilitbahir, the "bolt" that locks or unlocks the passage to the sea. The Ottoman fortress here, with its two stout towers linked by a curtain wall, was, together with that of the Kale-i-Sultaniye on the opposite bank, one of the key features in the plan of action prepared by Mehmet II for the final capture of Constantinople in 1453. The two fortifications would also play an important role during World War I, when the English and French attempted to force a passage through the Dardanelles, a major line of defense for inland Turkey.

THE GALLIPOLI CAMPAIGN

When World War One broke out, in July 1914, Ottoman Turkey hesitated to join the conflict. However, Germany, with which Turkey maintained extremely close ties, wasted no time in taking action. On the evening of August 10, the *Goeben*, a German warship feared for its speed and fire power, entered the Dardanelles and, together with the *Breslau*, blocked all access to the strait. On October 29, it bombarded Odessa, forcing Russia to issue an ultimatum and Turkey to choose a side, that of the Central Powers. On November 13 Sultan Mehmet V called for a Jihad, a holy war against the enemies of Islam. Rallied by three men – Mustafa Kemal, Enver Paşa, and the German General Liman von Sanders – a mixed band of soldiers, underequipped and raggedly uniformed, quickly assembled themselves into an army of liberation. Although at the price of heavy casualties, this ill-prepared Turkish army would force the Allies to pull back. In February 1915 ships from the Franco-British naval forces began bombarding the fortresses on either side of the strait. When these held firm against all attack, the Allies decided to send an armada to shell the

Gallipoli peninsula in preparation for a troop landing. But in a single day, March 18, mines set afloat by the Turkish ship *Nusret* sank three of the sixteen battleships, put four others out of action, and killed 2,750 British and French sailors. The Allies gave up on this naval tactic and, through some inexplicable strategic error, recalled their vessels and did not launch the long-anticipated land offensive until later, leaving the Turkish troops time to recover their strength and their leaders time to reorganize the defense. A first contingent of 8,000 Allied soldiers landed at the foot of the promontory at Cape Helles on April 25. In the eight months between this date and January 9, 1916, the day the Allied expeditionary force evacuated the peninsula, more than 110,000 men died in the effort to take possession of the narrow maritime corridor – just a few square miles – separating the Aegean Sea and the Sea of Marmara: 34,000 British and Commonwealth soldiers, including many troops from Australia and New Zealand; 9,000 French soldiers; 500 Senegalese infantrymen (who were killed during an attack on Kumkale); and 66,000 Turks.

MEMORIAL TO THE BATTLE OF GALLIPOLI. The battlefield at Gallipoli can be reached by driving along the coastal highway, north of Eceabat, to Anzac Cove, the site of numerous cemeteries and memorials. Kabatepe also has the Atatürk War Museum. You can also take the road that, beginning at Kilitbahir, descends along the coast and then veers inland before climbing the hills through a pine forest as far as Alçıltepe, the Greeks' Kritia. The main road then turns left and leads back out to Cape Helles at the end of the peninsula, where the British and Commonwealth Memorial is situated as well as the Turkish monument known as the Mehmetcik Anıtı, not far from the French War Memorial. The Turkish memorial at Cape Helles overlooks Morto Bay, another Allied landing site.

SEDDÜLBAHIR AND KUMKALE. Viewing the bay from the top of the promontory, you can see on the right the ruins of the

The Ottoman government purchased the German battleships sent to Istanbul. The Admiral in charge of the *Goeben*, renamed *Yavuz*, became a *paşa* and took to wearing a fez. On October 29, 1914, he sailed off to bombard Odessa, which resulted in an ultimatum being issued by Russia and Turkey's entry into the war.

MUSTAFA KEMAL PAŞA
The Dardanelles campaign made Mustafa Kemal Atatürk famous among his compatriots.

THE TURKISH FLEET ATTACKING THE SHIPS OF THE RUSSIAN NAVY
Russia declared war on the Ottoman Empire on November 2, 1914, dragging the country into World War One.

▲ THE DARDANELLES

The Ottoman Empire in 1913 as represented on a promotional label.

LANDING AT SEDDÜLBAHIR
To seize the fort at Seddülbahir, the Allied forces adopted a strategy reminiscent of the famous Trojan horse. The British transport ship *River Clyde*,

loaded with troops, ploughed into the beach and ran aground. Great ports fitted into the hull broke open, permitting the soldiers to pour down a pair of ramps, all the while covered by fire from cannons on the foredeck. With this tactic they managed to take the Turks by surprise.

A MEMORIAL IN THE TURKISH CEMETERY AT ÇANAKKALE.

Ottoman fortress of Seddülbahir, one of the two castles in the outer line of Turkish defense in the Dardanelles, with Kumkale on the opposite coast. Both were constructed in 1659 by Mehmet Köprülü Paşa, Grand Vizier to Mehmet IV, and rebuilt between 1773 and 1775 by Baron François de Tott, a Hungarian military engineer in the service of Abdül Hamit I.

THE SITE OF ELÆUS. The promontory on the left of the bay is known as Eski Hisarlık, meaning "old fortress." The name comes from the scattered ruins of ancient Elæus, the westernmost city of the Thracian Chersonese, the remains of which lay strewn all about until the Gallipoli campaign entirely destroyed them. Founded in the 6th century BC by colonists from Athens, Elæus sided with their native homeland throughout the Peloponnesian War. Heinrich Schliemann, the famous German archeologist who discovered Troy, studied the site and excavated a mound identified as the tomb of Protesilas, the uncle of Jason, a Thessalian King, who was the first Achaean victim of the Trojan War.

Homer mentions it in Book II of the *Iliad*, where he also lists the various contingents in Agamemnon's army at the siege of Troy. Herodotus and Thucydides also cite the tomb, which, in antiquity, sheltered an oracle frequently visited by Greek sailors crossing the Hellespont. Alexander the Great himself offered a sacrifice there before crossing the Strait on his way to invade Asia. His biographer, Arrien, assures us that he "performed this ceremony in the hope of knowing better fortune than Protesilas had." From there he landed at Elæus. Alexander, writes Arrien, made the crossing by "taking the helm of the flagship and, midway, cut the throat of a bull as an offering to Poseidon. Then, he poured into the sea wine

328

> "Heavy fighting has been going on in the Dardanelles. . .
> the situation is obviously very critical. Should the Dardanelles
> fall, the World War will have been decided against us."

Admiral von Tirpitz

from a golden cup to gain the favor of the Nereids." On the Asian side Alexander landed on the same beach where, long before, Agamemnon had assembled his army, and then went on a pilgrimage to Troy. Lord Byron, inspired by the story of Hero and Leander, swam the Hellespont on May 3, 1810.

ÇANAKKALE

To reach Çanakkale, on the Asian side of the strait, take a ferry at Eceabat. For the last two centuries this lively city has been the principal port on the Dardanelles. During the early Ottoman era the city was known by the name of the fortress – Kale-i-Sultaniye – which is still visible south of the quay. A great many Greeks, Armenians, and Jews once lived there, whereas today's population is almost exclusively Turkish. Since the 18th century the city has been famous for its earthenware potteries, which in Turkish are known as *Çanak*.

THE CEMETERIES IN ANZAC COVE Several military cemeteries, British, French, and Turkish, situated not far from the battle scene at Gallipoli, bear witness to the heavy casualties sustained by all sides.

THE MUSEUM OF ÇANAKKALE. The fortress of Kale-i-Sultaniye, renamed Çimenlik Kale, is still used by the Turkish Army, which makes it inaccessible to the public, save for the inner courtyard, where you can find the Military Museum devoted almost entirely to memorabilia of the Gallipoli campaign. The foremost exhibit is the famous mine ship *Nusret*. The Archeological Museum of Çanakkale is situated on the outskirts of town, near the national highway heading for Izmir. It houses a collection of archeological pieces unearthed during excavations at several sites in the Troad, the region extending south of the Dardanelles along the Aegean Coast. The museum also owns remarkable vases, clay statuettes, and obsidian jewelry from the collection of the archeologist Frank Calvert who was the first to direct Heinrich Schliemann to the site of Troy. Moreover, a room is reserved for the bronze utensils, terracotta pottery, and jewelry unearthed on the site of the tumulus of Dardanus, an antique cemetery located south of Çanakkale and excavated in 1974. Dated from the 4th to the 1st centuries BC, they are relics from the city of Dardanus, whose eponymous founder gave his name to the Dardanelles strait.

In 1915, *The Times* of London published this photograph of "a Turkish sniper cunningly camouflaged thanks to the branches that mask him."

BEAR TAMERS ON THE ROAD TO TROY Wandering gypsies used to perform with tame bears.

▲ THE DARDANELLES, MARCH 18, 1915

At the beginning of World War One, the Allies planned the Dardanelles operation in the hope of opening the strait, to enable the Allied fleet to resupply hard-pressed Russia with arms and munitions. The British Admiralty decided to launch a naval attack. In February 1915, an Anglo-French fleet of 90 vessels and 22,000 seamen assembled off the island of Mondros. From February 19 until March 17, the Allied ships bombarded the Turkish forts and swept the sea for mines. The main naval attack took place on March 18. At 9 a.m. a squadron of English battleships gathered at the entrance to the narrows and fired at long range upon the Turkish positions, particularly those at Çanakkale. At noon, the French squadron commanded by Admiral Guépratte entered the action and sailed into the first section of the strait. It was relieved thirteen hours later by an English flotilla.

BRITISH VICE-ADMIRAL DE ROBECK On March 16 de Robeck became commander of the Allied fleet, taking over from Vice-Admiral Carden, who had prepared the plan of attack.

REAR-ADMIRAL GUÉPRATTE Commander of the French squadron.

12 NOON. Of the eighteen vessels in the line, three, including the *Bouvet*, were sunk by floating mines; three other ships, the *Inflexible*, the *Gaulois*, and the *Suffren*, were seriously damaged.

PLAN OF DEPLOYMENT FOR THE ALLIED SHIPS AT THE ENTRANCE TO THE STRAIT
Admiral de Robeck launched the attack upon the Straits. The French squadron – *Suffren*, *Bouvet*, *Charlemagne*, and *Gaulois* – had the perilous honor of leading the engagement. Meanwhile, the most modern of the Allied vessels – HMS *Queen Elizabeth*, *Inflexible*, *Agamemnon*, and *Lord Nelson* – bombarded the Çanakkale forts at long range. On the front line, *Suffren*, *Charlemagne*, *Bouvet*, and *Gaulois* fired on the Turkish strongholds from a range of 7,000 to 8,000 yards. By noon all forces were engaged in the battle.

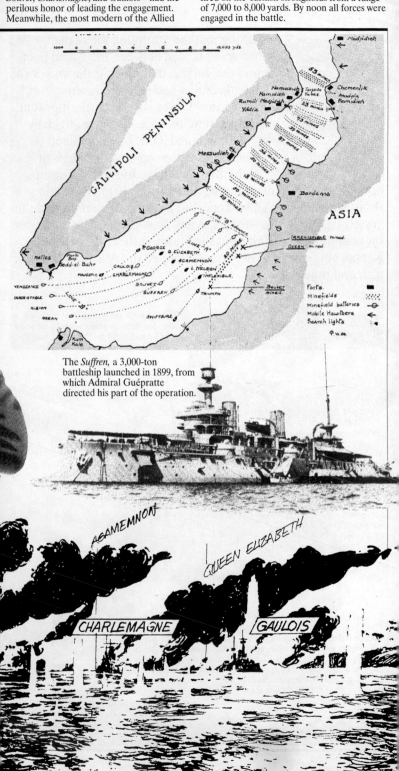

The *Suffren,* a 3,000-ton battleship launched in 1899, from which Admiral Guépratte directed his part of the operation.

▲ THE DARDANELLES, MARCH 18, 1915

The Times
HISTORY
OF THE WAR

VICE-ADMIRAL DE ROBECK.

PRICE 9d NET

PART 62
VOL. 5 OCT. 26 1915.

First Dardanelles Number.

In the foreground, one of the Gaulois' large guns and beyond it the silhouette of the Charlemagne.

Throughout the afternoon the exchange of fire never ceased between the Allied fleet and the Turkish defenses. At the end of the day the Allies had suffered heavy casualties. Of the sixteen battleships sent into action, six were lost. The attack by sea had failed. Only by a combined action of troops on land and ships at sea could the Allies hope to force the strait open. There was a new landing on April 25, 1915. The main thrust was aimed at Gaba-Tépé, but a strong current carried the vessels farther north. Australian and New Zealand forces began the assault upon the hills but the Turkish officer, Mustafa Kemal, at the head of his troops, stopped the Allied advance for a second time.

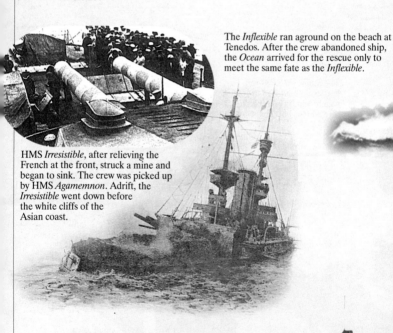

The Inflexible ran aground on the beach at Tenedos. After the crew abandoned ship, the Ocean arrived for the rescue only to meet the same fate as the Inflexible.

HMS *Irresistible*, after relieving the French at the front, struck a mine and began to sink. The crew was picked up by HMS *Agamemnon*. Adrift, the *Irresistible* went down before the white cliffs of the Asian coast.

11 A.M. On the front line, Britain's HMS *Queen Elizabeth* (below), *Lord Nelson*, *Inflexible*, and *Agamemnon* opened fire on the forts along both European and Asian coasts. The *Suffren*, under Admiral Guépratte, the *Bouvet*, the *Charlemagne*, and the *Gaulois* closed in to neutralize the defenses.

12 NOON. The duel intensified. The *Inflexible* caught fire; the *Agamemnon*, the *Bouvet*, and the *Gaulois* were hit. Admiral Guépratte stoped the *Suffren* in order to concentrate his fire on Kilit Bahir.

1 P.M.
The Turkish fire lessened. Admiral Guépratte decided to take advantage of the lull to force the strait open. Admiral de Robeck ordered him to pull back and accept relief from six English battleships.

2 P.M.
During these maneuvers, the *Bouvet* struck a mine and foundered. The *Gaulois*, hit at the waterline, was saved by her commander, who ran the ship aground on the beach at Tenedos.

7.30 P.M. Admiral de Robeck gave the order to withdraw. Of the eighteen ships which entered the battle, three battleships had been lost and four put out of action.

When Heinrich Schliemann discovered Hısarlık in 1868, he wrote: "The site fully agrees with the description that Homer gives of Ilium. The hill appears destined by nature to support a great city. No other place in the region is comparable to this one." The city

TROY

From Çanakkale you can reach the site of Troy (Truva in Turkish) by taking highway E87 in the direction of Izmir. After Güzelyak, the road no longer runs along the strait but turns inland, climbing the mountain through a forest of pine and oak as far as Intepe. At this point the view over the Trojan plain is panoramic and splendid. Thereafter the road descends towards Dürek Su, Homer's Simois, and then comes to the hamlet of Gökçay, where the exit for Hısarlık leads to ancient Troy. At the entrance to the archeological site stands a huge replica of the famous "Trojan horse."

HISTORY OF EXCAVATIONS

is entered by the East Gate in the walls erected about Troy VI. Here we see the remnants of two towers, Mycenaean houses, and the Temple of Athena. Farther along stand the *megarons* of Troy I and II, where

FRANK CALVERT'S DISCOVERY. There is very little doubt today that Hısarlık is indeed the site of Homer's Troy. Frank Calvert, the American and British Consul at Çanakkale in the second half of the 19th century, made an early contribution towards proving this. This diplomat owned a farm in Troad, which happens also to be the location of the Hısarlık mound, a place long associated with the site of Ilium, which specialists assumed to have been the flourishing Hellenistic and Roman city built upon the ruins of Troy. Convinced that an ancient city had once existed there, Calvert began to excavate the site in 1865.

SCHLIEMANN'S EXCAVATIONS. However, solid proof that Hısarlık was the site of ancient Troy did not come until Heinrich Schliemann, a German who had made a fortune in the United States, began to dig in 1870, following this

initiative with three further excavations from 1871 to 1873. Employing an average of 150 workmen daily, he cut right through the mound in a great north-south trench some 130 feet wide. As he made the cut, Schliemann noticed that the excavated earth was stratified in layers, which he correctly assumed represented a succession of settlements on the same site. Calling the lowermost stratum Troy , Schliemann thought he could discern seven distinct layers, of which he believed Troy II to be the Homeric city because of the wealth of jewelry and gold objects found there, a hoard that he called "Priam's Treasure." In 1883, Schliemann resumed digging, this time with the assistance of Wilhelm Dörpfeld, a young German archeologist. Eight years later the two men made an important discovery in the

Schliemann unearthed "Priam's Treasure." The Roman theater and the *bouleuterion* are situated outside the defense walls.

southern sector of the tumulus, at the level later called Troy VIIa, where they unearthed a palatial structure known as a *megaron*. It was so similar to the royal halls discovered at Mycenae and Tiryns that

Schliemann was forced to change his mind about the dating of the various strata. Finally, he decided that the sixth layer from the bottom was the Homeric city for which he was searching. This view is still generally held, though the numbering of the layers has been changed. After Schliemann's death in 1896, Dörpfeld took charge of the operation and, between 1893 1894, laid bare the massive fortifications of Troy VII.

THE TWENTIETH-CENTURY EXCAVATIONS. After a long delay, new excavations got underway in 1932, when a team of archeologists from the University of Cincinnati went to work at the Troy site under the direction of Carl W. Blegen. Blegen's group continued digging until 1938, but World War Two ended their project and delayed the publication of their findings until 1950. By this time, researchers had revealed

forty-six strata in all. They had also exposed the city's ring of defense walls, including several massive towers and two monumental gateways. This evidence confirmed Schliemann's hypothesis whereby Troy VIIa would have been the city of King Priam, destroyed around 1200 BC about the same time that Mycenae, Pylos,

and other Greek fortress cities met the same fate. The strata of Troy IV to V have been assigned to the Early Bronze Age lasting from 300 to 1800 BC (all dates are approximate); Troy VI to the Middle and Late Bronze Ages, that is 1800–1300 BC; and the various sublevels of Troy VII to the 1300–1100 BC period. In 1990, the University of Cincinnati launched a new program of excavation and research at the site, in collaboration with German and Turkish archeologists.

THE TROY MUSEUM
"Priam's Treasure," discovered at Troy II by Schliemann, comprised gold objects and jewelry that the archeologist sent to Berlin, where they disappeared during World War Two. Therefore, the artifacts exhibited at the Troy Museum in Turkey are the fruit of subsequent excavations. Many receptacles were found, among them *pithoi*, terracotta jars, and both vases and goblets made of glass, all with double handles. Other than utensils, the excavated articles include primarily arms, jewelry, and tools, fashioned of gold, silver, or bronze.

THE TROJAN HORSE

The main sources of information on the Trojan War are the *Iliad* and the *Odyssey*, the epic poems attributed to Homer. After Paris abducted Helen, Ulysses and other former suitors rallied behind Menelaus, her husband, whose honor they swore to avenge. For six years the Achaeans, under the command of Agamemnon, laid siege to Troy, during which time the great warriors of both sides confronted one

another: Ajax, Achilles, Nestor, and Ulysses in the Greek camp, and Aeneas and Hector on the Trojan side. Ulysses conceived the idea of taking the city by ruse. This involved building a colossal wooden horse inside which a contigent of soldiers would be hidden.. Believing the horse an offering to the gods, the Trojans allowed it to enter the city.

THE SITE OF TROY

THE PALACE OF PRIAM.

Archeologists now locate the main gateway into Troy on the south side of the city. This Southern Gate gave access to the citadel from the lower plain, and just inside it stands the most impressive of the dwelling places unearthed at Troy. This is the Pillar House, which by Mycenaean standards is a building of heroic proportions. It probably occupies the same site as Homer's Palace of Priam, while the Southern Gate would seem to stand on the exact site of the Skaian Gates, with the Great Tower of Ilium right beside it. Following the destruction of Troy VIIa, the site appears to have been only sparsely inhabited for about four centuries – the Dark Ages of the ancient Greek world – until Aeolian colonists arrived from Tenedos or Lesbos in c. 700 BC. Now came into being what Blegen identifies as Troy VIII, while Troy IX would be the *Ilium Novum* of the Hellenistic and Roman eras, venerated by the Classical world as the heir to Homeric Troy.

THE TEMPLE OF ATHENA. The most important monument from Ilium is the Temple of Athena, the ruins of which have been found in the northeast sector of the Hisarlık mound. Alexander the Great swore to reconstruct the sanctuary. In 323 BC, Lysimachus, Alexander's successor, honored the old promise and had a new, Doric temple built, architectural fragments of which were unearthed by Schliemann in the northwest sector of the excavation.

THE ROMAN ADDITIONS. After Troy was severely damaged during the first war waged by Mithridates the Great against Rome, the Romans, under Augustus, rebuilt the city. They also raised the peak of the tumulus in order to expand the sacred enclosure of the temple dedicated to Athena, reconstructing it with many elements from the older building. Other buildings dating from the period are the *odeum*, the theater, and the *bouleuterion*, all situated in the southeast.

Practical information

Key

✪	Editor's choice	🎵	Pets allowed
▥	Air conditioning	🎵	Pets not allowed
⊠	Children's rates	▢	Quiet
▤	Credit cards accepted	☎	Telephone
▤	Credit cards not accepted	◈	Tennis courts
		⬆	Terrace
♿	Disabled facilities	▢	TV in room
⬆	Garden	✂	Swimming pool
♫	Live music	🌿	View
P	Parking		

◆ GENERAL INFORMATION

USEFUL ADDRESSES
→ FORMALITIES
■ **Turkish Embassy**
43 Belgrave Square
London SW1X 8PA
Tel. 020 7393 0202
Fax 020 7393 0066
www.turkishembassy-london.com
2525 Massachusetts
Ave, NW Washington,
DC 20008
Consular section:
Tel. (202) 612 6740/41
Fax (202) 319 1639
www.turkey.org
■ **Consulate General of Turkey**
Rutland Lodge
Rutland Gardens
London SW7 1BW
Tel. 020 7589 0949
Fax. 020 7584 6235
www.turkeyconsulate-london.com
821 United Nations
Plaza, 5th Floor
New York, NY 10017
Tel. (212) 949 0160
Fax (212) 983 1293

→ INFORMATION
■ **Republic of Turkey Tourist Offices**
170–173 Piccadilly
London WV1 9DD
Tel. 020 7734 8681
Fax 020 7491 0773
Washington: see
Embassy (above)
Tel. (202) 612 6800
Fax (202) 319 7446
New York: see
Consulate (above)
Tel. (212) 687 2194
■ **Website**
www.turkey.org

ANIMALS
Vaccination book and
health certificate
signed by a vet 15
days before departure
is required by the
Turkish authorities.

MONEY
Take different means
of payment with you
(credit cards, foreign
currency especially
S dollars, and
eler's checks).

RENCY
ency
ish lira
TRL).
n TRL;
TRL
1).

→ CREDIT CARDS
■ **Payment**
International
credit cards
such as Visa,
Eurocard
and MasterCard,
are accepted by
hotels and major
restaurants.
■ **Autotellers**
Can be found in
tourist areas.

→ CHANGING MONEY
There is no restriction
on the amount of
currency you can
bring into Turkey.
There is also no need
to purchase TRL
before departure.
Because of
fluctuations in the
exchange rate
for the Turkish lira,
it is best to change
money only as and
when required.

GRAND BAZAAR, ISTANBUL

INSURANCE
You are advised to
purchase personal
insurance before
departure. This
usually covers both
local medical and
hospital treatment
and repatriation. Ask
your travel agent to
make the necessary
arrangements, or
check whether
insurance is included
in the services
offered by your credit
card company.

BUDGET
Istanbul is relatively
expensive compared
to the rest of
Turkey (especially
accommodation).
Expect to spend
between £38/$55
and £48/$70 per
person per day
(hotel included).

TIME DIFFERENCE
GMT + 2 (2 hours
ahead of London and
7 hours ahead of
New York).

ELECTRICITY
Alternating current,
220 V.

FORMALITIES
→ DOCUMENTS
UK citizens require a
visa (three-month
visa obtainable at the
border). US nationals
must also have a
visa, which they can
obtain in advance
from the nearest
Turkish Consulate
General or at the
entry point to Turkey
for a fee of $45 (visa
is valid for one year
from the date of
issue, with multiple
entries not exceeding
three months).

→ DRIVING LICENSE
A valid driving
license is required,
with registration
documents and
certificate of
insurance. The driver
must have a valid
passport and visa.

WHEN TO GO?
■ **Spring**
April–mid-June:
pleasant
temperatures and
fewer tourists.
■ **Summer**
Hot weather and blue
skies. Numerous
tourists until mid-
August.
■ **Fall**
Can last until
November. Rain from
October, but pleasant
temperatures and
few tourists.
■ **Winter**
Usually cold and wet.

HEALTH
→ FIRST-AID
Don't forget t
basic things su
antiseptic cream,
bandaids, aspirin
or paracetamol,
antidiarrhea tablets,
insect repellent and
sunblock cream.
Note
*Many antibiotics
and other medicines
are sold over the
counter in Turkey.
If you are taking
medication, bring a
spare prescription
with details of the
medication you need.*

→ VACCINATION
No specific
vaccinations are
required.

TELEPHONE
■ **From the UK/US**
00 90 + city code
omitting the 0, + the
subscriber number.

CLOTHING
→ GENERAL
Casual but tidy
clothes that cover
most of your body
(trousers, long skirts
or dresses, long-
sleeved shirts, scarf).
Slightly more formal
dress is expected in
the more expensive
restaurants and other
smart places.

→ SEASONS
■ **Spring–fall**
Take a sweater or
windproof jacket for
the rather cool
evenings (and be
prepared for heavy
rains in March and
October).
■ **Summer**
Light cotton
garments.
Sunglasses and
a hat are essental.
■ **Winter**
Warm clothes and
a heavy coat or
jacket.
Tip
*Take a windproof
jacket if you intend to
visit the Bosphorus or
make the ferry
crossing to the
Princes' Islands.*

UK TO ISTANBUL
→ BY AIR
Scheduled and charter flights from London and other other major UK cities direct to Istanbul. Return prices start from as little as £150.
■ **British Airways**
Tel. 08457 222 111
www.britishairways.com
■ **Turkish Airlines**
Tel. 020 7766 9300
www.turkishairlines.com

→ BY COACH
■ **Eurolines**
Tel. 01582 404 511
www.eurolines.com

→ BY TRAIN
FROM LONDON TO PARIS
■ **Eurostar**
Tel. 0990 18 61 86
www.eurostar.com
FROM PARIS TO ISTANBUL
■ **French railways**
Daily departures from Paris-Gare de l'Est, via Budapest. Allow for two days' traveling.
Tel. 08 36 35 35 35 (France); *www.sncf.fr*
■ **Orient-Express (from London)**
One scheduled departure per year. Allow for five days' traveling. Cost: about £3,000/$4,500 for a one-way ticket.
UK: Tel. 020 7805 5100
US: Tel. 800 524 2420
www.orient-express trains.com

→ BY CAR AND FERRY
By car ferry from Italy (Brindisi, Bari or Ancona) to Igoumenitsa in Greece, then by road via Thessaloniki. Allow for four to five days' traveling.

US TO ISTANBUL
Direct flights to Istanbul from New York, Chicago and Miami with Turkish Airlines and direct from New York with Delta Airlines.

Roundtrip prices start from $500. Flights from other US cities stopover in New York or major Europe cities.
■ **Delta Airlines**
Tel. 800-241 4141
www.delta.com
■ **Turkish Airlines**
Tel. 800-874 8875
www.turkishairlines.com

TOWARD BURSA
150 miles south of Istanbul.

→ TOURIST OFFICE
Off the Orhan Gazi Altgeçidi underpass crossing Atatürk Cad.

THE PRINCES' ISLANDS

BIRD SEED VENDOR, ISTANBUL

→ FROM ISTANBUL
■ **By bus**
The journey takes about four hours, with numerous stops. The bus terminal (*Santral Garaji*) is on Kıbrıs Şehitler Cad.
■ **By ferry and bus**
Take the hydrofoil from Kabataş (Istanbul) to Yalova (37 miles from Bursa). Departures: 3 to 6 a day; duration of the journey: 1 hour. Complete the journey by bus (the bus terminal is to the left of the piers). Duration of the journey: 1 hour 10 mins.

TOWARD THE DARDANELLES
180 miles southwest of Istanbul.

→ TOURIST OFFICE
At Gelibolu is located in the stone tower. At Çanakkale, it is located on Cumhuriyet Meydanı (landing pier).

→ FROM ISTANBUL
■ **By bus**
The bus terminal (*Otogar*) at Gelibolu is close to the stone tower. There are hourly departures throughout the day, and the bus journey from Istanbul takes about 4½ hours.
■ **By bus and ferry**
(Ferry crossing from the peninsula to the coast). Take the bus from Gelibolu to Kilitbahir (in the south), then the ferry to Çanakkale.

TOWARD EDIRNE
155 miles northwest of Istanbul.

→ TOURIST OFFICE
Hürriyet Meydanı 17, near the main square.

→ FROM ISTANBUL
■ **By bus**
The bus journey from Istanbul takes about 3½ hours. Departures every

20 mins. The bus terminal (*Otobüs Garaji*) is located 1¼ miles southeast of the town.
■ **By train**
Slow (takes about 6 hours) and not as convenient. The railway station is situated outside the town center.

→ FROM THE BORDER
■ **By car**
From Bulgaria, the Kapıkule border post (located 11 miles away) is open 24 hours a day. From Greece, the Pazarkule border post (located 4⅓ miles away) is usually open in the morning. From Istanbul, take highway E80 (make sure you have enough petrol before setting off as gas stations along the way are scarce).

TOWARD IZNIK
124 miles southeast of Istanbul and 50 miles northeast of Bursa.

→ TOURIST OFFICE
Kılıçaslan Cad. 130 (main town thoroughfare) on 3rd floor.

→ FROM ISTANBUL
■ **By bus**
The bus terminal (*Otogar*) is located south of the town. The journey from Istanbul takes about 3½ hours.

■ **By ferry and bus**
See under Bursa.

→ FROM BURSA
■ **By bus**
The bus journey from Bursa takes about 1½ hours. Hourly departures during the day. (The last bus leaves at about 6–7pm).

TOWARD TROY
About 16 miles south of Çanakkale.

FINDING YOUR WAY

Istanbul consists of three main zones (◆ A).

→ EUROPEAN SHORE

Divided into two zones by the Golden Horn.

■ **Eminönü-Fatih-Eyüp** (◆ B-D-E)
South of the Golden Horn the old Ottoman town of Eminönü (the tourist area) and Fatih, bound to the west by the old sea wall. Eyüp, further northwest, is another large district.

■ **Beyoğlu**
(◆ C) The modern, more European part of town, north of the Golden Horn. Further north are the commercial districts of Beşiktaş and Şişli.

→ ASIAN SHORE

This zone is separated from the other two by the Bosphorus.

■ **Üsküdar**
(◆ F) The most "Asian" district of Istanbul, together with Kadiköy, further south.

→ DISTRICTS

Most districts are named after a monument or mosque. They are traditional names, and do not reflect administrative divisions.

ADDRESSES

■ **British Consulate General**
Mesrutiyet
Caddesi 3–4
Tepebasi, Beyoğlu
80072 Istanbul
Tel. (0212) 293 7540
and 293 7545 to 49
Fax (0212) 245 4989
■ **US Consulate**
Mesrutiyet
Caddesi 104–108
Tepebasi, Istanbul
Tel. (0212) 251 3602

Fax (0212) 251 3218
www.usconsulate–istanbul.org

AIR TRAVEL

Atatürk Airport (Atatürk Havalimanı), located 15½ miles from the town center, has a new international terminal.

→ SERVICES

Buses, taxis and metro (change at Aksaray for the tramway).
■ **Fares**
The bus or metro fare to Sultanahmet is around $1; taxis are about $15.
Warning
Buses are often crammed.

→ TRANSFERS

Usually included in package tours (with flights and hotels). Some hotels offer a one-way transfer to individual travelers. Check conditions and prices.

BUS AND "DOLMUŞ"

Town buses (IETT) are painted red and cream. They only leave the stops when they have filled up. Tickets available at the main stops and in IETT kiosks. Routes are indicated on the side of the buses. The main *Dolmuş* terminals (minibuses that act as collective taxis) are at Taksim and Aksaray. Pay on board. Stops are rarely indicated.

COACHES

→ EUROPEAN SHORE

Istanbul's main bus terminal (*Otogar*) is about 6 miles west of the old town (◆ A).
■ **Services**
Metro link with Sultanahmet (change at Aksaray for the tramway). Buses and taxis.

→ ASIAN SHORE

This smaller bus station is in Harem.

DRIVING

Driving is not recommended in Istanbul. Only hire a car if you intend to go on an excursion.

ELECTRICITY

220 volts, plugs have two rounded pins.
Warning
Temporary powercuts can occur.

ETIQUETTE

→ SMOKING

Smoking is not permitted on public transport or in public places. The rule is not always strictly obeyed, but breaking it can mean to a heavy fine. In cafés and restaurants, however, smoking tends to be the norm and nonsmokers are expected to be tolerant.

→ HAGGLING

When prices are not displayed, it is acceptable to haggle. Do it with a smile and in an unhurried way.

→ TIPS

Tipping in major Turkish restaurants is similar to tipping in Europe and the US (5 to 10 percent is the norm). In smaller establishments and when paying for taxis, round up the amount. Always have notes ready for tipping hotel porters.

FERRIES

→ CATEGORIES

■ **"Vapur"**
Steamboats, often quite old but inexpensive.
■ **Hydrofoil**
Called *Deniz Otobüsü*, or sea buses, these cost twice as much as the *vapur*. They are faster and more comfortable, but have no deck.
■ **Ferry**
From Eminönü to Harem.

→ LOCATION

■ **Eminönü**
(◆ E C1) *vapur*-ferry
Main and most central landing pier in Istanbul. European and Asian shores, Bosphorus, Golden Horn and Princes' Islands (*vapur*).
■ **Beşiktaş**
(◆ A D3) *vapur*
Asian and European shores.
■ **Üsküdar**
(◆ F) *vapur*
Asian and European shores, Golden Horn, Bosphorus.
■ **Karaköy** (◆ C C6)
vapur-hydrofoil
Asian shore.
■ **Kabataş** (◆ C F3)
vapur-hydrofoil
Asian shore, Princes' Islands and Yalova (Bursa).
■ **Kadiköy**
(◆ F) *vapur*
European shore.

→ HOW TO USE THEM

Get there early. Start with single trips. For longer and more complex journeys, check out details the day before.
■ **Timetables**
Sailing times are displayed near the ticket office or on the piers. There are usually four columns (stops, times from Mon–Fri. and those for Sat. and Sun).
Note
For Bosphorus crossings, times are indicated in black for the European shore, and in red for the Asian shore.
■ **Frequency**
Short journeys
Usually by *vapur*. Roughly every 15 mins from Eminönü.
Long journeys
Usually by *vapur* or hydrofoil. There are more crossings in the morning and in the evening as they serve the suburbs.
Excursions
Frequency and operating times vary according to the day and the season

(e.g. from 3 to 5 departures a day for the Bosphorus). Find out at the departure point.

■ **Procedure**
Go to the ticket office that corresponds to your destination. Have the money ready and check your change. The token or ticket will remain in the turnstile as you go through.

Tip
For a long journey or an infrequent service, make sure you arrive 30 mins before departure in order to secure a seat.

FESTIVALS AND CELEBRATIONS

→ **PUBLIC HOLIDAYS**
■ **Jan. 1**
New Year's Day
■ **Apr. 23**
Children's Day and Festival of National Sovereignty
■ **May 19**
Commemoration of Atatürk and Festival of Youth and Sport
■ **May 29**
Commemoration of the taking of Constantinople by the Turks in 1453
■ **Aug. 30**
Commemoration of the victory of the Turks over the Greeks in 1922
■ **Oct. 29**
National Day (military parade)
■ **Nov. 10**
Commemoration of the death of Atatürk (not a public holiday). At 9.05am, a minute of silence is held in the whole country.

→ **RELIGIOUS CELEBRATIONS**
The dates follow the Muslim calendar (lunar) and vary from one year to the next.
■ **March**
Ras es-Sana, Muslim New Year
■ **Apr. 23**
Pilgrimage to the monastery of Saint George (▲ 273)

■ **May–June**
Sixth day of the Hegira (birthday of the Prophet Muhammad)
■ **Nov.**
Ramadan (*ramazan*) lasts for a month and ends with the Sugar Festival (*Şeker Bayramı*). The Festival of Sacrifice (*Kurban Bayramı*) takes place forty days later.

→ **FESTIVALS**
■ **Apr.–May**
International Film Festival and Tulip Festival (held in Istanbul).

HAYDARPAŞA STATION (ASIAN SHORE)

VAPUR AND FISH AUCTION MARKET

■ **June.**
Yağli güreş (traditional wrestling) in Sarayıcı (north of Edirne).
■ **June–July.**
International Festival of Art and Culture (Istanbul)
■ **Aug.**
Festival of Troy (Çanakkale)
■ **Sep.–Oct.**
Biennial Arts Fair (Istanbul)

HAMMAMS (▲ 365)
Hammans (public baths) are often found near mosques. Their quality can be variable. Mixed hammams tend to be

frequented by tourists.
Warning
Take sandals.
■ **Washing**
You do this yourself (with your own toiletries), or with the help of the staff. Then you put the wrap (*peştemal*) back on in the changing room.
■ **Saunas**
You relax on a heated marble bench. An attendant then soaps and rubs you with a massage glove. You then rinse with cold water.

■ **Massage**
Ask for information at the entrance. Turkish massage is very energetic and you will not feel its benefits immediately. You can recover in a relaxation room.
Warning
Only a masseuse can massage a woman: if a man is offered, refuse.

HEALTH
→ **DAILY LIFE**
■ **Food**
Avoid salads. If you have a delicate stomach, stick to grilled meat or plain dishes.

■ **Drinks**
Drink only from sealed bottles and avoid ice cubes.
■ **Traffic**
Take care at all times, even when crossing within "protected" zones or when you have right of way.
■ **Sun**
Very strong in the summer (especially on the Bosphorus). Use a quality sunblock cream, and wear a hat and sunglasses.
■ **Wind**
Wear glasses to protect your eyes from the dust, and a windproof jacket on the Bosphorus.

→ **PHARMACIES**
Turkish pharmacies sell many medicines over the counter, including antibiotics.

→ **EMERGENCIES**
Dial 112.

→ **IN CASE OF TROUBLE**
Contact your nearest consulate, which will recommend a registered doctor, or go to the relevant hospital (*hastane*). In the case of more serious medical problems contact your insurers before taking any steps.
■ **International hospital**
Istanbul Cad. Yesilköy
■ **American hospital**
Gühzelbahçe Sok. 20 Nişantaşı
■ **German hospital**
Sıraseviler Cad. 119 Taksim

HOTELS
The classification system of hotels in Turkey does not correspond to the one used in Europe.

→ **CLASSIFICATION**
■ **Three-star hotels**
Medium-category hotels with small, plainly furnished rooms. En suite bathroom (shower and toilets).

◆ STAYING IN ISTANBUL FROM A TO Z

■ **Four-star hotels**
All modern conveniences. Air conditioning, minibar and television.

■ **Five-star hotels**
Top-quality rooms and conveniences. Air conditioning, minibar and television.

Warning
Noise pollution affects many medium-category hotels both day and night.

→ **TIPS**
■ **Quiet**
Ask for a quiet room when you make a reservation, and don't hesitate to ask to be shown several rooms before deciding to stay, or to change rooms if the hotel is not full.

■ **Air conditioning**
Useful in spring and summer.

■ **Reductions**
Prices can be negotiated when making a reservation outside the high season (July and August).

→ **LOCATION**
■ **Sultanahmet**
Small, charming Ottoman-style hotels can be found here. The area is quiet at night and is ideal for a first visit or a short stay. The main sites and landing piers are within easy reach.

■ **Beyazit-Aksaray**
Where most middle-category hotels are located. These are reasonably priced but lack character. Select according to what you find.

■ **Beyoğlu**
This busy area has modern and major international chains hotels (Taksim, Nişantaşı).

MEDIA
→ **FOREIGN NEWSPAPERS**
Available from major hotels and bookstores.

→ **LOCAL NEWSPAPERS IN FOREIGN LANGUAGES**
■ *Turkish Daily News*
Main English-language daily, printed in Ankara.

■ *Orient Express* **and** *Newspot*
Weeklies published by the *Turkish Daily News*.

■ *Dateline*
Local weekly published in English.

METRO-TRAMWAY
The network is still being developed on the European shore. A tramway line links Tünel and Taksim, while another, more modern line, serves Sultanahmet and links up with the metro west of the sea walls. The metro departs from Aksaray and goes around

BOSPHORUS BRIDGE OVERLOOKING ORTAKÖY

the north and out to the airport. An underground line is currently being built between Taksim and Şişli.

MONEY
Prices displayed in places such as hotels and restaurants are usually in US dollars or German marks.

→ **DAILY EXPENSES**
Always keep Turkish liras for minor purchases, public transport, taxis and small restaurants. Foreign currency can be used for larger expenses (such as hotels and meals in the smarter restaurants).

■ **Cash**
Change money as and when you need it.

■ **Transactions**
Check the notes you give in payment or receive as change as they are very easy to confuse.

→ **CREDIT CARDS**
■ **Autotellers**
Autotellers that accept credit cards such as Eurocard, MasterCard or Visa can be found at major banks.

■ **Payment**
Use credit cards for top-class hotels and restaurants as well as in boutiques and for car hire companies.

Warning
Be sure to check in advance whether your particular type of card is accepted.

→ **TRAVELER'S CHECKS**
It is best to change traveler's checks at a post office or bank.

→ **EXCHANGE**
Foreign currency, traveler's checks and Eurocheques can be changed at the main tourist sites (present your passport).

Warning
Keep the receipts of all transactions until you leave Turkey.

■ **Bank representative agencies and Bureaux de Change**
Open Mon.–Fri. 8.30am–noon and 1.30–5pm

MOSQUES
Fatih is a very religious district where it is especially important to observe the following rules.

→ **DRESS CODE**
Bare legs and arms are forbidden, and women must wear a headscarf (major mosques lend scarves and wraps).

Advice
Always wear light garments that cover your whole body if you intend to visit mosques (trousers and a shirt for men; long skirts and a large headscarf for women).

→ **ETIQUETTE**
Take off your shoes before entering a mosque and keep your voice down. Do not enter the prayer area. Do not eat in the mosque or within its grounds.

→ **OPENING TIMES**
The main mosques are open all day (but avoid visiting them during prayer). Minor mosques often close; ask the imam's permission to visit.

OPENING TIMES
■ **Offices**
Open Mon.–Fri. 8.30am–12.30pm and 1.30–5.30pm

■ **Banks**
Open Mon.–Fri. 8.30am–noon and 1.30–5pm

■ **Mosques**
Avoid visiting mosques during prayers and on Friday mornings.

■ **Museums**
Usually open Tue.–Sun. 9am–4pm/5pm.

■ **Restaurants**
Restaurants in hotels and smart areas are open over the normal lunch and dinner hours. Local eateries stay open all day until late in the evening.

POST OFFICES
Identified by the yellow PTT sign. Major post offices are open Mon.–Fri. 8am–midnight and Sun. 9am–7pm.

Smaller offices keep normal office hours.
Warning
Some services, such as currency exchange, are not available in the evening.

RESTAURANTS
You can eat at any time of the day or the night in Istanbul.

→ DAILY LIFE
■ **Customers**
Use common sense and follow your intuition regarding the number and type of customers in a particular restaurant.
■ **Food**
Try to estimate the turnover and the freshness of the *meze*, and of the meat and fish in refrigerated displays.
■ **Prices**
If no prices are displayed, find out about them before you order or buy.
■ **Service**
Refuse any dishes that you have not ordered, and check that the bottles brought to you are still sealed.
■ **Bill**
Do not hesitate to query bills. Check the total and, if necessary, ask for a breakdown of the bill.

→ CATEGORIES
■ **Snacks**
Many cheap eateries offer simple, good food.
■ **Restaurants**
More expensive, with varied menus. Although the surroundings and service may be more sophisticated, the food is not necessarily better.
■ **Hotel restaurants**
Convenient, but the dishes, often based on Western cuisine, tend to be expensive and vary in quality. The surroundings (garden or view) may make up for it.

■ **Trendy restaurants**
The atmosphere, rather than the cuisine, is generally what makes these restaurants popular. Reservations recommended.

SAFETY
Istanbul is not a violent city and muggings are rare. This also applies to other Turkish towns.

→ WHERE TO TAKE CARE
Busy tourist areas (Grand Bazaar and Egyptian Bazaar).

→ TOURIST POLICE
Always present in tourist areas, and usually trained to answer queries from foreign visitors.
■ **Address**
Turizm Şube Müdürlüğü Yerebatan Cad. no. 6 Sultanahmet
■ **Emergency nos**
Police: 155
Municipal police: 153

→ PRECAUTIONS
■ **At the hotel**
Do not leave money or important documents lying about. Use a small padlock or the safe provided by your hotel.
■ **On the street**
Try not to carry your actual documents around with you (make photocopies before departure). Do not wear or carry valuable objects (camera, video recorder, jewelry, etc.) in an ostentatious manner, keep your wallet in a safe place and be discreet when you handle money.

TAXES
The local VAT or sales tax (KDV) is always included in the prices quoted.

TAXIS
Taxis, which are yellow, run day and night and tend to

travel at speed, when traffic allows.

→ DAILY LIFE
■ **Meter**
All taxis should have a meter. Make sure the driver switches it on when the journey begins. If he's unwilling to do so, get out of the car.
■ **During the ride**
Keep an eye on the meter as drivers sometimes change the established rate en route.
■ **Fixed fare**
Some drivers offer fixed fares, which tend to be quite high. If a taxi driver offers a fixed fare that you are not comfortable with, ask him to switch on the meter or get another taxi.

→ FARES
$3 to $5 for an average journey.
■ **Pickup charge**
Reasonable ($1 to $2), and higher at night.
■ **Day** (*gündüz*)
6am–midnight.
■ **Night** (*gece*)
Midnight–6am.

TELEPHONE
→ CALLING THE UK/US
Dial 00 44 (UK) or 00 1 (US) followed by the number you want, minus the 0.

→ CALLING WITHIN TURKEY
Each region has a three-digit area code, set within parentheses.

TOWN CODES	
Bursa	224
Çanakkale	286
Edirne	284
Istanbul (Europe)	212
Istanbul (Asia)	216
Yalova	226

■ **Istanbul**
Istanbul has two codes: 212 (European shore) and

216 (Asian shore). A call from one shore to the other counts as regional.
■ **Local**
Dial the seven-digit number, omitting the area code.
■ **Regional**
Dial 0 then the area code followed by the subscriber number.

→ PUBLIC TELEPHONES
Many public telephones (painted blue), to be found on streets and at post offices, accept both cards (*telekart*) and tokens (*jeton*).
■ **Tokens**
There are several types of token, for the various types of call (from local to international).
■ **Cards**
Sold in units ranging from 30 to 120.
■ **Sales points**
Post offices.

TOURIST OFFICES
■ **Atatürk airport**
■ **Sultanahmet**
Between Haghia Sophia and the Blue Mosque
■ **Galatasaray**
Meşrutiyet Cad. 57

WATER
■ **Tap water**
Do not drink the tap water or water from pitchers. Avoid ice cubes and water-based ice cream. If possible, use mineral water when you brush your teeth.
Warning
Temporary cuts to the water supply may occur.
■ **Mineral water**
Mineral water can be found at all corner shops: still (*şişe suyu/su*) or sparkling (*maden suyu*).
Warning
Check the date on the bottle and make sure the top is sealed before buying.

◆ USEFUL WORDS AND PHRASES

PRONUNCIATION

c: 'j'
ç: 'ch' as in chair
g: 'g' as in gift
ğ: silent
s: 'z'
ş: 'sh' or 's' as in sugar
e: 'e' as in bed
ı: 'i' as in flirt
ö: 'u' as in furniture
u: 'ou' as in you
ü: the French 'u'

ACCOMMODATION

Apartment: daire
Bag: çanta
Bathroom: banyo
Bed: yatak
  double: çift yatakli
  single: tek yatak
Board: pansiyon
  half-board: yarım pansiyon
  full board: tam pansiyon
Building: apartman
Cancel: iptal etmek
Double room: iki oda
Employee: memur
Furniture: mobilya
Gas water heater: şofben
Hotel: otel
Key: anahtar
Live (to): oturmak
Luggage: bagaj
Man: erkek, adam
"Night light": gece lambast
Owner: sahip
Person: (bir) kişi
Price of the room: oda fiyati
Quiet room: sakin oda
Reception (hotel): resepsiyon
Room with bath: banyolu oda
Room with shower: duşlu oda
Room with washbasin: lavabolu oda
Shower: duş
Single room: oda
Toilets: tuvalet, lavabo
Towel: havlu
Woman: kadın

ADJECTIVES

Bad: kötü
Beautiful: güzel
Big: büyük
Busy/Occupied: meşgul
Closed: kapalı
Cold: soğuk
Difficult: zor
Empty: boş
Free: boş
Fresh: taze
Full: dolu
Good: iyi
Hot: sıcak
Long: uzun
Necessary: lâzım
New: yeni
Old: eski
Open: açık
Ottoman: osmanlı
Possible: mümkün
Precious: değerli
Small: küçük
Well: iyi
Young: genç
Urgent: acele

CELEBRATIONS

Celebration: bayram
Festival of Sacrifice: kurban bayramı
Ramadan: ramazan
Saber and shield dance: kılıç-kalkan
Spoon dance: kaşik oyunu
Sugar festival: şeker bayramı

COLORS

Black: siyah
Blue: mavi
Bright: canlı renk
Brown: kahve rengi
Color: renk
Dark (color): koyu renk
Green: yesil
Light (color): açık renk
Orange: turuncu
Pale: solgun, soluk
Pink: pembe
Red: kırmızı
Purple: menekşe rengi
White: beyaz
Yellow: sari

DAYS OF THE WEEK

Monday: pazartesi
Tuesday: salı
Wednesday: çarşamba
Thursday: perşembe
Friday: cuma
Saturday: cumartesi
Sunday: pazar
Week: hafta
  weekend: hafta sonu
  during the week: hafta içinde
Weather: hava

DRINKS

Alcohol: içki
  wine: şarap
  red: kırmızı
  rosé: roze
  sparkling: köpüklü
  white: beyaz
Beer: bira
  dark: siyah
  lager/light: beyaz
  draft: fıçı bira
Coffee: kahve
  white coffee: sütlü kahve, fransız
  instant coffee: neskafe
  black coffee (no sugar): sade
  black coffee (little sugar): az şekerli
  black coffee (quite a lot of sugar): orta
  black coffee (a lot of sugar): şerkerli
  Coffee maker: cezve
Drink: içecek
Drink (to): içmek
Drinks included: içkili
Fruit juice: meyva suyu
Glass: bardak, cam
Glass of water: bardak su
Ice cubes: buz
Milk: süt
  warm milk made of orchid roots: salep
Orange juice: portakal suyu
Tea: çay
  light tea: açık
  strong tea: koyu
Tea room: çay-bahçesi
Water: suyu, su
  sparkling: maden suyu
  still: şişe suyu, su

EATING OUT

Bakery: ekmekçi (dükkânı)
Biscuit/Cookie: kuru pasta
Bread: ekmek
Breakfast: komple kahvaltı
  breakfast included: kahvaltı dahil
Buffet: büfe
Butcher's: kasap (dükkânı)
Butter: tereyağ
Cake: pasta
Cheese: peynir
Chicken: piliç
Chunk/Piece: parça
Cinnamon: tarçın
Dessert: tatlı
Dinner: akşam yemegi

[FOOD continued]

Dried fruit: kuru yemiş
Eat (to): yemek
Egg: yumurta
  soft-boiled egg: üç dakikalık, rafadan
  fried egg: sahanda yumurta
  hard-boiled egg: sert
Fig: incir
Fish: balık
  anchovy: hamsi
  bass: levrek
  bream: mercan
  caviar: havyar
  crab: yengeç
  fish eggs: tarama
  lobster: istakoz
  mackerel: uskumru
  mullet: kefal
  mussels: midye
  plaice: pisi
  red mullet: barbunya
  sea bream: karagöz
  shrimp: karides
  sardines (fresh): sardalya
  swordfish: kılıç
  bluefish: lüfer
  tunafish: palamut
  tunafish from the Aegean Sea: trança
  trout: alabalık
  turbot: kalkan
Fishmonger's: balık pazarı
Food: besin, yiyecek
Fork: çatal
Fritter: kızarmış
Fruit: meyva
Grapes: üzüm
Grilled meat: ızgara
Grocery store: bakkal (dükkânı)
Honey: bal
Hors-d'œuvre: meze
  eggplant paste: patlican salatast
  filled pastry: börek
  olive oil dressing: zeytinyağlı
  soft white cheese: beyaz peynir
  stuffed vine leaves: yaprak dolması, yalancı dolması
  sweet warm milk: sicak süt
  white beans in vinaigrette: pilaki, piyaz
  with spices: salep
  zucchini with meat stuffing (hot): etli kabak dolması
Hungry (to be): acıkmak
Jam: reçel

USEFUL WORDS AND PHRASES ◆

Knife: bıçak
Lamb: kuzu
Lunch: öğle yemeği
Meat: et
  beef: sığır
  chicken: tavuk, piliç
  chicken in a walnut
  sauce:
  çerkez tavuğu
  chicken kebab:
  tavuk/piliç şiş
  cutlets: pirzola
  dried spicy beef:
  pastırma
  mixed grill (lamb):
  karışık ızgara
  escalope/Wiener
  schnitzel:
  şinitzel
  fillet of beef: bonfile
  knuckle of lamb
  with vegetables:
  kağıt kebap
  roast lamb with
  onion: orman kebap
  liver: ciğer
  meat and vegetable
  stew: güveç
  meatballs: köfte
  mutton stew: tas
  kebap
  spit-roasted
  mutton:
  tandır kebap
  steak: şatobriyan
  roast mutton in
  tomato sauce:
  bursa kebap
  veal: dana
Meatball: köfte
Menu: menü,
  yemek listesi
Napkin: peçete
Onion: soğan
Olive: zeytin
Pasta: makarna,
  lazanya
Pastry (dessert):
  pastacı (dükkânı)
Pâté: ezme
Pepper (condiment):
  kara biber
Pepper (vegetable):
  biber
Pistachio nut: şam
  fıstığı, antep fıstığı
Pizza: pide
  minced lamb:
  kıymalı, etli
  cheese: peynirli
  eggs: yumurtalı
  minced meat:
  etli pide/ekmek
Pizzeria: pideci
Plate: tabak
Raisins: kuru üzüm
Reservation:
  rezervasyon
Restaurant: restoran,
  lokanta
Salad: salata

Salt: tuz
Soup: çorba
  chicken:
  tavuk çorbası
  egg and lemon:
  düğün çorbası
  fish: balık çorbası
  lentil: mercimek
  çorbası
  lentil and rice:
  ezo gelin çorbası
  mutton broth:
  haşlama / et suyu
  mutton trotters:
  paça
  tomato:
  domates çorbası
  tripe: işkembe
  çorbası
  vegetable: sebze
  çorbası
  vermicelli: şehriye
  çorbası
  yoghurt and millet:
  yayla çorbası
Spices: baharat
Spoon: kaşık
Sugar: şeker
Waiter: garson
Watermelon: karpuz
Vinegar: sirke

ELEVATOR

Busy: meşgul, "M"
Call: çağir, "Ç"
First floor: zemin, "Z"
Hall: lobi, "L"
Send: gönder, "G"
Stop: katta, "K"

EMERGENCIES / HEALTH

Look out!: dikkat!
Accident: kaza
Car breakdown:
  arızalı
Doctor: doktor
Hospital: hastane
Ill / Sick: hasta
Massage: masaj
Medical prescription:
  reçete
Medicine: ilaç
Pharmacy: eczane
Police: polis
Repair (to): tamir
  etmek
Repairs: tamir
Vaccine: aşı

FINDING YOUR WAY

I'm looking for:
  arıyorum
Is it far?: uzak mı ?
Where is?: nerede?
Close/Near: yakın
Come from (to):
  gelmek (-den)
Far: uzak
Here: burası,

  buraya, burada
Is: doğu (D)
Left: solda
Look for (to): aramak
Near: yakın
Nearby: çevrede,
  etrafta, cıvarda
North: kusey (K)
Over there: orada
Right: sağda
South: güney (G)
Straight on: doğru
There: şurada
West: batı B)

FORMALITIES

Family name/
  Surname: soyadı
Identity card:
  nüfus kağıdı
First name: isim, ad
Passport: pasaport
Sign (to): imzalamak

GETTING AROUND

Airlines: hava hatları
Airplane: uçak
Airport: havaalanı
Arrival: varış
Beltway/Ringroad:
  çevreyolu
Boat/Ship: gemi
Border: sınır
Bus stop: durak
Coach: otobüs
Collective taxi:
  dolmuş
Customs: gümrük
Departure: kalkış
Ferry: vapur
First class: birinci
  sınıf
Garage: garaj
Gas/Petrol: benzin
  (istasyonu)
Go out (to): çıkmak
Highway: otoban
Horse-dawn
  carriage: fayton
Landing pier: iskele
Leave (to): gitmek
Passport:
  pasaport
Railroad station:
  istasyon
Rental: kiralama, kira
Return: gidiş dönüş
Second class:
  ikinci sınıf
Single: gitmek
Sleeper (train):
  yataklı vagon
Stop: dur
Stop (metro): durak
Stop (to): durmak
Take a walk (to):
  gezmek
Taxi: taksi
Town plan:
  şehir planı
Train: tre

NUMBERS

One: bir
Two: iki
Three: üç
Four: dört
Five: beş
Six: altı
Seven: yedi
Eight: sekiz
Nine: dokuz
Ten: on
Eleven: on bir
Twenty: yirmi
Thirty: otuz
Forty: kırk
Fifty: elli
Sixty: altmış
Seventy: yetmiş
Eighty: seksen
Ninety: doksan
One hundred: yüz
One hundred and
  one: yüz bir
Two hundred: iki yüz
One thousand: bin
Two thousand: iki bin
Million: milyon

PAYMENT

Bank: banka
Bargaining:
  pazarlık
Bill: hesap
Bill/Invoice:
  hesap, fatura
Bill/Note: bilet
Buy (to): almak
Change money (to):
  bozdurmak
Cheap: ucuz
Check (a): çek
Coins: para
Credit card:
  kredi kartı
Exchange (currency):
  döviz
Expensive: pahalı
Gold: altın
In cash: gümüs
Money (cash): para
Pay (to): ödemek
Payment: ödeme
Perfume: parfüm,
  koku
Price: fiyat
Sell (to): satmak
Seller/Vendor: satan
Small change: bozuk
  para
Token: jeton
  telephone token:
  telefon jetonu
  ferry token: vapur
  jetonu

PLACE NAMES

Aqueduct: kemer
Avenue: caddesi
Beach: kumsal, plaj
Bridge: köprü

◆ USEFUL WORDS AND PHRASES

Country: ülke
Forest: orman
Fountain: çeşme
Garden: bahçe
Gate: kapı
Hammam: hamam
Harbor / Port: liman
Lake: göl
Mountain: dağ
Quarter / Zone:
 mahalle, semt
River: nehir, çay
Road: yol
Sea: deniz
Slope:
 yokuş
Square: meydan
Street: sokak
Town: şehir
Town center:
 şehir merkezi
Village: köy

POST OFFICE

Make a
 call/Telephone (to):
 telefon etmek
Letter: mektup
Paper: kağıt
Post office:
 postanen (büro)
Send (to): göndermek
Stamp: pul
Telegram: telgraf
Telephone: telefon

SEASONS

Season: mevsim
Autumn / Fall:
 sonbahar
Spring: bahar
Summer: yaz
Winter: kış

SHOPPING

I want to buy this:
 bunu almak
 istiyorum
How much is it?:
 bu ne kadar?,
 bu kaç lira?
It's too expensive:
 çok pahalı
Do you have
 anything a little
 cheaper? :
 daha ucuz
 bir şey yok mu?
Can you lower
 the price?:
 fiyatı indirebilir
 misiniz?
What's your final
 price?:
 En son ne olur ?
I'll take this:
 bunu alıyorum

Antique dealer:
 antikacı
Book: kitap
Bookstore: kitabevi
Carpet: halı
Copper: bakır
Fashionable:
 moda olan gözde,
 çok tutulan
Garment/Clothing:
 elbise
Handkerchief:
 mendil
Indoor bazaar:
 kapalı çarşı
Ivory: fildişi
Jade: yeşim taşı
Jewelry: mücevher
Leather: deri
Marble: mermer
Market:
 çarşı, pazar yeri
Miniature: minyatür
Newspaper: gazete
Porcelain:
 çini, porselen
Store/Shop:
 mağaza, dükkân
Tailor: terzi
Buy (to): almak

SIGHTSEEING

Architecture: mimarî,
 mimarlık
Art: sanat
Booking office /
 Ticket office: gişe
Closed: kapalı
Crafts: zanaat
Enter / Go in: girmek
Entrance giriş
Exit: çıkış
Free: ücretsiz, bedava
Guide: rehber,
 kılavuz
Historic buildings:
 eski eserler
Interpreter:
 tercüman
Monument: anıt
Mosque: camii,
 mescit
Museum: müze
Palace: saray
Painting
 (art gallery): resim
 (galerisi)
Panorama / Scenic
 view:
 manzara, görüntü
Photography:
 fotoğraf
Tourism: turizm
Tourist office:
 turizm bürosu
Visit: gezi
Visit (to): gezmek

TIME

At what time?:
 saat kaçta?
What time is it?:
 saat kaç?
Seven o'clock:
 saat yedi
A quarter past
 seven: saat yediyi
 çeyrek geçiyor
Half past seven:
 saat yedi buçuk
A quarter to seven:
 saat yediye
 çeyrek var
Afternoon:
 öğleden sonra
Century: yüzyıl
Date: tarih
Day: gün
Evening: aksam
Half: buçuk, yarim
Hour: saat
Midday: öğle, güney
Midday: öglede
Midnight: gece yarısı
Minute: dakika
Morning: sabah
Now: şimdi,
 şu anda.
Quarter: çeyrek
Time: zaman
Today: bugün
Tomorrow: yarın
Year: yil, sene
Yesterday: dün

USUAL PHRASES

All right: tamam,
 peki
Appointment/Date:
 sözleşme, randevu
Could you repeat
 that, please?:
 lüften tekrar eder
 misiniz?
Cheers!:
 şerefinize
Do you speak
 English?: Ingilizce
 biliyor musunuz
Don't mention it: rica
 ederim, birşey değil
Enjoy your meal!:
 afiyet olsun
Excuse me:
 özür dilerim
Good evening:
 iyi akşamlar
Good night:
 iyi geceler
Goodbye: iyi günler,
 Allaha ismarladık
Guest: misafir, davetli
Hear: işitmek
Invite (to): davet
 etmek

Hello: günaydın
Hi!: merhaba
How are
 you?: nasılsınız?
How much?: kaç?
I don't understand:
 anlamıyorum
I don't want it/any:
 Istemiyorum
I have to go:
 gitmeliyim
I'm American:
 Amerikalıy
I'mBritish:
 Ingilizim
Is it free?:
 bevada mi?
Is it a gift?:
 ikramiye mi?
Is there...?: var mı?
Madam: bayan
Misunderstanding:
 anlaşmazlık
My name is: Adim...
No: hayır, yok
Pardon?: nasıl?
Please: lütfen
Pleased to see you:
 hoş bulduk
Receive:
 kabul etmek, almak
Say: demek,
 söylemek
Speak/Talk:
 konuşmak
Sir: beyefendi
Talk (with):
 le görüşmek
There is: var
There isn't: yok
Thank you:
 teşekkür ederim,
 sagol, mersi
Thank you
 very much:
 teşekkürler, çok
 mersi
Understand:
 anlamak
Very well, thank you:
 çok iyiyim,
 teşekkür ederim
Welcome!: hoş
 geldiniz
What does it mean?:
 Ne demek
What's your name? :
 Adınız ne?
When?: ne zaman?
Where (movement)?:
 nereye?
Where from?:
 nereden?
Which?: hangi?
Which/What?: ne?
Why?: niçin, neden?
Yes: evet

The ◆ symbol followed by a letter and a number refers to the map section.
A list of other symbols can be found on page 337.

ISTANBUL
EMINÖNÜ

AKSARAY–LÂLELI

→ **HOTELS**

Avlonya Hotel
◆ **D** B5
Küçük Langa Cad. 59 Aksaray
Tel. (0212) 529 54 08 or 529 57 01/02
Fax (0212) 585 94 32
An old residential building that has been converted into a hotel. The rooms are small and clean. For the reasonable quality that it offers, this is one of the less expensive hotels in the area. View over the Sea of Marmara. Bar and restaurant. 56 rooms.
🖵🖥🖼🎀♿🅿🛎️🔲

Çara Hotel
◆ **D** D4
Koca Ragıp Paşa Cad. 19 Aksaray–Lâleli
Tel. (0212) 638 89 00
Fax (0212) 638 33 43
www.carahotel.com
There is a panoramic view from the terrace, where there is a sauna and a hammam. There is also a covered swimming pool on the roof. The rooms here are comfortable with standard décor. The bar-restaurant of the hotel is open from 2pm to 10pm. 105 rooms, including 6 suites.
🖵🔺🖥🖼🎀♿🛎️♿
🔲

Erden Hotel
◆ **D** C4
Azimkar Sok. 66–68 Aksaray–Lâleli
Tel. (0212) 518 48 52
Fax (0212) 518 48 57

Quite large and comfortable rooms. The surroundings are a little noisy, even at night, because the commercial district stays open late and attracts crowds of people.
🖵🖥🖼🅿🛎️🔲

Fuar
◆ **D** B4
Namık Kemal Cad. 26 Aksaray
Tel. (0212) 633 50 61
Fax (0212) 588 60 48
Although the décor is slightly flashy, this this four-star hotel is a high-class establishment. Courteous welcome and pleasant view over the Sea of Marmara (from all the rooms on the 5th floor). The rooftop bar commands a view over the Beyazıt and Fatih districts. Seven floors. 65 rooms.
🖵🖥🖼🎀🅿🛎️🔲

Gold Hotel
◆ **D** D4
Şair Haşmet Sok. 11 Aksaray–Lâleli
Tel. (0212) 518 74 30
Fax (0212) 518 74 35
Unremarkable hotel currently undergoing renovation. New carpets and furniture have been put in place and air conditioning installed. Small, clean rooms. Very noisy area at the heart of the cheap clothes shops district.
🖵🎰🖼🔲

Grand Ons Hotel
◆ **D** C4
Mesih Paşa Cad. Azimkar Sok. 32 Aksaray–Lâleli
Tel. (0212) 518 63 70
Fax (0212) 518 63 74
The 92 rooms, although rather small, are comfortable and have air conditioning. The hotel is located in a small street in the shopping district, some distance from the traffic but still not really quiet. Bar and restaurant.
🖵🖥🖼🎰🎀🎰🔲

Green Anka
◆ **D** A3
Findikzade Sok. 4 Molla Şeref-Aksaray
Tel. (0212) 631 17 21
Fax (0212) 525 37 78
The décor here is unremarkable but the rooms are comfortable and there is air conditioning throughout the hotel.
🖵🖥🖼🔲🅿🛎️🔲

Madrid Hotel
◆ **D** B3
Çıngıraklı Bostan Sok. 50 Aksaray
Tel. (0212) 635 78 91
Fax (0212) 525 21 08
Although the rooms overlook the street, they are quiet. The hotel has an ideal location near tramways leading to places of interest to tourists and near the Eminönü landing piers. Good service. The bar-restaurant has a terrace. 30 rooms.
🖵🖥🖼🎰♿🎀🅿
🛎️🔲

✪ Merit Antique Hotel
◆ **D** D4
Ordu Cad. 226 Aksaray–Lâleli
Tel. (0212) 513 93 00
Fax (0212) 512 63 90
One of the most luxurious hotels in Istanbul, with an ideal location. The marble and paneling décor is tasteful and attractive. Three restaurants: the Ocakbaşı (open 7.30am–11.30pm); the Dynasty, (open Mon.–Sat. 7.30–11.30pm) and the Metsou-Yan Kasher, the only kosher restaurant in Istanbul, (open 7–11pm). Babıalı Bar (Tue.– Sun. 6pm–midnight).

◆ USEFUL ADDRESSES
ISTANBUL, EMINÖNÜ

RESTAURANTS
- ◻ < $4
- ◨ $4–$7.5
- ◧ $7.5–$10
- ⊞ > $10

274 rooms including 11 suites.
◻◻◻Ⅲ☒P☒⊞

Orient Mintur Hotel
◆ **D** C5
Mermerciler Cad. 5
Aksaray–Yenikapı
Tel. (0212) 517 63 00
Fax (0212) 517 78 39
Average décor but some of the rooms have a sea view. Sauna and bar on the terrace. Bar-restaurant. 41 rooms including 2 suites.
◻◻◻Ⅲ⬆⬆☒P
☒◻

Prestige
◆ **D** C4
Koska Cad. 8
Aksaray–Lâleli
Tel. (0212) 518 82 80
Fax (0212) 518 82 90
Luxurious hotel located near the tramway. Outstanding décor. Offers all the comforts of a high-class hotel.
◻◻◻Ⅲ☒◻

Royal Hotel
◆ **D** C4
Aksaray Cad. 16
Aksaray
Tel. (0212) 518 51 51
Fax (0212) 518 51 60
A hotel of good standing, one of the best to be found in this district, located slightly away from the hubbub. The rooms are comfortable and guests receive a pleasant welcome.
◻◻◻☒☒◻

→ RESTAURANTS
Gaziantepli Cavuşoğlu
◆ **D** D4
Şair Fitnat Sok. 4/1, Ordu Cad.
Aksaray–Lâleli
Tel. (0212) 518 76 65
Open daily
noon–11pm
Located within easy reach of several medium-range hotels. Convivial atmosphere. Specialty: kebab in gravy.
◻

MERIT ANTIQUE, AKSARAY LALELI

THE PRESIDENT, BEYAZIT

ENGLISH PUB, BEYAZIT

SENATOR HOTEL, SEHZADE

Paçaci Hasan
◆ **D** B3
Şekerci Sok. 8/1
Gureba Hüseyinağa
Aksaray
Tel. (0212) 531 75 60
or 531 65 66
Open daily
7am–11pm
Unpretentious establishment that serves very good food. The specialties of the proprietor, Ahmet Usta, are kelle paça (soup made with chunks of tripe spiced up with garlic, vinegar and salt), kaburga dolmasi (mutton), and excellent Kurdish dishes. All the ingredients come from Diyarbekir, a town in southeastern Turkey. Make sure you get here before 2pm to have a chance to enjoy the specials. No alcohol.
◻◻

Sait Restaurant
◆ **D** B4
Mustafa Kemal Cad.
Inkılâp Cad. 10
Aksaray
Tel. (0212) 530 64 94
or 530 64 99
Open daily
11am–midnight
Closed on religious feast days
An extremely popular establishment that is halfway between a fast-food joint and a quality restaurant. Excellent kebab with yoghurt. Specialty: grilled lamb.
◻◻

Yöre Iskender Kebabşisi
◆ **D** B4
Inkılâp Cad. 12
Aksaray
Tel. (0212) 586 58 57
Good restaurant near Lâleli's main hotels. Copious, well-presented dishes. Turkish clientele. Specialties: mixed kebab (three types of lamb).
◻

HOTELS
- ▫ < $50
- ▣ $50 to $100
- ▤ $100 to $200
- ▦ > $200

→ SHOPPING
Gaziantepli Cavusoglu
◆ D DA
Ordu Cad.
Sair Fitnat Sok. 4
Aksaray Lâleli
Tel. (0212) 518 77 14
or 518 77 28
Open daily
8am–10pm
Tatli (Turkish pastries made with honey) on the first floor. The restaurant on the second floor can seat up to 60 people.
◻▪

BEYAZIT

→ HOTELS
Antik Hotel
◆ D E4
Sekbanbaşı Sok. 10,
Beyazıt
Tel. (0212) 638 58 58
Fax (0212) 638 58 65
www.istanbulhotels.com
New hotel in the university quarter. Well-equipped rooms (hairdryer, safe, etc.). Outdoor restaurant (7am–11pm) and indoor restaurant (Club Accademia, 6pm–2am), bars (5–11pm) and nightclub. 96 rooms including 4 suites.
◻◻◓Ⅲ⧝ ⬆⬇
♫P🅿◻

Inter
◆ D E4
Mithatpaşa Cad.
Efendi Sok. 29
Beyazıt
Tel. (0212) 518 35 35
Fax (0212) 518 35 38
Unremarkable but comfortable hotel. Breakfast with buffet served on terrace.
◻◻⬆P🅿◻

The President
◆ D E4
Tiyatro Cad. 25
Beyazıt
Tel. (0212) 516 69 80
Fax (0212) 516 69 99
www.thepresidenthotel.com.tr
Elegant hotel at the heart of old Istanbul. Rooftop swimming pool with panoramic view over the Sea of Marmara. Very beautiful traditional restaurant with screens and wrought-iron lamps. Restaurants: Ocakbaşı Garden and Marmara (7–10am, noon–2pm and 7–10pm). Two bars (English Pub and bar, Pool Bar: 11am–2am). 204 rooms including 8 suites.
◓◻◻◓Ⅲ⧝⬆⬇
🅿🌣◻

☯ Selman
◆ D E4
Soğan ağa Camii
Tavşantaşı Sok. 2
Beyazıt
Tel. (0212) 517 03 52
Fax (0212) 516 13 08
Very decent rooms with shower and telephone. Warm welcome. Rooftop cafeteria. Recommended.
◻⬆🌣◻

→ CAFÉS
Çay Bahçesi
◆ D E4
Sahaflar Çarşısı Sok.
Çınar Altı 1, Beyazıt
Tel. (0212) 513 56 89
Open daily 7am–8pm
Situated in a small shady garden opposite the entrance to the Sahaflar market. It serves tea, coffee and cold drinks as well as light snacks (such as döner and tosts).

English Pub
◆ D E4
The President Hotel
Tiyatro Cad. 25
Beyazıt
Tel. (0212) 516 69 80
Open daily 11am–2am
"The only English pub in Istanbul," according to the publicity. It is certainly the city's oldest pub. Elaborate décor. Popular with tourists and hotel residents.
◻

Evedikler
◆ D F4
Yeniçeriler Cad.
Çorlulu Alipaşa
Medreseni 36/28
Çarşıkapı Beyazıt
Tel. (0212) 528 37 85
Open daily
noon–10.30pm
Pleasant café with a courtyard where you can smoke a hookah and drink tea or coffee.
◻

→ NIGHTLIFE
Orient House
◆ D E4
The President Hotel
Tiyatro Cad. 27
Beyazıt
Tel. (0212) 517 61 63
Open daily
8pm–2am
The show (belly dancing and parade of traditional costumes) is better than the food. Fixed price for the dinner-show.
◻♫▦

KUMKAPI

→ HOTEL
Amber
◆ E B6
Cinci Meydani
Yusuf Aşkın Sok. 28
Küçük Ayasofya
Kumkapı
Tel. (0212) 518 48 01
Fax (0212) 518 81 19
www.hotelamber.com
Brand new hotel in a poor area of Sultanahmet, close to the sea. Comfortable rooms, saunas, hammam and bar (6pm–3am). Two restaurants: Tavern Restaurant and Damla Roof (noon–11pm). 58 rooms including 3 suites. Some rooms have air conditioning.
◻◻◓Ⅲ⬆⬇🌣P
🌣◻

→ RESTAURANTS
Kör Agop
◆ D E6
Ördekli Bakkal Sok. 7
Kumkapı
Tel. (0212) 517 23 34
Open daily
10.30am–1am
This is one of the best restaurants in the area, with a good reputation among the locals. Fine cooking. Huge choice and varied mezes. Fish specialties.
◻◻

Sehzade
◆ E A6
Kennedi Cad.
Balıkçılar Çarşısı 28
Kumcapı
Tel. (0212) 518 36 31
Open daily, 24 hours
Facing the road from Sultanahmet, Kumcapı has several fish restaurants: the Sehzade offers dishes made with the catch of the day. Hookah smokers have a designated area in the Anatolian-style dining rooms. Only a few steps away from the promenade along the Sea of Marmara. No alcohol.
◻Ⅲ⬆🌣◻

SEHZADE–SÜLEYMANIYE

→ HOTELS
Senator Hotel
◆ D C3
Gençturk Cad.
Şirvanizade Sok. 7
Şehzade
Tel. (0212) 520 18 65
Fax (0212) 522 73 93
www.senatorhotel.com.tr
The size and the decoration of the rooms in this new hotel are fairly average. A large staff ensures quick service. Historic and Brasserie Restaurant (noon–3pm and 7–11pm). Bar. 102 rooms, including 10 suites.
◓◻◻◓ⅢP🌣◻

Yigitalp Hotel
◆ D C3
Gençtürk Cad.
Çukur Çeşme Sok.
38 Şehzade

349

Tel. (0212) 512 98 60 or (0212) 512 20 72
www.yigitalp.com
Situated in a lively area of the city. The rooms are comfortable and extremely clean. Guests are warmly welcomed and treated to an impeccable service. Restaurant Alp (7am–10pm) and bar Kubbe (10am–midnight). 83 rooms.
▢◻◈▥P▨◨

→ RESTAURANTS
Darül Ziyafe
◆ **D** E1
Şifahane Sok. 6
Süleymaniye
Tel. (0212) 511 84 14
Open daily noon–11pm
Situated within the Süleyman the Magnificent Complex, this fine restaurant serves excellent traditional Turkish cusine, which is authentic and of the kind that is rarely found today because it simply takes too long to prepare. Specialties: yuftali köfte (meatball pastries) and fruit cordials. No alcohol.
▢◼

Güney Saray Restaurant
◆ **D** C2
Atatürk Bulvarı 126
Şehzade
Tel. (0212) 519 30 34
Open daily noon–midnight
Located close to the Valens Aqueduct, on a lively boulevard. Attractive European décor with paneling. Very clean. Good solid food. Specialty: karisik kebab.
◼

→ CAFÉ
Vefa Bozacisi
◆ **D** C2
Katip Çelebi Cad. 102, Şehzade

Tel. (0212) 519 49 22
Open Mon.–Sat. 10am–8pm
Near the Geographic Institute of Istanbul. The façade is rather forbidding, but once inside you will find the atmosphere rather pleasant. Try Boza, a winter drink made from fermented millet (£1/ $1.50 per glass).
▣

→ HOTELS
Askoç
◆ **E** C2
Istasyon Arkası Sok. 15 Sirkeci
Tel. (0212) 511 80 89
Fax (0212) 511 70 53
The unattractive

ARMADA HOTEL, SULTANAHMET

façade should not deter you from entering this agreeable air-conditioned and well-equipped hotel. The area is very lively during the day (near the station). Some rooms have a view over the Bosphorus. Rooftop bar.
▢◻▥▨P◨

Romance Hotel
◆ **E** C3
Hüdavendigar Cad. 7
Sirkeci

Tel. (0212) 512 86 76
Fax (0212) 512 87 23
Unremarkable but comfortable hotel close to Topkapı Palace. The rooms are quite large and decorated in a modern style. Prices may vary according to the season and the number of guests.
▢◻P▨◨

Ipek Palas
◆ **E** C2-C3
Orhaniye Cad. 9
Sirkeci
Tel. (0212) 520 97 24
Fax (0212) 526 13 02
Functional hotel located within a short walking distance of the Eminönü landing piers. Bar-restaurant with a terrace.
▢◻◈⬆▨P◨

Orsep
◆ **E** C2
Hoca Paşa Sok.
Ibni Kemal Cad. 34
Sirkeci
Tel. (0212) 513 35 86 or 526 76 29
Fax (0212) 513 35 91
www.orsephotel.com
Also close to the landing piers, this small hotel is both convenient and quiet although the rooms look onto the street. Bar and restaurant. 50 rooms.
▢◻◈▥⬇⬆▨◨

→ RESTAURANT
Pandeli
◆ **E** B1-B2
Egyptian market
Mısır Çasısı
Tel. (0212) 527 39 09
Open 11.30am–4pm
Closed Sun.
The large windows of this elegant restaurant look onto the Tahmis Caddesi on one side and the Grand Bazaar on the other. Impeccable service by attentive waiters. Specialties: grilled meats and kebabs.
◼

→ HOTELS
Acropol Hotel
◆ **E** D5
Akbıyık Cad. 25
Sultanahmet
Tel. (0212) 638 90 21
Fax (0212) 518 30 31
www.acropolhotel.com
Old wooden Ottoman house, recently restored and turned into a hotel. The rooms are comfortable and some have a sea view. The bar is open from 10am to 2.30am, and the Marmara Roof Restaurant from 7am to midnight. 26 rooms, 2 suites.
▢◻◈▥⬇⬆▨
P◨

Armada Hotel
◆ **E** D6
Ahır Kapı Sok. 24
Sultanahmet
Tel. (0212) 638 13 70
Fax (0212) 518 50 60
www.armadahotel.com.tr
In an old building that has been tastefully restored. Most rooms have a sea view, and all have ensuite bathrooms.
Three restaurants:
The Ahirkapi (6.30am–midnight), the Sera (7pm–1am), and the Garden (open in summer only, 7pm–midnight). Two bars:

HOTELS
- `•` < $50
- `•` $50 to $100
- `•` $100 to $200
- `•` > $200

*the Radio (5pm–2am)
and the Teras Bar
(5pm–midnight).
110 rooms, 4 suites.*

`□□▲Ⅲ□◎P♨&`
`┑⭡▣`

Avicenna Hotel
◆ **E** D5-D6
Amiral Tafdil
Sok. 33
Sultanahmet
Tel. (0212) 517 05 50
Fax (0212) 516 65 56
www.avicenna.com.tr
*Newly restored
Ottoman house,
charming and very
well situated. Some
of the rooms have
a view of the Blue
Mosque, and 13
out of the total of 16
are air conditioned.
The restaurant-
terrace boasts
views over the
Bosphorus.*
`□□◎Ⅲ♨▣`

AyaSofya Hotel
◆ **E** B6-C6
Küçükayasofya Cad.
Demirci Reşit Sok. 28
Sultanahmet
Tel. (0212) 516 94 46
Fax (0212) 518 07 00
www.ayasofyahotel.
com
*In a 19th-century
Ottoman house.
Comfortable rooms,
each with shower
and telephone.
Bar on the terrace.
20 rooms, 1 suite.*
`□□▲□◎Ⅲ┑⭡♨`
`P▣`

**✪ Ayasofya
Pansiyonlari**
◆ **E** D4
Soğukçeşme Sokağı
(closed to traffic)
Sultanahmet
Tel. (0212) 513 36 60
Fax (0212) 513 36 69
*Nine houses that
were built in the
18th century make
up this fine and
rather unusual hotel.
Charming 19th-
century décor. Very
quiet. Restaurants
Sera (6am–midnight)
and Sarniç (7.30pm–
midnight). Bar
(6am–midnight).
63 rooms, 6 suites.*
`□◎┑⭡P□▣`

AYASOFYA PANSIYONLARI, SULTANAHMET

ACROPOL HOTEL, SULTANAHMET

EMPRESS ZOE, SULTANAHMET

FOUR SEASONS, SULTANAHMET

✪ Empress Zoe
◆ **E** D5-D6
Akbıyık Caddesi.
Adliye Sok. 10.
Sultanahmet
Tel. (0212) 518 25 04
Fax (0212) 518 56 99
www.emzoe.com
*All the rooms in this
charming wood
and stone hotel are
decorated with kilims,
and have marble and
terracotta bathrooms.
The bar terrace (on
two levels) offers a
panoramic view of
the sights around the
Sea of Marmara. In
summer breakfast is
served in a garden
next to the ruins of a
former Turkish bath.
19 rooms, 3 suites.*
`□□◎◎⭡♨▣`

✪ Four Seasons
◆ **E** D5
Tevkifhane Sok. 1
Sultanahmet
Tel. (0212) 638 82 00
Fax (0212) 638 82 10
www.fshr.com
*The latest addition
to the international
chain, built near
Haghia Sophia on
the site of a former
prison. Spacious,
luxurious, air-
conditioned rooms.
Restaurant and bar.
54 rooms, 11 suites.*
`□□◎Ⅲ&⭡⭡♨`
`P▦`

Hali
◆ **E** B4
Klodfarer Cad. 20
Çemberlitaş
Sultanahmet
Tel. (0212) 516 21 70
Fax (0212) 516 21 72
www.halihotel.com
*Some rooms
overlook the Blue
Mosque. Restaurant
open in summer, and
a bar. 80 rooms.*
`□Ⅲ□◎♨┑&▣`
`⭡P▣`

Hippodrome
◆ **E** C5-D5
Mimar Mehmet Ağa
Cad. 17
Sultanahmet
Tel. (0212) 517 68 89
Fax (0212) 516 02 68
*The rooms in this old
Ottoman house are*

sparsely decorated, and there is no lift and no air conditioning. In summer, breakfast is served on the roof. Slightly overpriced for the comforts and facilities that it offers.
□□🖼🎣⛄・

Ibrahim Paşa Oteli
◆ E B5
Terzihane Sok. 5
Sultanahmet
Tel. (0212) 518 03 94
Fax (0212) 518 44 57
www.all-hotels.com
A charming small hotel located in an ancient building. The rooms are small but pleasant, and from the roof terrace there are superb views over Sultanahmet. Bar open daily 11am–midnight.
19 rooms, 1 suite.
□□🖼📺🎣⛄P
・

Konuk Evi
◆ E D4
Soğukçeşme Sokaği
Sultanahmet
Tel. (0212) 514 01 20
Fax (0212) 214 02 13
Charming Ottoman house hidden away in a quiet, secluded garden. Rooms with showers.
□⛄・

Küçük Aya Sofya
◆ E B5
Şehit Mehmet Paşa Sok. 25
Sultanahmet
Tel. (0212) 516 19 88
Fax (0212) 516 83 56
A typical Ottoman building located in the center of the Sultanahmet. A warm and friendly welcome.
・

Mavi Guesthouse
◆ E D5
Ishak Paşa Cad. Kutlugün Sok. 3
Sultanahmet
Tel. (0212) 516 58 78
Fax (0212) 517 72 87
www.maviguest house.8m.com
Situated between

SARNIÇ, SULTANAHMET

OBELISK, SÜMENGEN, SULTANAHMET

IBRAHIM PAŞA OTELI, SULTANAHMET

KONUK EVI, SULTANAHMET

Topkapı and Haghia Sophia, this small, quiet and inexpensive hotel offers basic comforts (including hot water). Breakfast is included. Around £15/$21 for two people. Bar.
12 rooms.
□⛄P・

Obelisk Sümengen Hotel
◆ E C5-D5
Mimar Mehmetağa Cad. Amiral Tafdil Sok. 17/19
Sultanahmet
Tel. (0212) 517 71 73
Fax (0212) 516 82 82
Charming hotel situated in a lovingly restored wooden Ottoman house. Despite its location close to the Blue Mosque and the Haghia Sophia, it is quiet. The terrace has a view over the Bosphorus. The restaurant is open daily 11am–11pm.
71 rooms, 3 suites.
□⛄□🖼📺🎣⛄
⛄P

Sari Konak Hotel
◆ E C5-D5
Mimar Mehmet Ağa Cad. 42-46
Sultanahmet
Tel. (0212) 638 62 58
Fax (0212) 517 86 35
Clean, new hotel in an old wooden house near Haghia Sophia. Very welcoming with a family atmosphere.
□📺・

Sokollu Paşa Hotel
◆ E B5
Küçük Ayasofya mah. Şehit Mehmet Paşa Sok. 5–7
Sultanahmet
Tel. (0212) 518 17 90
Fax (0212) 518 17 93
www.sokollupasa.com
Charming hotel surrounded by a pretty garden. There is a hammam. Breakfast and transfer from airport included.
2 restaurants: the Garden Restaurant and the Orient

HOTELS
- `•` < $50
- `•` $50 to $100
- `•` $100 to $200
- `•` > $200

Restaurant (noon–11pm). 37 rooms.
🔲🔲🔲🔲🔲🔲🔲

Terrasse Guesthouse
◆ **E** D5
Kutlugün Sok. 39
Tel. (0212) 638 97 33
or (0212) 638 01 15
Fax. (0212) 638 97 34
Set on three levels, this small, clean hotel has 6 quiet and well-equipped rooms with views over the Sultanahmet, Ayasofya and the Sea of Marmara. Very friendly atmosphere. Clients can use a communal kitchen, which has a splendid view over the sea. Owner Dogan Yildirim speaks English and is always available to provide any information or advice that guests may need. Kilims and suzanis are sold on the first floor (between £28/$40 and £60/$85). Book well in advance.
🔲🔲🔲🔲🔲🔲

Vezirhan
◆ **E** D3-D4
Alemdar Cad. 7
Sultanahmet
Tel. (0212) 511 24 14
Fax (0212) 511 17 85
Comfortable new hotel close to the entrance to Topkapı. Some rooms have a view over the Sultanahmet.
🔲🔲🔲🔲🔲

✪ Yeşil Ev
◆ **E** C5-C6
Kabasakal Cad. 5
Sultanahmet
Tel. (0212) 517 67 85
Fax (0212) 517 67 80
A splendid hotel with period furnishings hidden away in a large park. This is a place offering luxury and tranquillity in an attractive rural setting. Reservations essential. 24 rooms.
🔲🔲🔲🔲🔲🔲
Restaurant Yeşil Ev
◆ **354**.

→ RESTAURANTS
Altin Kupa
◆ **E** C4
Yerebatan Cad. 6
Sultanahmet
Tel. (0212) 519 47 70
Open daily
9am–midnight
Pleasant terrace overlooking Haghia Sophia. Specialty: fresh vegetable gratin.
🔲🔲🔲🔲

Café Medusa
◆ **E** C4
Yerebatan Cad. Muhteremefendi Sok. 19, Sultanahmet
Tel. (0212) 511 41 16
Open daily
9am–midnight
Situated inside a small four-story house. This pretty paneled restaurant has a pleasant atmosphere where a wide choice of Turkish dishes can be sampled at reasonable prices Specialty: diliç medusa.
🔲🔲

Doy Doy
◆ **E** C6
Şifa Hamami Sok. 13
Sultanahmet
Tel. (0212) 517 15 88
Fax (0212) 518 12 80
Open daily
11am–1am.
The restaurant is set on three levels. The terrace at the top offers truly stunning views over Sultanahmet, with Ayasofya on one side and the Sea of Marmara on the other. The views are even more spectacular at night, when all the monuments are lit up. Friendly waiters and reasonable prices.
🔲🔲

Kathisma Restaurant
◆ **E** D5-D6
Akbıyık Cad. 26
Sultanahmet
Tel. (0212) 518 97 10
Fax. (0212) 516 25 88
Open daily 9am–1am
Very pretty, elegant restaurant on three levels, in a quiet neighborhood. Sophisticated décor (the metal hull of a boat decorates the banisters, there is solid wood furniture and the tables are laid with fine cutlery). Unfortunately the terrace on the top floor only offers a restricted view of Istanbul. Top-quality service and English-speaking staff. Delicious, well-presented dishes of Turkish specialties (mostly grilled meats). Large choice of spirits and wines from various part of the world.
🔲🔲

Konyali
◆ **E** E3
De Palais Topkapı Sarayı Sultanahmet
Tel. (0212) 513 96 97
Open 9.30am–5pm
Closed Tue.
Sunny terrace and fine view. Essential stop after hours of sightseeing, despite prices that are high and waiters who can sometimes be rude.
🔲🔲🔲🔲🔲

✪ Sarniç
◆ **E** D4
Soğukçeşme Sok.
Sultanahmet
Tel. (0212) 512 42 91
Open Tue.–Sun.
8am–midnight
Old restored cistern. Candlelit dinners in the vaulted dining rooms. Sophisticated décor.
🔲🔲

Sultan
◆ **E** C4
Divanyolu Cad. 2
Sultanahmet
Tel. (0212) 528 17 19
Fa. (0212) 512 95 68
Open 6am–midnight
Located close to Haghia Sophia. Very quiet. International and Turkish cuisine. Small portions. Specialty: meat dishes. Meals are served on the rooftop terrace in summer.
🔲🔲
Sultan Pub ◆ **354**

Sultanahmet Köftecisi
◆ **E** C5-C6
Divanyolu Cad. 12/A
Sultanahmet
Tel. (0212) 513 14 38
Open daily
10am–11pm
Mehmet Seracettin Tezçakın is a great meatball specialist. His restaurant is popular with the citizens of Istanbul. This is definitely the place to go for the best köftes (grilled minced meat) in town. Haricot bean salad and semolina pudding are other specialties. Fast service.
🔲🔲

✪ Yeşil Ev
◆ **E** C5-C6
Kabasakal Cad. 5
Sultanahmet
Tel. (0212) 517 67 86
Fax (0212) 517 67 80
Open daily
10am–midnight
The restaurant has a splendid garden for al fresco lunches in summer. Very good international and Turkish cuisine, though prices tend be a little on the high side. Specialty: meats in various sauces.
🔲🔲🔲🔲

→ NIGHTLIFE
Sultan Pub
◆ **E** C4
Divanyolu Cad. 2
Sultanahmet
Tel. (0212) 528 17 19
Fax. (0212) 512 95 68
www.sultanpub.com.tr
Open 9am–1am
Pub located on the first floor of the restaurant of the same name. The atmosphere is reminiscent of that of an English pub. International music

and a wide range of cocktails. *Ideal stopping place for a cold drink after visiting the old town. £6–£30/$8.50–$42*
■ ◘ ⌂

→ **SHOPPING**
Baş-Pa
◆ **E** D5
Cankurtaran Mah. Kutlugün Sok. 31 Sultanahmet
Tel. (0212) 516 51 32 or 216 75 61
Fax. (0212) 216 51 33
www.asiaminor carpets.com
This manufacturer of carpets and kilims still uses traditional patterns and methods of weaving, even though it has a large distribution network both in Turkey and abroad.

GOLDEN HORN
→ **RESTAURANTS**
Café du Levant
◆ **B** D2-D3
Hasköy Cad. 27 Sütlüce, Golden Horn
Tel. (0212) 250 89 38
Open noon–2.30pm and 7.30–10.30pm. Closed Mon.
This is the restaurant of the Museum of Industry. The delicious and unusual dishes are basically French, but with carefully chosen Oriental ingredients. Specialty: breaded turbot.
■ ■

Sahil Restaurant
◆ **B** C3
Demirhisar Cad. 49 Sahil Yolu Balat–Karabaş
Tel. (0212) 525 61 85
Open daily 2–11pm
On the Golden Horn, near the Byzantine walls. Very good food. Specialty: saç kavurma (Turkish-style veal).
■ P ■

EDIRNEKAPI
→ **HOTEL**
✪ **Kariye Hotel**
◆ **B** B4
Kariye Camıı Sok. 18 Edirnekapı
Tel. (0212) 534 84 14
Fax (0212) 521 66 31
www.kariyeotel.com
This green wooden building, an Ottoman house that is quite typical of its kind, contains the Kariye Cami'i museum. The spacious, very tastefully decorated rooms overlook a lush, well-tended garden that is an oasis of greenery

YESIL EV SULTANAHMET

in the middle of the city. Restaurant Asitane (11am–midnight). 27 rooms, 2 suites, 2 deluxe.
■ ■ ◘ 🗂 🏊 ⌂ ☗ 🕍
P 🖥

→ **RESTAURANT**
Asithane
◆ **B** B4
Kariye Hotel Kariye Camıı Sok. 18 Edirnekapı
Tel. (0212) 534 84 14
Open daily noon–3pm and 7pm–1am
Situated opposite the Kariye Cami'i museum. Fine and flavorsome

Ottoman cuisine. *Good, efficient service. Meals are served on the pleasant terrace in summer.*
■ ■ ⌂ ◘ ■

EYÜP
→ **RESTAURANTS**
Ensar
◆ **B** A1
Eyüp Bulvari Eyüp
Tel. (0212) 612 77 38 or (0212) 613 50 53
Restaurant-pâtisserie
Open 4.30am–11pm
Following the times set by the mosque, the Ensar offers a typical Turkish breakfast of tomatoes, soft white cheese, olives, cucumbers, hard-boiled eggs, and soup made of lentils or tomatoes. Specialties: Turkish dishes and desserts made with honey. No alcohol. Fixed-price menu: 5 million TRL.
■ ■

Mihmandar Lokantasi
◆ **B** A1
Kalenderhane Cad. Eyüp Bulvari Sokollu Ikram Çarsısı 1

Eyüp
Tel. (0212) 612 59 98
Open daily 10am–11pm
Turkish cuisine and grilled meats. Terrace on the sunny square. Especially nice for dinner. No alcohol.
■ ■

→ **CAFÉ**
✪ **Pierre Loti Café**
◆ **B** A1
Gümüşsuyu Bal Mumcu Sok. 1 Eyüp
On the slopes overlooking Eyüp Cami'i. Leaving the mosque, follow a well-signed route on the right, which leads to the café.
Tel. (0212) 581 26 96
Open daily 8am–midnight
Located in the former house of the French writer Pierre Loti. Superb view over the Golden Horn, with small tables beneath a flower-filled arbor.
⌂ 🏊

YEDICULE
◆ **A** C4
→ **RESTAURANT**
✪ **Develi Restaurant**
Balıkçı, Gümüş Yüzük Sok. 7 Yedicule Samatya
Tel. (0212) 585 11 89
Fax (0212) 529 08 33
Open daily noon–midnight
This restaurant, founded in 1912, serves Anatolian specialties: kebabs with eggplant and pistachio, and the famous Künefe (dessert). Recommended.
■ ■

→ **HOTELS**
✪ **Çirağan Palace Kempinski Hotel**
◆ **A** D3
Çirağan Cad. 84 Beşiktaş

HOTELS
· < $50
⚐ $50 to $100
⚑ $100 to $200
⚏ > $200

Tel. (0212) 258 33 77
Fax (0212) 259 66 86
www.ciraganpalace.
com
*A former sultan's
palace that has
now been totally
restored. Today
this is the most
luxurious hotel in
Istanbul. It has been
used in the past by
various heads of
state, most
notably President
Mitterrand and the
former President
Bush. There is a
superb garden
overlooking
the Bosphorus and
the swimming pool is
a dream.*
🏊🍽🚭🛗🚖🅿🏧
🛗🚿🅿🗂🏧
Excellent restaurant
(see below).

Fuat Paşa
◆ **A** D2
Çayırbaşı Cad. 238
Büyükdere
Tel. (0212) 242 98 60
Fax (0212) 242 95 89
www.fuatpasa.com.tr
*Located in an
elegant 18th-century
Ottoman house,
painted pink and
green. A large
internal courtyard
is reached via
an impressive
staircase. The rooms
overlooking the
courtyard tend to
be quieter.*
🍽🛗🚖🚿🅿·

La Maison
◆ **A** D3
Müvezzi Cad. 63
Beşiktaş/Çırağan
Tel. (0212) 227 42 63
Fax (0212) 227 42 78
*Very quiet hotel.
The rooms are
pretty and the
terrace looks out
over the Bosphorus.*
🍽🔺🚖🛗🚿🅿🗂
🏧

→ RESTAURANTS
**✪ Çırağan Palace
Brasserie**
◆ **A** D3
Çırağan Cad. 84
Beşiktaş
Tel. (0212) 258 33 77

www.ciraganpalace.
com
Open daily
7am–11pm
*Situated on the
shores of the
Bosphorus in
the grand setting
of the former palace.
The brasserie's
sumptuous buffet,
with a great variety
of dishes, allows
gourmets to sample
a range of delicious
specialties. The
restaurant is pricey
for Istanbul, but
represents good
value for money.*
🍽🚿🅿🗂🏧

CAFÉ PIERRE LOTI, EYÜP

Deniz Park Gazinosu
◆ **A** D2
Daire Sok. 9
Yeniköy
Tel. (0212) 262 04 15
Open daily
noon–midnight
*This floating
restaurant is quite
difficult to find but
it is definitely the
best in Yeniköy. The
terrace commands
unbeatable views
over the Bosphorus.
Specialties: squid
and shrimps.*
🛗🚿🏧

**Divan Kuruçeşme
Restaurant**
◆ **A** D3
Kuruçeşme Cad. 36
Beşiktaş

Tel. (0212) 257 71 50
Open daily
8am–midnight
*Restaurant with a
pleasant setting
and a terrace for
relaxed, al fresco
eating in summer.
Fine Turkish cuisine
and attentive,
courteous and
efficient service.*
🍽🛗🏧

**Ece Bar
& Restaurant**
◆ **A** D3
Tramway Cad. 104
Kuruçeşme
Tel. (0212) 265 96 00
Open daily
8am–1.30am
*The owners of this
restaurant serve
specialties from
their own region
and the Aegean
coast (dishes cooked
in olive oil). In
summer the roof
of the dining room
opens up and you
can enjoy the
gentle breeze and
the views over the
Bosphorus.*
🍽🛗🚿🏧

Filiz Restaurant
◆ **A** D2
Çepelıköy Cad. 80
Tarabya
Tel. (0212) 262 01 52
Open daily
8am–2am

*The best-known
restaurant in Tarabya,
in a lovely wooden
house on a marina.
This restaurant is
good by any
standards. Excellent
fish dishes.
Specialties: fillets,
squid and shrimps.*
🍽🚿🏧

Iskele Restaurant
◆ **A** D3
Rumeli Hisarı Vapur
Iskelesi
Tel. (0212) 263 29 97
Open noon–5pm
and 6pm–2am
*Built on the old
pier, this restaurant
has a terrace
looking out over
the Bosphorus.
Huge choice of fish
and a selection of
delicious mezes.*
🛗🚿🗂

Kılçık Balıkçı
◆ **A** D3
Muallim Naci Cad.
130, Kuruçeşme
Tel. (0212) 287 10 24
Open noon–midnight
*Smart new restaurant
with beautiful views
of the Bosphorus.*
🚿🏧

Osmanli
◆ **A** D3
Kuruçeşme Cad. 42,
Kuruçeşme
Beşiktaş
Tel. (0212) 287 01 01
Open daily
10am–9pm
*Recommended
for breakfast and
dinner. Light cuisine
with Ottoman-style
köfte.*
🏧

Pafuli Restaurant
◆ **A** D3
Kuruçeşme Cad. 116
Kuruçeşme
Beşiktaş
Tel. (0212) 263 66 38
or 263 25 11
Open daily
9am–10pm
*Restaurant serving
specialties from Laz,
on the shores of the
Black Sea in northern
Turkey. Popular
with both local
and international*

◆ USEFUL ADDRESSES
ŞİŞLİ

celebrities, well-known intellectuals and politicians, for its stunning view over the Bosphorus, its excellent service and of course for its delicious cuisine. The dishes are based on Black Sea fish such as hamsi (a kind of anchovy) and alabalık (trout). Try the muhlama (a dish made with melted cheese) as a first course and the laz böreği (a warm specialty dessert made with honey) to finish. The homemade corn bread filled with hamsi is out of this world.
▢ ▥ ▥ P ▣

Palet 2
◆ A D2
Yeniköy Cad. 80
Tarabya
Tel. (0212) 262 02 20
Open daily
noon–midnight
This famous floating restaurant has a v ery pleasant atmosphere. Good choice of alcoholic drinks. Specialties: lüfer (bluefish), turbot.
▢ ▦

Pescatore Restaurant
◆ A D2
Kefeliköy Cad. 29/A
Kireçburnu
Tel. (0212) 223 18 19
Open daily
noon–midnight
Large fish restaurant offering a wide choice of dishes in a well chosen setting.
▢ ▥ ▦

Sirene Restaurant
◆ A D1
Mezarburnu Cad. 2
Sarıyer
Tel. (0212) 242 26 21
Open daily
10am–11pm
Carefully prepared and inventive dishes of numerous kinds of fish. This is one of the best restaurants

of its kind in the entire city. Specialty: balık kavurma.
▢ ▥ ▦

Sunset Ulus Grill, Bar & Restaurant
◆ A D3
Adnan Saygın Cad.
Yol Sok.
Ulus Parkı-Ulus 2
Tel. (0212) 287 03 57
Open daily noon–3pm and 7–9pm
The terrace of this restaurant has a splendid view over the Bosphorus. The Sunset Ulus is one of the most fashionable

PERA PALAS, KADIKÖY

restaurants in Istanbul. Specialty: sarma piliç, chicken with vegetables and mushrooms.
▢ ▯ ▲ ▥ ▦

Yeni Güneş Restaurant
◆ A D3
Cevdet Paşa Cad. 73
Küçük Bebek
Bebek
Tel. (0212) 263 38 23
Situated in an upmarket district of Istanbul, this restaurant looks out over the Bosphorus. It serves delicious freshly prepared mezes.
▢ ▥ ▣

→ CAFÉ
Bar of the Bebek Hotel
◆ A D3
Cevdet Paşa Cad. 113–115
Bebek
Tel. (0212) 263 30 00
Open daily
10am–10pm
A contemplative atmosphere pervades this unusually relaxing establishment. Its terrace overlooks the marina and has the advantage of being a good distance away from the road.
▲ ▥

ŞİŞLİ

→ RESTAURANTS
Efulli
◆ A C3 C D2-E1
Cumhuriyet Cad. 12/C
Tel. (0212) 247 35 68
Open daily
10am–11pm
This restaurant, where desserts are something of a specialty, offers traditional grilled meats served with pilav or vegetables. Delicious breakfasts are also served.
▯ ▯

Sehzane
◆ A C3
Açık Hava Tyatrosu

Demokrasi Park içi
Harbiye-Maçka
Tel. (0212) 231 79 09
Open daily
24 hours.
Turkish and Ottoman grilled meats are the specialties. Also excellent gozleme (flat bread with cheese or spinach toppings). Tranquil location in Maçka Park.
▯ ▦

→ HOTELS
Büyük Londra Oteli
◆ C B3
Meşrutiyet Cad. 117
Tepebaşı
Tel. (0212) 245 06 71
or 293 16 19
Fax (0212) 245 06 71
This hotel, was established in 1892. Its 54 rooms and 12 suites are very comfortable, and the service is impeccable. Bar on the first floor.
▢ ▯ ▣ ▯

✪ Pera Palace
◆ C B3
Meşrutiyet Cad. 98/100
Tepebaşı
Tel. (0212) 251 45 60
Fax (0212) 251 40 88
www.perapalas.com
This splendid hotel was designed as luxury accomodation targeted specifically to passengers from the Orient Express, and opened in 1892. Many famous guests, ranging from Greta Garbo to General Tito, have passed through its doors. It also inspired crime writer Agatha Christie, who wrote "Death on the Orient Express" there. The Pera Palace is virtually a national monument.
▢ ▯ ▣ ▥ ▯ ▲ ▥ P ▦
Restaurant of the Pera Palace
◆ 358.

HOTELS
- `⊡` < $50
- `⊡` $50 to $100
- `⊡` $100 to $200
- `⊞` > $200

Richmond
◆ **C** C3-D2
Istiklâl Cad. 445
Tünel / Beyoğlu
Tel. (0212) 252 54 60
Fax (0212) 252 97 07
Because the street on which it is located is closed to traffic, this hotel is very quiet. Some of the rooms overlook the Bosphorus. The hotel has two restaurants, the Café Lebon and Blue Cat, and a bar as well.
108 rooms.
⊟ ▣ ▤ ⊛ ⊪ ⊅ ⬆ ☒
🅿 ⊡

→ RESTAURANTS
Bilsak
◆ **C** D3
Soğanci Sok. 7
Cihangir Beyoğlu
Tel. (0212) 293 37 74
Open Mon.–Sat
10am–11.30pm
The windows of this café-bar-restaurant look out onto the Bosphorus. Its fine international cuisine (pasta, mixed salads, brownies, etc. feature on the menu) make it popular with Istanbul's affluent gay community. A lively atmosphere, with music and DJ every night.
🗐 ⊠ ⊞

Cafeteria of the Galata Tower
◆ **C** B5
Galata Tower, 9th fl.
Galata Kulesi Sok.
Karaköy
Tel. (0212) 293 81 80
Open daily
9am–8pm.
Closed Mon.
Located at a height of 174 feet, this restaurant offers superb views of the northern shore of the Golden Horn. Crepes, cakes, sandwiches (chicken, cheese and other filliwngs) and soups are served. No alcohol. Drinks: from 1 million TRL.
🗐 ⊠

Çiçek Pasaji
◆ **C** C3
Istiklâl Cad.
Galatasaray
Open daily
11.30am–1am
An ancient alley with a profusion of flowers, where a number of popular restaurants offering good simple cooking are located.
⊟ ⊠

Daphne Mediterranee
◆ **C** D2
Çukurlu Çesme Sok.
18 Taksim–Beyoğlu
Tel. (0212) 244 26 16
Open daily
11am–11pm
Restaurant serving a wide variety of Arab, Kurdish and Turkish seafood dishes.
🗐 ⊠

Evim
◆ **C** D2
Büyük Parmakkapı
sok 2/1
Beyoğlu
Tel. (0212) 293 40 25
Open daily
9am–11pm
Especially popular with young people, this restaurant serves simple, good food prepared by Talip Sentürk. The menu features Manty dishes (a kind of ravioli) and grilled meats. Especially recommended are the Bon Steak Evim (in a cheese and herb sauce), the mushrooms and spinach and the Laz-style pastries (with herbs and spices from the region of the Black Sea). Prices are very reasonable.
⊠

Haci Abdullah
◆ **C** C1-C2
Sakizağacı Cad. 19
Beyoğlu
Tel. (0212) 244 85 61
Open daily

CAFÉ LEBON, HOTEL RICHMOND, BEYOĞLU

11.30am–10pm
Located in a street that is at right angles to the tram line leading to Istiklal. Very pleasant interior design and excellent food (the stewed fruit is particularly delicious). Reasonable prices.
⊟ ⊠

Haci Baba Restaurant
◆ **C** D2
Istiklâl Cad. 49,
Taksim
Tel. (0212) 244 18 86
Open daily
10am–11pm
Extremely popular restaurant with well presented dishes and an impressive choice of desserts. Pleasant terrace. Specialties: mantarci sote (grilled mushrooms) and tandir kebab.
⊟ ⊠

Karakaş
◆ **C** D2
Istiklâl Cad.
Mis Sok. 14, Beyoğlu
Tel. (0212) 249 78 61
Open daily
10am–9.30pm
Small restaurant with a regular clientele. Five to six dishes are on offer every day; they include Turkish gratins, moussaka and white meat dishes served with pilau rice or bulgur wheat. If you want to try these specials make a point of arriving before 8pm, as there is usually nothing left after that time except kebabs.
⊡

Lades
◆ **C** C3
Istiklâl Cad.
Ayhan Işık Sok. 14
Galatasaray
Tel. (0212) 250 32 03
or 249 52 08
Open daily
10.30am–10.30pm
Restaurant serving Turkish specialties, including a great variety of delicious gratins. Quick, friendly service. Affluent clientele.
🗐 ⊠

Lale Iskemecisi
◆ **C** C3-D2
Istiklâl Cad. 238
Beyoğlu
Tel. (0212) 244 04 51
Open daily 24 hours
Ever since 1960, Lale Iskemecisi has been preparing the best soups, seasoned with chives, garlic and vinegar.
🗐 ⊠

Medi Şark Sofrasi
◆ **C** D2
Istiklâl Cad.
Küçük Parmakkapı

Sok. 46, Beyoğlu
Tel. (0212) 252 75 32
Open Mon.–Sat.
11am–10pm
*Local cuisine at
very reasonable
prices. Good,
generous dishes
of grilled meats,
with vegetables
and bulgur wheat.
Try the homemade*
salgam, *a Kurdish
drink made from
turnips.*
◼◼ ◼

Nature & Peace
◆ C D2
Istiklâl Cad.
Büyük Parmakappı
Sok. 21, Taksim
Tel. (0212) 252 86 09
Open Mon.–Sat.
11am–9pm
*Just a few steps
away from the
busy Istiklâl Caddesi,
this small vegetarian
restaurant offers
delicious white meat
dishes and crisp,
fresh salads.
A selection of
newspapers are
provided by
the establishment.*
◼◼ ◼

Parsifal
◆ C D2
Istiklâl Cad.
Kurabiye Sok. Taksim
Tel. (0212) 245 25 88
Open daily
noon–11pm
*Vegetarian
restaurant, meaning
that no red meat is
served although
the vegetables may
be mixed with
chicken or other
white meat.
Specialty: vegetable
pastry* proski böregi.
Moderate prices.
◼◼ ◼

Pazartesi
◆ C D2
Abdullah Sok. 9
Beyoğlu
Tel. (0212) 292 07 47
Open Mon.–Sat.
10.30am–10pm
*This restaurant offers
Caucasian specialties
prepared by Şelale
Yılal and Nesrin Uthu.
Try the* çerkès tavuğu

*(chicken in a white
sauce), the* Turşusu
*or the various savory
pastries (with
spinach, cheese and
other fillings), all
served with rakı.
This small restaurant
can be booked for
special events, and
Caucasian musicians
are provided free of
charge.*
◼◼ ◼◼ ◼

Refik's
◆ C B4
Sofyali Sok. 10
Tünel, Asmalı Mescit
Tel. (0212) 243 28 34
Open daily
noon–midnight
*Specialties from the
Black Sea region:
these include stuffed
red cabbage leaves,
mezes with hamsi, a
small Black Sea fish
similar to a sardine
but with a subtler
flavor.*
◼◼ ◼

Rejans
◆ C C3
Emir Nevruz Sok. 17
Galatasaray
Tel. (0212) 244 16 10
Open daily
noon–3pm and
6.30–11.30pm
*This restaurant was
opened by White
Russians after 1917
and it is still run by
the same family.
The menu features
Russian and Turkish
specialties. It is
located near the law
courts and is a
favorite among many
of Istanbul's
intellectuals.
Concerts of Georgian
music Fri., Sat. and
Sun.*
◼◼ ◼◼ ◼

**✪ Restaurant of the
Pera Palace Hotel**
◆ C B3
Pera Palace Hotel
Meşrutiyet Cad.
98–100 Tepebaşı
Tel. (0212) 251 45 60
Open noon–3pm
and 7–11.30pm
*Undoubtedly the
most beautiful
restaurant in*

*Istanbul. Fantastic
period décor
with sumptuous
ornamentation and
engravings. Very
reasonable prices.
Orchestra. Not to
be missed.*
◼◼ ◼◼ ◼

Yakup 2
◆ C B3-B4
Asmalımescit Cad.
35, Taksim 37
Galatasaray
Tel. (0212) 249 29 25
Open Mon.–Sat.
noon–1am,
Sun. 7pm–1am
*Not far from the
Pera Palace Hotel.
Warm rustic
atmosphere.
Renowned for its
succulent gratins
such as beef and
mushroom gratin.*
◼◼ ◼

Zencefil
◆ C D2
Kurabiye Sokak 3
Beyoğlu
Tel. (0212) 244 40 82
Open Mon.–Sat.
noon–9pm
*Small vegetarian
restaurant serving
a wide range of tasty
quiches and amazing
drinks made from
various herbs.*
◼◼ ◼

→ CAFÉS
Dinyar Cafe
◆ A D4
Caferağa Mah.
Moda Cad.
Dumulu Pînar Sok. 11
Kadıköy
Open daily
9am–11pm
*Café set in a quiet
garden. On the first
floor, you can play
Turkish games or
cards. No snacks.*
◼

**Passeport Cafe
Ve Bar**
◆ A D4
Mühürdar Cad. 62/A
Kadıköy
Open daily
2.30pm–3am
*Enjoy a drink or a
meal of grilled meats
while listening to*

*music. This bar
often puts on quality
concerts. A variety
of traditional music
(ranging from Turkish,
and Kurdish to Laz
and Georgian) is
played here. There
is also a dance floor.
Friendly atmosphere.*
◼

Vagzal Kahve
◆ C C2
Sakızağacı Cad. 25
Galatasaray
Tel. (0212) 249 70 48
Open daily 8am–2am
*Customers come
to smoke hookahs
here as well as to
enjoy sandwiches
and cakes.*
◼

→ NIGHTLIFE
Alman Bira Evi
◆ C D2
Istiklâl Cad.
Imam Adnan Sok. 10
Taksim
Tel. (0212) 251 69 38
Open daily
2pm–2am
*This café has a
billiard room and
projection room, as
well as a terrace with
a view over the city.
Jazz, blues and rock
concerts are put on
here. Turkish meals
are also served.*
◼◼ ◼ ◼

Artos
◆ C C3
Istiklâl Cad. 212
(1st basement of
the Aznavur Pasajı)
Galatasaray
Tel. (0212) 251 75 48
Open daily
10am–midnight
*Diverse clientele
and cosy ambience.
Pop concert during
the week and
Anatolian music
at weekends.*
◼◼ ◼

Bedaliza Sanat Evi
◆ C D2
Istiklâl Cad.
Imam Adnan Sok. 22,
Beyoğlu
Tel. (0212) 244 18 45
Open daily
2pm–3am

HOTELS
- ⊡ < $50
- ⊡ $50 to $100
- ⊞ $100 to $200
- ⊞ > $200

Concert 9pm–2am
*Traditional Turkish
music. Food (mostly
meat dishes) is also
available.
£10/$15*
🔲🎵

Hayal Kahvesi
◆ **C** D2
Istiklâl Cad.
Büyük Parmakkapı
Sok. 27, Beyoğlu
Tel. (0212) 244 25 58
Open daily
2pm–2am
*Concerts every night:
pop, rock, jazz, etc.
£10/$14*
🔲🎵

Jazz Stopp
◆ **C** D2
Büyük Parmakkapı
Sok. 9/15
Beyoğlu
Tel. (0212) 252 93 14
Open daily
2.30pm–3am
*Opened in 1992,
this bar has built its
reputation on the
quality of the
concerts that it puts
on. Different type of
music every day:
jazz, blues, rock,
folk performed by
Turkish or foreign
musicians. Light
snacks are available.
Drinks from £2/$3.
An admission fee
of £2.50/$3.60 is
charged for some
concerts.*
🔲🎵

Munzur Cafe
◆ **C** D2
Hasnun Galip Sok.
21/A
Galatasaray kulubü
Sok., Beyoğlu
Tel. (0212) 245 46 69
Open daily 2pm–2am
*A predominantly
Turkish clientele and
a good atmosphere.
Traditional music
and dance floor.*
🔲

Roxy
◆ **C** D3
Sıraselviler Cad.
Aslanyatağı Sok. 7
Cihangir
Tel. (0212) 249 13 01
Open Tue.–Sun.
10pm–4am

*Fashionable
place that can
accommodate up
to 300 people. Busy
at weekends. Live
music. Acid, jazz,
blues, salsa and
concerts.*
🔲🎵

SapphoRoxy
◆ **C** D2
Istiklâl Cad.
Bekar Sok. 14
Taksim
Tel. (0212) 245 06 68
Open daily
2pm–2am
*This wine bar
serves over 50
Turkish wines and
meze. Cellar-type
décor with brick
walls and a display
of bottles. It attracts
a youngish clientele,
who come for the
eclectic music.*
🔲🎵

Şarabi
◆ **C** C3
Istiklâl Cad. 174
Galatasaray
Tel. (0212) 244 46 09
Open daily noon–2am
*This bar is located
on three levels. The
basement resembles
a cistern with vaulted
ceiling and rough
stone walls. A
particular type of
music (Greek, Cuban,
etc.) is selected
and played for the
whole year. Wide
choice of Turkish
wines, including the
homemade Şarabi,
and a few dishes.
£10–15/$15–22*
🔲

Taksim Sanat Evi
◆ **C** D2-D3
Sıraselviler Cad.
69/1, Taksim
Tel. (0212) 244 25 26

Open daily
12.30pm–4am
*Disco, bar and
restaurant. Famous
for its transvestite
floor shows. From
the spacious dining
room there are
mesmerizing views
over the Bosphorus
The good hot or cold
food that is served
adds to the pleasure
of attending the live
concerts given by
local and
international
celebrities.*
🎭

→ **SHOPPING**
✪ **Hacı Bekir**
◆ **C** D2
Istiklâl Cad. 7
Tel. (0212) 244 28 04
Open daily 9am–9pm
*The first Bekir store
was opened as long
ago as 1817. In 1820
it was renamed Hacı
(the name given to
someone who has
made the pilgrimage
to Mecca) and it then
became the main
supplier to the court
of Sultan Abdülhamid
II. Tradition continues
to prevail, so that
to this day Hacı Bekir
still enjoys the
reputation of being
best maker of Turkish
delight and other
akide şekeri (chewy
sweets).*

--- **TAKSIM** ---
--- **NIŞANTAŞI** ---

→ **HOTELS**
Divan
◆ **C** D2-E1
Cumhuriyet Cad. 2
Taksim
Tel. (0212) 231 41 00

Fax (0212) 248 85 27
*Comfort is a priority
here: spacious rooms
with double glazing,
air conditioning,
marble bathrooms,
satellite television,
and all the amenities
you'd expect from a
quality hotel.
Bars and restaurants.
180 rooms, 11 suites.*
🔲🔲🔲🔲🔲🔲
Divan restaurant
◆ *360*

Eresin Taxim Hotel
◆ **C** D1
Topçu Cad. 34
Taksim
Tel. (0212) 256 08 03
Fax (0212) 253 22 47
www.eresintaxim.
com.tr
*Bright rooms with
air-conditioning,
minibar, and satellite
television. Large
conference room
available on the lower
floor. Bar and
restaurants.
75 rooms.*
🔲🔲🔲🔲🔲🔲

Feronya
◆ **C** D1
Abdülhakhamitt Cad.
70–72
Tel. (0212) 237 26 35
Fax (0212) 237 26 35
*Although the rooms
are small, this new
hotel, with its modern
décor, is comfortable
and has the
advantage of being
located away from
heavy traffic.*
🔲🔲🔲🔲

Hilton
◆ **C** D2-E1
Cumhuriyet Cad.
Harbiye
Tel. (0212) 231 46 50
Fax (0212) 240 41 65
*Large hotel complex
with 498 rooms,
4 restaurants, 3 bars,
shops, 2 tennis
courts and 2 squash
courts, a casino
and all the facilities
you'd expect from a
Hilton hotel.
498 rooms, 15 suites.
Breakfast not
included.*
🔲🔲🔲🔲🔲🔲🔲🔲
🔲🔲🔲🔲🔲

RESTAURANTS
🅭 < $4
🅭 $4–$7.5
🅭 $7.5–$10
🅭 > $10

Hyatt Regency
◆ C E1
Taşkışla Cad.
Tel. (0212) 225 70 00
Fax (0212) 225 70 07
www.istanbul.hyatt.
com
This is the latest
luxury international
hotel to be built in
the area, with
sumptuous Oriental-
style décor and
generously
proportioned rooms.
The excellent
restaurants serve
Turkish, Asian and
Italian food.
Minibars in rooms.
360 rooms, 28 suites
Breakfast not
included.
🔲🔲🔲🔲🔲🔲🔲🔲
🔲🔲🔲🔲🔲

HILTON, TAKSIM

Kervansaray
◆ C D1
Şehit Muhtar Bey
Cad. 61
Taksim
Tel. (0212) 235 50 00
Fax (0212) 253 43 78
A beautiful, new
four-star hotel near
Taksim Square in the
center of Beyofilu.
Particular attention
has been paid to
the decoration and
to such conveniences
as satellite television,
hairdryers and a
laundry service.
Two restaurants,
lounge, bar and
discotheque.
🔲🔲🔲🔲🔲🔲

HYATT REGENCY, TAKSIM

Lamartine
◆ C D1
Lamartin Cad. 25
Tel. (0212) 254 62 70
Fax (0212) 256 27 76
Notable for its marble
hall. The rooms are
simply decorated
but comfortably
appointed. Good
room service.
🔲🔲🔲🔲🔲🔲

HYATT REGENCY, TAKSIM

Nippon Hotel
◆ C D1
Topçu Cad. 10
Tel. (0212) 254 99 00
Fax (0212) 250 45 53
Small but
comfortable rooms.
There is also a
sauna, terrace

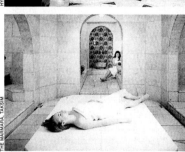

THE MARMARA, TAKSIM

THE MARMARA, TAKSIM

and small outdoor
swimming pool. Top-
quality service.
🔲🔲🔲🔲🔲🔲🔲🔲

The Marmara
◆ C D2
Taksim Square
Tel. (0212) 251 46 96
Fax (0212) 252 77 01
www.themarmara.
com.tr
This grand hotel
has 18 floors and
looks out over the
modern town of
Beyofilu. The simply
decorated rooms are
comfortable and
there is a hammam,
sauna, swimming
pool, casino and
patisserie. An
establishment with a
high level of luxury.
Three restaurants:
Panorama Restaurant
(7pm–midnight),
Brasserie (6.30am–
11pm) and Café
Marmara (7.30am–
1.30am), and 3 bars.
376 rooms, 15 suites.
Breakfast not
included.
🔲🔲🔲🔲🔲🔲🔲
🔲🔲🔲🔲

Vardar Palace
◆ C D2-D3
Sıraselviler Cad. 54
Taksim
Tel. (0212) 252 28 88
Fax (0212) 252 15 27
www.vardarhotel.
com
Small, moderately
priced hotel in the
bar and nightclub
district of Istanbul.
Definitely an ideal
place for night owls.
40 rooms.
🔲🔲🔲🔲🔲🔲🔲🔲🔲
🔲

→ RESTAURANTS
Divan Pub
◆ C D2-E1
Divan Hotel
Cumhuriyet Cad. 2
Harbiye
Tel. (0212) 231 41 00
Open Mon.–Fri.
noon–3pm and
7–11.30pm,
Sat. 7–11.30pm
Something of an old
world, colonial
atmosphere pervades

HOTELS
- ▫ < $50
- ▣ $50 to $100
- ▨ $100 to $200
- ▦ > $200

this beautiful restaurant, which is considered to be one of Istanbul's best. The food served in the pub is the same as in the restaurant, although at cheaper prices. The specialty is kebab in yoghurt.
▣ 🅿 🎵 ▦

Down Town Bar-Restaurant
◆ **A** D3
Abdi Ipekçi Cad. 7
Nişantaşı
Tel. (0212) 224 39 15
Open Mon.–Sat.
noon–midnight
Located in the same district as the smart European, American and Turkish clothes shops. The restaurant has a modern décor and specializes in Turkish nouvelle cuisine: particularly prominent on the menu are vegetable dishes (eggplant, tomatoes, peppers, carrots and green vegetables), which are invariably fresh and always served cooked, often grilled.
▣ 🎵 ⚡

Mezzaluna
◆ **A** D3
Abdi Ipekçi Cad.
Nişantaşı
Tel. (0212) 232 72 16
Open 12.30pm–midnight
Part of a small international chain of Italian restaurants, the Mezzaluna has a good reputation. The clientele includes many local celebrities.
▣ ⚡

Panorama
◆ **C** D2
The Marmara Hotel
20th floor
Taksim Meydanı
Tel. (0212) 251 46 96
Open 11am–midnight
A restaurant with a unique view of Istanbul. The city is literally at your feet as you dine in superb style. A pianist

performs every evening. This is a luxury restaurant with affordable prices. Specialty: fillet steak with three kinds of peppers.
▣ ⚖ 🅿 ▦

✿ Park Restaurant
◆ **C** E2
Dünya Sağlık Sok. 27
Tel. (0212) 245 38 73
Open 11am–midnight
Just behind the Marmara Hotel. Very pleasant terrace looking out onto a quiet street. The food is marvelous and the atmosphere unique. Recommended. Specialty: manti (raviolis).
▣ ⬆ ⚡

Rendez-Vous Restaurant
◆ **C** D1
Lamartin Cad. 7
Tel. (0212) 255 33 62
Open daily
noon–midnight
A perfect and courteous welcome in a richly decorated dining room. The dishes are meticulously presented and the portions are quite generous. Specialties: bluefish and fillets.
▣ ⚡

Susam
◆ **C** E3-E4
Susam Sok. 6
Cihangir, Taksim
Tel. (0212) 231 59 35
or 36
Just 10 minutes' walk from Taksim Square. Excellent food is served in a spacious area planted with trees.
▣ ⚡ ▦

Tatbak Kebab Salonu
◆ **A** D3
Akkavak 28/A
Nişantaşı
Tel. (0212) 248 04 25
Open Mon.–Sat.
11am–4pm and
7.30–9pm

Very welcoming with a wide choice of kebabs and rapid service.
▣ ⚡

Yekta Restaurant
◆ **A** D3
Valikonağı Cad. 39/1
Nişantaşı
Tel. (0212) 296 11 12
Open daily
noon–midnight
Eggplants, peppers and onions are hung up to dry from the ceiling. The dining room is refreshingly shaded and has a convivial atmosphere. At lunchtime the restaurant attracts local businessmen.
▣ ⚖ 🅿 ⚡

→ NIGHTLIFE
Exin Bar
◆ **C** D2
Sıraselviler Cad. 103
Taksim
Tel. (0212) 292 22 59
Open daily
7pm–4am
A young crowd comes here for the pleasant garden and reasonable prices. Admission fee Fri.–Sat.
▣ ⚡

Hayal Kahvesi
◆ **C** D2
Büyük Parmakkapı
Sok. Beyoğlu
Tel. (0212) 243 33 57
Open noon–3am
In a small street, this rock bar hosts shows by famous Turkish groups.
🎵

Kemansi Bar
◆ **C** D3
Sıraselviler Cad. 69
Cihangir
Tel. (0212) 251 30 15
Open daily
2pm–4am (bar) and 8pm–4am (discotheque)
Tarkan shot his Şıkıdım Şıkıdım scene on the first floor of this three-storey bar. Fine view of the Bosphorus. Concerts and plays.
▣ 🎵 ⚖

Roxy Bar and Disco
◆ **C** D2-D3
Aslanyatağı Sok.
Sıracevizler Cad.
Tel. (0212) 231 41 00
Open daily
9pm–6am
Bar and nightclub renowned in Istanbul. Busy at weekends. Live music. Admission fee.
▣ 🎵

Sdd
◆ **C** D2
Sıraselviler Cad.
Billurcu Sok. 25
Taksim
Tel. (0212) 244 24 82
Open Mon.–Sat.
5pm–midnight
Landmark of the Sinema Sevenler Derneği (Association of Cinema Lovers). One can be admitted as a mısafir (guest). Its luxurious surroundings and garden terrace are jealously guarded behind iron gates. Among regular customers are figures from the Turkish movie and theater world. Writers, including Yaşar Kemal, also frequent this venue.
▣ ⚡ ⬆

Sefahathane
◆ **C** C3
Atlas Pasajı Girisi
Istiklâl Cad.
Galatasaray
Tel. (0212) 251 22 45
Open daily
10am–2am
As darkness falls, the Sefahathane fills to capacity with a crowd of dancers moving to the sounds of jazz and acid-pop. Lively atmosphere.
▣ 🎵

Taksim Boğaz Çay Bakcesi
◆ **C** E2
Taksim Park
Tel. (0212) 243 23 53
Open daily
24 hours.
An ideal place to relax or throw a

◆USEFUL ADDRESSES
THE BOSPHORUS, ASIAN SHORE

RESTAURANTS
- ■ < $4
- ■ $4–$7.5
- ■ $7.5–$10
- ■ > $10

party. It also commands a wide view of the Bosphorus and of the Asian shore.

→ CAFÉ
Sütiş Taksim
◆ **C** D2
Istiklâl Cad. 7 (Taksim Square)
Tel. (0212) 251 32 70
Open daily
6am–2am
This traditional café and pâtisserie also serves delicious and satisfying breakfasts. Specialties: su boregi (cheese pastry) and sûtlaç (rice pudding). Breakfast: £5–10/ $7–15

ÜSKÜDAR

→ RESTAURANTS
Huzur
◆ **F** A2
Salacak Iskelesi 20
Üsküdar
Tel. (0216) 333 31 57
Open daily
noon–1am
Restaurant serving fish and red meat dishes and offering a wide choice of hot and cold meze. The terrace commands an open view over the Bosphorus, the heights of the Taksim district and Sultanahmet. Unfortunately, the service tends to be a little slow.

Kanaat Restaurant
◆ **F** C1
Selmanipak Cad. 25
Tel. (0216) 333 37 91
Open daily
6.30am–12.30am
This traditional Turkish restaurant offers plenty of choice as far as food is concerned. However, it does not serve alcohol.

Kiz Kulesi
◆ **F** A1-B1
Deniz restaurant
Seraglio Bar
Sahil Yolu
Salacak, Üsküdar
Tel. (0216) 341 04 03
Open daily
noon–1am
The fish restaurant on the second floor serves a wide range of meze. Quite apart from the food, the Kiz Kulesi is well worth a visit for its marble and brick décor and for the view of Leander's Tower from the terrace. Bar on the first floor.

SPLENDID PALAS HOTEL, BÜYÜKADA

THE PRINCES' ISLANDS

→ HOTELS
✪ **Merit Halki Palace**
◆ **A** E6
Refah Şehitleri Cad. 88, Heybeliada
Tel. (0216) 351 88 90
Fax (0216) 351 84 83
Closed Sep.–May
The Merit Halki Palace is widely considered to be the best hotel on the Princes' Islands. The beautiful wooden Ottoman house is surrounded by gardens and looks out over the sea. Its comfortable

rooms are in keeping with the Ottoman decoration, which is tastefully based on the many colors of traditional Turkish kilims. There is also a hammam, sauna, jacuzzi and open-air swimming pool. 45 rooms.

Princess
◆ **A** E6
Iskele Meydanı 2
Büyükada
Tel. (0216) 382 16 28
Fax (0216) 382 19 49
The Princess, located in the magical setting of the Princes' Islands, offers all the comforts, conveniences and services associated with a luxury hotel, including a good restaurant, swimming pool, bar, disco, casino and games room.

Splendid Palaş Hotel
◆ **A** E6
23 Nisan Cad. 71
Büyükada
Tel. (0216) 382 69 50
Fax (0216) 382 67 75
Closed Oct.–May

This majestic white building, which is crowned by two cupolas, has all the charm of old buildings coupled with the comfort of a modern hotel. The beautiful swimming pool and a pleasant view are additional features, as well as a restaurant and a bar. 70 rooms.

→ RESTAURANT
Kaptan Restaurant
◆ **A** E6
Liman Çıkmazı Sok. 11/A, Büyükada
Tel. (0216) 382 34 16
Open 10am–midnight
Situated on the promenade of the main island near the ferry dock. Superb views and a warm welcome. Specialty: turbot.

THE BOSPHORUS ASIAN SHORE

→ HOTEL
Bosphorus Paşa
◆ **A** D4
Yaliboyu Cad. 67
Beylerbeyi
Tel. (0216) 422 00 03
Fax (0216) 422 00 12
A 19th-century Ottoman house that has been converted into a hotel. Well-appointed rooms. Ideal location by the Beylerbeyi Palace on the Asian shore of the Bosphorus.

→ RESTAURANTS
Çecconi's
◆ **A** D4
Bosphorus Paşa
Yaliboyu Cad. 64
Beylerbeyi
Tel. (0216) 422 00 03
Open daily
noon–11pm
This restaurant has refined Italian cuisine and quality service. A boat can bring you here from the

HOTELS
· < $50
·· $50 to $100
··· $100 to $200
···· > $200

Çırağan Palace Hotel, by arrangement until 9pm. The dining area, located in the building that once housed the ferries crossing the Bosphorus, is at sea level. There is no terrace but the windows have a view of the constant traffic of passing boats.
□☼

Çengelkoy Iskele Restaurant
◆ A D3
Iskele Meydanı
Çengelkoy
Tel. (0216) 321 55 06
Open daily
noon–3pm and
6pm–midnight
A good fish restaurant situated on the Asian shore of the Bosphorus.
□☼▪

Hasir-Beykoz
◆ A E2
Abraham Paşa
Beykorusu içi 2
Beykoz
Tel. (0216) 322 29 01
Open daily
noon–midnight
Situated in the middle of a forest, which is rather unusual here, this restaurant serves excellent cuisine. The desserts are particularly delicious. A live band plays on Friday and Saturday.
□♫♪▪

Kavak Doğanay Restaurant
◆ A E1
Yalı Cad. 13
Anadolu Kavağı
Tel. (0216) 320 20 36
Open daily
11.30am–11pm
This is the most inviting establishment on the Anadolu Kavağı promenade. The service is discreet and efficient, and all kinds of fish and shellfish are served. Specialty: hot shrimps.
□☼▪

Korfez Restaurant
◆ A D3-E3
Korfez Cad. 78
Kanlıca
Tel. (0216) 413 43 14
Open daily
noon–3pm and
7pm–midnight
An elegant restaurant with a view over the Bosphorus and a terrace for dining in the open air during the summer. The cuisine is good, with fish the specialty. The restaurant has its own boat to ferry guests across the Bosphorus (by prior arrangement; departure opposite Rumeli Hisarı).
□⬆☼P▤▦

PRINCES' ISLANDS

BURSA MARKET

Sunset Balik Çubuklu
◆ A E6
Beykoz,
Burunbahçe–
Çubuklu
Tel. (0216) 425 07 22
This is a relatively new fish restaurant, situated on the Asian shore. The restaurant lays on a small private boat to transport guests across the Bosphorus from Istinye.
▦

IZNIK

→ RESTAURANT
Kirikçatal Restaurant
Göl Kıyısı
Tel. (0224) 757 12 02
Open daily
10am–11pm
Located in a quiet and isolated spot near Lake Iznik. A good fish restaurant.
□☼▪

BURSA

→ HOTELS
Almira
Ulubatlı Hasan
Bulvarı 5
Tel. (0224) 250 20 01
Fax (0224) 255 64 54
The Almira Hotel
has a 5 restaurants in addition to a wide range of other facilities, including a casino, nightclub, squash and tennis courts, a sauna and a swimming pool. The spacious air-conditioned rooms are comfortable even though they are not insulated from the noise from the rather busy street on which this hotel stands.
Ⅲ≋▪

Çelik Palace
Çekirge Cad. 79
Tel. (0224) 233 38 00
Fax (0224) 236 19 10
Located in a western suburb of Çekirge, this is a very high-quality establishment. Breakfast is not included.
▦

→ RESTAURANTS
Iskender Kebabçi
Heykel
Ünlü Cad. 7
Tel. (224) 221 46 15
Open 11am–9pm
The specialty of this establishment is Iskender kebab (grilled meat served on flat bread with plain yoghurt).
▪

Yusuf Restaurant
Kulturpark içi
Tel. (0224) 223 17 70
Open daily
11am–midnight
This restaurant has an open-air setting on a shady terrace in a park. Specialty: avci berefii.
□♦▪

→ NIGHTLIFE
Star
Bursa casino
nightclub
Inönü Cad. 113/E
Tel. (0224) 254 30 32
Open daily
11pm–4am
There is a bar and games room on the first floor, and a spacious bar and concert room in the basement where, Turkish stars perform.
□♫

EDIRNE

→ HOTEL
Yener
Demirciler Cad. 1
Kesan
Tel. (0284) 714 36 60
Fax (0284) 714 57 55
Breakfast and room with television available for an extra charge.
□▣P☼·

◆ PLACES TO VISIT

Places to visit are listed in alphabetical order under each town.
The ▲ symbol refers to the "Itineraries" section, and the ◆ symbol to the map section.

ISTANBUL

ADAM MICKIEWICZ MUSEUM (ADAM MICKIEWICZ MÜZESI) Bostan Mahalesi Serdar Ömer Paşa Sok. Tatlı Badem Sok. 23 Kurtuluş-Beyoğlu Tel. (0212) 253 66 98	*Open Wed.–Sun. 9am–5pm.*	◆ **C** C1
ARAP CAMI'I	*See Mosque of the Arabs.*	▲ 254
ARCHEOLOGICAL MUSEUM (ARKEOLOJI MÜZESI) Topkapı Palace, Sultanahmet Tel. (0212) 520 77 40	*Open Tue.–Sun. 9.30am–4.30pm.*	▲ 164 ◆ **E** D3
ATATÜRK MUSEUM (ATATÜRK MÜZESI) Halaskargazi Cad. 250 (north of Maçka Parkı) Şişli Tel. (0212) 240 63 19	*Open 9am–4pm. Closed Sun., Thur. and public hols.*	▲ 262 ◆ **A** C3
ATIK VALIDE CAMI'I	*See Old Mosque of Murat III's Mother.*	▲ 268
AYAZMA CAMI'I	*See Mosque of the Sacred Fountain.*	▲ 268
BASILICA CISTERN (YEREBATAN OR SARAYI) Yerebatan Cad. 13, Sultanahmet Tel. (0212) 522 12 59	*Open daily 9am–5.30pm.*	▲ 187 ◆ **E** C4
BEYAZIYE (MOSQUE) (BEYAZIDIYE CAMI'I) Hürriyet Meydanı, Beyazıt	*Open daily 4.30am–11pm.*	▲ 200 ◆ **D** E3
BEYLERBEY PALACE (BEYLERBEY SARAYI) Abdullah Ağa Cad., Beylerbey Tel. (0216) 321 93 20	*Open Wed.–Sun. 9.30am–5pm.*	▲ 289 ◆ **A** D4
BLACHERNAE PALACE Northern wall, Ayvansaray	*Free access.*	▲ 237 ◆ **B** B3
BLUE MOSQUE (SULTAN AHMET CAMI'I) Sultanahmet Parkı	*Open daily 4.30am–11pm.*	▲ 175 ◆ **E** C5
BOOK MARKET (SAHAFLAR ÇARŞISI) Sahaflar Çarşısı Sok. Beyazıt	*Open Mon.–Sat. 9am–7pm.*	▲ 198 ◆ **D** E4
BYZANTINE CHURCH OF HAGHIA EIRENE (AYA IRENE KILISESI) Courtyard of the Janissaries Topkapı Palace, Sultanahmet Tel. (0212) 522 09 89	*Currently being restored. Permission to visit must be arranged in advance.*	▲ 153 ◆ **E** D4
CAĞALOĞLU HAMMAM Corner of Ankara Cad. and Prof. Kazim Izmail Gürkan Cad. 34, Cağaloğlu Tel. (0212) 522 24 24	*Men: 8am–10pm. Women: 8am–8pm. Admission: $10 or $20 (massage included).*	▲ 133 ◆ **E** C3
CALLIGRAPHY MUSEUM (TÜRK VAFIK HAT SANATLARI MÜZESI) Beyazıt Meydanı, Beyazıt Tel. (0212) 527 58 51	*Open Tue.–Sat. 9am–4pm.*	▲ 202 ◆ **D** E4
CARAVANSERAIL OF ST PETER Eski Banka Sok., Tünel	*Open daily 10am–7pm.*	▲ 255 ◆ **C** B5
CASTLE OF SEVEN TOWERS (YEDIKÜLE KAPISI) Yediküle Cad., Yediküle Tel. (0212) 585 89 33	*Open Thur.–Tue. 10am–4.30pm.*	▲ 227
CATHEDRAL OF THE HOLY SPIRIT Cumhuriyet Cad. 205, Harbiye Tel. (0212) 248 09 10	*Open daily 8am–8pm.*	◆ **C** E1
ÇEMBERLITAŞ HAMMAM Yeniçeriler Cad., near Vezirhan Cad. 8, Çemberlitaş Tel. (0212) 522 79 74	*Open 6am–midnight. Admission: $6 or $15 (massage included).*	▲ 189 ◆ **E** B4
CHURCH OF CHRIST PANTOCRATOR	*See Zeyrek Mosque.*	▲ 240
CHURCH OF OUR LADY, MOTHER OF GOD (THEOTOKOS KYRIOTISSA)	*See Mosque of the Kalenderhane.*	▲ 205

CHURCH OF OUR LADY **OF THE MONGOLS (KANLI KILISESI)** Murat Molla and Manyasizade Cad., Draman	*Open during services.*	▲ *244* ◆ **B** D5
CHURCH OF OUR LADY **OF THE MONGOLS** Sancaktar Yokuşu Sok.	*Open daily 8am–8pm.*	◆ **B** D5
CHURCH OF ST ANTHONY OF PADUA **(SANT-ANTUAN KILISESI)** İstiklal Cad. 325, Beyoğlu Tel. (0212) 244 09 35	*Open Mon.–Sat. 8am–6pm, Sun. 10am–11am.*	▲ *260* ◆ **C** C3
CHURCH OF ST JOHN OF STUDIUS **(IMRAHOR CAMII)** İmrahor Ilyasbey Cad., Yedikule	*Open daily 8am–8pm.*	▲ *228*
CHURCH OF ST JOHN THE BAPTIST Kamış Sok., Balat	*Not open to the public.*	▲ *245* ◆ **B** C4
CHURCH OF ST MARY DRAPERIS İstiklal Cad. 429, Tünel Tel. (0212) 244 02 43	*Open 8am–6.30pm, Fri. 8am–5pm, Sun. 9am–5pm.*	▲ *258* ◆ **C** B4
CHURCH OF ST NICHOLAS Abdülezel Paşa Cad., between Cibali kapı and Aya kapı, Fener	*Open during services.*	▲ *241* ◆ **B** E5
CHURCH OF ST PETER AND ST PAUL Galata Kulesi Sok. 44a, Tünel	*Open during services.*	▲ *255* ◆ **C** B5
CHURCH OF ST SERGIUS **AND ST BACCHUS**	*See Little Mosque of Haghia Sophia.*	▲ *181*
CHURCH OF ST STEPHEN **OF THE BULGARS (BULGAR KILISESI)** Balat Vapur Iskelesi Cad., Balat	*Open during services.*	▲ *244* ◆ **B** C4
CHURCH OF THE HOLY TRINITY **(AYA TRIADA KILISESI)** Meşelik Sok. 11, Taksim Tel. (0212) 244 13 58	*Open Mon.–Fri. 9am–2pm, Sat.–Sun. 9am–noon.*	▲ *262* ◆ **C** D2
CHURCH OF THE **JOYOUS MOTHER OF GOD** **(THEOTOKOS PAMMAKARISTOS)**	*See Mosque of the Conquest.*	▲ *223*
ÇINILI CAMII	*See Tiled Mosque.*	▲ *270*
CISTERN OF A THOUSAND-AND-ONE **COLUMNS (BINBIRDIREK SARNICI)** Işık Sok., Sultanahmet	*Not open to the public.*	▲ *189* ◆ **E** C4
DOLMABAHÇE PALACE **(DOLMABAHÇE SARAYI)** Dolmabahçe Cad., Beşiktaş Tel. (0212) 258 55 44 Fax (0212) 227 34 41	*Open 9am–3pm. Closed Mon. and Thur.*	▲ *278* ◆ **C** F2
FENERIOTE MANSIONS Vapur Iskelesi Cad., Fener	*Open daily 10am–7pm.*	◆ **B** D5
FORTRESS OF ASIA **(ANADOLU HISARI)** Tel. (0212) 263 53 05	*Permanent access.*	▲ *287* ◆ **A** D3
FORTRESS OF EUROPE **(RUMELI HISARI)** Tel. (0212) 263 53 05/265 04 10	*Open Thur.–Tue.. 9am–5pm.*	▲ *281* ◆ **A** D3
FRENCH RESIDENCE Tomtom Kaptan Sok. 20 Galatasaray	*Open (Italy Gate) 7.50–8.20am* *and 1.05–5.20pm. École Pierre-Loti.*	▲ *259* ◆ **C** C3
GALATA TOWER (GALATA KULESI) Galata Kulesi Sok., Tünel Tel. (0212) 293 81 80 Fax (0212) 245 21 33	*Open daily 8.30am–8pm.*	▲ *256* ◆ **C** B5
GALATASARAY HAMMAM Turnacı Başı Sok. 2, Galatasaray Tel. (0212) 249 43 42/244 14 12	*Men: 8am–10pm.* *Women: 8am–8pm.* *Admission: 15 million TRL.*	◆ **C** C3
GEDIK PAŞA HAMMAM Gedik Paşa Cad., Beyazıt Tel. (0212) 516 26 12	*Open 6am–midnight.* *Admission: $8 or $12 (massage included).*	▲ *199* ◆ **D** F4
GOTHS' COLUMN (GOTLAR SÜTUNU) Parc de Gühlane, palais de Topkapı Sultanahmet	*Park open daily 8am–11pm.*	▲ *129* ◆ **E** E2

◆ PLACES TO VISIT

GRAND BAZAAR (KAPALI ÇARŞI) Çarşıkapı Cad., Beyazıt	*Open Mon.–Sat. 9am–7pm.*	▲ 193 ◆ D F3 ◆ E A3
GREAT CEMETERY OF EYÜP Eyüp	*Open daily 9am–9pm.*	▲ 249 ◆ B A1
GREEK ORTHODOX CHURCH OF THE HOLY TRINITY (AYA TRIADA KILISESI) Istiklal Cad., Taksim	*Open during services.*	▲ 262 ◆ C D2
GÜL CAMI'I	*See Mosque of the Roses.*	▲ 242
GÜLHANE PARK (GÜLHANE PARKI) Topkapı Palace, Sultanahmet	*Open daily 8am–11pm.*	▲ 129 ◆ E E4
HAGHIA SOPHIA (AYA SOFYA) Sultanahmet Meydanı Sultanahmet Tel. (0212) 522 92 41/523 30 09	*Open Tue.–Sun. 9.30am–4.30pm.*	▲ 138 ◆ E D4
HAMMAM OF ROXELANA (HASEKI HAMMAMI) Sultanahmet Parkı Sultanahmet	*Open Wed.–Mon. 9.30am–5pm.*	▲ 174 ◆ E C5
IMPERIAL BEYLERBEY MOSQUE (BEYLERBEY CAMI'I) Beylerbeyı-Üsküdar landing pier	*Open daily 4.30am–11pm.*	▲ 289 ◆ A D4
ISTANBUL LIBRARY (ISTANBUL KÜTÜPHANESI) Soğuçeşme sokak, Sultanahmet Tel. (0212) 512 57 30	*Open to students only.*	▲ 137 ◆ E D4
KANTARCILAR MESCIDI	*See Mosque of the Scale-makers.*	▲ 238
KARIYE CAMI'I	*See Mosque of Kariye.*	▲ 232
KAZANCILAR CAMI'I	*See Mosque of the Cauldron-makers.*	▲ 239
KIOSK OF THE BASKET-WEAVERS (SEPETÇILER KÖŞKÜ) Kennedy Cad., Sirkeci	*International Press Center.* *Not open to the public.*	▲ 129 ◆ E E1
KÜÇÜK AYA SOFYA CAMI'I	*See Little Mosque of Haghia Sophia.*	▲ 181
LÂLELI CAMI'I	*See the Tulip (or Lily) Mosque.*	▲ 203
LEANDER'S TOWER (KIZ KULESI)	*Not open to the public.*	▲ 267 ◆ F A2
LITTLE MOSQUE OF HAGHIA SOPHIA (KÜÇÜK AYA SOFYA CAMI'I) Küçük Ayasofia Cad. Sultanahmet	*Open daily 4.30am–11pm.*	▲ 181 ◆ E B6
LYCÉE GALATASARAY (GALATASARAY LISESI) Istiklâl Cad., Galatasaray	*Not open to the public.*	▲ 260 ◆ C C3
MAUSOLEUM OF ABDÜL HAMIT (HAMIT TÜRBESI) Hamidiye Türbe Sokak, Eminönü	*Not open to the public.*	▲ 133 ◆ E B2
MAUSOLEUM OF AHMET I (SULTAN AHMET TÜRBESI) Mosquée Bleue, Sultanahmet	*Open Wed.–Sun. 9.30am–4.30pm.*	▲ 177 ◆ E C5
MAUSOLEUM OF EYÜP (EYÜP TÜRBESI) Eyüp	*Open Tue.–Sun. 10am–4pm.*	▲ 247 ◆ B A1
MAUSOLEUM OF MAHMUT II (MAHMUT TÜRBESI) Divan Yolu Cad., Çemberlitaş	*Not open to the public.*	▲ 189 ◆ E B4
MAUSOLEUM OF MAHMUT PAŞA (MAHMUT PAŞA TÜRBESI) Mahmut Paşa Mahk. Sok. Cağaloğlu	*Open daily 10am–10.30pm.*	▲ 190 ◆ E B3
MAUSOLEUM OF SINAN (SINAN TÜRBESI) Mimar Sinan Cad., Süleymaniye	*Open daily 10am–10.30pm.*	▲ 216 ◆ D E1
MAUSOLEUMS OF SÜLEYMAN AND ROXELANA Mosque of Süleyman the Magnificent, Süleymaniye	*Open daily 10am–10.30pm.*	▲ 215 ◆ D E1
MEDRESE LIBRARY (MILLET KÜTÜPHANESI) Macar Kardeşler Cad. 85, Fatih Tel. (0212) 631 36 07	*Open 9am–5pm.*	▲ 221

Mosques are usually open daily from the first to the last prayer.
Smaller mosques may close during the day, in which case wait or call for the guard
(often the imam himself) who will open the mosque for you.

MEDRESE OF DAMAT IBRAHIM PAŞA Corner of Dede Efendi Sok. and Şehzade Başı Cad., Mercan	*Open daily 10am–5pm.*	▲ 205 ◆ D D2
MIHRIMAH MOSQUE (MIHRIMAH CAMI'I) Ali Kuşcu Sok., Edirnekapı	*Open daily 4.30am–11pm.*	▲ 231 ◆ B B5
MILITARY MUSEUM (ASKERI MÜZESI) Valikonağı Cad. (north of Maçka Parkı) Harbiye Tel. (0212) 240 62 55	*Open Wed.–Sun. 9am–5pm.*	▲ 262 ◆ C F1
MONASTERY OF JESUS CHRIST Büyük Ada (Princes' Islands)	*Open daily 9am–6pm.*	▲ 273 ◆ A E6
MONASTERY OF ST GEORGE **(AYA YORGI KARIPI MONASTIRI)** Ayios Yorgios Hill Büyük Ada (Princes' Islands)	*Open daily 8am–8pm.*	▲ 273 ◆ A E6
MONASTERY OF THE WHIRLING **DERVISHES (TEKKE)** Gelip Dede Cad., near Tünel Beyoğlu	*Open Tue.–Sun. 9.30am–5pm.* *See Museum of Literature of the Divan.*	▲ 257 ◆ C B4
MOSAIC MUSEUM (MOZAIK MÜZESI) Torun Sok., Arasta Çarşısı Sultanahmet	*Open Tue.–Sun. 9.30am–4.30pm.*	▲ 184 ◆ E C6
MOSQUE OF ABDÜL MECIT/ORTAKÖY **(MECIDIYE/ORTAKÖY CAMI'I)** Ortaköy	*Open daily 4.30am–11pm.*	▲ 280 ◆ A D3
MOSQUE OF ATIK ALI PAŞA **(ATIK ALI PAŞA CAMI'I)** Medrese Sok., Çemberlitaş	*Open daily 4.30am–11pm.*	▲ 191 ◆ E A4
MOSQUE OF ATIK MUSTAFA PAŞA **(ATIK MUSTAFA PAŞA CAMI'I)** Ayvansaray Cad., Ayvansaray	*Open daily 4.30am–11pm.*	▲ 246 ◆ B C3
MOSQUE OF BEŞIR AĞA (AĞA CAMI'I) Alay Köşkü Cad., Sultanahmet	*Turks of Western Thrace Cultural Center.*	▲ 134 ◆ E C5
MOSQUE OF ÇORLULU ALI PAŞA **(ÇORLULU ALI PAŞA CAMI'I)** Yeni Çerler Cad., Beyazıt	*Open daily 4.30am–11pm.*	▲ 192 ◆ E A4
MOSQUE OF DOLMABAHÇE **(DOLMABAHÇE CAMI'I)** Dolmabahçe Cad.	*Open daily 4.30am–11pm.*	▲ 277 ◆ C F2
MOSQUE OF EYÜP (EYÜP SULTAN CAMI'I) Eyüp	*Open daily 4.30am–11pm.*	▲ 249 ◆ B A1
MOSQUE OF FATIH (FATIH CAMI'I)	*See Mosque of Mehmet the Conqueror.*	▲ 221
MOSQUE OF FETHIYE	*See Mosque of the Conquest.*	▲ 223
MOSQUE OF FIRUZ AĞA **(FIRUZ AĞA CAMI'I)** Divan Yolu, Sultanahmet	*Open daily 4.30am–11pm.*	▲ 188 ◆ E C5
MOSQUE OF KANLICA **(KANLICA CAMI'I)** Kanlıca-Beykoz	*Open daily 4.30am–11pm.*	▲ 286 ◆ A D-E3
MOSQUE OF KARA MUSTAFA PAŞA **(KARA MUSTAFA PAŞA CAMI'I)** Yeniçeriler Cad., Çemberlitaş	*Open daily 4.30am–11pm.*	▲ 192 ◆ E A4
MOSQUE OF KARIYE (KARIYE CAMI'I) Kariye Camii Sok. 28, Edirnekapı Tel. (0212) 523 30 09	*Museum (Kariye müzesi): open Wed.–Mon.* *9.30am–4.30pm.*	▲ 232 ◆ B B4
MOSQUE OF KILIÇ ALI PAŞA **(KILIÇ ALI PAŞA CAMI'I)** Necatibey Cad. Beyoğlu	*Open daily 4.30am–11pm.*	◆ C D4
MOSQUE OF KOCA SINAN PAŞA **(KOCA SINAN PAŞA CAMI'I)** Yeniçeriler Cad., Çemberlitaş	*Open daily 4.30am–11pm.*	▲ 191 ◆ E A4
MOSQUE OF MAHMUT PAŞA **(MAHMUT PAŞA CAMI'I)** Mahmut Paşa Mahk. Sok. Cağaloğlu	*Open daily 4.30am–11pm.*	▲ 190 ◆ E B3
MOSQUE OF MEHMET PAŞA THE GREEK **(RUM MEHMET PAŞA CAMI'I)** Şemsi Paşa Cad. Üsküdar	*Open daily 4.30am–11pm.*	▲ 268 ◆ F A1
MOSQUE OF MEHMET THE CONQUEROR **(MEHMET FATIH CAMI'I/FATIH CAMI'I)** Aslanhane Sok., Kirmasti	*Open daily 4.30am–11pm.*	▲ 221

◆ PLACES TO VISIT

Mosques are usually open daily, from the first to the last prayer.
Smaller mosques may close during the day, in which case wait or call for the guard
(often the imam himself), who will open the mosque for you.

MOSQUE OF RÜSTEM PAŞA (RÜSTEM PAŞA CAMII) Hasırcılar Cad., Eminönü	*Open daily noon–2pm.*	▲ 132 ◆ E A1
MOSQUE OF (SULTAN YAVUZ) SELIM I/ (SELIMIYE/YAVUZ SELIM CAMI'I) Yavus Selim Cad., Fener	*Open daily 4.30am–11pm.*	▲ 222 ◆ B D5
MOSQUE OF ŞEMSI AHMET PAŞA (ŞEMSI AHMET PAŞA CAMI'I) Sahil Yolu Cad., Üsküdar	*Open daily 4.30am–11pm.*	▲ 267 ◆ F A1
MOSQUE OF SINAN PAŞA (SINAN PAŞA CAMI'I) Beşiktaş Cad. (opposite the Naval Museum), Beşiktaş	*Open daily 4.30am–11pm.*	◆ A D3
MOSQUE OF SOKOLLU MEHMET PAŞA (SOKOLLU MEHMET PAŞA CAMI'I) Şehit Mehmet Paşa Sok. Sultanahmet	*Open daily 4.30am–11pm.*	▲ 180 ◆ E B5
MOSQUE OF SÜLEYMAN THE **MAGNIFICENT (SÜLEYMANIYE CAMI'I)** Süleymaniye Cad., Süleymaniye	*Open daily 4.30am–11pm.*	▲ 214 ◆ D E1
MOSQUE OF SULTANA MIHRIMAH (MIHRIMAH SULTAN CAMI'I) Paşa Limanı Cad., Üsküdar	*Open daily 4.30am–11pm.*	▲ 265 ◆ F B1
MOSQUE OF SULTANA ZEYNEP (ZEYNEP SULTAN CAMI'I) Alemdar Cad., Sultanahmet	*Open daily 4.30am–11pm.*	▲ 136 ◆ E D3
MOSQUE OF THE ARABS (ARAP CAMI'I) Hoca Hanım Sok., Karaköy	*Open daily 4.30am–11pm.*	▲ 254 ◆ C B5
MOSQUE OF THE CAULDRON-MAKERS (KAZANCILAR CAMI'I) Kazancılar Cad., Küçükpazar	*Open daily 4.30am–11pm.*	▲ 239 ◆ E A1
MOSQUE OF THE CONQUEST (FETHIYE CAMI'I) Fethiye Kapısı Sokak, Draman	*Mosque: open daily 4.30am–11pm.* *Museum: open Wed.–Mon. 9.30am–4.30pm.*	▲ 223 ◆ B C5
MOSQUE OF THE KALENDERHANE (KALENDERHANE CAMI'I) Kalender Camii Sok., Şehzade	*Open daily 4.30am–11pm.*	▲ 205 ◆ D D2
MOSQUE OF THE KÖPRÜLÜ FAMILY (KÖPRÜLÜ CAMI'I) Divan Yolu Cad., Çemberlitaş	*Open daily 4.30am–11pm.*	▲ 189 ◆ E B4
MOSQUE OF THE LEATHER-WORKERS (SAĞRICILAR CAMI'I) Ragıp Gümüşpala Cad. Küçükpazar	*Open daily 4.30am–11pm.*	▲ 239 ◆ E A1
MOSQUE OF THE PRINCE (ŞEHZADE CAMI'I) Şehzadebaşı Cad., Şehzade	*Open daily 4.30am–11pm.*	▲ 204 ◆ D C2
MOSQUE OF THE ROSES (GÜL CAMI'I) Kara Sarlıklı Sok., Fener	*Open daily 9am–5pm and during prayer.*	▲ 241 ◆ B E6
MOSQUE OF THE SACRED FOUNTAIN (AYAZMA CAMI'I) Eşretsaat Sok., Üsküdar	*Open daily 4.30am–11pm.*	▲ 268 ◆ F A1
MOSQUE OF THE SACRED LIGHT **OF OSMAN/OSMAN II** (NURUOSMANIYE CAMI'I) Nuruosmaniye Cad., Beyazıt	*Open daily 4.30am–11pm.*	▲ 190 ◆ E B4
MOSQUE OF THE SCALE-MAKERS (KANTARCILAR CAMI'I) Ragıp Gümüşpala Cad., Küçükpazar	*Open daily 4.30am–11pm.*	▲ 238 ◆ E A1
MUSEUM OF CARPETS AND KILIMS (HALI VE KILIM MÜZESI) Blue Mosque, Sultanahmet Tel. (0212) 518 13 30	*Open Tue.–Sun. 9am–4pm.*	▲ 185 ◆ E C5
MUSEUM OF LITERATURE **OF THE DIVAN** (DIVAN EDEBIATI MÜZESI) Galipdede Cad. 15, Tünel Tel. (0212) 245 41 41	*Open Wed.–Mon. 9.30am–4.30pm.*	▲ 257 ◆ C B4

MUSEUM OF THE ANCIENT ORIENT (TANZIMAT MÜSEZI) Topkapı Palace, Sultanahmet Osman Hamdi Bey Yoku'su Tel. (0212) 520 74 40 Fax (0212) 527 43 00	*Open Tue.–Sun. 9am–4.30pm.*	▲ 165 ◆ E D3
MUSEUM OF TURKISH AND ISLAMIC ART (TÜRK-ISLAM ESERLERI MÜZESI) Ibrahim Paşa Sarayı (racecourse) Sultanahmet Tel. (0212) 518 18 05	*Open Tue.–Sun. 9am–4.30pm.*	▲ 179 ◆ E C5
MUSEUM OF TURKISH TILES (ÇINILI KÖŞKÜ) Archeological Museum garden Topkapı Palace Hamdi bey Yoküşü, Sirkeçi Tel. (0212) 520 77 40	*Open Tue.–Sun. 9am–4.30pm.*	▲ 164 ◆ E D3
NAVAL MUSEUM (DENIZ MÜZESI) Cezayir Cad., Beşiktaş Tel. (0212) 261 00 40	*Open Wed.–Sun. 9am–12.30pm and 1.30–5pm.* *Ouvert mar.-sam. 9 h-16 h.*	▲ 277 ◆ A D3
NEW MOSQUE (YENI CAMI'I) Eminönü Meydanı (opposite Galata Bridge)	*Open daily 4.30am–11pm.*	▲ 130 ◆ E B1
NEW MOSQUE OF THE DOWAGER SULTAN (YENI VALIDE CAMI'I) Hakimiyeti Milliye Cad., Üsküdar	*Open daily 4.30am–11pm.*	▲ 267 ◆ F B1
NURUOSMANIYE CAMI'I	*See Mosque of the Sacred Light of Osman/Osman II.*	▲ 190
OLD MOSQUE OF MURAT III'S MOTHER (ATIK VALIDE CAMI'I) Valide Imaret Sok., Üsküdar	*Open daily 4.30am–11pm*	▲ 268
ORTHODOX CHURCH OF THE HOLY TRINITY (AYA TRIADA KILISESI) Meşelik Sok. 11, Taksim Tel. (0212) 244 13 58	*Open Mon.–Fri. 9am–2pm, Sat.–Sun. 9am–noon.*	▲ 262 ◆ C D2
OTTOMAN LIBRARY (KÖPRÜLÜ KÜTÜPHANESI) Divan Yolu Cad. 29, Çemberlitaş	*Not open to the public.*	▲ 189 ◆ E B5
PALACE OF KÜÇÜKSU (KÜÇÜKSU SARAYI) Küçüksu-Beykoz Tel. (0216) 332 33 20	*Open 9.30–4pm.* *Closed Mon. and Thur.*	▲ 287 ◆ A D3
PATRIARCHAL CHURCH OF ST GEORGE Sadrazam Ali Paşa Cad. 35, Fener	*Open daily 8am–8pm.*	▲ 242 ◆ B E5
PROTESTANT CHURCH Kumbaracı Yokuşu., Tünel	*Open during services.*	▲ 258 ◆ C C4
REVIEW PAVILION (ALAY KÖŞKÜ) Gülhane Park, corner of Alemdar Cad. and Soğuçeşme Sok.,Sultanahmet	*Open daily 10am–5pm.*	▲ 135 ◆ E D3
RUMELI HISARI MUSEUM Rumeli Hisarı, Bebek Tel. (0212) 263 53 05	*Open Tue–Sun. 9.30am–4.30pm.*	▲ 281 ◆ A D3
SACRED SPRING OF THE BLACHERNAE Ayvansaray Cad., Ayvansaray	*Free access.*	▲ 246 ◆ B C3
SADBERK HANIM MUSEUM Piyasa Cad. 25–29 Büyükdere-Sariyer Tel. (0212) 242 38 13	*Open Thur.–Tue. 10.30am–6pm.*	▲ 283 ◆ A D2
SAĞRICILAR CAMI'I	*See Mosque of the Leather-workers.*	▲ 239
ST SAVIOR- IN-CHORA	*See Mosque of Kariye.*	▲ 232
SANCTUARY OF EYÜP Defterdar Cad., Eyüp	*Open daily 9am–9pm.*	▲ 247 ◆ B A1
ŞEHZADE CAMI'I	*See Mosque of the Prince.*	▲ 204
SOĞUK ÇEŞME MEDRESE Bazaar of Ottoman arts and crafts Caferyie Sok., Sultanahmet	*Open daily 10am–5pm.*	▲ 137 ◆ E D4
SPANISH CHAPEL Tomtom Kaptan Sok. 28 Galatasaray	*Open during services.*	◆ C C4

◆ PLACES TO VISIT

SPICE MARKET OR **EGYPTIAN BAZAAR (MISIR ÇARŞISI)** Opposite Yeni Camii, Eminönü	*Open Mon.–Sat. 8.30am–6.30pm.*	▲ 132 ◆ E B2
SULTAN AHMET CAMI'I	*See Blue Mosque.*	▲ 175
PALACE OF IBRAHIM PAŞA **(IBRAHIM PAŞA SARAYI)**	*See Museum of Turkish and Islamic Art.*	▲ 179
PALAZZO DI VENEZIA **(VENICE PALACE)** Embassy of Italy Tomtom Kaptan Sok. 21 Galatasaray	*Open Mon.–Fri. 9am–6pm.*	▲ 259 ◆ C C4
TARIHI AĞA HAMMAM Turnacı Başı Sok. 66 Kuloğlu Mahallesi, Galatasaray Tel. (0212) 249 50 27	*Men: 6pm–9am. Women: 9am–6pm.* *Open Sun. only for men.* *Admission (men): 5 million TRL.* *Admission (women): 2.5 million TRL.*	◆ C D3
TEKFUR PALACE (TEKFUR SARAYI) between Edirnekapı and Eğrikapı Along the ramparts, Edirnekapı Tel. (0212) 522 09 89/522 17 50	*Visit by special appointment only.* *Contact the Tourist office.*	▲ 236 ◆ B B4
THEOTOKOS PAMMAKARISTOS	*See Mosque of the Conquest.*	▲ 223
TILED MOSQUE (ÇINILI CAMI'I) Valide Imaret Sok., Üsküdar	*Open daily 4.30am–11pm.*	▲ 270
TOPKAPI HAREM Topkapı Palace Sultanahmet	*Open Wed.–Mon. 10am–4pm.* *Special ticket: limited number of visits and visitors.* *Reserve ticket as soon as you arrive at Topkapı.*	▲ 160 ◆ E E3
TOPKAPI PALACE (TOPKAPI SARAYI) Access through Bab ı Hümayun Cad., Sultanahmet Tel. (0212) 512 04 80/512 04 84	*Open Wed.–Mon. 9am–4.30pm.*	▲ 150 ◆ E E3
TULIP MOSQUE (LÂLELI CAMI'I) Ordu Cad. (near Ramada Hotel), Lâleli-Aksaray	*Open daily 4.30am–11pm.*	▲ 203 ◆ D C4
YENI CAMI'I	*See New Mosque.*	▲ 130
YENI VALIDE CAMI'I	*See New Mosque of the Dowager Sultana.*	▲ 267
YILDIZ PALACE (YILDIZ SARAYI) Yıldız Parkı Çırağan Cad., Beşiktaş Tel. (0212) 259 45 70/259 89 77	*Open 9am–5pm.* *Closed Mon. and Thur.*	▲ 280 ◆ A D3
ZEYREK MOSQUE **(ZEYREK CAMI'I/KILISE)** Ibadethane Sok., Vefa	*(Also Church of Christ Pantocrator)* *Open daily 4.30am–11pm.*	▲ 240 ◆ D D1

IZNIK

CHURCH OF THE KOIMOISIS **(OF THE ASSUMPTION OF THE VIRGIN)** Istiklâl Cad., near Horoz kapı (southwest of town)	*Open daily 8am–8pm.*	▲ 295
FORMER BASILICA OF HAGHIA **SOPHIA (AYA SOFYA)** Corner of Atatürk Cad. and Kılıçaslan Cad. (main roundabout)	*Open Tue.–Sun. 9am–noon and 2–5pm.* *Key available from the museum if necessary.*	▲ 294
GREEN MOSQUE (YEŞIL CAMI'I) Corner of Müze Sok. and Kılıçaslan Cad. (east of town)	*Open daily 4.30am–11pm.*	▲ 294
HACI ÖZBEK MOSQUE **(HACI ÖZBEK CAMI'I)** Kılıçaslan Cad.	*Open daily 4.30am–11pm.*	▲ 294
IMARET OF NILÜFER HATUN	*See Archeological Museum.*	▲ 295
IZNIK ARCHEOLOGICAL MUSEUM Imaret de Nilüfer Hatun Müze Sok. (near the Green Mosque)	*Open Tue.–Sun. 8.30am–noon and 1–5pm.*	▲ 295
ROMAN AMPHITHEATER Yakup Sok., near Saray kapısı (southwest of town)	*Open daily 10am–7pm.*	▲ 296

BURSA

ARCHEOLOGICAL MUSEUM **(ARKEOLOJI MÜZESI)** Kültür Park	*Open Tue.–Sun. 8.30am–noon and 1–5pm.*	▲ 305

ESKI KAPLICA HAMMAM **(OLD THERMAL BATHS)** (on the western edge of town, at the foot of Çekirge Hill)	*Open daily 8am–11pm (men and women).*	▲ 305
GREAT MOSQUE (ULU CAMI'I) Orhan Gazi Meydani	*Open daily 4.30am–11pm.*	▲ 298
GREEN MAUSOLEUM (YEŞIL TÜRBE) (near the Green Mosque)	*Usually open 8.30am–noon and 1–5.30pm.*	▲ 306
GREEN MOSQUE (YEŞIL CAMI'I) (1¼ miles east of the city center)	*Open daily 4.30am–11pm.*	▲ 305
MOSQUE OF BEYAZIT I **(YILDIRIM BEYAZIT CAMI'I)** Yıldırım Cad.	*Open daily 4.30am–11pm.*	▲ 306
MOSQUE OF MURAT II **(MURADIYE CAMI'I)** Kaplıca Cad. (high town, 1¼ miles west of the city center)	*Open daily 4.30am–11pm.* *Mausoleums open Tue.–Sun. 8.30am–noon and* *1–5.30pm.*	▲ 302
MOSQUE OF ORHAN **(ORHAN GAZI/ORHANIYE CAMI'I)** Atatürk Cad.	*Open daily 4.30am–11pm.*	▲ 299
MOSQUE OF THE CREATOR **OF THE WORLD** **(HÜDAVENDIGAR/MURADIYE CAMI'I)** (1½ miles west of the town center)	*Open daily 4.30am–11pm.*	▲ 304
MUSEUM OF TURKISH AND **ISLAMIC ARTS** **(TÜRK-ISLAM ESERLERI MÜZESI)** Yeşil Cad.	*Open Tue.–Sun. 8.30am–noon and 1–5pm.*	▲ 306
OTTOMAN MUSEUM (OSMANLI EVI **MÜSEZI)** Kaplıca Cad. (opposite Muradiye)	*Open Tue.–Sun. 8.30am–noon and 1–5pm.*	

EDIRNE

ARCHEOLOGICAL MUSEUM **(ARKEOLOJI VE ETNOLOJI MÜZESI)** (former *medrese* of the Mosque of Selim II)	*Open Tue.–Sun. 8am–noon and 1–5pm.*	▲ 312
MOSQUE OF MURAT II **(MURADIYE CAMI'I)** (northeast of the Mosque of Selim II, at the end of Mimar Sinan Cad.)	*Open daily 4.30am–11pm.*	▲ 313
MOSQUE OF SELIM II (SELIMIYE CAMI'I) (center-east of town, on the Mimar Sinan Cad.)	*Open daily 4.30am–11pm.*	▲ 311
MOSQUE OF THREE BALCONIES **(ÜÇ ŞEREFELI CAMI'I)** (near the main station)	*Open daily 4.30am–11pm.*	▲ 310
MUSEUM OF TURKISH AND ISLAMIC **WORKS (TÜRK-ISLAM ESERLERI MÜZESI)** (former *darü'l-hadis* of the Mosque of Selim II)	*Open Tue.–Sun. 8am–noon and 1–5pm.*	▲ 312
OLD MOSQUE (ESKI CAMI'I) (corner of Talatpaşa Cad. and Mimar Sinan Cad.)	*Open daily 4.30am–11pm.*	▲ 309

ÇANAKKALE

ARCHEOLOGICAL MUSEUM **(ARKEOLOJI MÜZESI)** corner of Atatürk Cad. and 100 Yil Cad. (southwest of town)	*Open Tue.–Sun. 10am–5pm.*	▲ 329
MILITARY MUSEUM **(ASKERI VE DENIZ MÜZESI)** Park of the Çimenlik Kale (fortress, south of the landing piers	*Open 9–11am and 2.30–7.30pm.* *Closed Mon. and Thur.* *Access to the park: daily 9am–10pm.*	▲ 329

TROY

		▲ 336
SITE OF TROY	*Open daily 8am–5pm.*	

◆ BIBLIOGRAPHY ◆

ESSENTIAL READING

◆ FREELY (J.): *Istanbul* (Blue Guide), London and New York, 1987.
◆ HAUSSIG (H.W.): *Byzantine Civilization* (trans. J. Hussey), London, 1971.
◆ KINROSS (J.B. Lord): *The Ottoman Centuries, the Rise and Fall of the Turkish Empire*, London, 1977.
◆ NORWICH (J.J.): *Byzantium, the Early Centuries*, London 1988 *Byzantium, the Apogee*, London, 1991.
◆ SUMNER-BOYD (H.) and FREELY (J.): *Strolling through Istanbul, a Guide to the City*, Istanbul, 1973.

GENERAL

◆ AMICIS (E. de): *Constantinople* (trans. C. Tilton), London, 1878.
◆ BUTLER (R.): *City Breaks in Istanbul*, London, 1991.
◆ CRAWFORD (F. MARION) *Constantinople*, New York, 1895.
◆ DWIGHT (H.G.): *Constantinople Old and New*, New York, 1915.
◆ EKREM, (Selma), *Turkey Old and New*, New York, 1967
◆ FREELY (J.): *The Companion Guide to Turkey*, London, 1979.
◆ HÖFER (H.): *Istanbul (City Insight Guides)*, Istanbul, 1991.
◆ JACOBS (D.): *Constantinople, City on the Golden Horn*, New York, 1969.
◆ KELLY (L.): *Istanbul, a Traveller's Companion*, London, 1987.
◆ LEWIS (J.F.): *Illustrations of Constantinople*, London, 1835–6.
◆ MACLAGAN (M.): *The City of Constantinople*, London, 1968.
◆ PARDOE (J.): *The Beauties of the Bosphorus*, London, 1861.
◆ PENZER (N.M.): *The Harem*, London, 1965.
◆ RICE (D. Talbot): *Constantinople; Byzantium; Istanbul*, London, 1965.
◆ YOUNG (G.): *Constantinople*, London, 1926.

BYZANTINE HISTORY

◆ ANNA COMNENA: *The Alexiad* (trans. E.R.A.

Sewter), London, 1969.
◆ BARKER (J.W.): *Justinian and the Later Roman Empire*, Madison, Wis.,1960.
◆ BROWNING (R.): *The Byzantine Empire*, London, 1980; *Justinian and Theodora*, London, 1971.
◆ DE CLARI (R.): *The Conquest of Constantinople* (trans. E.H. McNeal), New York, 1936.
◆ DIEHL (C.): *Byzantine Empresses* (trans H. Bell and T. de Kerpely), London, 1964.
◆ FINLAY (G.): *A History of the Byzantine Empire*, London, 1854.
◆ GRABAR (A.): *Byzantium, from the Death of Theodosius To the Rise of Islam* London, 1967.
◆ HUSSEY (J.) (ed): *The Byzantine Empire* (Cambridge Medieval History, Volume IV), Cambridge, 1966–7; *The Byzantine World*, London, 1957.
◆ JENKINS (R.): *Byzantium, the Imperial Centuries*, London, 1966.
◆ JONES (A.H.M.): *Constantine and the Conversion of Europe*, New York, 1962.
◆ MICHAEL PSELLUS: *Fourteen Byzantine Rulers (Chronographia)*, (trans. E.R.A. Sewter), Harmondsworth, 1966.
◆ OSTROGORSKY (G.): *History of the Byzantine State* (trans. J. Hussey), Oxford, 1968.
◆ PROCOPIUS: *The Secret History* (trans. R. Atwater), Ann Arbor, 1967.
◆ RUNCIMAN (S.): *The Fall of Constantinople*, Cambridge, 1969.
◆ URE (P.N.): *Justinian and his Age*, Harmondsworth, 1951.
◆ VASILIEV (A.A.): *History of the Byzantine Empire* (trans. S. Ragozin), Madison, Wis., 1928, and Oxford, 1952; *Justin the First. An Introduction to the Epoch of Justinian the Great*, Cambridge, Mass., 1950.
◆ VILLEHARDOUIN (G. de): *The Conquest of Constantinople* (trans. F Marzials), London, 1908.

OTTOMAN HISTORY

◆ ALDERSON (A.D.): *The Structure of the*

Ottoman Dynasty, Oxford, 1956.
◆ BABINGER (F.): *Mehemed the Conqueror and his Time* (trans. R. Mannheim), Princeton, 1978.
◆ EVLIYA ÇELEBI EFFENDI: *Narrative of Travels in Europe, Asia and Africa* (trans. J. von Hammer-Purgstall), London, 1834.
◆ HORNBY, Lady: *Constantinople during the Crimean War*, London, 1863.
◆ INALÇIK (H.): *The Ottoman Empire, The Classical Age, 1300–1600* (trans. N. Itzkowitz and C. Imber), London, 1973.
◆ KRITOVOULOS (M.): *History of Mehmed the Conqueror* (trans. C.T. Riggs), Princeton, 1954.
◆ SHAW (S.J.): *Between Old and New, the Ottoman Empire under Selim III*, Cambridge, Mass., 1971.
◆ SHAW (S.S. and E.K.): *History of the Ottoman Empire and Modern Turkey*, Cambridge, Mass., 1976–77.
◆ WITTEK (P.): *The Rise of the Ottoman Empire*, London, 1938.

BYZANTINE ARCHITECTURE AND ART

◆ GRABAR (A.): *From Theodosius to Islam*, London, 1966.
◆ HAMILTON (J.A.): *Byzantine Architecture and Decoration*, London and New York, 1934.
◆ KINROSS (J.B. Lord.): *Hagia Sophia*, London, 1973.
◆ KRAUTHEIMER (R.): *Early Christian and Byzantine Architecture*, Harmondsworth, 1965.
◆ LEACROFT (H.): *The Buildings of Byzantium*, London, 1977.
◆ LETHABY (C.) and SWAINSON (H.): *Santa Sophia Constantinople: A Study of Byzantine Building*, London, 1894.
◆ MAINSTONE (R.J.): *Hagia Sophia: Architecture, Structure and Liturgy of Justinian's Great Church*, London, 1988.
◆ MANGO (C.): *Byzantine Architecture*, London, 1979.
◆ MATHEWS (T.F.): *The Byzantine Churches of Istanbul*, Pennsylvania State University, 1976.
◆ MILLINGEN (A. van): *Byzantine*

Constantinople: the Walls of the City, London, 1899; *Byzantine Churches in Constantinople, their History and Architecture*, London, 1912.
◆ RICE (D. Talbot): *The Art of Byzantium*, London, 1959; *The Great Palace of the Byzantine Emperors*, Oxford, 1947–58.
◆ WITTEMORE (T.): *The Mosaics of Haghia Sophia at Istanbul*, Oxford, 1933–52.

OTTOMAN ARCHITECTURE AND ART

◆ CAGMAN (T.) and TANINIDI (Z.): *The Topkapı Saray Museum: The Albums and Illustrated Manuscripts* (trans. J.M. Rogers), London, 1986
◆ ÇIĞ (K.): *Treasury: Guide, Topkapı Palace Museum*, Istanbul, 1966.
◆ ETTINGHAUSEN (R.): *Turkey: Ancient Miniatures*, UNESCO, 1954.
◆ FREELY (J.) AND BURRELL (A.R.): *Sinan: Architect of Suleyman the Magnificent and the Ottoman Golden Age*, London, 1992.
◆ GOODWIN (G.): *A History of Ottoman Architecture*, London, 1971.
◆ GOODWIN (G.): *Sinan*, London, 1993.
◆ KOSEOGLU (C.): *The Topkapı Saray Museum: The Treasury* (trans. J.M. Rogers), London, 1987.
◆ STRATTON (Arthur), *Sinan*, New York, 1972
◆ VOGT-GÖKNIL (U.): *Living Architecture: Ottoman*, London, 1966.

RELIGION CHRISTIAN

◆ HUSSEY (J.): *The Orthodox Church in the Byzantine Empire*, London, 1986.
◆ STANLEY (A.P.): *The Eastern Church*, London, 1861.

RELIGION ISLAM

◆ ARBERRY (A.J.): *The Koran Interpreted*, Oxford, 1964.
◆ GUILLAUME (A.): *Islam*, Harmondsworth, 1956.

LITERATURE

◆ BLANCH (L.): *Pavilions of the Heart*, London, 1974.
◆ BYRON (Lord): *Letters and Journals, Vol I, 'In My Hot Youth'*, London, 1973.
◆ CARLISLE (Earl of): *Diary in Turkish and Greek Waters*, London, 1854.
◆ CHANDER (R.): *Travels in Asia Minor*, London, 1776.
◆ COLTON (W.): *A Visit to Constantinople and Athens*, New York, 1836.
◆ DOLLOWAY (J.): *Constantinople, Ancient and Modern*, London, 1797.
◆ ELIOT (T.): *Diary of an Idle Woman in Constantinople*, London, 1893.
◆ GRAVES (R.): *Count Belisarius*, London, 1955.
◆ HAYES (B.): *Midnight Express*, London, 1977.
◆ HOBHOUSE (J.C.): *A Journey through Albania ... to Constantinople during the years 1809 and 1810*, London, 1813.
◆ LOTI (P.): *Constantinople (Aziyadé)* (trans. M. Lowrie), London, 1927
◆ MACAULAY (R.): *The Towers of Trevizond*, London, 1956.
◆ MONTAGU (Lady Mary Wortley): *Letters*, London, 1763 (many later editions).

TRADITIONS

◆ ATAZOY (Nurhan) and RABY (Julian), Petsopoulos (Yanni) (ed.) *Iznik, the Pottery of Ottoman Turkey*, London, 1989.
◆ BALPINER (Beluis) and PETSOLPOULOS (Yanni), *100 Kilims, Masterpieces from Anatolia*, London, 1991.
◆ BEKTAS (C.): *Living in Turkey*, London, 1992.
◆ DWIGHT (H.G.): *Constantinople, Settings and Traits*, London, 1927.
◆ GARNETT (L.M.J.): *Turkish Life in Town and Country*, London, 1904.
◆ HUBBARD (G.E.): *The Day of the Crescent: Glimpses of Old Turkey*, Cambridge, 1920.
◆ HULL (A.) and BARNARD (N.): *Living with Kilims*, London, 1988.
◆ LEWIS (R.): *Everyday Life in Ottoman Turkey*, London, 1971.
◆ ORGA (I.): *Portrait of a Turkish Family*, London, 1950.
◆ PARDOE (J.): *The City of the Sultan and Domestic Manners of the Turks in 1836* London, 1838.
◆ PEARS (E.): *Forty Years in Constantinople* London, 1916.
◆ PETSOPOULOS (Yanni) *Kilims*, Fribourg, 1979; *Tulips, Arabesques and Turbans*, London, 1982
◆ SPRY (W.J.J.): *Life on the Bosphorus*, London, 1895.

COOKING

◆ EDMONDS (A.G.) (ed.): *Cooking in Turkey*, Istanbul, 1986.
◆ HALACI (N.): *Nevin Halaci's Turkish Cookbook*, London, 1989.
◆ HAROUTUNIAN (A. der): *A Turkish Cookbook*, London, 1987.
◆ YAYINLARJ (A.): *The Turkish Kitchen*, Istanbul, 1988.
◆ YAYINLARJ (M.): *The Famous Turkish Cookery*, Istanbul, 1988.

We would like to thank the following publishers or copyright-holders for permission to reproduce the extracts on pages 97–120.

◆ THE BODLEY HEAD: Extract from *My Autobiography* by Charlie Chaplin (published 1964). Reprinted by permission of the Bodley Head.

◆ MARION BOYARS PUBLISHERS: Excerpt from *Berji Kristin – Tales from the Garbage Hills* by Latife Tekin, translated by Saliha Paker and Ruth Christie (Marion Boyars Publishers, New York and London, 1993). Reprinted by permission.

◆ CARROLL & GRAF PUBLISHERS: Excerpt from *The Towers of Trebizond* by Rose Macaulay (published 1956). Reprinted by permission of Carroll & Graf Publishers.

◆ HARCOURT, BRACE & CO.: Excerpt from *Orlando* by Virginia Woolf (published 1928). Reprinted by permission of Harcourt Brace & Co. (in the UK by permission of the Hogarth Press Ltd)

◆ INDIANA UNIVERSITY, TURKISH STUDIES: Excerpt from essay by Sait Faik, translated by Talat Sait Ralman from *Turkish Studies*, edited by Ichan Basqoz (1930). Reprinted by permission.

◆ MACMILLAN PUBLISHING CO: "Sailing to Byzantium" from *The Poems of W. B. Yeats: A New Edition*, edited by Richard J. Finneran, copyright © 1928 by Macmillan Publishing Company, copyright renewed 1956 by Georgie Yeats. Reprinted by permission.

◆ MARLBORO PRESS: Excerpt from *The Spirit of Mediterranean Places* by Michel Butor (published 1986), translated by Lydia Davis. Reprinted by permission of Marlboro Press.

◆ RUSSELL & VOLKENING INC: Excerpt from *Sinan* by Arthur Stratton (Charles Scribner's) copyright © 1972 by Arthur Stratton. Reprinted by permission of Russell & Volkening, Inc., as agents for the author.

◆ CHARLES SCRIBNER'S & SONS: Excerpt from *Turkey Old and New* by Selma Ekrem (published 1967). Reprinted by permission of Charles Scribner's & Sons).

◆ THAMES & HUDSON: Excerpt from INTRODUCTION TO *Turkey* by Lord Kinross, edited by Robert Mantran, 1959. Reprinted by permission of Thames & Hudson.

◆ VIKING: Excerpt from *Stamboul Train* by Graham Greene (published 1932). Reprinted by permission of Viking (in the UK by permission of Heinemann).

◆ LIST OF ILLUSTRATIONS

LIST OF ILLUSTRATIONS ◆

◆ LIST OF ILLUSTRATIONS

◆ LIST OF ILLUSTRATIONS

◆ LIST OF ILLUSTRATIONS

LIST OF ILLUSTRATIONS ◆

Interior of Mosque of Selim II (Selimiye), Edirne. Photo idem. *The architect Sinan*, painting by Sabri Berkel, 1952. Private coll. Architects in procession in Hippodrome with model of Süleymaniye, miniature from *Book of Festivals*, 1582. Topkapı Palace Museum. Statue of architect Sinan, Edirne. Photo H. Özözlü.

316 Window in Mosque of Rüstem Paşa. Photo Ara Güler. Section and elevation plan of Mosque of Süleyman I (Süleymaniye), prod. by R. Petruzzi.

317 Windows in mausoleum of Süleyman the Magnificent. Photo Ara Güler. Interior of mosque of the Prince Şehzade Cami'i. Photo idem. Pulpit (mimbar) in the Atik Valide Cami'i. Photo Ara Güler.

318 Mosque of Selim II (Selimiye), Edirne, postcard. EDM coll. Fountain and courtyard of the Mosque of Selim II (Selimiye), Edirne. Photo Ara Güler. Fountain (şardivan) of the Mosque of Süleyman I (Süleymaniye). Photo idem.

319 Example of wood carving, detail from a door. Photo idem.

318–319 Longitudinal section of the precinct of Selim II (Selimiye), Edirne. Drawn by P. Carnelutti.

320 Zurna player (kind of oboe). Photo H. Özözlü. Flight of Turkish peasants to Istanbul, illustration from *Petit Journal* 1913.

320–321 Meriç (Maritza), river near Edirne. P. de Gigord coll.

321 *Wrestlers*, painting by L.-F. Cassas (1756–27). Private coll. Festival of Wrestling in Kirkpinar, Edirne. Photo Ara Güler.

322 General view of Gallipoli (Gelibolu), postcard. EDM coll.

323 *Buccaneer in Dardanelles*, painting by L. Garneray (1783–57). Photo Marine Museum, Paris. Hero bewailing the death of Leander, engraving.

324–325 Auction sale in outer district of Gallipoli (Gelibolu), postcard. EDM coll.

324 Constantinople and Dardanelles, 1711 engraving. EDM coll. Cart transporting sheafs of corn in trades district of Gallipoli (Gelibolu). Photo H. Özözlü.

325 Municipal offices and court in Gallipoli (Gelibolu), postcard. EDM coll. Goddess. Archeological museum in Çanakkale. Photo H. Özözlü. Fortress of Kilitbahir, Dardanelles straits. Photo idem.

326 German cruisers *Goeben* and *Breslau*. Photo Match, 1939. Viribus Unitis, postcard. P. de Gigord coll.

326–327 Caricature, November 1914, postcard. Coll. idem.

327 German cruiser renamed by Turks. Drawing N. Boussot. Mustafa Kemal Paşa, postcard. Drawing N. Boussot. Confrontation of Turkish and Russian fleets in Dardanelles strait, postcard. EDM coll.

328 Poster from turn of century. Drawing N. Boussot. Landing of the British at Seddülbahir. Illustration from *Miroir*, 1914. Memorial in Turkish cemetery in Çanakkale. Photo H. Özözlü.

328–329 Imprisoned Turkish sniper. Photo *The Times* 1915.

329 Sign at approaches to military cemetery in Çanakkale. Photo H. Özözlü. Military cemetery and memorial to the dead, Çanakkale. Photo idem. Bear tamers on road to Troy. Photo idem.

330 Vice-admiral Robeck. Photo *The Times*, 1915. Admiral Guépratte, photo idem.

330–331 British and French ships exploding on mines in the Strait. Drawing N. Boussot.

331 Map of the battle of March 18, 1915. Cruiser *Le Suffren*. Marine Museum.

332 Cover of *The Times History of the War*, October 1915. Survivors of *The Irresistible*, on board *The Agamemnon*, archives photo. Sinking of *The Irresistible*. Times archives.

332–333 The Queen Elizabeth, archives photo.

333 Allied flags flying over the Dardanelles forts. Marine Museum, Paris. Cruiser of the fleet, *Bouvet*, archives photo. Crew of *Le Gaulois* leaving seriously damaged ship, archives photo.

334 Section plan of successive settlements of the site of Troy. Heinrich Schliemann, archeologist (1822–90), archives photo. Ancient theater, Troy. Photo Ara Güler. Remains of tower, gateway and walls, Troy. Photo idem.

335 Battle around the body of Patrocles. Reconstruction of the Trojan Horse. Photo Ara Güler. The Trojan Horse ruse, sculpture in bronze. Warrior in chariot. Silhouette, guide to Troy.

336 Stone axes, cup, Troy II. Ajax and Achilles throwing dice. The Trojan Horse ruse, drawings by N. Boussot.

337–363 General view of a shopping arcade. H. Özözlü coll. Bird seed vendor. E. De Pazzis coll. Haydarpafla station, H. Özözlü coll. Fish mongers. A. Thévenart coll. Bridge over the Bosphorus, Ortaköy. G. Rossi coll.. Princes' Islands, Splendid Palafl hotel, Büyükada. Bursa market. Cl. Ara Güler.

347–363 we thank the following establishments for the pictures they have sent us Çara Hotel, Grand Ons, Merit Antique, The President, English pub, Senator Hotel, Armada hotel, Ayasofia Pansiyonlari, Acropol Hotel, Empress Zoé, Four Seasons, Sarniç, Obelisk Sumengen, Ibrahim pafla Oteli, Konuk Evi, Yeflil Ev, Café Pierre Loti, Pera Palas, Café Lebon, Richemond Hotel, Eresin Taxim Hotel, Hilton, Hyatt Regency, The Marmara, Splendid Palafl Hotel.

Maps of itineraries
Pierre-Xavier Grézaud, assisted by Jean-François Binet, Philippe Pradel and Samuel Tranlé.

D. T. P. Maps
Édigraphie (endmaps and 354–359)

Diagrams
Emmanuel Calami: 340-343, 345, 347

Abbreviations :
Coll.: Collection.

We have not been able to trace the heirs or publishers of certain documents. An account is being held open for them at our offices.

A

Ağa: schoolteacher, lord, honorary title in the Turkish army.
Arasta: covered street with shops; shopping mall.
Avlu: large square or courtyard in front of a mosque.
Ayazma: sacred fountain.

B

Bayram: festival.
Bedesten: structure in the center of a covered bazaar where objects of value are displayed and sold.
Bent: dam; water in a reservoir.
Bey: governor of a town or district (*beylicat*).
Beylerbeyi: "bey of beys", governor-general of a province.

C–Ç

Caique: small sailboat with oars used on the Bosphorus and Golden Horn until the early 20th century.
Camekan: reception area and cloakroom (apodyterium) of a hammam.
Cami'i: mosque with a mimbar.
Çarsi: market, bazaar.
Çelebi: Turkish gentleman.
Çeşme: fountain.
Cumhuriyet: Republic.

D

Darül'hadis: Koranic college.
Darü'ş-şifa: Ottoman hospital.
Dershane: amphitheater, lecture room in a *medrese*.
Dervish: member of a religious brotherhood (Kalender, Mevlevi etc.).
Devşirme: Christian child offered as tribute by family for enrollment in the service of a sultan.
Divan: Imperial Ottoman council; by extension, the Ottoman government in general.

E

Eyvan: vaulted or domed areas positioned round the central chamber of a mosque.

F

Firman: edict of the sultan.

G

Grand Vizier: VIZIER: the equivalent of a prime minister in the Ottoman Empire.

H

Hadım: eunuch.
Halı: carpet with knotted stitches.
Hammam: Turkish baths.
Han: caravanserai, inn for merchants and their caravans.
Hararet: hot-water and steam-bathing room (*caldarium*) in a hammam.
Harem: section reserved for women in Ottoman houses and palaces.
Haseki: the sultan's favorite.
Hégire: Islamic calendar, in which year 1 corresponds to 622 in the Christian calendar.
Hisar: Ottoman fortress.
Hübte: sermon given on Fridays in large mosques.
Hünka Kasri: lodge or gallery reserved for a sultan in an imperial mosque.
Hücre: student's study room in a *medrese*.

I

Imam: leader of prayers attached to a mosque.
Imaret: institution where free meals are served to the poor.

J

Janissary: member of the élite guard serving the sultan.

K

Kadin: a sultan's legal spouse.
Kalender: mendicant order of the wandering dervishes.
Kapi: gate.
Kemer: aqueduct.
Kethüda: steward, manager.
Kiblah: the wall facing Mecca at the rear of the prayer chamber in a mosque; the direction Moslems must face when at prayer.
Kilim: woven carpet.
Kilise: church.
Konak: private Ottoman town house.
Köpru: bridge.
Köşkü: Turkish summerhouse or pavilion.
Köy: village, hamlet.
Kule: tower.
Külliye: socioreligious precinct in a mosque comprising various public buildings.
Kuran Kürsü: pulpit from which the Koran is read.

L

Lâle Devri: the "Tulip Period", the latter part of Ahmet III's reign.

M

Medrese: school of higher education in a külliye.
Mektep: primary school.
Mescit: small mosque without a mimbar.
Mevlevi: brotherhood of the wandering dervishes.
Mihrab: in a mosque, a recess in the wall of the kiblah.
Mimar: architect.
Mimarbaşı: chief architect.
Mimbar: pulpit in a mosque from which the preacher delivers the Friday sermon.
Minaret: tower from which the muezzin calls the people to prayer.
Müezzin: official in a mosque whose role is to call the faithful to prayer.

N

Narghile (or hookah): water pipe with a long tube connected to a flask where water is cooled in scented water; the tobacco burns in a small bowl above the water.

O

Oda: public or private room, chamber.
Osmanlı: Ottoman dynasty founded by Osman in the 13th century, which held power until 1923.

P

Paşa: title given to high officials, governors and generals in Turkey.

S–Ş

Şardıvan: fountain for ablutions, usually to be found in the courtyard of a mosque.
Saray: Ottoman palace, harem.
Sarnıc: water tank.
Sebil: public fountain.
Selamlik: area reserved for men in Ottoman houses and palaces.
Şerefe: balcony of a minaret.
Şehzade: prince, son of a sultan.
Sofa: raised platform, ceremonial rostrum.
Soğukluk: moderately warm, medium-temperature bathing room (*tepidarium*) in a hammam.
Sublime Porte: entrance to the palace of the Grand Vizier; by extension, the Ottoman government in general.
Sultan: sovereign of the Ottoman empire.
Sultana: wife or daughter of a sultan.
Suterazi: Turkish water tower.
Sütun: column.

T

Tabhane: hospice for wandering dervishes.
Tekke: dervish monasteries.
Tuğra: calligraphic signature of a sultan, attached to all official documents.
Türbe: Ottoman mausoleum.

U

Ulu Cami'i: the Great Mosque, also known as the Friday Mosque.

V

Valide Sultane: a sultan's mother, the mother of a reigning sultan.

Y

Yalı: private town house, built of wood and located on the water's edge.

Z

Zâviye: religious establishment whose purpose is to accommodate pilgrims and dervishes.

◆ NOTES

Map section

◆ STREET INDEX

◆ ISTANBUL–BOSPHORUS

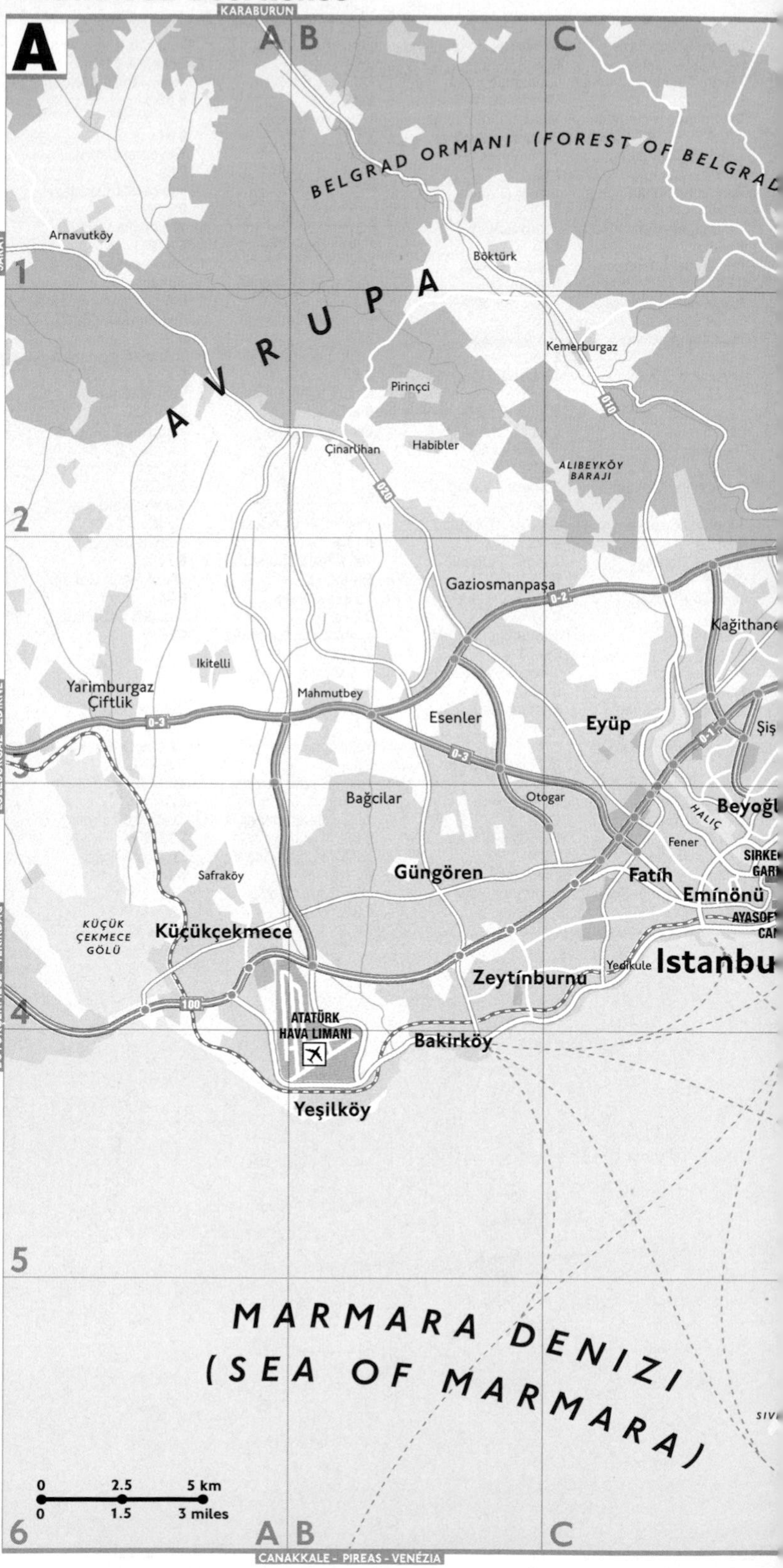

A

KARABURUN

BELGRAD ORMANI (FOREST OF BELGRAD)

Arnavutköy

Böktürk

A V R U P A

Kemerburgaz

Pirinçci

Çinarlihan   Habibler

ALIBEYKÖY
BARAJI

Gaziosmanpaşa

Kağithane

Ikitelli

Yarimburgaz
Çiftlik   Mahmutbey

Esenler   Eyüp   Şiş

Bağcilar   Otogar   Beyoğl

HALIÇ

Safraköy   Fener

Güngören   Fatíh   SIRKE
GARN

Emínönü

KÜÇÜK
ÇEKMECE   Küçükçekmece   AYASOF
CAI
GÖLÜ

Yedikule   Istanbu

Zeytínburnu

ATATÜRK
HAVA LIMANI   Bakirköy

Yeşilköy

M A R M A R A   D E N I Z I
(S E A   O F   M A R M A R A)

SIV

| 0 | 2.5 | 5 km |
| 0 | 1.5 | 3 miles |

A B   C

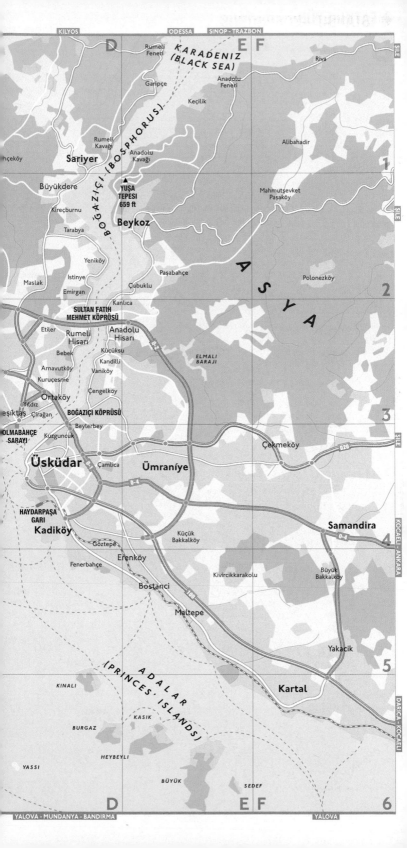

B

EYÜP İSKELESİ

CAMİ-İ KEBİR C.

YENİ SAHİL YOLU

B BOYACI C.

FESHANE C.

EYÜP SULTAN BULVARI

ESKİ SOĞULAR CAD.

BALCI YOKUŞU

ZALPAŞA CAD.

KUMBARAHANE CADDESİ

FATİH KÖPRÜSÜ

1

EYÜP

HAYDAR BABA CAD.

ÇÖMLEKÇİLER C.

DEFTERDAR CAD.

DEFTERDAR İSKELESİ

ESKİ GALATA KÖPRÜSÜ

AYVANSARAY İSKELESİ

ZAHİRECİ SOKAĞI

DAVUTAĞA CAD.

AŞHANE SOKAĞI

ALACA TEKKESİ SOKAĞI

YENİ MAHALLE S.

AYVANSARAY CAD.

DEMİRHİSAR CAD.

2

PAŞMACI ÇAYIRI CADDESİ

MOBİLYACI S.

AYVANSARAY

ATİK MUSTAFA PAŞA CAMİ

DERVİŞZADE CAD.

EBE SOKAĞI

DEĞİRMEN YOLU S.

BOĞAZIÇI KÖPRÜSÜ ÇEVRE YOLU

KIRIMLI ÇEŞME S.

EĞRİKAPI C.

ŞİŞHANE

SAKALAR YOK.

PÜSKÜLCÜ S.

BALAT

3

FETHİ ÇELEBİ C.

CEBECİBAŞI CAD.

OTAKÇIBAŞI SOKAĞI

SAVAKLAR CADDESİ

TEODOS II. SURU

HOCAÇAKIR CADDESİ

TEKFUR SARAYI

ŞİŞHANE CADDESİ

BEŞİRGAZI S.

SULTAN PAŞA HAMAMI

KÜRKÇÜ ÇEŞMESİ CAD.

AYAN CADDESİ

RAMİ KIŞLA CADDESİ

EDİRNEKAPI ŞEHİTLİĞİ

KARİYE CAMİ

NESTER SOKAĞI

ŞEYH EYÜP

DRAMAN

ZÜLÜFLÜ

FENER

4

EDİRNEKAPI CADDESİ

EDİRNEKAPI CADDESİ

BOSTAN A.S.

TOPKAPI - EDİRNEKAPI CADDESİ

MİHRİMAH SULTAN CAMİ

HOCAÇAKIR CAD.

ALİ KUŞCU SK.

FEVZİ PAŞA CADDESİ

SALMA TOMRUK C.

KURT AĞA ÇEŞMESİ

SENA SOKAĞI

FETHİYE CADDESİ

FETHİYE CAMİ

DİLMAÇ S.

DOLAPLI BOSTAN CADDESİ

SARAY AĞASI CAD.

5

EDİRNEKAPI

TEODOS II. SURU

SULUKULE CADDESİ

SARMAŞIK S.

ÇEŞME SOKAĞI

UZUN YOL S.

HOCA CADDESİ

LODOS S.

CEMALİ S.

BEYCEĞİZ FIRNI S.

ADNAN MENDERES

KEÇECİ MEYDANI S.

SOFALI ÇEŞME S.

GÜL DEDE S.

MELEK HOCA CADDESİ

KABAKULAK S.

ATİK ALİ PAŞA CAMİ

FATİH NİŞANCA C.

FEVZİ PAŞA CADDESİ

FATİH

YAVU

6

A B C

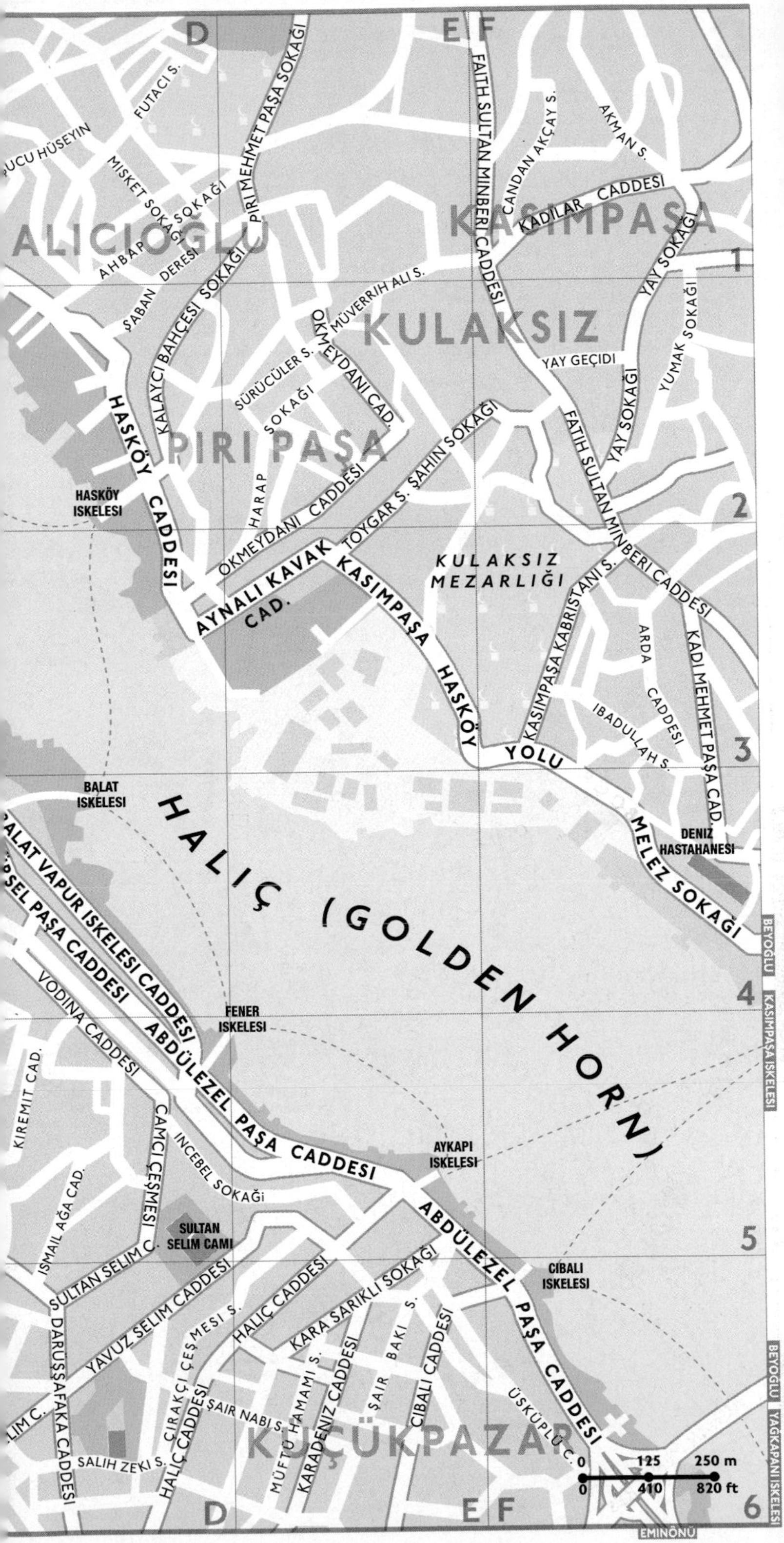

ALICIOĞLU

KASIMPAŞA

KULAKSIZ

PIRI PAŞA

HASKÖY CADDESI

HASKÖY ISKELESI

PIRI MEHMET PAŞA SOKAĞI

FATIH SULTAN MINBERI CADDESI

KADILAR CADDESI

CANDAN AKÇAY S.

AKMAN S.

YAY SOKAĞI

YAY GEÇIDI

YUMAK SOKAĞI

YAY SOKAĞI

MÜVERRIH ALI S.

SÜRÜCÜLER S.

MEYDANI CAD.

FUTACI S.

MISKET SOKAĞI

KALAYCI BAHÇESI SOKAĞI

ŞABAN DERESI

AHBAP SOKAĞI

UCU HÜSEYIN

HARAP SOKAĞI

ÖKMEYDANI CADDESI

AYNALI KAVAK CAD.

KASIMPAŞA HASKÖY YOLU

TOYGAR S. ŞAHIN SOKAĞI

FATIH SULTAN MINBERI CADDESI

KULAKSIZ MEZARLIĞI

KASIMPAŞA KABRISTANI S.

IBADULLAH S.

ARDA CADDESI

KADI MEHMET PAŞA CAD.

MELEZ SOKAĞI

DENIZ HASTAHANESI

BALAT ISKELESI

HALIÇ (GOLDEN HORN)

BALAT VAPUR ISKELESI CADDESI

SEL PAŞA CADDESI

ABDÜLEZEL PAŞA CADDESI

VODINA CADDESI

KIREMIT CAD.

ISMAIL AĞA CAD.

CAMCI ÇEŞMESI

INCEBEL SOKAĞI

FENER ISKELESI

AYKAPI ISKELESI

CIBALI ISKELESI

SULTAN SELIM CAMI

SULTAN SELIM C.

YAVUZ SELIM CADDESI

DARÜŞŞAFAKA CADDESI

ÇIRAKÇI ÇEŞMESI S.

HALIÇ CADDESI

ŞAIR NABI S.

MÜFTÜ HAMAMI S.

KARADENIZ CADDESI

ŞAIR BAKI S.

KARA SARIKLI SOKAĞI

CIBALI CADDESI

ABDÜLEZEL PAŞA CADDESI

ÜSKÜPLÜ C.

SALIH ZEKI S.

LIM C.

KÜÇÜKPAZAR

BEYOĞLU KASIMPAŞA ISKELESI

BEYOĞLU YAĞKAPANI ISKELESI

EMINÖNÜ

0   125   250 m
0   410   820 ft

D   E   F

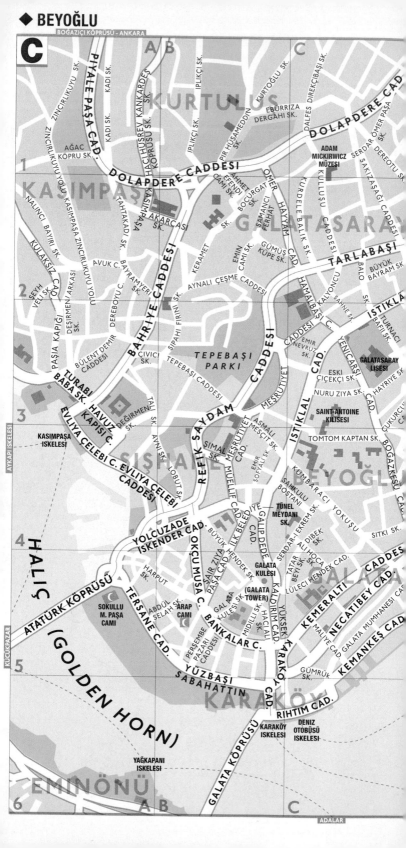

◆ BEYOĞLU

BOĞAZIÇI KÖPRÜSÜ - ANKARA

C

KURTULUŞ

KASIMPAŞA

GALATASARAY

TARLABAŞI

İSTİKLAL

TEPEBAŞI PARKI

SİŞHANE

BEYOĞLU

HALİÇ

(GOLDEN HORN)

KARAKÖY

EMİNÖNÜ

ADAM MICKIRWICZ MÜZESİ

GALATASARAY LİSESİ

SAINT-ANTOINE KİLİSESİ

TOMTOM KAPTAN SK.

TÜNEL MEYDANI

GALATA KULESİ (GALATA TOWER)

KASIMPAŞA İSKELESİ

SOKULLU M. PAŞA CAMI

ARAP CAMI

KARAKÖY İSKELESİ

DENİZ OTOBÜSÜ İSKELESİ

YAĞKAPANI İSKELESİ

GALATA KÖPRÜSÜ

RIHTIM CAD.

DOLAPDERE CAD.

DOLAPDERE CADDESİ

PİYALE PAŞA CAD.

BAHRİYE CADDESİ

EVLİYA ÇELEBİ CADDESİ

ATATÜRK KÖPRÜSÜ

TERSANE CAD.

YÜZBAŞI SABAHATTİN

BANKALAR C.

İSTİKLAL CAD.

KEMERALTI CADDESİ

NECATİBEY CAD.

KEMANKEŞ CAD.

YOLCUZADE İSKENDER CAD.

OKÇU MUSA C.

KARAKÖY CAD.

AYKAPI İSKELESİ

KÜÇÜKPAZAR

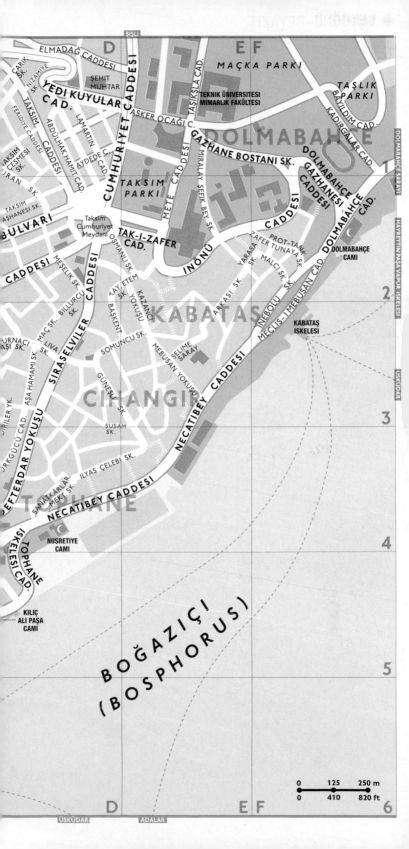

D

EYUP

A B C

BOĞAZIÇI KÖPRÜSÜ - ANKARA

ATATÜRK -

SARI GÜZEL CADDESI

FEVZI PAŞA CADDESI

BÜYÜK KARAMAN CADDESI

MUTAFLAR SK.

ÖMER EFENDI SK.

CADDESI

SERDAR SU YOLU SK.

BOZDOĞAN KEMERI
(AQUEDUCT OF VALENS)

ATATÜRK BULVAR

1

HALICILAR CADDESI

CADDESI

KIZANLIK CAD.

MACAR KARDEŞLER CAD.

KIZTAŞI

DOLAP CAD.

CADDESI

ITFAIYE

SARACHANE PARKI

BURMALI MESCIT ☪

ŞEHZADEBAŞI CAD.

SEHZAD CAMI

VATANPERVER SK.

ISKENDER PAŞA SK.

HACI SALIH SK.

CADDESI

YEŞIL TEKKE SK.

MOLLA HÜSREV SK.

KAVALALI SK.

HORHOR

BULVARI

BELEDIYE SARAYI

BURMALI DEDE SK.

AHMEDIYE CADDESI

ADNAN MENDERES CADDESI

SOFULAR

SARACHANE

HORHOR CADDESI

CINGIRAKLI BOSTAN SK.

IMAM MURAT SK.

ÖMER YILMAZ SK.

ATATÜRK

BUKALIDEDE SK.

FEVZIYE CAD.

CADDESI

YOKUŞU SK.

GENÇTÜRK

2

MURAZT PAŞA SK.

MURAT PAŞA CAMI

VALIDE CAMI ☪

YEŞIL TULUMBA SK.

MAHFIL SK.

LÂLELI CAMI

3

HASEKI CADDESI

CERRAH PAŞA

CAD.

SORGUÇU SK.

AKSARAY LÂLELI

ORDU

KÜRKÇÜBAŞI KÜLHANI SK.

CEZMI SK.

TECCEDÜT SK.

SAIT EFENDI SK.

ŞAIR

INKILÂP

CADDESI

VALIDE CAMI SK.

HASAN PAŞA SK.

TIRYAKI

AKSARAY CAD.

MESIH

AZIMKÂR

LÂLELI CADDESI

PAŞA

SK.

4

KÜÇÜK LANGA CADDESI

KÜÇÜK LANGA CAD.

KEMAL CADDESI

MUSTAFA KEMAL CADDESI

LANGA BOSTANLARI SK.

HAYRIYE TÜCCARI CADDES

KÂTIP KASIM CAMI SK.

KÂTIP KASIM BOSTANI SK.

NAMIK KEMAL CADDESI

KÂTIP

KASIM BOSTANI SK.

YENIKAPI IST.

MERMERCILER CADDESI

5

BOSTAN ARKASI

YENIKAPI KUMSALI

SK.

KENNEDY CADDESI

KENNEDY CADDESI

YENIKAPI FERIBOT ISKELESI

KENNEDY CADDESI

MARMARA

ZEYTINBURNU

6

A B C

BAKIRKÖY

ÜSKÜDA